Challenging the 'European Area of Lifelong Learning'

Lifelong Learning Book Series

VOLUME 19

Aims & Scope
"Lifelong Learning" has become a central theme in education and community development. Both international and national agencies, governments and educational institutions have adopted the idea of lifelong learning as a major theme in the coming years. They realize that it is only by getting people committed to the idea of education both life-wide and lifelong that the goals of economic advancement, social emancipation and personal growth will be attained.

The *Lifelong Learning Book Series* aims to keep scholars and professionals informed about and abreast of current developments and to advance research and scholarship in the domain of Lifelong Learning. It further aims to provide learning and teaching materials, serve as a forum for scholarly and professional debate and offer a rich fund of resources for researchers, policy-makers, scholars, professionals and practitioners in the field.

The volumes in this international Series are multi-disciplinary in orientation, polymathic in origin, range and reach, and variegated in range and complexity. They are written by researchers, professionals and practitioners working widely across the international arena in lifelong learning and are orientated towards policy improvement and educational betterment throughout the life cycle.

For further volumes:
http://www.springer.com/series/6227

George K. Zarifis • Maria N. Gravani
Editors

Challenging the 'European Area of Lifelong Learning'

A Critical Response

 Springer

Editors
George K. Zarifis
Faculty of Philosophy
School of Philosophy and Education
Department of Education
Aristotle University of Thessaloniki
Thessaloniki, Greece

Maria N. Gravani
School of Humanities and Social Sciences
Open University of Cyprus
Latsia, Cyprus

ISBN 978-94-007-7298-4   ISBN 978-94-007-7299-1 (eBook)
DOI 10.1007/978-94-007-7299-1
Springer Dordrecht Heidelberg New York London

Contents

Contributors

Eva Andersson is a senior lecturer at the Department of Education and Special Education, University of Gothenburg, Sweden. Her research mainly concerns adult education and popular adult education and the significance these study forms have for individuals as well as for local communities. Within this field, she has also studied ICT-supported distance education. Further, she has participated as a research expert in conducting European studies on the adult education sector with specific focus on the Nordic countries.

Fátima Antunes holds a Ph.D. in education/sociology of education and works as an associate professor at the Institute of Education, University of Minho, Portugal. Her recent work includes *New Educational Order: Actors, Processes and Institutions – Subsidies to Debate* (2008, Portugal) and several publications on education, Europeanisation and globalisation in Portuguese, Brazilian and English journals. Her research and teaching interests focus on (European) education policy analysis, public policies and state reforms, (sociology of) education and work and vocational education and training.

Nils Bernhardsson obtained his degree in educational science and adult education in 2006 at the University of Education, Freiburg, Germany. He is currently employed as a researcher at the German Institute for Adult Education – Leibniz Centre for Lifelong Learning, Bonn (Germany). His main interests are professionalisation of staff in adult education, ethics and values in the context of adult education and qualitative research methods.

Patrick Bettinger is a research fellow at the Johannes Gutenberg University of Mainz and the University of Augsburg, Germany. His emphases lay on adult education and media education, especially theories and research in teaching and learning with digital media.

Simon Broek is a senior researcher at Panteia/Research voor Beleid, the Netherlands. The main focus of his work concerns lifelong learning, adult education, European policies related to qualifications (European Qualifications Framework) and mobility (Lifelong Learning Programme). He is involved in many European and national research projects on education and labour market policies. Simon has a background in philosophy.

Kristiina Brunila is an adjunct professor and works as a postdoctoral researcher in the Unit of Sociology, Politics and Culture of Education, Institute of Behavioural Sciences, University of Helsinki.

Bert-Jan Buiskool is a senior account manager at Panteia/Research voor Beleid (the Netherlands). He is responsible for a high number of research projects and evaluations for the European Commission, European Parliament and several member states in the field of lifelong learning, adult learning qualifications and mobility. He is an appointed member of the 'Thematic Working Group' on Quality in the Adult Learning Sector of the European Commission. Bert-Jan has a background in economic geography.

Micaela Castiglioni is a researcher and also teaches general pedagogy and adult education at the University of Milano Bicocca, Italy, and coordinates a research group on adult lives and educational processes. She collaborates in research projects with public and private organisations in the fields of health, care and social work. She is vice president of 'Libera Università dell'Autobiografia' (Anghiari) and codirector of the series 'Condizione adulta e processi formativi', Unicopli (Milano).

José Tomás da Silva is an associate professor of psychology at the University of Coimbra, Portugal. He is currently the coordinator of a research group at the Institute of Cognitive Psychology, Vocational and Social Development (R&D unit). His research interests are in the areas of career psychology, counselling psychology, motivation and academic achievement. He is also involved in researching the impact of cognitive-motivational constructs (psychological needs, achievement goals, instrumentality and time perspective) on vocational development, school performance and well-being.

Regina Egetenmeyer is a professor (Juniorprofessur) for lifelong learning at the Johannes Gutenberg University of Mainz, Germany. Her emphases of research are international and comparative adult educational research, informal learning in the workplace and academic professionalisation in adult and lifelong learning.

Andreas Fejes is an associate professor in education at the division for education and adult learning, Linköping University, Sweden. His research interests relate to lifelong learning and adult education. Fejes is one of the founding editors of the *European Journal for Research on the Education and Learning of Adults* and has been the secretary of the *European Society for Research on the Education of Adults* since 2007.

Laura Formenti is an associate professor and teaches general and family pedagogy at the University of Milano Bicocca, Italy, and researches on vocational education, family and socio-educational work. She is a co-convenor of the research network 'Life History and Biography in Adult Education' and a member of the steering committee of ESREA (European Society for Research on the Education of Adults), as well as journals and series devoted to narrative and reflexive methods in education.

Martin Gough attained his Ph.D. in philosophy some time ago and is currently a lecturer in Higher Education and Academic Practice in the University of Kent Unit for the Enhancement of Learning and Teaching and the Centre for the Study of Higher Education. He convenes the Postgraduate Issues Network of the Society for Research into Higher Education and the South-East Branch of the Philosophy of Education Society of Great Britain.

Maria N. Gravani is a lecturer in continuing/adult education at the School of Humanities and Social Sciences of the Open University of Cyprus and coordinator of the continuing education strand of the Master's programme in Education Studies. She previously worked in the UK (Bristol University, University College London), in the Republic of Ireland (Trinity College Dublin) and in Greece (University of Peloponnese, Hellenic Open University, General Secretariat for Adult Education). Her publication and research interests engage such areas as continuing education, lifelong learning, adult education, adult distance teaching and learning in university and professional learning.

Paula Guimarães is an assistant professor of the Institute of Education of the University of Lisbon, Portugal. She is also a member of the steering committee and vice president of ESREA. Recently she has published on adult education policies in the *European Journal of Education*, the *European Journal for Research on the Education and Learning of Adults* (RELA) and *Journal of Adult and Continuing Education* (JACE) as well as in Portuguese journals.

Barry J. Hake is a comparative and historical policy analyst in the area of lifelong learning. He has worked at universities in a number of European countries and was the founder and secretary of the European Association for Research on the Education of Adults (ESREA) 1991–2007. He is retired and is now a consultant (Eurolearn Consultants) working for the European Commission in the areas of lifelong learning and intergenerational learning. He has a long-standing record of publications in scientific journals, edited volumes of research papers and empirical research reports.

Alexandra Ioannidou is an adjunct lecturer at the Open University of Cyprus and researcher. She worked as a project manager at the German Institute for Adult Education in Bonn, as a lecturer and researcher at the University of Tübingen and as an advisor to the Greek Minister of Education and Lifelong Learning in Athens. Her research interests are comparative adult education, education policy, lifelong learning, educational governance and education monitoring.

Larissa Jõgi has a Ph.D. in adult education and is working as an associate professor and as the head of Adult Education Department in the Institute of Educational Science at Tallinn University, Estonia. Her current research interests include adult learning, learning during the life course, emotional learning experiences and teaching and learning in university. She is a member of the steering committee of the European Society for Research on the Education of Adult (ESREA) and co-convener of ESREA's Research Network on Adult Educators, Trainers and their Professional Development (ReNAdET).

Lynette Jordan is a lecturer on the Bachelor of Arts in Community Development (BACD) at the University of Glasgow. She has worked with women's community organisations in Croatia, Turkey and Zambia. She recently worked with Hawler Medical University in Erbil, Kurdistan, Iraq, providing academic development on *student-centred learning*. She is currently PI for the EUROlocal project which provides a website for those interested in promoting and establishing learning regions and cities.

Erik Kats is a sociologist of education. He works at the Centre for Research and Development in Education and Lifelong Learning (PLATO) of Leiden University in the Netherlands. His special interest as a lecturer and researcher is in the transformation of organisations in a knowledge economy and in the integration of learning and working. He is especially involved in comparative research into practices in vocational learning in diverse European countries.

Françoise F. Laot is a socio-historian, specialised in adult education and training. She is a professor at the University of Reims Champagne-Ardenne in France and a member of the Centre for Research on Employment and Professionalisation (CEREP). She works on the history of adult (men and women) education and training policies after WWII, on the links between the 'social question' and adult education in the nineteenth century and on the history of educational research.

Norman Longworth has been a visiting professor at several European universities. He was the project manager of seven European Commission lifelong learning projects and the author of influential books and web-delivered courses on Lifelong Learning and Learning Cities and Regions. He is also the author of the European Commission's policy document on the Local and Regional Dimension in Lifelong Learning, president of the European Lifelong Learning Initiative and consultant to the European Commission, UNESCO and OECD.

Emilio Lucio-Villegas holds a Ph.D. in pedagogy with a thesis on participatory research in adult education. His works are mainly focused on adult education. Publications include books (as author or editor), chapters in books and articles in journals in English, Portuguese, Spanish and Catalan. Since 2008, he is the head of the 'Paulo Freire Chair' at the University of Seville.

Peter Mayo is a professor at the University of Malta where he teaches/researches in adult education, sociology of education, comparative/international education and political sociology in general. His many publications include the recent authored books: *Learning with Adults* (with Leona English, Sense, 2012), *Politics of Indignation* (single authored, Zero/John Hunt, 2012) and *Echoes from Freire for a Critically Engaged Pedagogy* (single authored, Bloomsbury, 2012). He edits the book series *International Issues in Adult Education* (Sense) and coedits the journal *Postcolonial Directions in Education* and the book series *Postcolonial Directions in Education* (Palgrave Macmillan).

Marcella Milana is an associate professor at the Department of Education, Aarhus University, Denmark, and specialises in comparative and adult education. Her current research focuses on the relations between globalisation processes and adult education and the interplay between national and transnational levels. Since 2010, she co-convenes the research network on Policy Studies in Adult Education, under the European Society for Research on the Education of Adults (ESREA). She has recently gained Marie Curie Fellowship status and is currently based at the University of California-Los Angeles (USA).

Stephen O'Brien is a college lecturer at the School of Education, University College Cork. His publication and research interests engage such areas as educational policy studies; social inclusion and the theory of social capital; multicultural education; curriculum and assessment; adult, community and continuing education; and the theory and practice of learning. His latest research critically examines the role of higher education in society.

Albertina L. Oliveira is an assistant professor of adult education and adult learning and development at the Faculty of Psychology and Educational Sciences, University of Coimbra, Portugal. Her research interests include adult education, self-directed learning, epistemological development and well-being and quality of life of adults and older people.

Michael Osborne is a professor of adult and lifelong learning at the University of Glasgow and codirector of the Research Cluster in Social Justice, Place and Lifelong Education. He is experienced in adult education, VET and higher education research, development and evaluation. He is the director of the Centre for Research and Development in Adult and Lifelong Learning within the Faculty of Education and codirector of the PASCAL Observatory on Place Management, Social Capital and Lifelong Learning.

Maria Paula Paixão is an associate professor of psychology at the Faculty of Psychology and Educational Sciences of the University of Coimbra, Portugal. She is the director of the Psychology Doctoral programme and subdirector of the Faculty of Psychology and Educational Sciences. She has several national and international publications on the topics of counselling psychology, lifelong guidance and counselling and motivation and time perspective. She is a founding member of the 'European Society for Vocational Designing and Career Counselling'.

Katarina Popović is an assistant professor at the Department of Andragogy, Faculty of Philosophy, University of Belgrade, Serbia; a researcher at the Institute for Pedagogy and Andragogy of the same university; and a visiting professor at several European universities. She is the vice president of EAEA (European Association for the Education of Adults), president of the Serbian Adult Education Society, coordinator of regional projects of German 'dvv international' and editor-in-chief of the journal *Andragogical Studies*. She is also a member of several relevant European and international organisations and member of International Adult and Continuing Education Hall of Fame.

Simona Sava is a professor at the Faculty of Sociology and Psychology, Department of Education Sciences, West University of Timisoara, Romania, and the director of Romanian Institute for Adult Education (IREA).

Bernhard Schmidt-Hertha is a full professor for educational research with a focus on vocational continuing education and on-the-job training at the University of Tübingen, Germany. He studied educational research, psychology and sociology in Munich, where he finished his Ph.D. in 2004. He is an editor of an online journal, a reviewer for the German Research Association and different national and international journals and a member of the ESREA steering committee.

Claudia Strobel-Dümer is an educational researcher at Socio-Educational Institute of SOS-Kinderdorf e.V., Germany. She previously worked as a researcher at the Faculty of Psychology and Educational Sciences at the Ludwig Maximilians University, Munich. Her field of work include practical research and evaluation in youth welfare services and research projects in the fields of children village families, child protection and early support.

Despina Tsakiris is an associate professor in the Department of Social and Educational Policy at the University of Peloponnese, and she has also worked at the Hellenic Education Research Centre (1998–2005). She studied and lived in France at the University of Paris X-Nanterre. Her background is on sciences education, and she largely focuses her research on evaluation aspects in education and training.

Jaap van Lakerveld is an educationalist. He is the director of the Centre for Research and Development in Education and Lifelong Learning (PLATO) of Leiden University in the Netherlands. His field of expertise is learning. It includes learning within educational settings as well as learning of professionals in work environments. He works as a researcher and consultant in in-service teacher education, vocational and adult education and learning and human resources development.

Gun-Britt Wärvik Ph.D., is a senior lecturer at the Department of Education and Special Education, University of Gothenburg, Sweden. Her research interest concerns the study of educational restructuring, subsequent institutional change and governing technologies related to notions of performance and competence. Her studies take a 'bottom-up perspective', meaning that the implications of restructuring for occupational and professional knowledge are a main focus, which also includes studies of the VET sector.

George K. Zaritis is an assistant professor of continuing education at the Faculty of Philosophy, School of Philosophy and Education, Department of Education, Aristotle University of Thessaloniki, Greece. His research interests focus on adult educators' training and professionalisation, university continuing education and comparative examination of adult learning policies and practices in Southeastern Europe. He is an elected member of ESREA steering committee and co-convener of ESREA's Research Network on Adult Educators, Trainers and their Professional Development (ReNAdET).

Chapter 1
Introduction

Maria N. Gravani and George K. Zarifis

Lifelong Learning as a European policy initiative has not yet been proven as beneficial as the European Commission might have expected when it launched the 'Memorandum on Lifelong Learning' in 2000.[1] Despite the strong rhetoric on promoting the idea of lifelong learning in Europe and after over a decade of ongoing adjustments, relevant European Union (EU) policies have neither responded to nor have they fulfilled any concrete social demand or a coherent attitude towards learning (as a mode of development) amongst Europeans. Policy analysis so far (see English and Mayo 2012) explains very well the genuine drive behind the construction of dubious terminology and the problematic application of a series of political decisions that brought forward the semantics of globalisation with terms and ideas like 'citizenship', 'employability', 'social cohesion' and 'flexibility'. It is still hard for a generation that was literally brought up using in their everyday language such terminology veiled under the benefits of 'lifelong

---

[1] The Memorandum opens by stating the case for implementing lifelong learning and notes that promoting active citizenship and promoting employability are equally important and interrelated aims for lifelong learning. It also argues that the scale of current economic and social change in Europe demands a fundamentally new approach to education and training with lifelong learning as the common umbrella under which all kinds of teaching and learning should be united. In response, it highlights six key messages which offer a structured framework for an open debate on putting lifelong learning into practice (European Commission 2000: 4). These messages are based on experience gathered at European level through Community programmes and the European Year of Lifelong Learning (1996) and are the following: new basic skills for all, more investment in human resources, innovation in teaching and learning, valuing learning, rethinking guidance and counselling and bringing learning closer to home.

M.N. Gravani
School of Humanities and Social Sciences, Open University of Cyprus, Latsia, Cyprus
e-mail: maria.gravani@ouc.ac

G.K. Zarifis (✉)
Faculty of Philosophy, School of Philosophy and Education, Department of Education,
Aristotle University of Thessaloniki, Old School of Philosophy Building,
Office 208, GR-54124, Thessaloniki, Greece
e-mail: gzarifis@edlit.auth.gr

G.K. Zarifis and M.N. Gravani (eds.), *Challenging the 'European Area of Lifelong Learning': A Critical Response*, Lifelong Learning Book Series 19, DOI 10.1007/978-94-007-7299-1_1, © Springer Science+Business Media Dordrecht 2014

learning', to contest the neo-liberal turn[2] of the actual concept. The 'Memorandum' has tried to respond (probably very persuasively) to the ongoing debate amongst European policymakers, social partners and scholars on the reasons why the time is right to promote active citizenship and employability as two equally important and interrelated aims for our societies. As such the Memorandum remains the most influential but also the most dissimulated policy document that the European Commission has produced, and as such it rests as a basis of any debate on lifelong learning policies in Europe. Along the same line, the Communication on 'Making a European Area for Lifelong Learning a Reality' that was released, a year after the 'Memorandum' (see European Commission 2001),[3] became the modus operandi of all education and training initiatives that were introduced thereafter. What these policy documents really do is to legitimise the overemphasis on work, employability and ICT. As English and Mayo (2012: 18) note, however, this legitimisation indicates that the discourse is removed from a broad conception of education that takes on board the different multiple subjectivities characterising individuals and is gravitating around the notion of the knowledge economy. The current socio-economic crisis, which still threatens the foundations of the European imagery, has brought about by force a series of social and economic challenges for many Europeans. After a period of gut reaction to what is forcefully regulated for most of us by those defining the late neo-liberal state of mind, it is now the time to contemplate on the validity of the semantics of globalisation and the authority that resides behind them.

The purpose of this book is to critically reflect on the context in which lifelong learning policies and practices are organised in Europe with the contribution of people who are working in the field either as researchers or as policymakers. Through a critical lens, the book reinterprets the core content of the messages that are conveyed by the European Commission in the 'Memorandum on Lifelong Learning',

---

[2] As it is so convincingly debated by Aspin and Chapman (2000: 2), lifelong learning's meaning – although it is used in a wide variety of contexts and has a wide currency – is still unclear. It is perhaps for that reason that its operationalisation and implementation have not been widely practised or achieved, and such application as it has had has been achieved primarily on a piecemeal basis.

[3] As it is stated in the relevant text (European Commission 2001: 2), the Communication contributes to the establishment of a European area of lifelong learning, the aims of which are both to empower citizens to move freely between learning settings, jobs, regions and countries, making the most of their knowledge and competences, and to meet the goals and ambitions of the European Union and the candidate countries to be more prosperous, inclusive, tolerant and democratic. This development will be facilitated by bringing together within a lifelong learning framework education and training and important elements of existing European level processes, strategies and plans concerned with youth, employment, social inclusion and research policy. This does not imply a new process, nor can it involve the harmonisation of laws and regulations. Rather, it calls for more coherent and economical use of existing instruments and resources, including through the use of the open method of coordination. In order to achieve the Lisbon aim of a knowledge-based society, close links will be established between the European area of lifelong learning and the European research area, particularly with a view to raising the interest of young people in science and technology careers.

the vehicle for all current developments in lifelong learning in Europe. With references to research findings, proposed actions and applications to immediate practice that have an added value for Europeans – but either do they not appear to correspond directly to what is stipulated by the European Commission or they are completely ignored as part of the lifelong learning process – the book offers an analytic and systematic outlook of the main challenges in creating the 'European Area of Lifelong Learning'.

Scope and Significance

As Borg and Mayo (2005: 218) argue, the EU 'Memorandum on Lifelong Learning' and a number of projects it inspired indicate, in no uncertain terms, the extent of the distortion that has occurred with respect to the once humanistic concept of 'lifelong education'. Some of the humanistic considerations were co-opted in the service of a document seeking to provide a humanistic facade to what is, in effect, a neo-liberal-inspired set of guidelines. Today it is clear that policymakers in countries, agencies and institutions across Europe are devoting increasing attention to the notion of 'lifelong learning' as an idea to be promoted in education policies but also as a strong foundation to underpin education and training provision.

The real challenge however for today's educational and learning policies in Europe does not lie with the promotion of a narrative that prioritises the needs of the market,[4] but with the truthful delivery of a narrative that corresponds to valid learning needs of Europe's citizens. It has been over a decade since Preston (1999) was arguing into the positivist narratives of lifelong learning as the Janus face.[5] As she aptly put it, lifelong learning

> …is a mechanism of social control mediated by the market. As promoted in this context, the word "learning" does not refer to those reflective incidentally acquired understandings which enable us to navigate our daily lives. In most cases contemporary usage of the term lifelong learning refers to the process of allowing ourselves to be exposed to pre-packaged gobbits of knowledge, allowing ourselves to be assessed on the mastery of that knowledge, accepting the implications of the resulting indicators of our performance for access to the labour market and our resultant positioning within it. Lifelong in some contexts lives up to its promise: the presentation of a variety of opportunities from the cradle to the grave. In other contexts it more narrowly refers to work-related education and training (Preston 1999: 562).

---

[4] As Borg and Mayo (2005: 218) figuratively note as far as the concept of lifelong learning is concerned, it is like old wine that has been placed in new bottles but has been adulterated in the process. They further argue that the neo-liberal set of guidelines, contained in the *Memorandum*, serves to heighten competitiveness in a scenario characterised by the intensification of globalisation.

[5] Janus (Iānus) was the Roman god of beginnings and transitions.

The undebatable focus of European lifelong learning policies on the latter, cloaked under an attractive vocabulary that was associated with personal development, empowerment and citizenship, has gradually led to the uncritical recognition of lifelong learning as Europe's way towards economic development. The current economic crisis as well as the lack of political vision for a social Europe is partly the result of a persistent and ongoing rhetoric of the benefits of like policies that have prevented people from asking the usual critical questions of who exactly has access to it (lifelong learning that is), in what form, under what conditions and who gains what from it.

Over a decade after the release of the Memorandum and the Communication on a European area of lifelong learning, the dominant discourse in lifelong learning (as a concept, as a policy objective but also as terminology) in Europe is essentially framed within the human capital approach in which a pragmatist and also a systemic approach are also engaged. Less apparent is the social capital approach, whereas the ecological and ethical approaches (as extensions of the humanistic façade in the relevant policy documents) are standing in the periphery of the discourse.

In the book contributing authors are looking critically at these types of discourse with direct reference to the Memorandum. All chapters touch upon the contribution of lifelong learning policy research in Europe and how it affects (or not) the current lifelong learning perspective (a misleading yet commanding linguistic manifestation of Europe's demand to become the world's leading knowledge economy). For the majority of the contributors, it does not come as a surprise that the way in which lifelong learning is defined by the European Commission (2001: 33) – as an all learning activity undertaken throughout life, with the aim of improving knowledge, skills and competences within a personal, civic, social and/or employment-related perspective[6] – is obfuscating rather than elucidating on how learning contributes to promoting employability and active citizenship and combating social exclusion. It is in this respect that lifelong learning has become the 'Trojan horse' of Europe's own vision for prosperity.

The driving force behind most member states' policies on lifelong learning so far has been employability and adaptability to economic drifts and demands. Especially today there is a growing recognition of the inevitable relationship between education and the economic and social well-being of individuals as something undisputable. This monosemantic[7] approach has largely misguided both policymakers and politicians who lost focus while orbiting their decisions around conservative practices and old-school explanations of newfangled social

---

[6] That is (…) not limited to a purely economic outlook or just to learning for adults. In addition to the emphasis it places on learning from pre-school to postretirement, lifelong learning should encompass the whole spectrum of formal, non-formal and informal learning. The objectives of learning include active citizenship, personal fulfilment and social inclusion, as well as employment-related aspects. The principles which underpin lifelong learning and guide its effective implementation emphasise the centrality of the learner, the importance of equal opportunities and the quality and relevance of learning opportunities (European Commission 2001: 3–4).

[7] By monosemantic, we mean the 'single-mindedness' or 'unambiguous' meaning of particular traits that are attributed to learning as a lifelong process in European policy documents.

anomalies that are directly related to, and occasionally explained based on, an equally monosemantic interpretation of economic figures.

It is exactly this undisputed persistence on the relation between something so profound as learning and something so mundane as economic figures that asks for a closer look to policy research, and for the formation of an ongoing critical debate on the benefits of lifelong learning for Europe's citizens, as well as for a critical examination of the structural and social changes that lifelong learning both as a policy concept and as a principle has or has not brought forward in the last 10 years. In times as decisive (in social and in economic terms) as the ones we are going through today, a critical viewpoint of the practices and policies adopted by member states – in an effort to culminate the European area for lifelong learning – and a holistic approach to lifelong learning in Europe is essential.

Outline of the Book

The chapters in the book are organised into five parts that quasi trail the structure of the Memorandum in order to debate and critically approach in separate sections the core issues that Europe faces today in relation to the idea of making a 'European Area of Lifelong Learning' a reality. The parts are as follows:

1. Part I: Lifelong Learning and New Basic Skills for All
2. Part II: Lifelong Learning and More Investment in Human Resources
3. Part III: Lifelong Learning, Innovative Teaching and Learning and Rethinking Guidance and Counselling
4. Part IV: Lifelong Learning and Valuing Learning
5. Part V: Lifelong Learning and Bringing Learning Closer to Home

Part I of the book reflects on the first message of the 'Memorandum', the aim of which was to guarantee universal and continuing access to learning for gaining and renewing the skills needed for sustained participation in the knowledge society. Contributing authors argue on whether basic skills – as a response to the crisis that Europe faces – have become a 'chimera' of modern education, the role of computer literacy as part of the new basic skills, the contribution of new basic skills to the development of active citizenship and the relationship between new basic skills, knowledge practices and judgement.

More specifically now in the second chapter of the book, Popović discusses the notion of skills, basic skills and competencies and their relation to the broader concepts of lifelong learning and knowledge society, as paradigmatic representatives of educational policy. She argues that the idea of basic skills is not new, but in the contemporary European context, the 'Memorandum' emerged as the best response to the challenges of the fast-changing society and economy. She notices that the serious problem with skills is their value-free character, and that attempts to include attitudes to the definition of skills are not grounded, while some of the most important questions of human life, such as values, ethics and emotions, are untouched by skills. The real question for Popović is how to move from traditional '*l'art pour l'art*' approach of non-pragmatic and remote-from-life-education to the current, applicable one, without losing integral approach, value-based issues and long-term perspective.

In the third chapter, Schmidt-Hertha and Strobel develop their analysis around the concept of computer literacy as an important basic skill postulated in the 'Memorandum' and discuss the problem of digital divide between different groups of people. The authors report on two qualitative studies in Germany that recently investigated the participation of elderly people in digital technologies and the role of intergenerational communication within this context. The results of the studies contribute greatly to the discussion of lifelong learning policies in Europe and reveal how far the goal has been achieved to enable all people to participate. Additionally, the studies give helpful suggestions for further measures within this field.

In Chap. 4, Lucio-Villegas reflects on the process of building a democratic citizenship beyond the construction of a hegemonic social cohesion, as it seems to derive from the Lisbon Strategy and the 'Memorandum'. He starts with the idea of Enlightenment and John Dewey's thought on democratic school, in an attempt to define the skills to edify a democratic citizen from both the field and practices of adult education and learning. The chapter presents the experience of the 'Participatory and Citizenship School' in Seville, from 2005 to 2007, as an example for the development of basic skills for active citizenship in Europe.

In Chap. 5, Gough claims that the emphasis, in the service of promoting lifelong learning, in various national and European level government policy initiatives on developing basic skills in their populations for the workplace and for other uses in life has been, and is still, in different ways both appropriate and not appropriate. He argues that it is appropriate if we place the emphasis on the term 'skill' as a form of knowledge, and if we place emphasis on 'basic' in the context of providing a focus for increasing life's opportunities for those relatively dispossessed; it is inappropriate if we are forced to pretend that skills are discrete, specific entities that can, along with the people in possession of them, 'transfer' unproblematically from one learning context to another. It is inappropriate further if we were to treat skills as always basic and technicist, as if lower knowledge levels are the limit of entitlement for citizens, or always a contextually generic. The English conception of 'skill' promotes this inappropriate emphasis, which is also an economic and employment-led perspective, fuelled by neo-liberal hegemony. Domination of the English language, and hence prevalence of the English term 'skill', across the European Community will be reinforcing this particular conception as if it were universally appropriate. The key question concerning how we serve the appropriate policy for lifelong learning is ultimately an ontological one about the nature of skills. Certain amongst both proponents and opponents of the skills agenda are stuck in a 'realist' mindset which demands critique. It promotes, on the one hand, an unhelpful deficit model of skills as discrete concrete requirements and, on the other hand, gives licence to the equally unhelpful challenge that skills and higher knowledge attainments are worlds apart. He concludes that reconceptualising skills as 'knowledge practices' enables us to open up analysis of the term and avoid the unhelpful connotations. In turn, we can understand better how an agent can exploit knowledge from one context of use into another and can develop judgement, the most important of all 'skills', and get closer to the 'Good Life'.

Part II of the book reflects on the second message of the 'Memorandum', the aim of which was to visibly raise levels of investment in human resources in order to place priority on Europe's most important asset: its people. The issues that are debated in this part of the book include incentives and disincentives given and approaches adopted by European governments to ensure mechanisms that encourage investment in human resources; lifelong learning and adult education policy towards economic growth; tensions between two important aims of lifelong learning – educational flexibility and predictability; the relationship between lifelong learning and employability; the influence of governance on employability and the influence of human capital theory in the mission and role of lifelong learning and human action in the work activity.

In particular, in Chap. 6, Milana explains that the objective of 'investing' in human resources expressed in the 'Memorandum' finds its *raison d'être* in the conception that the acquisition of skills and knowledge at the individual level increases a person's productive value. Within this line of argument, economic investment in skill upgrading amongst the adult population produces a return of investment in terms of both economic and noneconomic benefits at micro, meso and macro levels. Milana reviews available data and existing literature on governments' approaches and mechanisms to encourage investment in human resources and puts under critical scrutiny the potentials as well as the limitations of the human capital paradigm.

In Chap. 7 Guimarães and Antunes discuss the ways by which the EU lifelong learning agenda, specifically the guidelines for basic skills, has been interpreted according to the Portuguese realities, at national and local levels. They suggest that basic skills for all, as intended in the framework of the European area of lifelong learning, have somewhat loose roots on the cultural and civic dimensions of education in a human and social development perspective. As they suggest competitiveness and social cohesion, the dual centrality of lifelong education and learning for Europe, stated in the Lisbon Strategy, has been interpreted and translated in Portugal through a dynamic imbalanced agenda fed by two major strands: the prosecution of a social right long-time in debt to adult population and a search for so-called employability and qualification, as a way to tackle Portuguese 'distance' from European educational standards. According to these options that frame the EU agenda, their chapter stresses adults' understanding of adult education based on research findings. These understandings are congruent with EU orientations; adults see adult education as a promise for a better life. Thus, given the inconsistency of lifelong learning, fulfilling this promise is a hard task to achieve.

In Chap. 8, Andersson and Wärvik discuss the new picture of vocational education in Sweden in the light of the European policies on lifelong learning. In their chapter, two issues are discussed: the extent to which the new picture matches or not the ambitions outlined in the European lifelong learning policies and the tensions and contradictions identified as permeating the new educational reform in Sweden. The argument made is that the new reform implies a return to a previous school form with two tracks: one preparing for higher education and one for vocational work. Moreover, it is argued that the organisation of upper secondary education in Sweden is moving away from the lifelong learning imagery towards one in which vocational education is in the centre. This is manifested in the reduction of study hours in subjects close to the key competences related to democratic and civic issues.

In Chap. 9, Fejes identifies that in the last couple of decades, there has been a shift from speaking about employment to speaking about employability. He goes on to analyse how discourses on employability are mobilised in the wider discursive terrain of governance. A discourse analysis is performed inspired by the concepts of governmentality and the enabling state. The analysis indicates that the individual is constructed as responsible for their own employability, and the state and the employer are construed as enablers. However, this is not clear-cut or deterministic as diverse texts produce different kinds of positioning. The analysis helps to open up a new space for thought and action.

In Chap. 10, Tsakiris seeks to explore the tenacious influence of certain capitalist economic ideologies, which find application in the educational policies of lifelong learning. The chapter focuses on the human capital as it is presented in education policy texts, as an economic theory that seeks to explain human action in the work activity. Emphasis is placed on the way this theory is interwoven with the mission and the role of lifelong learning. Her analysis of the 'Memorandum' shows that the strategy of defending human capital as a form of rationality is an imaginary social construction which both in the project level and in the level of facts seems to invalidate the defended form of rationality. The analysis reveals that the text contains certain opposing or contradictory goals that are incompatible with those openly advocated. In this sense, the 'Memorandum' is a social exemplar of how capital is understood in the project of human action in work activity specifically and in the social activity generally.

Part III of the book focuses on the development of effective teaching and learning methods and contexts for the continuum of lifelong and life-wide learning, as well as access to good quality information and advice about learning opportunities throughout Europe (messages three and five of the 'Memorandum'). This part of the book revolves around the following issues: the meaning of 'innovation' and its relevance to teaching and learning, the Memorandum's understanding of professional teaching and the link between teaching and learning methods on the one hand and professional teaching on the other, the importance placed in certain European policy documents on the professionalisation for adult learning staff and the changes that have taken place over the years, a discussion on how adults as learners understand learning and how understandings of learning differ throughout generations in the life-course context and guidance and counselling services and their coordination in Portugal in the light of the Memorandum.

More specifically in Chap. 11, O'Brien suggests that 'innovation' messages, such as those that relate to teaching and learning in the 'Memorandum', need to be seriously questioned. With specific attention to the message on teaching and learning and set within an Irish policy context, he argues that the strategy connects with neo-liberal meanings, standpoints and practices that oversee an incomplete educational representation. He further debates that there are aspects to the Memorandum that are to be welcomed but are chiefly diluted by the strategy's insubstantial analysis of education as a field of power – specifically, the concern that education reflects and produces diverse interests and effects. The chapter responds to a professed need to interrogate the educational sensibility of particular power 'interests' in education. The evidence presented indicates an over-representation of the education-economy relation that obviates against education being seen as a moral and social practice. Consequently, the chapter's evidence indicates the need to establish a stronger intellectual and teacher-professional presence at the educational 'partnership' table. Ultimately, O'Brien concludes that if there is to be innovation in teaching and learning, this is best served, and can only be effectively engaged, via a more complex and authentic representation.

In Chap. 12, Egetenmeyer and Bettinger question the close link between teaching and learning methods on the one hand and professional teaching on the other. Their chapter focuses on teachers and trainers in adult education. Under the perspective of professionalisation, the chapter questions the role of teaching and learning methods within the professionalisation of teachers and trainers in adult education. The authors see a need for further development of the issue of the Memorandum's understanding of professional teaching. They argue that it needs to go beyond teaching methods and the role of professionals in teaching and learning scenarios. As adult education plays a central role in the realisation of lifelong learning in Europe and has various target groups, a fixed set of teaching methods is neither appropriate nor sufficient. In order to cope with the demands in adult education, the authors suggest that a complex competence set is necessary for professional teaching.

In Chap. 13, Sava reviews the relevant European documents from 2000 to 2010 aiming at identifying aspects of 'professionalisation' for adult learning staff. She uses three sets of criteria to select the relevant documents, and her analysis points out that in the last part of the decade, there is more emphasis on the need to professionalise adult learning staff, considering that the quality of professional behaviour is seen as determinant for the quality of learning.

In Chap. 14, Jõgi identifies tensions between the understandings of learning amongst educational policymakers and experts and adult learners and argues that this tension brings misunderstanding and confusion in the educational policy discussion. In her chapter she presents findings from a research study conducted between 2004 and 2006 that used semi-structured interviews in order to discuss how adults as learners understand learning and how understandings of learning differ throughout generations in the life-course context. She concludes that these findings help us understand and reflect on how unique and subjective personal learning experience is, and how different are the attitudes and understandings of learning that adults as learners bring to social and educational process.

In Chap. 15, Paixão, da Silva and Oliveira focus on guidance and counselling services and their coordination in Portugal, in the light of lifelong learning policies fostered in Europe. They present the history of guidance and counselling services in

Portugal and critically discuss the implementation of lifelong learning and guidance structures and services within adult education. They argue that in the case of Portugal, the responsibility for guidance and counselling services is fragmented across a number of ministries and governmental entities, some of which are created and dissolved according to strictly political and governmental aspirations. Moreover, the authors argue that gradual osmosis between structures of guidance provision, as advocated in the Memorandum, is far from being a reality and that there is a state of confusion both in terms of how policies are adapted and the structures developed and also on how language is used to create new realities in the already existing ones.

Part IV of the book reflects on the fourth message of the 'Memorandum', the aim of which was to significantly improve the ways in which learning participation and outcomes are understood and appreciated, particularly in non-formal education and informal learning. The issues that are debated in this part of the book include the contradicting values inherent in the concept of lifelong learning and their impact in the development of lifelong learning discourse, quality in adult learning and how policymakers and member states approach quality in adult learning, the influence of EU and OECD within the transnational educational space and the appearance of new instruments of educational governance, the shifting relationships between education and working life in the Netherlands, the influence of EU-project-based work on learning and academic research in the era of lifelong learning and the importance of autobiographical research in adult education.

In Chap. 16, Bernhardsson identifies that lifelong learning has so far been implemented insufficiently. His main argument is that there are fundamental contradictions between the values of the original idea of lifelong learning and the values inherent to the concept currently in use. The chapter illustrates that the development of lifelong learning and the reconstruction of the '*Social Imaginaries*' – on the basis of Charles Taylor's theory – which emerged in the policy discourse show that all political attempts of developing a comprehensive system of lifelong learning cannot overlook anymore the fact that the core of values which could carry or prevent such a system is being shaped by social discourses and learning processes of individuals.

In Chap. 17, Buiskool and Broek identify a shift in the interpretation of what 'quality' in adult learning means and how policymakers approach the term. Their chapter tracks the ways in which the concept of quality is used in relation to adult learning. The authors conclude by arguing that the analysis of quality developments in Europe is seriously hampered by the fact that until this moment no European-wide overview of quality is available. Moreover, a critical reflection is lacking on the issues and challenges that are specific to the adult learning sector in relation to assuring quality of its providers and provision.

In Chap. 18, Ioannidou focuses on two influential actors of education policy within the transnational educational space: the EU and OECD. She pinpoints the appearance of new instruments of educational governance, which coincide with and support an emerging governance model in the educational realm: the evidence-based education policy. The author argues that education and education policy have been set up and ran under the control of the nation-state since the origins of modern education systems. Even if this is still true to varying extent in many countries, recently we witness a shift in the examination of issues concerning educational governance. Regarding the governance of lifelong learning, Ioannidou claims that it is the emergence of a transnational educational space that brings about a blend of actors from different levels that interact in various patterns and influence policy formation at the international as well as at the national level. This policy arena shows characteristics of a multilayered system with horizontal and vertical policy interweaving, with network-like structures from state and non-state actors and with interaction patterns that are based more on coalitions, negotiations and mutual adjustment rather than on hierarchical regulations.

In Chap. 19, Kats and van Lakerveld argue that the development of systems of education is strongly connected to the development of industrial society. Relationships between education and the vocational practice of people in the companies and organisations where they work are however variable through the times, and there is always some room between both spheres. By describing shifts in the way vocational learning is situated in the growing room between formal education and working life in the Netherlands, the authors go into the way vocational learning relates to the traditional broad humanistic approach to adult education and conclude that these shifts are not exclusively tied to specific historic circumstances, neither are they irreversible, but have an actual meaning for the debate on lifelong learning.

In Chap. 20, Brunila analyses how EU-project-based work represents a form of power that regulates academic research linked to education in accordance to lifelong learning discourse. She identifies that in Europe, funded projects with economic aims and discourses for lifelong learning have permeated the public sector and pinpoints the consequences by analysing project-based academic research in the field of education in Finland.

In Chap. 21, Formenti and Castiglioni put learners, with their experience, questions and knowledge, at the centre of the debate in adult education. As they identify, the 'Memorandum' does not give any indication of the role of the learner in developing self-reflective competence as part of the lifelong learning process. Their chapter focuses on auto/biographical methods as ways to bring forth a new perspective on identity and knowledge in adult education and research. The authors conclude that from the subject's point of view, telling the story of a learning experience, and thinking about it in due ways, is a means to value, celebrate and accompany lifelong and life-wide transformation.

Part V of the book essentially reflects on the sixth message of the 'Memorandum'. This message addressed the need to provide lifelong learning opportunities as close to learners as possible, in their own communities and supported through ICT-based facilities wherever appropriate. The issues that are debated in this part of the book include the theoretical and methodological issues involved in the development of mobilisation strategies which are based upon locating learning closer to home, key aspects of a national curriculum draft policy framework in relation to lifelong learning focusing on Malta, the creation of learning cities and regions and collective dimensions in lifelong education and learning with focus on France.

More specifically in Chap. 22, Hake argues that while one of the key messages in the 'Memorandum' stressed the need to bring learning closer to home and the daily lives of European citizens, the Lisbon Declaration emphasised the need to raise the levels of participation in adult learning in most of the member states. His chapter focuses on the theoretical and methodological issues involved in the development of mobilisation strategies which are based upon locating learning closer to home and thus to raise levels of participation. As such, the chapter departs from an analysis of the so-called articulation problem which involves the different sets of assumptions about the relation between the supply of and demand for adult learning. Hake's subsequent analysis focuses on the prevailing patterns of participation and non-participation in adult learning, the identified barriers to participation and the potential effectiveness of different mobilisation strategies.

In Chap. 23, Mayo argues that a series of volumes providing guidelines, key principles and aims for the Maltese national curriculum framework are currently the target of debate and the focus of reactions by various stakeholders in education including teachers who were asked to read the volumes and provide reactions in the form of answers to a set questionnaire. According to Mayo, the dominant discourse on lifelong learning, as adopted in the National Curriculum Framework, is one that shifts the onus of responsibility onto the individual rather than the state and the social collectivity. Learning and adequate provision for it become a matter of individual rather than social responsibility. He concludes that the overarching notion that emerges from the main policy documents thus far is that of lifelong learning for employability and a narrowly defined notion of active citizenship which overlooks the collective dimension of education for social change and which provides a very problematic notion of individualised learning.

In Chap. 24, Jordan, Longworth and Osborne provide an overview of an aspect of lifelong learning implementation that has waxed and waned in importance over since the 1970s, the notion of creating learning cities and regions. The authors provide a brief history of developments within the field of learning cities and regions in Europe in recent decades and then focus on one particular project, EUROlocal, which has sought to gather and analyse the current state of development within the continent.

In Chap. 25, Laot discusses the pedagogical arguments for the collective development of adult education in France. Drawing on sources from archives from the 1950s and 1960s, she examines the different understandings and who defended them from a political point of view. Her analysis reveals the fundamental role attributed to the family circle (notably the couple) in these discussions. Then the decline of intensity of these debates within the framework of the European area of lifelong learning is examined, as well as their evolution or transposition into other social spheres.

Chapter 26 is the concluding chapter of the book. In this chapter Zarifis and Gravani review the main issues and challenges as these appear in the book and present a revised framework for a 'European Area of Lifelong Learning' from the people and for the people adopting a social capital approach and focusing on aspects of ethical values in learning, learning quality, learning ecologies and learning collectives.

References

Aspin, D. N., & Chapman, D. C. (2000). Lifelong learning: Concepts and conceptions. *International Journal of Lifelong Education, 19*(1), 2–19.

Borg, C., & Mayo, P. (2005). The EU Memorandum on lifelong learning. Old wine in new bottles? *Globalisation, Societies and Education, 3*(2), 203–225.

English, L. M., & Mayo, P. (2012). *Learning with adults – A critical pedagogical introduction.* Rotterdam: Sense Publishers.

European Commission. (2000). *A memorandum on lifelong learning* (Commission Staff Working Paper, 30.10.2000, SEC(2000) 1832). Brussels: European Commission.

European Commission. (2001). *Making a European area of lifelong learning a reality* (Communication from the Commission, 21.11.01 COM(2001) 678 final). Brussels: European Commission.

Preston, R. (1999). Critical approaches to lifelong education. *International Review of Education, 45*(5/6), 561–574.

Part I
Lifelong Learning and New
Basic Skills for All

Chapter 2
The Skills: A Chimera of Modern European Adult Education

Katarina Popović

Introduction

The concepts of *recurrent education, continuing education* and *permanent education* (introduced by the Council of Europe) began to appear in discussions from the 1960s both in Europe and UNESCO. The *learning to be* approach of Edgar Faure and the International Commission on the Development of Education influenced the European understanding of adult education from the 1970s. This approach agreed with the type of humanism that UNESCO's policy was rooted in (having a person, its needs, well-being and self-fulfilment at the core of its philosophy) but also in line with the democratic vision of European society with equal opportunities, active participation and autonomy of citizens and learners. Together with *lifelong education, learning to be* influenced policy, legislation and practice of adult education in many European countries, although OECD's *recurrent education* seemed to respond to the need for a more flexible relationship between education, training and work and thus to the needs of fast technological development. Even the CoE's recommendations from 1970 pointed out need for permanent education to meet the contemporary demands of both social justice and economic progress (Council of Europe 1970).

Lifelong learning emerged as a conceptual framework able to balance these approaches and was renewed as a concept with the *European Year of Lifelong Learning* in 1996 and the *White Paper on Teaching and Learning: Towards a Europe of Knowledge* in 1997, promising answers to the challenges of the coming millennium. Lifelong learning policy in Europe, as the dominant discourse which gained currency in the 1980s and 1990s after the other concepts had been slowly abandoned, seemed to be the only approach including the 'old', somewhat naive humanism (believing in changing the world through education) and the socio-economic needs of the modern times. The increased speed of science, technology, economy and politics created new demands, and in 2000 Europe experienced a paradigm shift in many areas, including education.

K. Popović (✉)
Department for Andragogy, Faculty of Philosophy, University of Belgrade, Belgrade, Serbia
e-mail: kpopovic@f.bg.ac.rs; aes@sbb.rs

G.K. Zarifis and M.N. Gravani (eds.), *Challenging the 'European Area of Lifelong Learning': A Critical Response*, Lifelong Learning Book Series 19, DOI 10.1007/978-94-007-7299-1_2, © Springer Science+Business Media Dordrecht 2014

Memorandum on Lifelong Learning: Message and Language

In 2000 it was obvious that Europe was influenced by global trends and reacted quickly by changing its approach to education and learning: 'The European Union was confronted with a quantum shift resulting from globalisation and the challenges of a new knowledge-driven economy. The Union has today set itself a new strategic goal for the next decade: To become the most competitive and dynamic knowledge-based economy in the world, capable of sustainable economic growth with more and better jobs and greater social cohesion' (European Council 2000: 1–2). These changes, new demands and new political and economic challenges shaped the lifelong learning and adult education policy. This was further expressed in the Commission's *Memorandum on Lifelong Learning*[1] in 2000, a document that counts as one of the milestones of the development of European educational policy and the *Communication from the Commission: Making a European Area of Lifelong Learning a Reality*[2] in 2001.

The main goal, ambition and tone of these texts expressed the conception in which education was encompassing multiple purposes and dimensions. The rhetoric of the *Memorandum* and the *Communication* was (and probably still is) an enticing one; employability and social inclusion going hand in hand, the availability of lifelong learning to everyone, the promotion of active citizenship and the promotion of vocational skills and self-development; they were all supposed to pave the way to a knowledge-based society, allowing full participation in social and economic life for everyone.

The achievements of the *Memorandum* are undeniable, and a significant step has been taken towards Europe as a common educational area. A number of aspects have also been improved – the quality of adult teaching and education has increased, professionalisation is progressing, there is a constant growth in research volume, and mobility of learners and staff in adult education is higher than ever. Still, some concepts, approaches and ideas are questionable and need to be analysed, because they are persistent and represent the basis of the new European educational policy in spite of obvious failures in many aspects, such as widening access to education, increasing level of participation and so on. *Skills* and *basic skills* are such concepts, even being transferred to the new main policy documents of the European Commission ('Europe 2020' 2010a; 'ET 2020' 2009; 'Agenda New skills for new jobs' 2010b).

The *Memorandum* represents an obvious attempt to balance human resources and citizens, learning and training, self-development and new technologies, e-learning and mobility. Even the six key messages have this multiple character, recognising the range of the roles of a person and needs of both personal and socio-economic development. But the overall goal stands for 'the shift towards more integrated policies that combine social and cultural objectives with the economic rationale for lifelong learning'

---

[1] Hereafter *Memorandum*.

[2] Hereafter *Communication*.

(European Commission 2000: 9). The ongoing globalisation and international influences, especially the OECD, supported this approach, which reflected the changes in the socio-economic, political and demographic contexts and were seeking transnational solutions for the growing national and global problems (such as changing production, trade and investment patterns, high levels of structural unemployment, densely populated urban areas and others).

Having both Commission's 1993 *White Paper on Growth, Competitiveness and Employment* and 1995 *White Paper on Teaching and Learning: Towards the Learning Society* embedded in its approach – the *Memorandum* attempts to foster the development of a coherent and comprehensive lifelong learning strategy, but for some researchers:

> … it was a neo-liberal set of guidelines that serves to heighten the member states' and candidate countries' competitiveness in a scenario characterised by the intensification of globalisation. (Borg and Mayo 2005: 218)

The focus of this analysis is the notion of skills, basic skills and competencies and their relation to the broader concepts of lifelong learning and knowledge society, as paradigmatic representatives of educational policy.

> The notion is, of course, hopelessly vague, masking many different policy approaches, but it captures something real and significant in modern policy trends…. (Green 2003: 2)

What does the language of the *Memorandum* reveal, and why is the language important? We use it here as the main criterion for our research approach: discourse analysis (combined with the interpretive approach), known as *critical language study* (Fairclough 1989, 1992), because of its power to decode the paradigms behind language. The starting premise is that the use of language is defined by the sociocultural norms or meta-level factors and frames which regulate talk and through which meaning-making occurs (Fairclough 1992), and, coming closer to the user, his language is constructed by the policy discourse and educational paradigm. Even decoding some formal aspects of language and relating them to the context may reveal much about the discourse behind it. Therefore, the 'language can be seen as a form of action' (Fairclough 1989: 9); thus, the critical language analysis opens a base for the interpretation of planning elements and possible actions based on conceptual premises in the text of document.

So, the language of *Memorandum* shows, at a first glance, the deep commitment to lifelong learning. The term appears more than 130 times in the document, *nonformal* and *informal learning* are mentioned around 10 times, *citizens* and *civil society* many times, *competitiveness* just 7 times, *employability* 10 times; similar quotes apply to the term 'Communication'. Obviously, this discourse does not deserve to be called 'neo-liberal' – it is not, at least not in its intention. But the devil is in the detail, and the messages reveal a kind of naivety suggesting steps and solutions that do not respond to the real nature of the proclaimed goals and do not give a realistic direction of reaching them. The most important 'detail' – even more, one of the pillars of the whole document – is 'skills' and 'basic skills', being explicitly mentioned 27 times in the first message and at least once in all other messages. But even more important is the conceptual and relational analysis of these concepts. Moreover, the relevance, consistency and coherence of the ideas around basic skills will be used as the criteria for a discourse and interpretive analysis.

Conceptual and Relational Analysis

The *Memorandum* frequently uses the pair 'education and training', which might imply the reduction of the understanding of education. Since 'general education' does not appear at all and 'basic education'? appears just two times, the text thus suggests that it is through 'training' and 'skills' that the ambitious goals defined in the introduction to *Memorandum* could be fulfilled. It is still not clear how Europe could move to the 'Knowledge Age' ensuring equal participation for everyone, full employment and self-development of citizens. The *knowledge* component remains rhetorically in the document, while the *training* component is clearly and defined in detail through *basic skills*: '…this Memorandum defines new basic skills as those required for active participation in the knowledge society and economy' (European Commission 2000: 10). Education remains in between, as taken for granted, implying a formal education system. How could the high expectations of a knowledge society be achieved just by a skilled labour force? Creativity, innovation, responsibility, capacity to face risks and uncertainties – all these traits and activities are supposed to be implemented by *trained* and *skilled* people. The goals that Europe sets for the future and the way they should be achieved are paved by undefined knowledge, vocational training and skills reduced to basic ones; this is inconsistent with the model of development given implicitly in the text.[3] The problem of moving from rhetoric to realistic development (from theory to praxis) is not analysed or thoroughly mapped.

A further inconsistency is related to the new vision of society and ways to achieve it. This should be (according to both *Memorandum* and *Communication*) a knowledge-based, inclusive society with intelligent use of resources where people

> live positively with cultural, ethnic and linguistic diversity… participate in all spheres of social and economic life… feel that they belong to and have a fair say in the society in which they live (European Commission 2000: 5).

On the other hand, both documents point decisively to the ways of reaching it, whereby one of the most important mechanisms is adaptation: individuals have to adapt to changes… Europe's education and training systems must adapt to the new realities… adaptability of the workforce is crucial… employers demand adaptation to new challenges and situations… the employability and adaptability of citizens is vital for Europe… There is even the statement that the *adaptation* of lifelong

---

[3] Development of learning organisations, use of creativity and innovation in all spheres of life, full mobilisation of resources, active participation of each person in the shaping of Europe's future – in modern public life, especially in social and political life at all levels of the community….

learning facilitators' should be supported! (European Commission 2001: 12).[4] The adaptation to the individual needs of the participants, citizens and local communities is also pointed out in both documents, but adaptation to economic needs and changes is more strongly argued. The necessity of this kind of adaptation is clearly pointed out as the only way for the new vision of Europe to function, while the adaptation to the individual needs has a kind of *l'art pour l'artistic* touch – something which should be done for the sake of itself and for some abstract humanistic purpose, but not really necessary for an economically successful, functioning society. Obviously, the important task of initiating social changes, participating actively in them and taking them forward is not high on the European agenda. Even more so, people educated and trained in skills will not be able or motivated to conduct such changes, because they are expected mainly to learn how to adapt, which is raised to the level of a generic skill: 'Learning how to learn, to adapt to change and to make sense of vast information flows are now generic skills that everyone should acquire' (European Commission 2000: 11), while technological, social and political changes come as an unavoidable *vis* major, beyond the influence of citizens.

The criticism points to the choice of non-relevant means to achieve these goals. The desired kind of economy demands proactive, creative people and a kind of education that will unlock people's creative potential, demand deeper knowledge and a higher level of cognitive and professional competences. In the context of global competition, just acquiring skills will not make a crucial difference and people who 'have adapted' will not be able to make the relevant change. Adaptation preserves the set of given circumstances and supports a development that goes in only one direction. It has a conservative character, because it does not allow one to initiate changes, being thus directly opposite to the development agenda which is set in the European documents.

Even the definition of lifelong learning adopted in the documents – with the aim of improving knowledge, skills and competence – reveals the theoretical conception and ideological approach on which it is based; it implies an increase in the amount of information and development of abilities but no qualitative changes, transformation or personal development. It is not a philosophy of life and of development but more an instrument to achieve some instrumental goals. Even if lifelong learning is perceived as a continuum, it is rather a narrow one:

> High quality basic education for all, from a child's youngest days forward, is the essential foundation. Basic education followed by initial vocational education and training, should equip all young people with the new basic skills required in a knowledge-based economy. (European Commission 2000: 7)

So, the proposed actions are not equally relevant for the two groups of objectives outlined in these documents – firstly, promoting active citizenship and secondly, promoting employability. The first objective is treated more on a declarative level, and there are no further attempts to show concretely how it will be reached, while

---

[4] Furthermore, DG Employment has today in its structure the unit called 'New Skills for New Jobs, Adaptation to Change, CSR and EGF.'

the second objective is higher on the agenda and clearly justified. The documents neglected the power general education, civic education or cultural education might have for the defined purposes:

> Education and training were also narrowed by the qualification-competence pairing, which also forbade the adoption of broader and more complex conceptions of AE, and the implementations of actions that encouraged the training of democratic, independent, thinking, and critical citizens. (Lima and Guimaraes 2011: 109)

Still, the attempt to balance these two approaches is obvious throughout both documents, specific target groups have been mentioned, as well as the intercultural character of European societies and different ways and paths of teaching and learning. Basic skills, as the fundamental idea and the leading mechanism, seemed to be in accordance with these important aspects and tasks – but they turned out to be a 'Trojan horse', paving the way to a completely different approach, marked nowadays with the dominance of vocational education and training, upskilling and reskilling, qualifications and employability.

Difficulties Around the Concept of 'Skills'

The concept of skills started to dominate European policy recently, not playing an important role in European documents about lifelong learning until the *Memorandum* and the *Communication* were launched. This was primarily due to the pressure from the world of economy, to the need for global competitiveness and to the demands from the changing technologies and labour market. The other reason was the transnational influence, particularly from World Bank and the OECD.

Why is the notion of skills limited in its appropriateness for the area of education? As the term comes from human capital theory, reflecting in its nature the world of work, it is not really adequate for the world of education. The basic meaning of 'skills' is usually associated with manual skills, acquired in a short time, based on very little knowledge and almost value-free. Skill refers to the capacity (in the beginning just manual, later also cognitive or intellectual) of performing certain tasks according to certain procedures. The attributes *efficient*, *exact* and *routine* are usually added to skills. No matter if they are defined by various authors as the personal ability of performing a task, or description of activities and ways of performing, they have a strong behavioural character, and a bit a narrow reductionist meaning.

It is seldom that a concept makes such a successful carrier and has such impact at both international level and among the EU members as *skills* did; to mention, for example, the situation in the UK: the Department for Education and Skills (DfES), the Learning and Skills Council (LSC) and The National Skills Task Force (see DfES 2004) have influenced the overall national agenda on skills. Widely accepted, hardly ever critically reflected, further developed in many aspects (basic skills, key skills, generic skills, high and low skills), skills have a fascinating attractiveness for all those seeking a closer relation between education and work, for more effectiveness and standardisation, for establishing procedures, quality criteria and measuring. This kind of popularity made 'skills' a kind of *deus ex machina* for any problem, be it in the field of policy, research or practice.

Indeed, the introduction of this approach helped European education to progress, raised many new issues and supported many developments in the field of vocational education and training. It inspired new critical discussion about traditional, old-fashioned and outdated approaches to learning and education, which really could not meet the demands of the new, modern times. But coming back to the question; does this approach have unlimited relevance and functionality for the European agenda?

The variety of meaning attached to 'skills' and the numerous definitions and approaches applied may suggest that it could be the answer to all problems in the field of vocational education. But closer analysis of the context, relations and interdependencies of the term shows that it is mainly about production, technology, jobs and qualifications. One example from England, a country that adopted the EU skills policy extensively, illustrates this: Although the book *Skills in England: The Research Report* promises a broader approach, the starting definitions point to the dominant paradigm:

> Overall, we have sought to use four sets of proxies for skills: occupations (the actual jobs that people do); qualifications (the level of certified competence that people possess); individuals' assessment of their own skills; and employers' assessment of their skill requirements. In assessing many aspects of skills in England we examine the evidence in terms of sectors, occupations and qualifications. (Campbell et al. 2001: 3)

Looking closer to the *Memorandum* and the *Communication*, the skills are put either in the context of mobility, labour market and employability or in something which remains very much as a somewhat enriched traditional conception of basic literacy: literacy, numeracy, ICT and 'the others', as they are called in the *Memorandum* (European Commission 2000: 11). It is interesting that 'the others' mostly just remain 'the others', and if they are specified, they include entrepreneurship, foreign languages and technology. Social skills are mentioned just marginally. It is much more than language bizarreness when *science* is considered as one of the *new basic skills* in the *Communication*: '...new basic skills, including entrepreneurship, science and technology' (European Commission 2001: 12).

The criticism towards a skills approach is even more justified when it comes to the definition where 'skills' do include 'knowledge'. Subsequent analysis shows that the level of required knowledge does not allow raising the concept of 'skills' above that of 'knowledge' (even if the policy level might allow one to define 'everything by everything', the research approach could hardly define skills by knowledge). Almost every activity of an adult person demands some kind or some level of knowledge, it is not in the very nature of skills; knowledge is not *differentia specifica* of skills. Therefore, the reductionist character of skills remains one of the main points of criticism – it denies the integral, holistic approach to human being, leaves less space for creativity, freedom, flexibility and critical thinking. This criticism does not deny the usefulness and positive impact of the skills approach; it applies to the attempt to raise skills to the highest level in the European policy, to the main mechanism and all-encompassing concept.

Even more, the serious problem with skills is their *value-free* character. Similar to knowledge, attempts to include attitudes to the definition of skills are not grounded, and some of the most important questions of human life are untouched by skills – values, ethics and emotions. It could be additionally argued that skills help the shift to the neoliberal approach through their feigned neutralism, since they do fulfil some goals and do have certain functions, but in the domain of production rather than in the domain of citizenship. Further on, skills are almost *context-free* and could not be transferred easily from one setting to another – whether a work or life situation – and cannot be simply related to the situation of the individuals, with their life context and the meanings they give to it. An additional aspect is that a reductionist approach to skills helps to shift the whole responsibility for education and learning process to an individual (not to an employer, institutions or state) but without really giving people the opportunity to think and reflect on their own learning goals, paths and preferences.

A serious attempt to overcome the difficulties of a skills approach is made by the use of the term *competences*. Many authors use these words as synonyms, thus giving an *alibi* to the shortcomings of skills, ascribing some qualities of the *competencies* to the *skills*, which are not in the nature of skills. The competences indicate the tendency to combine skills (including cognitive, social and personal), particularly those not related to employment and employability and not exclusively outcome oriented. The concept of *key competences* suggests this even more, trying to include *attitudes* and elements of *values* in it.

This seems to be a perfect compromise. The *Memorandum* and the *Communication* (European Commission 2001: 23) have announced 'a shift from 'knowledge' to 'competence'', opening thus the new 'era' – an attempt to integrate all aspects of human being and life into a list of various competences. This ambitious task resulted in a powerful skills/competencies combination: Together with vocational training, ICT and soft skills became a *deus ex machina* that should enable employability, competitiveness and adaptability. Soft skills (called also *interpersonal/communicative competences*) are also meant to cover all personal (even if not strictly measurable) abilities, traits, characteristics and qualities. Similarly, the concept of competences was extended beyond its real capacity encompassing an extremely broad range of areas: culture, aesthetics, critical thinking, problem solving, creativity and innovation (OECD even adds terms like reflectiveness to the list). Common sense alone would dictate that competences cannot be easily trained and transferred but have to be developed through long-term processes and via complex learning experiences.

The terminology and conceptual confusion was increased by introducing expressions like *functional literacy* and *multiliteracies* by some authors. For example, these expressions should include also 'historic and cultural literacy' (Doukas 2003: 30), which is far beyond the standard meaning of skills and competencies.

The concept of competences also gains popularity and developed further, *generic, broad, intersectoral, transversal,* creates an artificial, anthropologically strange idea of the person, who consists of a set of implausible competencies, but with no recognisable characteristics of a human being, whose performances – even in a strictly professional setting – are also determined by emotions, motivation, satisfaction and very much by a value system.

Developments After the *Memorandum* and *Communication*

Both documents could be seen as milestones in European educational policy. They adopt a balanced approach, a broad and all-encompassing understanding of teaching and learning and an openness to the new tendencies in education and related areas. This contains some elements of the best traditions of European education. The set of messages in the documents was given favourably and with commitment. On the other hand, these texts heralded a new development in this field, which was becoming the dominant paradigm in European educational policy. It was the concept of skills in these documents that announced the positivist, pragmatist discourse and the prevalence of the labour-/job-oriented function of education and learning. Ten years after that, developments progressed swiftly:

> EU education and training policies have gained impetus since the adoption of the Lisbon Strategy in 2000, the EU's overarching programme focusing on growth and jobs. The strategy recognised that knowledge, and the innovation it sparks, are the EU's most valuable assets, particularly in the light of increasing global competition. The Member States and the European Commission strengthened co-operation in 2009 with strategic framework for 'European Cooperation in Education and Training' (ET 2020), a follow-up to the earlier 'Education and Training 2010 Work Programme' launched in 2001. (European Commission 2009)

Appearing under the *Lifelong Learning Policy* title on the web portal of the Commission, this document demonstrates one of the main contradictions of this approach, since *lifelong learning* is supposed to be the main concept, but it almost disappears from the text, which was not the case with the *Memorandum.*

Obviously, the shift from education to learning, which is a part of common rhetoric and generally accepted as *factum est* in the European area, was not really developed in its entirety as it was assumed. To put it another way, the process was like *peeling an onion*, and lifelong learning remained as the outside layer, when everything inside were turning more and more to skills and competencies. If the strategy documents are taken as the illustration for the policy which is about to be adopted or implemented, or even just made public at the rhetoric level, lifelong learning is not a pillar of this policy at all. The titles of the new documents show that (e.g. *Agenda New Skills for New jobs, Education and Training 2020*). But a closer look reveals that *education* is still the dominant term, in two meanings: either in the context of formal system (schooling), where the minimal use of *nonformal and informal education* proves that formal education still widely dominates, or together with *training*, which speaks strongly for the dominance of vocational education.

The fact that two strategic documents *Europe 2020* and *ET 2020* are accompanied by an *Agenda* which has just the word *skills* in the title, leaving out other terms related to education and learning (without having some new *Action Plan on Adult Learning*), sheds the light on the central concept and main paradigm of these strategies and dominant approach.[5] Lifelong learning is obviously not recognised as a

---

[5] Compare how OECD is putting the terms 'education' and "skills" as opposite poles in the title of the book: 'Skills, not just diplomas...' (Sondergaard et al. 2011).

concept helpful for achieving the European goals for 2020, but *education and training* together with *skills* are recognised as useful. *ET 2020* does recognise life-long learning as a fundamental principle, including adult learning, but in the *Agenda New Skills for New Jobs,* they are hardly mentioned. If adults have such a low rank as a target group in all these documents, then *lifelong learning* as the overall title for the policy and programme is not justified. Adults *disappear* to a certain extent from the scene, learning also – what remains dominantly is educa-tion, training, formal system and young people as the prevailing target group. Formal and/or formally recognised training and acquirement of skills turned out to be not just the main instrument in the above-mentioned strategies, but they are even raised to the paradigm level, appearing as the goal or key objective. Some examples can be found in the documents, such as the title *Agenda New Skills for New Jobs* or a quotation from it: 'Implementing flexicurity principles and enabling people to acquire new skills to adapt to new conditions and potential career shifts will be key' (European Commission 2010a: 16). The other example shows that acquisition of skills even changes the importance of rank within the lifelong learn-ing strategy: 'The key importance of acquiring skills and competences throughout the working life requires comprehensive strategies for Lifelong Learning' (Agenda New skills for new jobs: 8). So, skills attained the status of the key objec-tive, method and mean – the development that begun already with *Memorandum* and *Communication.*

The following view illustrates the function of skills and competencies in the actual European educational policy:

> Europe 2020 boosts the idea of lifelong learning becoming both the global agenda and a new 'fashion', as argued by Field… Furthermore, it retails the relation between the educa-tion, training, and economic development by granting adult education the status of an instrument for human resources management, and by establishing complex technical process for that link, especially after the adoption of the EQF. (Lima and Guimaraes 2011: 108)

So, skills and competencies achieved the central role in translating the philosophy and concept of lifelong learning into a tool, i.e. a simplified, pragmatic list of measurable abilities oriented to economic purposes.

Skills might be an important instrument in the global competition, but it is a 'weapon' that was produced elsewhere and imported under the pressure of economic reasons into educational processes. As Lima and Guimaraes (2011: 108) state:

> Lifelong learning favoured by European Union […] also met the demands of globalisation and the economy. It therefore considered orientations that focused on encouraging the adaptability of individuals, flexibility, competitiveness, and growth in the service of the knowledge-based economy.

By imposing the concept of skills to the world of education, the world of work has successfully replaced the narrative typical for education and learning, thus disempowering the traditional educational concept. Terminology and vocabulary proved to have power to subordinate the field or the group that they had been imposed to.[6] Educational sector is thus developing (actively, engaged and convinced) the 'imported' concepts and narratives, neglecting completely its own field of responsibility, issues and problems that it should focus on.

By using skills and competencies, European strategies put learning into the function of economy, implying that it was something that could be commodified or measured quantitatively and therefore be transferred, sold or exchanged as a product. No doubt education and world of work need a common understanding, concepts and terminology enabling dialogue, but skills as a concept are introduced from the world of production; therefore, they omit some of the most important features of the learning and education process.

The risk of such a narrow development focusing on skills is twofold. The strength of European education and learning policies could hardly lie in a concept which is not rooted in the European tradition, not consequently integrated into the whole policy (economic, social, educational) and not related to the achievement of overall goals, especially not in the long run. One of the strong points of the European tradition – close connections between general and vocational education and good general education *for all* – is jeopardised now. The artificial separation which is done for the sake of faster economic growth can harm both types of education but also both sectors of society – economy (in the long run, because jobs are becoming more knowledge intensive) and the inclusive society where personal growth is seen as the value for both individual and the society. The artificial division between general and vocational education does not withstand interrogation – neither from a formal-logical nor a functional point of view. The attempt to incorporate them under the umbrella of *skills*, as *vocational and soft skills, basic and high, generic and scientific* is artificial and mainly disadvantageous for the second group. The relationships between them has to be redefined, and some new paradigms (not just mechanisms) for their functional connections should be found, which is far more challenging (and more difficult) for educational policy than the provision of basic or similar skills. It is perhaps easier to create a common approach to problems like 'skills shortage assessment' than to address the question Europe once shared with UNESCO – 'How to live together?'[7] But it does not make this question less important.

Furthermore, there is a danger in the process of translating the European policy at the national level. Considering the variety of approaches, traditions and learning cultures, training could be easily understood as drill, and skills acquisition implemented simply as short-term courses on elementary skills. Very strong orientation to employment would certainly lead to the reduction of funding for any other kind of

---

[6] The anthropology of gender focused a lot to the ways that vocabulary developed from the point of view of male researchers influenced the whole area of anthropological researches, creating the distorted picture of social development. Imposing narrative through vocabulary creates an illusion of equality and 'cooperation', while at the same time the group or field concerned loses the power to develop its own concepts and to contribute genuine to the crosscutting issues and to 'cooperation'.

[7] It is interesting that UNESCO is still very much trying to balance these two approaches - see for example 'Belém framework for action' (UNESCO 2009).

education (such as civic education, intercultural and peace education), which is embedded in the fundaments of European history and community and is an inseparable part of its identity. Oriented to short-term goals, European societies will not have long-term and common solutions for challenges like ageing societies, mobile workforce, mixed societies, growing nationalism and aggression, fragile democracies and so forth.

The global socio-economic crisis puts this discussion high on the global agenda; approaches, paradigms and concepts have to be critically reflected and rethought. The way this is done does not promise affirmative change because it contains a logical fallacy which shows the deep lack of understanding. Einstein has formulated it in the following way[8]: 'We can't solve problems by using the same kind of thinking we used when we created them'. Not just in Europe, but globally, only the consequences of the crises have been addressed, not the causes and the question: What education can do about that remains to be answered. Most certainly value-free education, which is just a mask for vocational training in the function of a neoliberal economy, will not prevent any further crises – neither economic and monetary nor social and value crises. Missing values is a more important challenge than missing skills. Still adult education which is remote from everyday life and from economic reality, being somewhat *for its own sake,* is not a good approach to address the challenges of the modern time and the global world. But using skills and competencies as the main instrument to respond to these challenges may lead to another kind of impasse. As a matter of fact, Europe is already facing serious crises of its value system, crises of identity and solidarity, combined with nationalism and violence. The adult education response to these crises, in the shape of skills, is a chimera – an illusion that is composed from fragments of learning and work but not the most relevant and adequate fragments. The need to rethink and re-evaluate our concepts and need to create new paradigms remains.

References

Borg, C., & Mayo, P. (2005). The EU 'Memorandum' on lifelong learning. Old wine in new bottles? *Globalisation, Societies and Education, 3*(2), 203–225.

Campbell, M., Baldwin, S., et al. (2001). *Skills in England 2011. The research report.* Leeds: Policy Research Institute Leeds Metropolitan University.

Council of Europe. (1970). *Permanent education.* Strasbourg: COE.

DfES. (2004). *Key skills. Policy & practice. Your questions answered.* London: DfES.

Doukas, C. (2003). New topologies in European policies: The framework of lifelong learning policies. In C. Medel-Anonuevo (Ed.), *Lifelong learning discourses in Europe* (pp. 27–35). Hamburg: UNESCO, UIL.

Einstein, A. (2013). Resource document. *Wikiquote.* http://en.wikiquote.org/wiki/Albert_Einstein#1940s

European Commission. (2000). *A 'Memorandum' on lifelong learning.* Resource document. European Commission. http://www.bologna-berlin2003.de/pdf/'Memorandum'Eng.pdf

---

[8] Probably the paraphrases of the Einstein's 1946 quote (2013), not confirmed.

European Commission. (2001). *'Communication' from the commission. Making a European area of lifelong learning a reality*. Brussels: European Commission.

European Commission. (2009). *Strategic framework for education and training*. Resource document. European Commission. http://ec.europa.eu/education/lifelong-learning-policy/framework_en.htm

European Commission. (2010a). *Europe 2020: A European strategy for smart, sustainable and inclusive growth*. Resource document. European Commission. http://europa.eu/press_room/pdf/complet_en_barroso_007_-_europe_2020_-_en_version.pdf

European Commission. (2010b). *An agenda for new skills and jobs: A European contribution towards full employment*. Resource document. European Commission. http://eur-lex.europa.eu/lexuriserv/lexuriserv.do?uri=com:2010:0682:fin:en:pdf

European Council. (2000). *Presidency conclusions: Lisbon strategy*. Resource document. European Council. http://www.mpn.gov.rs/resursi/dokumenti/dok282-eng-lisbon_strategy.pdf

Fairclough, N. (1989). *Language and power*. London: Longman.

Fairclough, N. (1992). *Discourse and social change*. London: Polity Press.

Green, A. (2003). The many faces of lifelong learning: Recent education policy trends in Europe. *Journal of Education Policy, 17*(6), 611–626.

Lima, L., & Guimaraes, P. (2011). *European strategies in lifelong learning*. Leverkse/Opladen: Barbara Budric Publishers.

Sondergaard, L., Murthi, M., Abu-Ghaida, D., Bodewig, C., & Rutkowski, J. (2011). *Skills, not just diplomas. Managing education for results in Eastern Europe and Central Asia*. Washington, DC: The World Bank.

The Council of the European Union. (2009). Strategic framework for European cooperation in education and training ('ET 2020'). *Official Journal of the European Union*. Resource document. http://eur-lex.europa.eu/lexuriserv/lexuriserv.do?uri=oj:c:2009:119:0002:0010:en:pdf

UNESCO. (2009). *Harnessing the power and potential of adult learning and education for a viable future. Belém framework for action*. CONFINTEA VI. Brazil. Resource document. http://www.unesco.org/fileadmin/multimedia/institutes/uil/confintea/pdf/working_documents/bel%c3%a9m%20framework_final.pdf

Chapter 3
Computer Literacy Among the Generations: How Can Older Adults Participate in Digital Society?

Bernhard Schmidt-Hertha and Claudia Strobel-Dümer

Introduction

The ability to participate in society is considered a central aim of every educational process in the memorandum, and lifelong learning is seen as a way *"to encourage and equip people to participate more actively once more in all spheres of modern public life, especially in social and political life at all levels of the community, including at European level"* (European Commission 2000, p. 5). Looking at contemporary ways of participating in modern societies, knowing how to deal with digital media, especially the computer and the Internet, constitutes a crucial and basic educational content. Digital media play a crucial role not only in accessing information but also in communication in the private, the commercial, and the political sector. Furthermore, the fact that many services – such as counseling, banking, or administrative processes – are increasingly handled via Internet has a significant impact on older people's lives. For people who do not have access to a computer or to the Internet, this development implies that they are excluded from a steadily growing sector of social life. Active participation in social life and societal processes is thus significantly limited, which is why the acquisition of just this ability to participate is formulated as one of the foremost aims of media-pedagogical approaches (Hurrelmann 2002).

Digital media thus constitute a significant content of education and learning processes in every phase of life. At the same time, these media – the Internet, in particular – provide rich resources for learning processes and thus offer the possibility to support informal learning which can take place independent of institutional

B. Schmidt-Hertha (✉)
Institute of Education, University of Tübingen, Tübingen, Germany
e-mail: bernhard.schmidt-hertha@uni-tuebingen.de

C. Strobel-Dümer
Socio-Educational Institute of SOS-Kinderdorf e.V., Munich, Germany

G.K. Zarifis and M.N. Gravani (eds.), *Challenging the 'European Area of Lifelong Learning': A Critical Response*, Lifelong Learning Book Series 19, DOI 10.1007/978-94-007-7299-1_3, © Springer Science+Business Media Dordrecht 2014

infrastructures within the educational system. Thus, modern information and communication technologies on the one hand offer the chance to make up for infrastructural disadvantages, when access to services and information does no longer depend on local facilities; on the other hand, structures of inequality may well be (re-)produced through the medial infrastructure. The more important it is to have access to digital media for social participation and individual learning opportunities, the more problematic it becomes if entire groups of the population are excluded from this use of digital media (Remtulla 2010, p. 309).

Computer Competence, Digital Divide, and Participation

Participation is an elementary component of civil society. Accordingly participation is formulated as a central goal of European policy, as mentioned above. The memorandum also points on the revolutionary meaning of digital media for knowledge societies (European Commission 2000, p. 7) and consequently claims IT skills as one of the necessary basic skills for people in Europe (ibid. p. 10). We can observe an increasing transfer of information processing, opinion making, and also learning resources into digital worlds. This means the exclusion of people who don't have access to the Internet in many central parts of civil life and informational resources. Looking at this, it seems only consequent, to make demands on fostering IT skills for all. Nevertheless, in same way the question could be posed, if it is necessary or beneficiary to bound participation in many fields exclusively to digital media (e.g., evaluation of political ideas or products but also processes of daily living like ticket sale). On the one hand, it can be criticized that many parts of daily life and civil society depend more and more on the use of digital media; on the other hand, it can be argued, developing IT skills in all social groups and generations is the only way to cope with this irreversible development.

In current reality this trend means exclusion of parts of the population from more and more important societal resources, named with the catchword "digital divide" (Warschauer 2004). The divide between people with and people without access to the Internet can essentially be discussed related to three aspects:

Firstly, on the global level, strong disparities between North and South are discernible. While large parts of the population of the rich and mostly industrialized northern hemisphere have been provided with Internet access, large parts of the population of the economically less developed countries of the southern hemisphere remain excluded from participation in the World Wide Web (Warschauer 2004).

Secondly, in modern industrial societies another form of the "digital divide" within society becomes apparent. Not so much the possibility to access digital media, but rather the competence to use these media is unequally distributed among the different social strata and milieus. While the number of users suggests a quite thorough distribution of computer and Internet throughout all social milieus, the ways in which these media are used differ significantly. For instance, some social groups focus more on informational aspects of media while others prefer to use the same media for entertainment (Pietraß et al. 2005).

Thirdly, there runs a digital divide between different generations – if diverse studies on the use of digital media are reliable. Those born after 1980 grew up with modern digital media; they use these media with great routine and naturalness due to their medial socialization and are therefore also referred to as "digital natives" (Trinder et al. 2008). In contrast, older adults, in particular, especially those born before 1950, seem to be less familiar with the use of digital media (Hargittai 2002). At least, the number of individuals not using the computer and the Internet is (still) much higher among those older than 60 than among the younger age groups (Jones and Fox 2009). This is due, on the one hand, to different socialization experiences and, on the other hand, to habitualized media practices determined by the use of media during adolescence. Following Karl Mannheim's considerations on generational location and on "generations in actuality" (Mannheim 1928), media experiences in adolescence can be expected as crucial for media use during the lifetime. It can be assumed that those media which played a crucial role during adolescence as well as the respective patterns of media use will remain defining during the later phases of a person's life. This assumption was further substantiated through empirical studies (Schäffer 2003). Looking at the aims formulated in the memorandum (strengthening social participation and developing ICT skills), it has to be seen as a great challenge not to exclude older people when information and participation is more and more based on digital media.

Cultures of media practice specific to certain generations do not only have an impact on the way media are dealt with or on the attitude toward media. These cultures also correspond with the development of knowledge and competencies regarding the handling of media. Knowledge about media and the ability to employ them effectively can be considered essential prerequisites for media use and are closely linked with the terms "media competence" and "media literacy" or – when referring to digital media – "computer literacy". Although these three central terms are sometimes used as synonyms, different definitions apply to each.

Media competence is a term well established in European media pedagogy, in the German literature, in particular. According to the concept evolved by Baacke (1996), media competence comprises four fields:

- Media knowledge refers to basic information and knowledge about media and media formats.
- Media use emphasizes more strongly the knowledge concerning the application of media. The focus is on enabling people to choose and use appropriate media.
- Media design is, according to Baacke (1996), the ability to actively partake in the design and production of medial contents. Nowadays, at times of an interactive use of the Internet, media design is turning into a mass phenomenon and, thus, is becoming a fundamental competency requirement in modern societies (Pikalek 2010, p. 151).
- Media critique comprises the skill to critically question medial contents and their design, to recognize inherent manipulation strategies and manipulative intentions, and to be aware of the influence of media on the social level (Remtulla 2010). Empirical findings indicate that this ability to remain critical is more pronounced among older adults than among the younger ones (Eshet-Alkalai and Chajut 2010).

As a counterpart to the term competency, the concept of literacy is used above all in American and internationally determined educational research; this term originally referred to the skill to read and understand texts. In a broader sense, *media literacy* refers to "people's ability to access and process information from a form of transition" (Potter 2011, p. 12). Thus, the concept of media literacy is not limited to a certain medium but rather comprises almost all forms of medial presentation, although most of the scientific discourses focus on mass media. From a cognitive-psychological perspective, Potter (2011) argues that habituated attentional processes, individual knowledge and the ability to deal with media are central components of media literacy.

Computer literacy, on the other hand, refers exclusively to computer and Internet applications and is therefore much easier to grasp empirically. Computer literacy comprises the use of programs and applications in solving well-structured problems (Bers 2010). Furthermore, there are indications that the development of computer software (in the sense of media design, see above) may also promote meta-cognitive competencies (Papert 1980).

Learning and Media Competency in Old Age: The Research Projects CiLL and IGeL-Media

In the context of lifelong learning and the EU memorandum, which points on the meaning of ICT skills in every age and for every social group, some central questions related to ICT use in higher age become significant. Looking at media use, what differences between age groups and generations can be found? Is the ability to develop media competence related to age? What are motives and barriers for older adults to deal with digital media? To what extent is intergenerational learning a meaningful way of developing media competence in higher age? All these questions are addressed by different research projects, which will be presented briefly in the following passages.

With regard to adults, the digital literacy model proposed by Eshet-Alkalai (2004), which also takes into consideration socio-emotional aspects, provides a differentiated alternative to the concept of computer literacy. Empirical studies revealed that younger computer users could better orientate themselves in multimedia environments and were faster in grasping graphically processed contents than older users; however, these differences are clearly reduced after several years of computer use. In contrast, older computer users showed a much higher performance with regard to critical reflection and creative (re)organization of multimedia presentations. The gap between the age groups related to these aspects of digital literacy actually increased with the growing experience in dealing with the computer in all age groups (Eshet-Alkalai and Chajut 2010). The authors consider these findings a clear proof of the ability to build up or broaden digital literacy in old age.

The results of the abovementioned study are thus consistent with gerontological and cognitive-psychological studies on the ability to learn during old age.

It is by now beyond dispute that the ability to learn is not primarily a question of age but rather can be maintained well into old age (Kruse and Schmitt 2000; Schaie 2005). A prerequisite for this is that one never grows out of the habit of learning and that the mental performance is practiced through cognitive activation (Saczynski et al. 2002). Forms of learning and learning preferences change with age; however, these developments differ considerably from one individual to the other. They are determined, e.g., by biographical experiences and the current life situation (Strobel et al. 2011), and it is due to these diverse developments that older adults are an extremely heterogeneous target group for adult education (Schmidt 2010a, b).

This heterogeneity is reflected in the interest in dealing with digital media and in the ways in which older adults choose to approach these media. The further development of one's computer literacy can be targeted or rather casual. The motivational basis for learning processes then results from an actual challenge to act (e.g., the necessity to solve a problem) or from a merely intrinsic interest (e.g., being curios on new IKT). Computer literacy may be obtained in organized courses or through informal channels, alone or together with friends or family members. These different ways of learning and learning motives, learning opportunities, and situations as well as the significance of computer literacy for older adults in everyday life are the subject of several studies presently carried out in Germany. In this contribution, results from two ongoing research projects – "Competencies in Later Life (CiLL)" and "Informal Intergenerational Learning for Media Competence (IGeL-Media)" – will be presented.

One of the components of the CiLL project is an extension of the national PIAAC survey carried out in Germany. Within the framework of PIAAC, the Program for International Assessment of Adult Competencies of the OECD, the competencies of 19–65-year-old adults in three different fields are surveyed through standardized tests: literacy, numeracy, and problem solving in a technology-rich environment (Schleicher 2008). The last mentioned field of competency – problem solving in a technology-rich environment – essentially refers to the skill to solve everyday problems with the use of the computer or the Internet. Thus, the underlying competency construct is closely linked to the concept of computer literacy or digital literacy (OECD 2009). In the CiLL project, the abovementioned fields of competency are surveyed among the group of 66–80-year-old adults in Germany by using the same instruments. The competency tests, which are still being prepared, are supplemented by qualitative data, some of which has already been collected. These qualitative case studies primarily aim at clarifying in what way the competencies surveyed are relevant to older people's ability to deal with everyday life and what learning opportunities the respective living environments provide for older people to develop these competencies (Strobel et al. 2011).

IGeL-Media - a research project funded by the German Research Association DFG (SCHM 2391/3-1) - focuses exclusively on the acquisition of media competency among those older than 60, with the emphasis on informal learning processes triggered, for instance, through the exchange with children, grandchildren, or other significant members of a younger generation. This approach is based on the assumption that older adults mainly develop their competencies in dealing with digital media through the exchange with younger contact persons. Through a secondary analysis of a representative survey on the interests in learning and further education among older adults living in Germany (Schmidt 2007) and through qualitative interviews with older people, these intergenerational learning processes and their contribution to the acquisition of media competencies are to be revealed (Schmidt-Hertha and Thalhammer 2012). So far, only first results of the secondary analysis have been reported, while the qualitative results will not be available until the end of 2012.

In the following, we refer to the results of the secondary analysis of 2.142 standardized interviews with adults aged between 60 and 80 living in Germany, carried out within the framework of the IGeL-Media project, as well as to the first results of the case studies from the CiLL project. These case studies are mainly based on qualitative guideline interviews which have been fully transcribed and analyzed following the principles of qualitative content analysis (Mayring 2000).

Computer Literacy Among Older People

Throughout the different countries, it can be seen that younger generations are much closer to digital media than the older ones. In practically all of the European countries – and also in non-European states – the percentage of computer and Internet users in the older cohorts is clearly below average. Although, for the year 2010, the percentage of Internet users among people older than 65 varied in the European countries from 3 % (in Rumania and Bulgaria) to 64 % (in Luxemburg). While the Scandinavian countries, in particular, belong to the lead group with more than 40 %, the quota of the so-called silver surfers is below 15 % throughout all of the Southern and Eastern European countries. At the same time, data from the Federal Statistical Office (2011, p. 35) show that the growth rates in Internet users have been highest among the older population groups during the last few years.

Computer Use Among Older Adults

According to the data collected by the German Federal Statistical Office (2011, p. 32) for the year 2010, the percentage of Internet users among those aged 45–64 had already reached 75 %, and that among adults older than 65 had reached 31 %, with a clear upward trend. In the context of the IGeL-Media project, the point of interest was not so much the percentage of users but rather in how far users and nonusers differ with regard to their life situation and their environment. By means of a logistic regression analysis, the influence of different factors was determined. Among these factors were in addition to socio-demographic variables, attitudes, and lifestyles, above all activities in the social field and leisure activities.

As was to be expected, both gender and educational level proved to be strong predictors for computer use. Older adults are significantly more likely to be among those using the computer if they are male and if they have higher school-leaving qualifications than if they are female and have a lower education. About as important as gender for the probability of computer usage is the influence of calendrical age, even within the group of those aged 60–80. The influence of migration background and of employment status, although statistically relevant, is much smaller than that of the variables mentioned before. Nonetheless, older people with migration background and those not or no longer employed use the computer less often than other older adults. The most striking result of the regression analysis was that participation in cultural activities and programs was as meaningful with regard to computer use as was educational background or age. Older adults who regularly participate in cultural activities or who are themselves active in the fields of music or art are much more often among those using a computer than other older people.

Learning Processes: Why and How Do Older People Learn to Deal with the Computer?

We are now faced with the question of why and how people who never systematically learned to deal with the computer or the Internet (can) catch up on this in old age.

Here, the influence of educational and vocational biographies, hinted at above, manifests itself, as is confirmed by first evaluations of the CiLL project. Persons who actively used a computer during their vocational lives were able to acquire first competencies through measures of in-service training or through the exchange with younger colleagues. Often, interest was aroused through those experiences, and in the following a computer was bought for private use. Especially these people who had fun in dealing with the computer and who considered it to be a great asset improved their computer literacy through adequate courses offered in adult education.

A somewhat different picture presents itself with regard to people who had no contact with computers or the Internet during their working life. Here, the evaluation of the case studies often reveals a strong rejection of or lack of interest in the digital world. Frequently, persons from the immediate environment (especially one's own children and grandchildren) are drawn upon whenever information to be found on the Internet is required.

Another group of older adults deliberately and specifically learned how to use digital media once they had retired. Thus, they learn either by trial and error or by attending a course of further education or – as was true for many of the cases investigated – through the exchange with younger generations (again, above all, children and grandchildren). Often, these individuals display a strong interest in technology, and they are open to new things.

For many of the older people, contact with the younger generations can be cause and motivation for dealing with the Internet at the same time. For instance, if the grandchild studies in a foreign country and contact can be maintained through e-mail communication, digital media become relevant for the grandparents, too.

In many instances, the motivation to deal with the computer and to learn how to use digital media results from a consideration of their immediate usefulness.

But also the life situation of older adults plays an important role. Seniors with an active lifestyle and a stable social network seem to be more open toward the computer (Strobel et al. 2011). Here, patterns for an active shaping of one's life take effect, which enable a person to learn something new and to ask for help from people who accompany this process. The influence of the social environment seems to be just as strong in this age group as IT is the influence of the individual educational biography.

When looking at the results of the case studies, it becomes apparent that older adults are much more careful than younger adults in dealing with the computer or the Internet. Often, it is reported that, although the Internet is used as a medium to gain information, websites which require a registration or the revelation of personal data are avoided. Thus, a pronounced critical distance does not necessarily lead to a complete rejection of specific medial applications. For instance, being skeptical about security of e-business offers doesn't always mean to avoid all forms of financial transfers via Internet but could lead to limited e-business activities exclusively with well-known providers.

The Participation of Older Adults in Digital Worlds: Challenges for Society and Science

The social inclusion of older adults and also of the very old in aging societies has to be considered as one of the crucial challenges of the coming years and decades. In this context, modern information and communication technologies may have both integrative and ostracizing effects. On the one hand, they have the potential of allowing partaking in many areas of both public and private life, independent of any physical impediments or factors of mobility. On the other hand, generation-specific habits of media use and a lack of access to a computer or the Internet often mean that older adults, in particular, remain excluded from this increasingly more important medium. The aim to promote participation in public life for all, like it is defined in the memorandum on lifelong learning, is closely related to the use of digital media. When public life is more and more transferred into digital worlds and at the same time a significant number of people don't have access to these media worlds, this aim has to be missed. The partial coercion to use computer and Internet – e.g., when certain products or services are no longer available but online – is considered impertinence by older people. It would be just as presumptuous to require older people per se to have computer literacy on a specific level without considering their respective individual living environments and the related everyday demands.

The results of the CiLL study that are available so far clearly show that many older people like to resort to modern media if they recognize their immediate added value. Communication with children and grandchildren has proven to be a further source of motivation for dealing with modern media. Still, media use and media competence must not become an end in themselves; rather, their relation to the living environment of older people has to be meaningful and useful. An important strategy to encourage more people to use ICT for participating in public life would be to strengthen and support the development of media competence especially for those groups which are excluded from digital worlds so far.

In order to support media use among older adults – depending on regional and social background – two different approaches seem to be of significance. On the one hand, participation in modern information and communication technologies can only be made possible for older adults if both the infrastructural basis and certain economic preconditions for Internet use are given. On the other hand, such participation requires not only basic knowledge of how to handle this medium but also knowledge of the risks and dangers connected with the Internet and about possible ways of minimizing these risks. While the first requirement describes a sociopolitical challenge, the second points to a task of adult education. Not only is it necessary to offer adequate educational programs for older people but also informal learning processes within the social environment have to be initiated and supported. These self-controlled learning processes can, for instance, take place in self-organized computer groups or on Internet forums which, in turn, can be initiated and accompanied by educational institutions. One such initiative which specifically promotes self-controlled learning among older adults is, for example, the EU project PALADIN (www.projectpaladin.eu). This project focuses on the development of instruments which are meant to provide older people as well as professionals and institutions working in this field with printed material and support resources.

Finally, it has to be noted that the differences revealed in the context of media use are not differences between age groups but between generations. Future generations of older adults are already much more familiar with digital media and have integrated these quite naturally in their everyday lives. Thus, for the future, it can be assumed that among the very old generations, too, computer and Internet applications will be used in various ways and that the opportunities of social participation connected with these will become more and more important.

References

Baacke, D. (1996). Medienkompetenz – Begrifflichkeit und sozialer Wandel. In A. von Rein (Ed.), *Medienkompetenz als Schlüsselbegriff* (pp. 112–124). Bad Heilbrunn: Klinkhardt.

Bers, M. U. (2010). Beyond computer literacy: Supporting youth's positive development through technology. *New Directions for Youth Development, 128*, 13–23.

Eshet-Alkalai, Y. (2004). Digital literacy: A conceptual framework for survival skills in the digital era. *Journal of Educational Multimedia and Hypermedia, 13*, 93–106.

Eshet-Alkalai, Y., & Chajut, E. (2010). You can teach old dogs new tricks: The factors that affect changes over time in digital literacy. *Journal of Information Technology Education, 9*, 173–180.

European Commission. (2000). *A Memorandum on lifelong learning*. Brussels: European Commission.

Federal Statistical Office. (2011). *Im Blickpunkt: Ältere Menschen in Deutschland und der EU*. Wiesbaden: Federal Statistical Office.

Hargittai, E. (2002). Second level digital divide: Differences in people's online skills. *First Monday, 7*(4). Retrieved from http://firstmonday.org/htbin/cgiwrap/bin/ojs/index.php/fm/article/view/942/864

Hurrelmann, B. (2002). Zur historischen und kulturellen Relativität des „gesellschaftlichen handlungsfähigen Subjekts" als normative Rahmenidee für Medienkompetenz. In N. Groeben & B. Hurrelmann (Eds.), *Medienkompetenz. Voraussetzungen, Dimensionen, Funktionen* (pp. 160–197). Weinheim: Juventa.

Jones, S., & Fox, S. (2009). *Generations online in 2009.* Retrieved from http://www.floridatechnet. org/Generations_Online_in_2009.pdf

Kruse, A., & Schmitt, E. (2000). Adult education and training. In N. J. Smelser & P. B. Baltes (Eds.), *International encyclopedia of the social and behavioural sciences* (pp. 139–142). Oxford: Pergamon.

Mannheim, K. (1928). Das Problem der Generationen. *Kölner Vierteljahreshefte für Soziologie, 7*(2), 157–185; (3), 309–330.

Mayring, P. (2000). Qualitative content analysis [28 paragraphs]. *Forum: Qualitative Social Research, 1*(2), Art. 20. Retrieved from: http://nbn-resolving.de/urn:nbn:de:0114-fqs0002204

OECD. (2009). *PIAAC problem solving in technology-rich environments: A conceptual framework* (OECD Education Working Papers, 36). Paris: OECD Publishing. Retrieved from http://dx.doi. org/10.1787/220262483674

Papert, S. (1980). *Mindstorm. Children, computers, and powerful ideas.* New York: Basic Books.

Pietraß, M., Schmidt, B., & Tippelt, R. (2005). Informelles Lernen und Medienbildung. *Zeitschrift für Erziehungswissenschaft, 3*(05), 412–426.

Pikalek, A. J. (2010). Navigating the social media learning curve. *Continuing Higher Education Review, 74*, 150–160.

Potter, W. J. (2011). *Media literacy* (5th ed.). Thousand Oaks: Sage.

Remtulla, K. A. (2010). 'Media mediators': Advocating an alternate paradigm for critical adult education ICT policy. *Journal for Critical Education Policy Studies, 7*(3), 299–324.

Saczynski, J. S., Willis, S. L., & Schaie, K. W. (2002). Strategy use in reasoning training with older adults. *Aging Neuropsychology and Cognition, 9*(1), 48–60.

Schäffer, B. (2003). *Generationen – Medien – Bildung. Medienpraxiskulturen im Generationenvergleich.* Opladen: Leske + Budrich.

Schaie, K. W. (2005). *Developmental influences on adult intelligence.* Oxford: The Seattle Longitudinal Study.

Schleicher, A. (2008). PIAAC: A new strategy for assessing adult competencies. *International Review of Education, 54*, 627–650. Retrieved from http://www.oecd.org/dataoecd/48/5/41529787.pdf

Schmidt, B. (2007). Educational behaviour and interests of older adults. In E. Lucio-Villegas & M. del Carmen Martrinez (Eds.), *Adult learning and the challenges of social and cultural diversity: Diverse lives, cultures, learnings and literacies 1. Proceedings of the 5th ESREA European research conference* (pp. 157–166). Seville: University of Seville.

Schmidt, B. (2010a). Educational goals and motivation of older workers. In S. Bohlinger (Ed.), *Working and learning at old age. Theory and evidence in an emerging European field of research* (pp. 127–136). Göttingen: Cuvillier.

Schmidt, B. (2010b). Perception of age, expectations of retirement and continuing education of older workers. In Cedefop (Ed.), *Working and ageing: Emerging theories and empirical perspectives* (pp. 210–226). Luxembourg: Publications Office.

Schmidt-Hertha, B., & Thalhammer, V. (2012). Intergenerative Aneignung von Medienkompetenz in informellen Kontexten. In A. Hartung, B. Schorb, & C. Kuttner (Eds.), *Generationen und Medienpädagogik. Annährungen aus Theorie, Empirie und Praxis* (pp. 129–148). München: kopaed-Verlag.

Strobel, C., Schmidt-Hertha, B., & Gnahs, D. (2011). Bildungsbiografische und soziale Bedingungen des Lernens in der Nacherwerbsphase. In *Magazin erwachsenenbildung.at, 13.* Wien. Retrieved from http://www.erwachsenenbildung.at/magazin/11-13/meb11-13.pdf

Trinder, K., et al. (2008). *Learning from digital natives: Bridging formal and informal learning.* Retrieved from http://www.academy.gcal.ac.uk/ldn/LDNFinalReport.pdf

Warschauer, M. (2004). *Technology and social inclusion: Rethinking the digital divide.* Cambridge, MA: MIT Press.

Chapter 4
Basic Skills for Becoming a Citizen

Emilio Lucio-Villegas

Introduction: *'It Is Always a Good Time to Learn'*, What?

This chapter aims to re-examine the concept and practice of an education focused on people as citizens. Against the narrow idea of people as workers – if they can have a job – or consumers, I think that education must be useful to encourage people to take part in social and community life.

In the scope of the current policies and practices in Lifelong Learning, I will only focus on those related to Active Citizenship and will present the experience of the Participatory and Citizenship School developed in the city of Seville (Spain) from 2006 to 2007 as an example of other perspectives that allow us to create – or better re-create – different practices on adult education and learning beyond the suffocating pressure for training disciplined workers.

In the last 10 years, one of the most interesting and surprising achievements in education and learning has been the diverse attempts for a gradual unification of educational policies in the European Union. As Lima and Guimarães (2011) state, this is an important process that has moderated national sovereignty. 'A Memorandum on Lifelong Learning' could be considered the foundational document of the so-called Lisbon Strategy, primarily aiming to promote a 'comprehensive strategy on lifelong learning' (CEC 2000, p. 6). The 'Council Resolution of 27 June of 2002 on Lifelong Learning' stresses that the main goal of this policy convergence is 'to achieve a comprehensive and coherent strategy for education and training' (OJEC 2002, p. 2). Lifelong Learning is defined as follows:

> [A]ll learning activity undertaken throughout life, with the aim of improving knowledge, skills and competences within a personal, civic, social and/or employment-related perspective (CEC 2001, p. 9).

E. Lucio-Villegas (✉)
Faculty of Education, University of Seville, Seville, Spain
e-mail: elucio@us.es

G.K. Zarifis and M.N. Gravani (eds.), *Challenging the 'European Area of Lifelong Learning': A Critical Response*, Lifelong Learning Book Series 19, DOI 10.1007/978-94-007-7299-1_4, © Springer Science+Business Media Dordrecht 2014

The 'Memorandum', then, differentiates three types of learning: formal learning, non-formal learning and informal learning (CEC 2000, p. 8). The Memorandum also states the main aims for this common policy on lifelong learning through six key messages, all of which stress on the importance of lifelong learning (CEC 2000, pp. 10–20). These messages are meant to edify a 'knowledge-based economy and society' (CEC 2000, p. 3) that will transform Europe into 'the most competitive and dynamic knowledge-based society in the world by 2010' (CEC 2007, p. 2). The key message, 'New skills for all', aims to 'Guarantee universal and continuing access to learning for gaining and renewing the skills needed for sustained participation in the knowledge society' (CEC 2000, p. 10). These basic skills for sustained participation include IT skills, foreign languages, technological culture, entrepreneurship and social skills. One of the goals of these basic skills is:

> [T]o encourage and equip people to participate more actively once more in all spheres of modern public life, especially in social and political life at all levels of the community, including at European level (CEC 2000, p. 4, bold type in the original).

Basic skills are always associated with two different domains: active citizenship and employability. As active citizenship is not presented as an objective in and of itself, an important double discourse arises, distinguishing concept from practice. This double discourse specifically concerns particular lifelong learning practices, with the stronger discourse focusing on the labour market rather than citizens' rights and participation. Policymakers seem to have forgotten that education and learning should span an entire lifetime, rather than using education just for job preparation defined by competiveness. This is evident in the 2007 document 'It is always a good time to learn', where the practices evidently become the dominant discourse. 'The Action Plan on Adult Learning' (CEC 2006) focuses on giving responses to the following challenges: competitiveness, demographic change and social inclusion. Responses to the last challenge, social inclusion, is meant to eliminate poverty among marginalised groups. 'The Action Plan', however, does not reference active citizenship. In fact, the discourse had been changed. The document 'It is always a good time to learn' affirms the following:

> A key element of the agenda proposed in Lisbon was the promotion of employability and social inclusion through investment in citizens' knowledge and competence at all stages of their lives (CEC 2007, p. 2).

It has been forgotten, however, that the Lisbon Agenda 'argues that promoting active citizenship and promoting employability are equally important and interrelated aims for lifelong learning' (CEC 2000, p. 4).

I think that the most powerful and important critique that can be made to lifelong learning's current policies and practices is that the aims of the education must be for education itself. According to Dewey (1995), the most important achievement in a democratic society is education's role to encourage both personal and collective development. However, lifelong learning's policies subordinate these educational aims to professionalisation and business. As Dewey (1995) states, in a democratic society, learning and teaching cannot become mere resources to achieve aims disconnected from the educational means.

On Citizenship and Participation

It is commonly argued that the concepts of citizen and citizenship were born in Athens, during the period of 'Classic Greece'. This is a myth that young people – at least in Spain – learn at school. Citizenship is a concept that has been used throughout history, and perhaps is still used in the present, to introduce differences among people: owners and slaves; men, women and children; native and foreigner; and others. These differences mark individuals 'who were not allowed to participate in the decision-making about the polis' (Biesta 2011, p. 3).

The ideas of democracy and citizenship return in different historical moments. I would like to stress the role of the Scottish Enlightenment, which included intellectuals such as Hume, Robertson, Smith, Millar, Ferguson and others (Wences 2007). As Devine (2003, p. 165) states:

> [O]ver the century between 1680 and 1780 some 818 colleges – or university – educated men came to the American colonies from Britain and Europe. About the third of this total (211) had been educated at three Scottish universities, Glasgow, Edinburgh and Aberdeen.

Migratory movements shaped by educational needs went both ways: people from the American colonies went to Europe to study in universities, including higher education institutions in Scotland. They learnt from Smith, Millar, Ferguson and others. Importantly, the teaching was in English, not Latin. According to Devine's figures, the first teachers in new colleges and universities throughout North America's New England were both educated and recruited from Scottish institutions. Beyond the 'accusations of exceptionalism and chauvinism' (Devine 2003, p. 171), the influence of the Scottish Enlightenment is evident, for example, in the works of James Wilson, one of the signers of the Declaration of Independence of the United States. According to Wilson,

> Rights are the outward expression of an inner truth available to all who are fit for life under law. It is the inner truth, part of the very constitution of the human nature that makes government possible. Thus government is not the source but the product of that exercise of power and judgments available to a being capable of self-government (in Robinson 2011, p. 4).

One of the heirs of this democratic tradition is John Dewey. Perhaps it is very hazardous to connect Dewey with the Scottish Enlightenment, yet it could be argued that one of the sources of Dewey's thoughts is the democratic tradition deriving from Wilson and others. As Dewey states, learning for democracy is acquired while living within a democratic environment such as the community.

Community refers to a democratic setting arising from one's environment. According to Raymond Williams (1985, p. 76), the notion of community 'express particular kinds of social relations [...] the warmly persuasive word to describe an existing set of relationship, or the warmly persuasive word to describe an alternative set of relationship'. Deriving from Williams, then, community is a public space where debate takes place. A community is not homogeneous; on the contrary, the community is a heterogeneous place where conflict is a fundamental part of quotidian living. It also leads to the political understanding of citizenship (Biesta 2011). Thus, in the public arena, debate, contradiction and deliberative democracy should be the norm.

Gaventa (2006) distinguishes four stages in the evolution of participation: first, in the 1960s, the notion that communities could organise themselves to urge their demands arose. Gaventa connects this period with Paulo Freire's seminal work, *Pedagogy of the Oppressed* (1970). Second, the expansion of NGOs in the 1980s overlapped with the concomitant growth in programmes related to water, health, agriculture and other fields. Both were understood as forms of development defined by modernisation theory (Youngman 2000). This era also can be associated with a new term: beneficiaries. Consequently, only participants of development programmes were allowed to take part in communities, as all individuals were not involved. Third, during the 1990s, the scope of community was made even narrower with the introduction of another new term: stakeholder. According to Gaventa (2006), this ambiguous word represents the abandonment of community itself. Stakeholders are presented as 'representatives of civil society's private sector, government, and donors, but not necessarily with any view to whether they indeed represented the poor or excluded *within* these sectors' (Gaventa 2006, p. 56, italic type in the original). Lastly, by the late 1990s, there was a return to the first model: participation as focused on exercising the rights of citizenship. On this account, citizenship was understood as a practice and an engagement rather than as something defined by law. Thus, citizenship entails the following characteristics: the existence of democratic institutions, the inclusion of disadvantaged people, the obligation to protect and promote rights and a wide participation beyond the political (e.g. participation in economic, cultural and social dimensions). Gaventa (2006) defines this shift as one of participation, representing a change from opportunities to rights, beneficiaries to citizens, projects to policies, consultation to decision-making and micro to macro. This shift has other implications, not the least of which is the inclusion of disadvantaged groups. Mohanty and Tandon (2006) describe participatory citizenship as bringing previously excluded or marginalised social actors back into the political arena:

> Participatory citizenship offers an elaboration of both citizenship and participation. In this elaborated version, citizenship is rescued from its universal legal status to include the differential positioning of powerless groups (2006, p. 10).

According to Heller and Thomas Isaacs (2003), citizenship is defined by a specific relationship between individuals and groups. Ideally, this relationship would be constructed in an egalitarian manner. However, citizenship is subverted by social differences (e.g. class, gender, ethnic and other differences). Hence, Santos (2003) stipulates that participatory democracy is a redistributive democracy based on egalitarian principles.

With this approach, participation is a strategic element of becoming a citizen, but participation can also be hijacked: 'Who speaks on behalf of whom? Who sets the framework for participation? Who creates boundaries and dismantles them?' (Mohanty and Tandon 2006, p. 15). Managing these questions and answers requires training, which is not only important for the acquisition of citizenship but also for the maintenance of citizenship. When studying the participatory process in Porto Alegre (Brazil), Santos (2003) concludes that training people by encouraging them to take part in the participatory democracy process (in this case, a budgetary process) is fundamental.

Important here are also the works of Paulo Freire. Of particular importance are his notions of codification and decoding, as well as his description of people becoming literate. His concept of literacy goes beyond simply being able to read words: people come to read to understand the world better. According to Freire, the most important pedagogical issue for adult education (and for education in general) is to start from peoples' own daily lives and, from this standpoint, encourage them to reflect on their own realities. Codification, decoding and dialogue allow people to 'recognize the situation in their own lives' (Kirkwood and Kirkwood 1989, p. 140). In this process, individuals become more aware of their problems, desires, resources, potentialities and their own expertise.

In the experiences considered by Gaventa, I stress those linked with the Participatory Budget – the most well known in Porto Alegre (Brazil) – as well as others, such as the Popular Planning Campaign in Kerala (India). This last is important in terms of linking participation to training in order to participate. The 'Kerala's model' (Thomas Isaacs and Franke 2005) is very stimulating because one of the most important goals to develop the *Participatory and Citizenship School* was to potentiate training as a key element to the development of democracy.

The background of Participatory Budgets offers up a diverse analysis based on politics, participation and descriptions of both methodologies and experiences (e.g. Avritzer 2003; Lucio-Villegas et al. 2009; Santos 2003). Looking for educational results, one interesting work is the analysis performed by Lerner and Schugurensky (2007) on the Participatory Budget in Rosario, Argentina. According to the authors, it is possible to differentiate four different assets that lead to both learning and changes in people's participation (pp. 92–95): first, increased knowledge relates to people becoming more aware of their citizen rights; second, changes in skills address how to 'monitor governments' actions, contact government agencies and officials' (p. 93); third, changes in attitudes translate to increased self-confidence; and lastly, changes in practices lead to people becoming more committed to community life.

Participation in Process

Following the model of Porto Alegre (Brazil), Seville's City Hall, in Spain, launched the Participatory Budget as an experiment to manage people's participation in public issues concerning the city. The experimentation ran from 2003 to 2007. One of the main problems that arose was that people had considerable difficulty in understanding the decision-making processes that they had previously been excluded from. City Hall decided to confront this problem with a specific adult education programme (2005–2007), which broadened to include social movements. By its second year, the programme included the development of the Participatory and Citizenship School. The primary goal here was to help people to overcome obstacles that made participation difficult in participatory budget activities. Towards this end, it was important for people to learn how to research their own communities, undertake a project, translate the project into official documents, fill out forms and present a proposal in a public forum. As previously mentioned, the programme adopted a model derived from the Popular Planning Campaign in Kerala (Thomas Isaacs and Franke 2005).

Adult education is uniquely suited to the study of citizenship. However, adult education is a broad concept related to diverse educational tasks and educational spaces. From a Gramscian perspective, adult education is a contested space, a battle-field between hegemony and counter-hegemony, each seeking to prevail over the other. In this case, it is the success of the ideas of participatory democracy and representative democracy that are at stake.

According to Santos (2003) as well as Thomas Isaacs and Franke (2005), I sug-gest that education is essential to both edify and strengthen participatory democracy and citizenship. Consequently, the adult education programme mentioned has integrated participatory democracy into the classroom and has constructed a corresponding set of teaching materials. These teaching materials improve literacy skills, encouraging people to participate. The link between literacy skills and a democratic education to help people to participate was able to achieve this by selecting a few generative words (Freire 1965), such as desire, necessity, democracy and participation. By starting with these words, as well as with people's real situations (in their own communities and in their neighbourhoods), individuals not only became more aware of their situations and resources but also simultaneously improved their literacy skills by enlarging their vocabulary. As Freire (1970) states, through dialogue people become more aware of their reality in the double perspective of 'naming the world, or saying your own *word*' (Kirkwood and Kirkwood 1989, p. 141, italic type in the original). For instance, when doing a household budget (itself an exercise in numeracy), people can also reflect on the larger municipal budget because the concept of budget is not far from a domestic budget where people should decide their own priorities deriving from the money that they have available. By doing this, people discover how the money that the City Hall collected from their taxes is spent – or wasted

Now, I will focus on the Participatory and Citizenship School. The major goal here was to achieve a democratic balance inside social movements but also to create democratic practices at a community level. While Offe (1990) suggests that new social movements have a nonhierarchical structure, this did not seem to be empirically true. The Participatory and Citizenship School, then, sought to change the structure of social movements in order to edify a democratic power within social movements:

> In the arena of more visible power – who participates with what effect in public processes – the capacity building strategy may be about strengthening the abilities of the relatively powerless groups [...] to have an impact on such processes, through improved advocacy skills, organization, and research (Gaventa 2006, p. 63).

It is also important to stress that individuals do not participate alone but participate in organised groups aiming to articulate specific claims.

In short, the school was devoted to empower people by teaching them skills to take responsibility for research so that their work might transform their communities and associations. As Dewey (1995, Chapter XI; see also Dewey 1938) notes, people learn by doing. Applying this in a relevant way, then, people learn to participate by participating, and individuals who participate become citizens. However, participation needs to take place in venues where people can learn from their own practices, which can then bring about changes both in spaces and procedures (*conscientização* in the Freirean way). Usually this transpires in scenarios where people live their everyday life. Thus, this process of *conscientização* can take place through non-formal learning. It 'may be provided in the workplace and through the activities of civil society organizations and groups (such as in youth organizations, trades unions and political parties)' (CEC 2000, p. 8).

To summarise, the Participatory and Citizenship School in Seville during the time of the Participatory Budget experiment was planned and organised through 14 courses that amounted to 24 h, spanning 2 weeks from Monday to Thursday, usually in the evening. The courses focused on participation, conflicts, mediation skills, community analysis and, finally, the development of a community project. In short, every course was divided into four components: (1) definitions of community problems, (2) a reflection on democracy and citizenship at both a macro (community) and micro (association) level, (3) the development of a project (4) and, finally, a section on how to look for and manage resources. Courses took place in community centres located in different districts around the city of Seville. This became a very important issue: these public places were, at that time, privileged spaces in terms of public and popular participation. The average number of people who attended the courses was 12, with the prerequisite that participating students had not had previous roles in leading association groups. Another important aspect of each course was that the collective of participating associations was heterogeneous. For instance, a course might include a flamenco association, a fishing club, an immigrant workers association, a neighbours association and a cyclist group. An outcome of this process was that membership in these different groups created networks in each district. Finally, two courses were addressed to specific groups: a gypsy women's association and adults attending an adult education school.

The Participatory and Citizenship School has also produced a teaching material entitled *Projecting Dreams*. *Projecting Dreams* is an attempt to present a journey of learning from the social constructions of problems and the making of both community projects and actions, to produce changes in communities. This teaching material is meant to support the courses, as well as encourage people to take part in more democratic social movements aimed at edifying participatory democracy.

Finally, the evaluation of these courses was generally positive, but the change in the municipal government did not allow the people involved to change and/or enlarge the courses.

Conclusion

Popular education is linked to the struggle for social justice. As Freire stipulates, our starting point must always be people's real situations. Through the process of *conscientização,* people can interpret, understand and change their world. Hence, as I suggest in this paper, the essence of popular education is the making of people into citizens, 'the idea that the democratic experiment should be understood as a process of *transformation*' (Biesta 2011, p. 5, italic type in the original). Popular education is linked both to communities and to people's everyday lives, as the neighbourhood becomes a classroom. The places and spaces for education certainly extend beyond the restrictions of lifelong learning policies and practices. As Lima states:

> In education, managerial speeches have been occupying the position previously assumed by educational theories and pedagogical thinking, building narratives of a managerial type that legitimize a new social order based on the market, the private sector, economic competition and in client-centred management (2000, p. 243).

According to this critique, nowadays the most relevant issue seems to be the reduction of training to dedicate it only for employment. As Olesen points out: 'In the last couple of decades, the needs for work competence-building have tended to prevail over traditional forms and rationales of adult education and training in developed western societies' (2010, p. 4).

Lifelong learning policies and practices seem to have become a kind of race for competitiveness and not for people´s development. Following Lima (2000), this race aims at delivering diplomas according to a 'countable paradigm'.

At present time, in this age of financial crisis, Europe seems to be more a place of merchants and consumers than the birthplace of the ideas of democracy and the cradle of the Enlightenment. I think that we need to rethink the lifelong learning's policies – only focussed on employment – and promote a shift to focus it on the building of democracy and citizenship.

What are the skills needed to become a citizen? As Biesta (2011, p. 5) states, 'as long as we see citizenship as a positive, identifiable identity, we can indeed see the learning involved as a process of knowledge, skills and dispositions that are needed to bring out this identity as citizens'.

Some of these skills are related to the acquisition of literacy skills, but sometimes they do not include the acquisition of oral skills or public speaking. In a participatory democracy, the process of deliberation is very important. These deliberation processes are usually oral performances; they involve speaking in the public arena and presenting one's own ideas and proposals to others. This means, then, that participatory democracy also involves people improving their capacities to speak in public arenas, as well as strengthening their ability to organise speeches with respect to alternative and/or antagonistic ideas.

On the other hand, as the Portuguese sociologist Boaventura de Sousa Santos (2003) notes, participatory democracy is a complicated system of rules. As mentioned above, people do indeed have difficulties understanding the processes of deliberation and, presumably, its rules. Training and learning are not only significant means of overcoming these difficulties, but educating disadvantaged individuals on educational processes connect them to exercise their rights. Generally, to need means to lack something that one must have or that one must obtain. However, people tend not to think that needs are also rights. The right to participate, then, must be guaranteed:

In situation of highly unequal power relations, simply creating public spaces for more participation to occur, without addressing the other forms of power, may do little to affect pro-poor or more democratic change. New public spaces will simply be filled by the already powerful (Gaventa 2006, p. 63).

The challenge of the Participatory and Citizenship School – as a model of other educational practices – was to encourage people to fill up the public spaces in a learning process for the edification of a participatory democracy.

References

Avritzer, L. (2003). Modelos de deliberação democrática: uma análise do orçamento participativo no Brasil. In B. S. Santos (Org.), *Democratizar a democracia. Os caminhos da democracia participativa* (pp. 467–496). Porto: Afrontamento.

Biesta, G. (2011, February 17). *Learning in public places: Civic learning for the 21th century.* Inaugural lecture on the Occasion of the Award of the International Francqui Professorship to Prof. Gert Biesta, Ghent.

Commission of the European Communities. (2000). *Commission staff working paper. A memorandum on lifelong learning.* Brussels: European Union. SEC (2000) 1832.

Commission of the European Communities. (2001). *Making a European area of lifelong learning.* Brussels: European Union. COM (2001) 678 final.

Commission of the European Communities. (2006). *Adult learning: It is never too late to learn.* Brussels: European Union. COM (2006) 614 final.

Commission of the European Communities. (2007). *It is always a good time to learn.* Brussels: European Union. COM (2007) 558 final.

Devine, T. M. (2003). *Scotland's empire 1600–1815.* London: Penguin.

Dewey, J. (1938). *Experience and education.* New York: McMillan.

Dewey, J. (1995). *Democracia y Educación.* Madrid: Morata. (First edition 1916).

Freire, P. (1965). *Educação como prática da liberdade.* São Paulo: Paz e Terra.

Freire, P. (1970). *Pedagogy of the oppressed.* New York: The Continuum Publishing Company.

Gaventa, J. (2006). Perspectives on participation and citizenship. In R. Mohanty & R. Tandon (Eds.), *Participatory citizenship. Identity, exclusion, inclusion* (pp. 51–67). New Delhi: Sage Publications.

Heller, P., & Thomas Isaac, T. M. (2003). O perfil político e institucional da democracia participativa: lições de Kerala, India. In B. S. Santos (Org.), *Democratizar a democracia. Os caminhos da democracia participativa* (pp. 497–535). Porto: Afrontamento.

Kirkwood, G., & Kirkwood, C. (1989). *Living adult education. Freire in Scotland.* Milton Keynes: Open University Press.

Lerner, J., & Schugurensky, D. (2007). Who learns what in participatory democracy? In R. van der Venn, D. Wildemeersch, J. Youngblood, & V. Marsick (Eds.), *Democratic practices as learning opportunities* (pp. 85–100). Rotterdam: Sense Publishers.

Lima, L. C. (2000). Educação de Adultos e construção da cidadania democrática: Para una crítica do Gerencialismo e da educação contabil. In L. C. Lima (Org.), *Educação de Adultos. Forum I* (pp. 237–255). Braga: Universidade do Minho.

Lima, L. C., & Guimarães, P. (2011). *European strategies in lifelong learning. A critical introduction*. Opladen/Farmington Hills: Barbara Budrich Publishers.

Lucio-Villegas, E., et al. (2009). Educating citizenship in the background of participatory budget. In E. Lucio-Villegas (Ed.), *Citizenship as politics. International perspectives from adult education* (pp. 105–144). Rotterdam: Sense Publishers.

Mohanty, R., & Tandon, R. (2006). Identity, exclusion, inclusion: Issues in participatory citizenship. In R. Mohanty & R. Tandon (Eds.), *Participatory citizenship. Identity, exclusion, inclusion* (pp. 9–26). New Delhi: Sage Publications.

Offe, C. (1990). *Contradicciones en el Estado de Bienestar*. Madrid: Alianza.

Official Journal of the European Communities. (2002). *Council Resolution of 27 June of 2002 on lifelong learning*. Brussels: Official Journal of the European Communities. Brussels: European Union. 2002/C 163/01.

Olesen, H. S. (2010, September 23–26). *Adult learning, economy and society: Modernization processes and the changing functions of adult education*. Paper presented to the 6th European research conference. Linkoping, Sweden.

Robinson, D. N. (2011). *James Wilson and Natural Rights Constitutionalism: The influenced of the Scottish Enlightenment*. Natural Law, Natural Rights and American Constitutionalism. http://www.ninrac.org/american/scottish-enlightenment. Accessed 16 Nov 2011.

Santos, B. S. (2003). Orçamento Participativo em Porto Alegre: para uma democracia redistributiva. In B. S. Santos (Org.), *Democratizar a democracia. Os caminhos da democracia participativa* (pp. 375–465). Porto: Afrontamento.

Thomas Isaacs, T. M., & Franke, R. W. (2005). *Democracia Local y desarrollo*. Barcelona: Diálogos.

Wences, I. (2007). *Teoría Social y Política de la Ilustración Escocesa*. México: Plaza & Valdés.

Williams, R. (1985). *Keywords*. London: Fontana.

Youngman, F. (2000). *The political economy of adult education & development*. Leicester: NIACE.

Chapter 5
'New Basic Skills', Nonbasic Skills, Knowledge Practices and Judgement: Tensions Between the Needs of Basic Literacy, of Vocational Education and Training and of Higher and Professional Learning

Martin Gough

Policy Emphasis on Skills and Lifelong Learning Across Europe

The European Commission's (2000) 'Memorandum on Lifelong Learning', defines new basic skills as those required for active participation in the knowledge society and economy' (sec. 4.1, p. 11). Field (2006, pp. 11 and 17) explains that EU policy on lifelong learning, when it had got round to formulating one, before and since the issue of the Memorandum, has been driven by economic concerns, to increase competitiveness rather than to enhance citizenship or other facets of a 'Good Life'[1] for people. This is, however, a fact not in any way occluded in the Commission's own publications and therefore needing revelation, with one such opening: 'Over the last four years the overall performance of the European economy has been disappointing.[...] Few European countries score high on competitiveness and performance'.[2] The Memorandum itself spells out similar priorities.[3]

---

[1] This phrase is, of course, handed down to us from Aristotle through his concept of *Eudaimonia*: 'human flourishing' (White 1997) is a modern equivalent alternative.

[2] c.f. Tessaring and Wannan (2004, p. 3); they go on (pp. 5 and 23) to advocate that job-related skills and competences, not just academic excellence, are the key to progress.

[3] '[...] to ensure that people's knowledge and skills match the changing demands of jobs and occupations, workplace organisation and working methods' (sec. 1, p. 5); 'The driving force that brought lifelong learning back onto policy agendas in the 1990s has been the concern to improve citizens' employability and adaptability' (sec. 3.2, p. 9); 'Europe has moved towards a knowledge-based society and economy. More than ever before, access to up-to-date information and knowledge, together with the motivation and skills to use these resources intelligently on behalf of oneself and the community as a whole, are becoming the key to strengthening Europe's competitiveness and improving the employability and adaptability of the workforce' (sec. 2, p. 5).

M. Gough (✉)
Education Studies, De Montfort University, The Gateway, Leicester, LE1 9BH, UK
e-mail: a.m.gough@kent.ac.uk

G.K. Zarifis and M.N. Gravani (eds.), *Challenging the 'European Area of Lifelong Learning': A Critical Response*, Lifelong Learning Book Series 19, DOI 10.1007/978-94-007-7299-1_5, © Springer Science+Business Media Dordrecht 2014

We can acknowledge that explicit policy does also promote wider social and personal, rather than just work-oriented, goals.[4]

However, it may not be just incidental happenstance that the result of policy debate has encouraged the presumption that 'those who will not upgrade their skills [...] do not deserve support from the rest of us' (Field 2006, p. 6). This presumption, coupled with work and the economy being the primary concern, is one where the individual worker is seen as responsible for their own work-related development and is certainly how the UK government policy has taken forward its own national agenda,[5] through exploitation of the fervour around lifelong learning at the European level. The UK approach could be seen as reconceptualising work as being the most important part of you, the individual, the main thing that should concern you.[6] The implications of this are that if it is social and personal goals which motivate you then ultimately you want to fulfil them through work and will want to improve your work performance to enhance your goals.

The clue to critique of this lies within the richer conceptual framework of lifelong learning and the understanding of learning generally (as opposed to just from within the resources of economic, political or sociological analysis). And recognition, through cross-lingual comparison of concepts, of problematic issues inherent in attempts to achieve a European Qualification Framework (EQF) for occupational competence highlight the clue. The EQF would consider key terms for vocational education and training (VET) as *prima facie* equivalent across different national languages and systems. However, many such terms in any one language have no equivalent in another or cannot strictly be translated and hold the same connotations.

To illustrate, the term 'knowledge' in English does not in itself allow explicitly for the distinction between systematic and nonsystematic knowledge captured in the German terms *Wissen* and *Kenntnis*. In general, the UK perspective does not promote the notion of the worker, even as 'competent', being able to direct their own work and make sound judgements within it, favouring compliance in the workplace and shunning the use of intelligence.[7] *Kompetenz* in German and *competénce* in

---

[4]c.f., subsequently· European Commission (2001), Eurydice and CEDEFOP (2001). Indeed, a 'Eurobarometer' survey shows that this better reflects people's motivations to engage in future learning (van Rens and Stavrou 2003, p. 19); c.f. Davies (2001). Aside from varieties of individual motivation, the Memorandum does 'not take account of learning as a social, collective activity' (Summers 2000, p. 231). Arguably, any humanistic language is largely rhetorical, even pre-Memorandum: 'the EU's action programmes are relentlessly vocational, utilitarian and instrumental in their emphasis' (Field 1998, p. 8).

[5]Field (2006, pp. 79, 161–163). This approach amounts to short-term, on-the-job specific skill development, at the expense (as in Germany, for instance) of investment in initial formal training setting the individual up properly with a broader working competence: Dehmel (2005, p. 62).

[6]And so for you to be responsible for and to fund as well, skills talk being about individual responsibility and not the State's, according to this realization of neo-liberalism: Borg and Mayo (2004, 2005, p. 20).

[7]c.f. Winch, 'Skill – a concept manufactured in England?' Chapter 6, in Brockmann et al. (2011), p. 88.

French do have the connotation of the worker being intelligent enough to make judgements autonomously. The most important term for current purposes is 'skill', and, whilst this can connote a broad ability, such as an occupational capacity, it normally connotes a specific task ability; the term *Fähigkeit* in German by contrast includes not just the broad occupational but also extra-functional personal and social capacities, with *Fertigkeit* being reserved for the more specific and functional.[8] The prevalent conception of 'skill' in the UK links it to tasks where performance of that task is observable and measurable, so with bias towards ostensive behaviour in typically manual functional tasks.[9] This urge for measurability in turn encourages further the process signalled by Adam Smith of analysis rather than synthesis, the specifying further still in simpler terms of the tasks to be done, and which in their specificity can be observed more easily. This leaves a fragmented view of work and the occupation when reassembled as just the bundle of those 'skills', the sum of its mechanical parts.[10]

The non-UK reader might agree with the above account and yet be satisfied that it describes fairly a problem for the UK conception of its own domains of education and of work: the terms translated back into the other languages could keep their connotations and so maintain, unbothered, the more holistic conceptions of knowledge for work in, for instance, Germany, the Netherlands and France.[11] Unfortunately, it is not so easy for the non-UK world. The Anglo-Saxon tradition, still drawing from the Rylean legacy, has introduced and embedded the vehicle of learning outcomes as a way to account for success in learning (and so success in teaching too). One of the features of learning outcomes is the placing of emphasis upon outputs of the process and paying less attention to inputs, i.e. how the learning is effected, such as through national culturally established education systems. Furthermore, as regards VET at least, the form of the learning outcomes in the UK is driven by labour market interests rather than educational concerns.[12] The learning outcomes approach has been adopted as a way to recognise knowledge, skills and competences across the labour market Europe wide, as the realization of the goals of the Memorandum, and so it is no surprise, then, that this approach has infected the French, German and Dutch systems,[13] if not others'. Now that it has the opportunity, the EQF translates terms such as 'skill' from the English using the intellectually

---

[8] c.f. Hanf, 'The changing relevance of the *Beruf*', Chapter 4, in Brockmann et al. (2011), p. 57.

[9] Regrettably inspired by contributions to Western thought such as from Gilbert Ryle: Winch, 'Skill – a concept manufactured in England?' Chapter 6, in Brockmann et al. (2011), pp. 90–93.

[10] Reflection upon which would become redundant: Brockmann, Clarke, Winch, Hanf, Méhaut and Westerhuis, 'Interpretive dictionary: competence, qualification, education, knowledge', Chapter 10, in Brockmann et al. (2011), pp. 180–184.

[11] c.f. Méhaut, *'Savoir* – the organising principle of French VET', Chapter 3, in Brockmann et al. (2011), pp. 45–46; also Griffiths and Guile (2004, p. 63).

[12] c.f.: Winterton et al. (2006, p. 17); Clarke and Westerhuis, 'Establishing equivalence through zones of mutual trust', Chapter 9, in Brockmann et al. (2011), p. 138.

[13] c.f. Westerhuis, 'The meaning of competence', Chapter 5, in Brockmann et al. (2011), p. 81.

more impoverished and reductionist option amongst terms in other languages, for instance, *Fertigkeit* rather than *Fähigkeit*.[14]

The linguistic and conceptual imperialism of English seems to be the problem, for all, not just the UK. This demands a proper consideration of the nature of 'skill', by means of the English language, in order to uncover the flaw in the analytic reductionist thinking behind the policy developments now infecting all of Europe. An alternative conception of 'skill' in the English context is then the means for revising such policy.

What Skills 'Are'

One of the problems with the term 'skill', in the English language at least, is its ambiguity. It is used on the one hand to describe an attribute of an individual agent and on the other hand to refer to procedures which the agent performs for a task.[15] So, for instance, I could say 'you have the skill of sawing wood'; at the same time, we might say 'sawing wood is a skill'. This externalising of skills, the latter sense, makes them seem especially thing-like, as separate from our personal identity and somehow acquirable from the external world to become our instrumental possessions. Even if we say that the primary usage of the term 'skill' is the former sense, as an attribute of a person if it is anything, the analytical reductionist view given to us by Adam Smith encourages us to consider skills as a multitude of discretely identifiable aspects of the person, of their body at least.

The ontological classification I give to this view of skills is 'naïve realist'. Naïve realism about skills, then, is a view which maintains that skills are some sort of independently existing and identifiable entities, different from other entities, and they would primarily be alluded to explicitly by means of noun terms. For most realists, the identifiable entities which are skills are abilities acquired or formed in the bodies of persons for conducting various practical activities.

The drive, fuelled by the (false) assumption of realism, to be increasingly specific, and to specify all that would be relevant for work, leads some subject leaders across VET and higher sectors, such as in nursing,[16] to include intrinsically worthy educational outcomes such as understanding and moral values in the list of skills.

---

[14] Méhaut and Winch, 'EU initiatives in cross-national recognition of skills and qualifications', Chapter 2, in Brockmann et al. (2011), suggest (pp. 30–31) that and this is probably a political decision, given licence by the conceptual bias prevalent in the UK usage against autonomy in the workplace (once English is granted dominant language status, a prior political decision in turn). The political decision would ostensibly be aimed to benefit employers who would want a compliant workforce, although, ultimately, such a policy will benefit no one, in terms of facilitating neither the Good Life universally nor the higher potential of workers to be more productive.

[15] c.f. Winch, 'Skill – a concept manufactured in England?' chapter 6, in Brockmann et al. (2011), pp. 99–100.

[16] c.f. Winch, 'Skill – a concept manufactured in England?' Chapter 6, in Brockmann et al. (2011), pp. 90–93.

This illustrates well how the realist is in a logical muddle, since these are neither skills nor 'things'. On a more holistic conception of nursing, and of any other occupation, we can say that doing it well requires care. It may happen that students (of many disciplines) do learn about the general importance of caring as a discrete topic and act more morally subsequently. But this is the wrong way to understand the 'caring professions'. Graduates do not transplant into the new work context the general virtue of caring: the point is that workers should care about their work and how well they do it,[17] and this requires a high degree of autonomy in directing that work and a work environment conducive to this. The introduction of values into such 'skills' lists should make us suspicious that employers are taking further advantage of the political climate to demand that educational institutions form their students by the time of graduation with the 'right' attitudes or virtues, such as being humbly compliant. It may be that the more you decide to comply, the more competitive you appear to be for the labour market, but at the same time the more you lose your important values. Likewise, motivation cannot, even in a realist framework, be a skill (Winterton et al. 2006, p. 44), even if being motivated makes for better work in the event.

The realist way of thinking leads policymakers to identify for special attention a sub-degree-level 'skills sector'. True, if there is a shortage of skilled plumbers in a country or area, then there is a shortage of plumbers. And the education or training required for this work does not have to be higher education degree level. One problem with this situation, however, is that it creates, or, rather, bolsters, a false division between the world of 'skills' for 'skilled' work and higher levels of attainment for more prestigious work.

Instead of taking one side, I disagree with both proponents and opponents of the skills agenda on grounds of the ontology which they share.[18] I reject their realism about skills as entities transferable eo ipso into new situations[19] and adopt 'irrealism' instead. With irrealism, we use the problematic word as an adjectival term instead of a noun term and place skills firmly in the category of being attributable to an individual agent, and intrinsically linked to their actions, rather than being

---

[17] In nursing this would mean caring for a patient as a person with feelings and with a biological welfare, but, rather than just having consideration for the person as an end in itself, the nurse needs to focus on carrying out the job of work conducive to that end in the medical context; thus the caring is analogous to the context of the plumber caring for good design and maintenance of a plumbing system. Winch correctly emphasises just this point, that care to do the job well is what matters, but then expands this view fallaciously to claim that the important task to this end is ultimately to cultivate the virtues of general living to make 'the way one exercises a skill in this sense […] partly constitutive of one's character' (*ibid.*, p. 100).

[18] Lum (2009, pp. 22–24) adopts the same stance as I do against what he calls the 'orthodox' view of skills shared by the skills 'lobby' and certain opponents of it.

[19] As if via an automatic mechanistic process: Winterton et al. (2006, p. 8). We need to wrest the concept of skill away from the automaton conformity fetishists – with apologies to Erich Fromm; but not to opponents of the skills agenda, e.g. Maskell and Robinson (2001, Chapter 5), Furedi (2004) and Rowland (2006, Chapter 4), who are yet beguiled by this conception of skills per se.

detached entities: formally, to say 'person A has skill X' is equivalent in meaning to saying 'A is skilled at doing X'.[20]

Against the opponents of the skills agenda, the above accounts for how the language of skills is at home in higher learning and thinking as it is in manual activities, once we have cleared away the metaphysical obfuscation about the nature of skills presented to us by the realists.[21] The whole point of this debate is, or should be, how we can talk about people doing activities competently. Those activities lie on a multidimensional spectrum: if they are ostensibly behavioural, they will still variously contain intellectual or other mental components; and some activities will be mainly intellectual or otherwise mental, whether, for instance, working out directions for travelling or interpreting Martin Heidegger. These will all be 'skills', understood as a figurative term in the irrealist framework, and will lie on one dimension of the spectrum between basic and nonbasic skills, therefore.

Knowledge Practices and Judgement: Resolving the Tensions

Despite my argument above offering qualified support on behalf of the skills agenda, the English term 'skill' will forever carry connotations of remedial educational provision and sub-degree-level manual work. So I propose that we endorse the alternative term 'knowledge practice'.[22] This helps us place the focus on practice as a concept without dispensing with a (high or low level) cognitive framework. The whole (as well as an aspect) of an academic discipline is a (knowledge) practice, and the same is true for nonacademic relatively physically active domains such as plumbing or football. This allows us to get away from Adam Smith's legacy of analytical specification, where skills have to be discrete parts, and to say that it makes more sense to speak (in English!) of being skilled in your occupation taken holistically.

If this is right, then a more intellectual (i.e. cognitively challenging) education[23] makes for the better worker, in exercising good judgement,[24] as well as for the better in any other respect. This is also why 'skills talk' in the mouths of people who want and have the power to get you to do things or to do things to you is inevitably suspicious, when the drift is one of downplaying the importance of subject disciplines in

---

[20] So I still draw from Ryle but more appropriately, I would say! I illustrate irrealism further in Gough (2011), section on 'Dimensions of (knowledge) practices'.

[21] Albeit perhaps attributable ultimately to the quirk of language which encourages us all to use primarily the noun term in English.

[22] c.f. Barnett (1990, p. 42) uses this term in his own way and others more recently.

[23] And, arguably, of a humanistic rather than technological sort, a point implicitly entertained by Chisholm et al. (2004, p. 34).

[24] I go into greater detail explaining the dimensions of knowledge practices and how the key dichotomies of discursive/nondiscursive, thin/thick and primary/secondary explain the place of judgement and the translation of 'skills' from learning environment to context of use, with the illustration of academic Philosophy as one such, in Gough (2011).

their own terms and one of promoting employability as if that were achievable only by means other than learning academic subjects. The *Memorandum* declares: 'The new basic skills [...] are IT skills, foreign languages, technological culture, entrepreneurship and social skills' and goes on 'this is not a list of subjects or disciplines as we know them from our schooldays and beyond' (sec 4.1, pp. 10–11). Throughout the document it highlights the importance of 'knowledge and skills', as referred to together, but ultimately to force a contrast between them and give predominance to the latter. As Field notes, our attempts to articulate key skills reduce to 'a rather instrumental minimum of literacy and numeracy skills combined with some familiarity with the new technologies' (2006, p. 152), alongside that investment in provision of basic skills gives proportionately higher economic returns than in higher education provision (2006, pp. 140 and 160). Although Field supports such investment as a good *ceteris paribus*, it also demonstrates that a mainly economic model will always go against what would be a greater emancipatory potential of the higher education experience.[25] It is a way of policymakers saying that you can have your lifelong learning but only by learning basic technicist 'skills' components applicable to less prestigious work.

My alternative stance claims that intellectual learning and acting through attuned judgement are not out of place together, whether in professional or sub-degree-level work and learning, or anywhere else, these being knowledge practices, on a spectrum containing much variety, all deserving of prestige and resourcing. The 'new basic skills' are worthy in themselves, but the failure to promote subject knowledge means ultimately that the authors do not really value human flourishing through this policy initiative. The list of skills, and the sentiments of the rest of the *Memorandum*, should be reconceived so that they celebrate higher knowledge as well, and so higher knowledge practices, which happen to enhance economic productivity anyway. This would enhance the opportunity for the individual, as a good worker, to pursue the Good Life and serve as a richer and more appropriate conception of lifelong learning.

References

Barnett, R. (1990). *The idea of higher education*. Buckingham: Society for Research into Higher Education & Open University Press.
Borg, C., & Mayo, P. (2004). Diluted wine in new bottles: The key messages of the memorandum. *LLinE: Lifelong Learning in Europe, 9*(1), 18–25.
Borg, C., & Mayo, P. (2005). The EU Memorandum on lifelong learning. Old wine in new bottles? *Globalisation, Societies and Education, 3*(2), 203–225.
Brockmann, M., Clarke, L., Winch, C., Hanf, G., Méhaut, P., & Westerhuis, A. (2011). *Knowledge, skills and competence in the European labour market: What's in a vocational qualification?* Abingdon: Routledge.

---

[25] And perhaps the 'hysteria' (Borg and Mayo 2005, p. 213) around ICT shows that it is something of a fetish; c.f. Clarke and Englebright (2003).

Chisholm, L., Larson, A., & Mossoux, A.-F. (2004). *Lifelong learning: Citizens' views in close-up: Findings from a dedicated Eurobarometer survey*. Luxembourg: Office for Official Publications of the European Communities.

Clarke, A., & Englebright, L. (2003). *ICT: The new basic skill*. Leicester: NIACE.

Davies, P. (2001). New tasks for university continuing education and EUCEN. *LLinE: Lifelong Learning in Europe, 6*(1), 6–7.

Dehmel, A. (2005). *The role of vocational education and training in promoting lifelong learning in Germany and England*. Oxford: Symposium Books.

European Commission. (2000). *A memorandum on lifelong learning*. SEC(2000) 1832. Brussels: European Commission.

European Commission. (2001). *Making a European area of lifelong learning a reality*. Brussels: European Commission.

Eurydice & CEDEFOP. (2001). *National actions to implement lifelong learning in Europe*. Brussels: Eurydice.

Field, J. (1998). *European dimensions: Education, training and the European Union*. London/ Philadelphia: Jessica Kingsley Publishers.

Field, J. (2006). *Lifelong learning and the new educational order* (2nd ed.). Stoke-on-Trent: Trentham Books.

Furedi, F. (2004, September 24). It's now no longer critical and nor is it thinking. *The Times Higher Education Supplement*, 58. http://www.timeshighereducation.co.uk/story.asp?sectioncode=26 &storycode=191406. Accessed 9 July 2012.

Gough, M. (2011). Education as philosophy, philosophy as education and the concept of practice: Considerations of disciplinarity arising out of learning and teaching development work. *Discourse: Learning and Teaching in Philosophical and Religious Studies, 10*(3). http://prs. heacademy.ac.uk/publications/discourse/10_3.html. Accessed 9 July 2012.

Griffiths, T., & Guile, D. (2004). *Learning through work experience for the knowledge economy: Issues for educational research and policy*. Luxembourg: Office for Official Publications of the European Communities.

Lum, G. (2009). *Vocational and professional capability: An epistemological and ontological study of occupational expertise*. London: Continuum.

Maskell, D., & Robinson, I. (2001). *The new idea of a university*. London: Haven Books.

Rowland, S. (2006). *The enquiring university: Compliance and contestation in higher education*. Maidenhead: Society for Research into Higher Education & Open University Press.

Summers, J. (2000). A memorandum on lifelong learning commission staff working paper. *LLinE: Lifelong Learning in Europe, 5*(4), 230–232.

Tessaring, M., & Wannan, J. (2004). *Vocational education and training: Key to the future: Lisbon, Copenhagen, Maastricht, mobilising for 2010*. Luxembourg: Office for Official Publications of the European Communities.

van Rens, J., & Stavrou, S. (2003). *Lifelong learning: Citizens' views*. Luxembourg: Office for Official Publications of the European Communities.

White, J. (1997). *Education and the end of work*. London: Cassell.

Winterton, J., Delamare-Le Deist, F., & Stringfellow, E. (2006). *Typology of knowledge, skills and competences: Clarification of the concept and prototype*. Luxembourg: Office for Official Publications of the European Communities.

Part II
Lifelong Learning and More Investment in Human Resources

Chapter 6
Incentives and Disincentives to Invest in Human Resources

Marcella Milana

Introduction

The Memorandum on lifelong learning states that its second objective is to 'visibly raise levels of investment in human resources in order to place priority on Europe's most important asset – its people' (EC 2000, p. 12). As well as outlining this objective, the Memorandum on lifelong learning also suggests possible ways for member states to increase the annual per capita investment in human resources. These include specific agreements between social partners for the continuation of employee training, as well as incentive measures to support individual investment in training and education. Both options identify the need to adopt cofinancing arrangements as a means of creating shared responsibility between the state, private enterprises, social partners and individuals.

The objective of 'investing' in human resources clearly finds its raison d'être in the notion that, at an individual level, the acquisition of skills and knowledge increases a person's productive value, an idea that is grounded in human capital (HC) theory, and which still informs much of the debate in adult education today. Within this line of argument, economic investment in skill upgrading among the adult population produces a return on investment in terms of both economic and noneconomic benefits at micro, meso and macro levels. Accordingly, human resource management (HRM) researchers argue that a competitive advantage at enterprise level can be achieved 'by putting people first'.

The scope of this chapter is to critically examine the arrangements that European governments, in dialogue with trade unions and social partners, have put into place to encourage employers to invest in education and training. In doing so, this chapter reflects on the potential benefits and limitations of the HC paradigm for

M. Milana (✉)
Department of Education, Aarhus University, Aarhus, Denmark
e-mail: mami@dpu.dk

G.K. Zarifis and M.N. Gravani (eds.), *Challenging the 'European Area of Lifelong Learning': A Critical Response*, Lifelong Learning Book Series 19, DOI 10.1007/978-94-007-7299-1_6, © Springer Science+Business Media Dordrecht 2014

'Making a European Area of Lifelong Learning', at a time when European countries are being strongly affected by the economic crisis.

This chapter is divided into four sections. Following this first, introductory section, in section "Investing in an organisation's most valuable asset: its human capital", I address the relations between HC and HRM, in order to shed light on what underpins the political interest to invest in human resources. Against this background, in section "Participation in formal or nonformal education and training of employed people", I look at the rate of participation in education and training by employed people and the main job-related obstacles identified by people who wished to, but did not, participate in such arrangements. In section "Governments' contribution (if any) to support employers' investment in education and training", I review the relation between public policy and investment in human resources, with a specific focus on the multiplicity of arrangements in place in selected European countries (i.e. Austria, Belgium, Denmark, France, Germany, Ireland, the Netherlands, Norway, Sweden, Switzerland and the United Kingdom), which aim to increase employer investment in employee training. Finally, in section "Concluding remarks", I conclude with few remarks on the previous analysis. I suggest that the most beneficial government arrangements are those that favour HRM strategies built on a shared social commitment towards workers' development. These have the potential to increase employer expenditure on employee training, and also to produce a better return on investment in education and training for both enterprises and individuals.

Investing in an Organisation's Most Valuable Asset: Its Human Capital

HC theory was first developed in the late 1950s and early 1960s, thanks to the contribution of a limited number of economists, who were mostly concentrated around two Northern American higher education institutions: the University of Chicago (Becker 1993; Schultz 1960, 1961) and Columbia University (Mincer 1958, 1974). Since then, HC theory has spread across geographical borders and academic disciplines. Furthermore, it has reached out to the policy environment and still informs much of the policy debate surrounding governmental arrangements to encourage employer investment in education and training.

Originated by an interest in the return rate of investment in education and training, the early studies in HC research were concerned with 'activities that influence future monetary and physic income by increasing the resources in people. These activities are called investments in human capital' (Becker 1993, p. 11).

The above studies were grounded on the belief that HC, contrary to other forms of capital, is embodied in people, and that 'earnings mainly measure how much workers had invested in their skills and knowledge' (Burton-Jones and Spender 2011, p. xiii). These beliefs have led to extensive analysis of investment in HC, which aims to understand people's behaviour from an economic point of view, given that investment in education and training is considered a rational response to a calculus of expected costs and benefits (Becker 1993).

HC theory does not deny nonmonetary benefits of investment in people; in fact, it also recognises other types of investment in supporting knowledge and skills that form a person's HC. Nonetheless, HC theory still claims, from a macro economic perspective, that investment in education and training is the most powerful factor in explaining economic growth. This claim is grounded on two beliefs: firstly, that high technology plays a significant role in many jobs in modern societies, but, secondly, that the specific knowledge and skills required to cope with advancements in high technology are difficult to acquire outside the education and training system.

However, an increased interest in HC theory is also the result of convergent views, which link information, knowledge and job productivity, and which arose through the predicted shift to a post-industrial society (Bell 1973) and the rise of knowledge workers (Drucker 1959), in other words, employees who work primarily with information or develop and use knowledge in the workplace for the benefit of the organisation. This gave rise to the idea that an organisation's knowledge represents the most relevant economic and strategic resource, which was widely accepted in the 1990s and laid the foundation of new practices in the workplace, such as knowledge and human resource management, as we shall see.

Rethinking Human Capital

Traditional economic theories identify physical capital as a homogeneous, quantifiable and measurable object of study. Accordingly, capital is considered a factor of production that is itself an output of other productive activities and is owned by some party of the production process. HC theory first applied and expanded this notion to include a form of capital that is embodied in people. The analogy between physical capital and HC assumes that HC can be the output of working and personal experience, but it is primarily the output of education and training, which is owned by the workers. However, while the investors of other forms of capital may not participate in productive activities, the owners of HC must work in the productive activity; thus, a higher HC renders workers more productive (Blair 2011).

Several scholars have questioned the validity of such an analogy, as well as its instrumental approach of reducing people to commodities. Thus, over time, researchers have argued for the concept of capital to be revised so as to apply to all productive resources, thereby recognising the importance of existing connections between types and forms of tangible/physical and intangible/nonphysical capital (Burton-Jones and Spender 2011). According to this argument, whether it is constituted by a knowledge representation, i.e. a tool, or by embodied knowledge, i.e. people, Lewin (2011) argues that capital is always knowledge based. This way of conceptualising capital not only emphasises all type of resources as capital, it also stresses that, although all forms of capital are intrinsically involved with knowledge, in HC, this knowledge is inalienable (Lewin 2011, p. 146). In doing so, it also highlights that the development of capital in general and, in particular, in HC is never the product of autonomous workers, but rather the result of workers' interactions.

This way of rethinking HC theory shifts the focus away from a strictly quantitative analysis, which still informs much of HC research (cf. Hartog and Maassen Van Den Brink 2007), towards a qualitative approach to theorising the knowledge economy. This is achieved through, what Burton-Jones and Spender (2011) call, an 'HC-based theory of the firm'. This theory distinguishes 'between the human capital that characterizes efficient markets and that which characterizes productive organizations' (Burton-Jones and Spender 2011, p. 8). When it comes to investments in HC, this approach seems more suitable to reintegrate economic and practice perspectives. In fact, while traditional economic perspectives consider HC as a mere factor of production, an 'HC-based theory of the firm' views HC as a result of learning processes – occurring through organisational practices – which bring HC into play. Furthermore, it also presents human resource management (HRM) as a critical factor that cannot be reduced to performance measurement and rational goal setting.

Human Resource Management

As with HC theory, this field of research and practice find its roots in the Northern American context, which still heavily influences it. In fact, HRM emerged in the mid-1980s as a development of personnel management (PM), thanks to the contribution of a group of scholars based at the Harvard Business School (Beer et al. 1984).

PM represented an established approach to the management of people in planned, stable economies; hence, it distinguished between management and strategic planning within an organisation. By contrast, HRM considers the management of people as a serious organisational activity, which is intertwined with the business strategy of an organisation in at least two ways. First, HRM contributes to the achievement of an organisation's strategic objectives. Second, HRM's decisions depend on the organisation's business strategy (Rowley and Jackson 2011). In other words, HRM represents 'a strategic and coherent approach to the management of an organization's most valuable assets – the people who are working there, who individually and collectively contribute to the achievement of its objectives' (Armstrong 2006, p. 3); hence, from the employee's recruitment to the employee's future development, HRM – like HC theory – emphasises human resources.

In practice, HRM covers diverse domains of activity, which Rowley and Jackson (2011) categorise as:

- Employee resourcing, dealing with decisions relevant to recruitment and selection
- Employee rewards, concerned with decisions about payment and promotion
- Employee relations, dealing with perceptions, processes and institutions of relations between employers and employees
- Employee development, concerned with decisions about increasing skills and competences of individuals and teams, mostly through 'on-the-job' and 'off-the-job' training

With this in mind, I shall now look at participation rates in education and training among the employed (as a proxy for employee development), using the Adult Education Survey (AES) data for the EU-27 and Turkey.

Participation in Formal or Nonformal Education and Training of Employed People

According to the AES, almost 40 % of employed people aged 25–64 participated in formal or nonformal education and training during the last 12 months preceding the interview, i.e. 2007. However, participation rates at national level vary extensively (cf. Fig. 6.1). The highest rates of participation (60 % or more) are found in Sweden, Finland and Norway. However, relatively high rates of participation (40–60 %) are found in other Northern European countries (the United Kingdom, Denmark), as well as in a number of countries scattered in Central and Eastern Europe. By contrast, but with the exception of Cyprus and Malta, participation rates are far below the EU-27 mean in Southern Europe, especially in Greece, Hungary and Romania (below 20 %).

The AES also collected information on how the education and training was funded. Unfortunately, only data on individual expenditure can be accessed publically (cf. Fig. 6.2). The greatest individual expenditure (200–400 EUR) occurs primarily in countries showing the highest or relatively high participation rates, such as Norway, Denmark, Germany, Austria, the Netherlands, Cyprus and Malta.

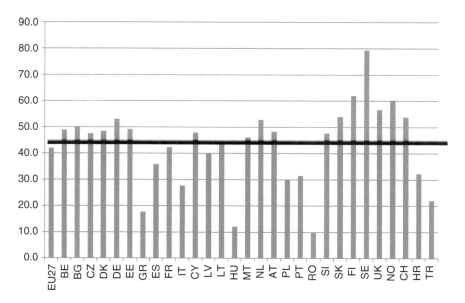

Fig. 6.1 Employed people aged 25–64 by participation in formal or nonformal education and training, reference year: 2007 (%) (*Source*: Eurostat, Adult Education Survey, 2007)

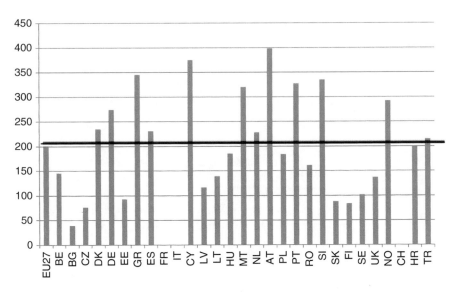

Fig. 6.2 Individual expenditure by employed people aged 25–64 for participation in formal or nonformal education and training, reference year: 2007 (Euro) (Note: Missing values for FR, IT and CH; *Source*: Eurostat, Adult Education Survey, 2007)

It is interesting to notice, however, that equal individual expenditure also occurs in countries like Greece and Portugal (300–350 EUR), where participation of employed people in education and training is low.

It is also worth considering the job-related obstacles that were perceived by the population aged 25–64, who wished to, but did not, participate in formal or non-formal education and training (cf. Fig. 6.3). The major job-related obstacle is a conflict between training and work schedules, with a European mean of 35 %, which increases to 40 % or more in various Southern and Eastern European countries, as well as in Finland and the United Kingdom. A second job-related obstacle is the lack of employer support, perceived, on average, by 15 % of the population, with important exceptions in Denmark, Lithuania, Hungary and Romania (28 % or more). It is worth noticing that, although this type of obstacle is ill-defined – as it leads to different interpretations at an individual level – it generally makes reference to a lack of economic support by the employer to cover expenditure for participation in education and training, as well as to the impossibility of negotiating time off work for the same purpose.

To recapitulate, in Europe, almost one out of two employed people aged 25–64 participated in formal or nonformal education and training in 2007. However, participation rates vary extensively across countries, from 79 % in Sweden to less than 10 % in Romania. On average, individuals contribute 200 EUR to the total cost. In the majority of cases, a higher level of individual expenditure is positively correlated with participation rates, with only a few exceptions (Greece and Portugal). Approximately one in three of the European population aged 25–64, who did not

Fig. 6.3 Respondents aged 25–64 who wanted to but did not participate in formal or nonformal education and training, by job-related obstacles, reference year: 2007 (%) (*Source*: Adult Education Survey, 2007)

participate in education and training but wanted to, addressed conflicts between education or training and work schedules as a major obstacle; while less than one in six explicitly addressed the lack of employer support.

Having dealt with perceived obstacles, participation rates and individual investment in education and training among employed people, I shall now move my attention to government–employer arrangements, which stimulate employer investment in education and the training of employees.

Governments' Contribution (if Any) to Support Employers' Investment in Education and Training

European governments, in dialogue with trade unions and social partners, have put into place a multiplicity of arrangements to increase employer investment in education and training. Billet and Smith (2003, 2005) identify four purposes for governments to introduce such policies. These purposes are not mutually exclusive:

– A shift of expenditure from the public to the private purse
– Equity in expenditure and funding
– Development of skills
– Strategic development of skills

A shift of expenditure from the public to the private purse is often an implicit policy purpose that may result in the imposition of mandated training levies, which are often resisted by employers and their associations. However, it is also possible to make the expenditure more attractive for the employer and, therefore, to alter the employer's view on the value of such expenditure. Equity in expenditure and funding is an alternative policy goal for governments to ensure that the diverse need for skill development across industry sectors is met and costs for skills development are shared across enterprises and workplaces. Related to this is the goal for governments to leverage skills development, in order to secure a better balance between the demand and supply of skilled work at national level. This goal is generally achieved by improving the quality of skill development, as well as by increasing the commitment in skills development by enterprises. Finally, government policy may also aim at maintaining national competitiveness through the development of new types of skills and the increase in knowledge creation and sharing, via the education and training of employees (Billett and Smith 2005).

Although specific policy purposes may differ, government policy is always concerned with how best to encourage employer expenditure for employee training and is, ultimately, dependent on the nature of the market failure for which the government intends to adjust (Trendle and Siu 2005). A market failure exist, for instance, when the employee's demand for education and training decreases in the face of capital constraints, together with uncertainty regarding the future salary gain, which will result from undertaking additional education and training (i.e. capital market imperfection). Alternatively, a market failure may arise when skilled workers earn less than their marginal product; in this scenario, the wage gain from additional education and training is lower and so is the employee's desire to invest in it (Stevens 1996). Finally, market failures may also result from an asymmetry of information between employees and providers on the type and quality of the education and training supply.

In order to adjust for market failures, European governments have set in place diverse mechanisms for prompting employer investment in education and training. These mechanisms include both incentives and compulsory measures. Incentives relate to government cofinancing of the education and training of employees or tax incentives for employers investing in education and training. Compulsory measures comprise the creation of sectorial training funds with residual government subsidies, revenue-generating levies remitted to the government budget for training or for training institutions and levy exemption schemes, in which the government fixes the percentage of payroll employers that must take advantage of employee training.

Gasskov (2001, p. 36) has mapped incentives and compulsory measures in place in various European countries and, on this basis, distinguishes between the following typologies, which are not mutually exclusive:

- Countries in which governments have introduced compulsory financing of training by employers (e.g. Denmark, France and Ireland)
- Countries in which governments offer tax exemptions to training enterprises (e.g. Belgium and Germany)

- Countries in which enterprises have no legal obligations regarding training and its financing (e.g. the Netherlands, Sweden and the United Kingdom)
- Countries in which employers voluntarily take significant responsibility for financing of employee training (e.g. Germany and Switzerland)
- Countries in which employers and unions set up training development funds under the training clauses of collective labour agreements (e.g. Belgium, Denmark and the Netherlands)

Gasskov's (2001) mapping also devotes ample attention to subsidised schemes set in place by governments to cofinance enterprise training with the aim of maintaining or increasing the level of training for specific targets. These are targets for which the enterprise is not solely responsible and, therefore, targets that are not prioritised; they include educating those employees at risk of unemployment, as well as imparting transferable (as opposed to company specific) skills to the unemployed. In addition, governments sustain employer investment in human resources through tax-related incentives, which include the exemption of all training facilities from property and land tax and the possibility for companies to deduct training expenses from their total taxable revenue.

More recently, Smith and Billett (2004) suggested a different categorisation of government–employer financing arrangements aimed at encouraging greater employer investment in employee training. This categorisation distinguishes between:

1. Laissez-faire systems (e.g. the United Kingdom)
2. High employer commitment systems (e.g. Finland, Denmark, Germany and Norway)
3. Sectorial training funds (e.g. the Netherlands)
4. Levy schemes (e.g. Austria and France)

In laissez-faire systems, governments impose only a limited number of regulations on employers to train employees. These systems are characterised by a low-skill equilibrium, work simplification and deskilling in a mass-production environment, with persistent skill shortages as proof of market failure in education and training (cf. Ashton and Green 1996). An example of this type of system is the United Kingdom, where ad hoc government initiatives to increase employer investment in employee training have, apparently, benefitted only those employers already investing significantly in this area. Unfortunately, such ad hoc initiatives have not encouraged employers with little or no commitment to employee training to begin or increase investment in this sphere (Smith and Billett 2004).

By contrast, in high employer commitment systems, there are legal obligations on employers to provide employee training, even if the employer is primarily responsible for the cost. Typical examples of countries in which this system prevails are Germany and Denmark. According to Gosskov (2001), employers in both of these countries assume a high degree of responsibility for employee training at either initial or continuing education levels. In Germany, this is exemplified by the dual system for the initial vocational education and training of youngsters.

This scheme is organised and funded by the federal government, the state (Lander) governments and employers, through their associations. However, when it comes to the continuing education of employees, legal obligations are insufficient to increase employer investment in training, which means that employees, as opposed to employers, are left to finance much of their continuing vocational training. Denmark is a different case. In Denmark, the employer commitment to employee training is rooted in a combination of governmental, financial support and a strong role for social partners; together, they reach a consensus on the importance of training at enterprise level. However, high employer commitment systems can also be found in countries that do not impose legal obligations on employers, such as Norway and Finland. In these countries, employer investment is guaranteed through a common, social desirability for worker development via employee training (Smith and Billett 2004).

Sectorial training funds are characteristic of those countries in which either the government or the employers have established training funds based on industrial agreements between social partners. This model is exemplified by the Netherlands, where sectorial training funds have been established as a result of a national agreement on wages. Over time, these have become the basis for a strong social partnership and the foundation for regulating established, diverse employment-related aspects (Smith and Billett 2004). Other countries are following this example, albeit at a relatively slower pace (e.g. Italy).

Finally, in countries such as France or Austria, levy schemes represent the key mechanism for boosting employer investment in employee training (Smith and Billett 2004).

Smith and Billet (2004) conclude that policy mechanisms adopted by governments to increase investment in employee training are still limited, and, without the employer's voluntary participation in cofinancing and/or increasing investment in employee training, these schemes remain largely ineffective.

In short, the literature on public policy to encourage employer investment in education and training highlights that an institutional responsibility of governments to adjust for market failures is often combined with an implicit goal to shift expenditure for education and training from the public to the private purse, which is much in line with neoliberal policy approaches to education and training in general. To this aim, some governments assume stronger regulatory functions than others, although this does not necessarily result in higher employer commitment towards employee training.

Concluding Remarks

The new way of thinking HC, as interconnected with other types and forms of physical and nonphysical capital, takes HC to be an essential part of an enterprise's assets. However, simply emphasising its presence does not guarantee an enterprise's success. Consequently, Nahapiet (2011, p. 78) suggests redirecting the attention of HC research 'from exclusive interest in individual attributes to include the emergent features of social relations and social interactions'.

In the meantime, the return of investment in education and training at individual level has been put into doubt by the simple observation that a general rise in investment has de facto been accompanied by a universal worsening of working conditions. This has been documented by Brown et al. (2011). Accordingly, these commentators denounce the existence of 'a race to the bottom'. In other words, they claim that competitive advantage enterprises look after highly educated and trained workers to which they can offer low wage jobs!

These observations, by themselves, do not deny the need for governments to provide incentives for employers to invest in employee training; they rather suggest that higher investment in the education and training of workers, although important, is not sufficient. Furthermore, they acknowledge that employee development decisions are not only influenced by government interventions but also by the type of HRM strategy adopted within a given organisation.

Several approaches to HRM can be found in the relevant secondary literature. Among these approaches is the so-called European model, proposed on the basis of international comparisons of human resource practices in European organisations (Brewster 1995; Brewster et al. 2004). The model differentiates between the environment and the organisation and considers the interconnections that exist between and within them. The environment is constituted by the international context (which includes the European Union), the national context (with its cultural, political, economic and social characteristics) and the national HRM context (which refers to labour market structures, industrial relations, trade union representation and existing opportunities and/or support for education and training). The organisation is constituted by the corporate strategy of a given company, its HRM strategy (i.e. employment, involvement and rewards policies) and its HRM practice (i.e. employee selection, appraisal and development).

Although the European model does not include distinctive factors, such as the diverse availability of skills and qualifications at national level or the degree of employee participation in decision-making processes (Rowley et al. 2011), it nonetheless reflects a certain degree of integration that results from adopting common EU legislation, without denying the differences between countries and clusters of countries, which are the manifestation of their historical and cultural traits.

For example, in countries such as Finland or Norway, which are characterised by a broad employer commitment to employee training and the highest education and training participation rates in Europe, it is a shared sociocultural desire for worker development, rather than fiscal or financial measures by the government, which has had the most positive impact on employer expenditure on education and training. However, a closer look at other countries, such as Germany or Denmark, which also boast high participation rates in education and training, questions whether a clear-cut distinction between neutral and intervening governments can capture the complexity of the phenomenon under consideration. In fact, the 'voluntarism' of German enterprises is indirectly sustained by tax exemptions, as well as by compulsory measures, such as training levies by the German government. In Denmark, collective labour agreements go hand in hand with the compulsory financing of training programmes (introduced by the Danish government) and a governmental contribution to the sectorial funds established through collective bargaining.

In light of the above, it is reasonable to suggest that the most beneficial institutional or legislative arrangements are those that favour HRM strategies that are built on a shared social commitment towards employee development (as opposed to those which favour a 'race to the bottom' approach). Such approaches have the potential to encourage employer expenditure on employee training but also to enable both enterprises and individuals to gain a better return on investment in education and training.

References

Armstrong, M. (2006). *A handbook of human resource management practice*. London: Kogan Page.

Ashton, D., & Green, F. (1996). *Education, training and the global economy*. Aldershot: Edward Elgar Adelaide: National Centre for Vocational Education Research.

Becker, G. S. (1993). *Human capital: A theoretical and empirical analysis with special reference to education* (3rd ed.). Chicago/London: University of Chicago Press.

Beer, M., Spector, B., Lawrence, P. R., Quinn-Mills, D., & Walton, R. E. (1984). *Managing human assets*. New York: Free Press.

Bell, D. (1973). *The coming of post-industrial society. A venture in social forecasting*. New York: Basic Books.

Billett, S., & Smith, A. (2003). Compliance, engagement and commitment: Increasing employer expenditure in training. *Journal of Vocational Education and Training, 55*(3), 251–269.

Billett, S., & Smith, A. (2005). Enhancing enterprise expenditure on VET: Policy goals and mechanisms. *Journal of Vocational Education and Training, 57*(1), 5–23.

Blair, M. M. (2011). An economic perspective on the notion of 'human capital'. In A. Burton-Jones & J.-C. Spender (Eds.), *The Oxford handbook of human capital* (pp. 51–70). Oxford: Oxford University Press.

Brewster, C. (1995). Towards a European model of HRM. *Journal of International Business Studies, 26*(1), 1–21.

Brewster, C., Morley, M., & Mayrhofer, W. (2004). *HRM in Europe: Evidence of convergence*. Oxford: Butterworth-Heinemann.

Brown, P., Lauder, H., & Ashton, D. (2011). *The global auction. The broken promises of education, job and incomes*. Oxford: Oxford University Press.

Burton-Jones, A., & Spender, J.-C. (Eds.). (2011). *The Oxford handbook of human capital*. Oxford: Oxford University Press.

Drucker, P. F. (1959). *Landmarks of tomorrow*. New York: Harper & Bros.

EC. (2000). *Memorandum on lifelong learning*. Brussels: Commission of the European Communities.

Gasskov, V. (2001). *Government interventions in private financing of training*. Geneva: International Labour Organization.

Hartog, J., & Maassen Van Den Brink, H. (Eds.). (2007). *Human capital: Advances in theory and evidence*. Cambridge: Cambridge University Press.

Lewin, P. (2011). A capital-based approach to the firm. In A. Burton-Jones & J.-C. Spender (Eds.), *The Oxford handbook of human capital* (pp. 145–161). Oxford: Oxford University Press.

Mincer, J. (1958). Investment in human capital and personal income distribution. *Journal of Political Economy, 66*, 281–302.

Mincer, J. (1974). *Schooling, experience and earnings*. New York: Columbia University Press.

Nahapiet, J. (2011). A social perspective – Exploring the links between human capital and social capital. In A. Burton-Jones & J.-C. Spender (Eds.), *The Oxford handbook of human capital* (pp. 71–95). Oxford: Oxford University Press.

Rowley, C., & Jackson, K. (Eds.). (2011). *Human resource management: The key concepts*. London/New York: Routledge.

Rowley, C., Hon-fun Poon, I., Zhu, Y., & Warner, M. (2011). Approaches to IHRM. In A.-W. Harzing & A. P. Pinnington (Eds.), *International human resource management*. London: SAGE.

Schultz, T. W. (1960). Capital formation by education. *Journal of Political Economy, 68*(6), 571–583.

Schultz, T. W. (1961). Investment in human capital. *American Economic Review, 51*(1), 1.

Smith, A., & Billett, S. (2004). *Mechanisms for increasing employer contributions to training: An international comparison: National Centre for Vocational Education Research* (under licence from Australian National Training Authority). Adelaide: National Centre for Vocational Education Research.

Stevens, M. (1996). Transferable training and poaching externalities. In A. L. Booth & D. J. Snower (Eds.), *Acquiring skills* (pp. 19–37). Cambridge: Cambridge University Press.

Trendle, B., & Siu, J. (2005). *Investment in training and public policy – A review*. Labour Market Research Unit Department of Employment and Training Working (Working Paper No. 35). Queensland.

Chapter 7
An Inconsistent Policy: Lifelong Learning and Adult Education Policy Towards a Competitive Advantage

Paula Guimarães and Fátima Antunes

Introduction

This chapter focuses on the ways in which the EU lifelong learning agenda, specifically the guidelines for basic skills, has been interpreted according to the Portuguese realities, at national and local levels. We suggest that basic skills for all, as intended in the framework of the European area of lifelong learning, have somewhat loose roots in the cultural and civic dimensions of education from a human and social development perspective. Competitiveness and social cohesion, the dual centrality of lifelong education and learning for *Europe*, stated in the Lisbon Strategy, have been interpreted and translated in Portugal through a dynamic, imbalanced agenda fed by two major strands: the prosecution of a social right for a long time indebted to the adult population and a search for so-called employability and qualification as a way to tackle Portuguese *distance* from European educational standards. According to these options that frame the EU agenda, this article also stresses the adults' understandings of adult education which come out in the research findings presented later. The data analysis shows that these understandings are congruent with EU guidelines; adults see adult education as a promise of a better life. Thus, given the inconsistency of lifelong learning, fulfilling this promise is a hard task to achieve.

This paper was written within the research project "EDUQUAL - Educar e Qualificar: o caso do Programa Novas Oportunidades" (PTDC/CPE-CED/105575/2008) funded by the Foundation for Science and Technology (Fundação para a Ciência e Tecnologia - FCT - in Portuguese). In addtion, this article was developed with the support of Centre of Research in Education (in Portuguese CIEd), University of Minho, and also financed by National Funds by the FCT in the scope of the project Pest-OE/CED/UI1661/2011.

P. Guimarães (✉)
Institute of Education, University of Lisbon, Lisbon, Portugal
e-mail: pguimaraes@ie.ul.pt

F. Antunes
Institute of Education, University of Minho, Braga, Portugal

A Rationale for Interpreting Adult Education Policies Under Development

On a first level, in the context of globalisation we have witnessed the emergence of international and supranational organisations such as the European Union (EU). This organisation is increasingly intervening in several domains, in particular that of education. In this arena the production of guidelines that are being adopted by many member states has taken place. National policies may show a wider or narrower convergence towards supranational orientations. The lifelong learning guidelines fostered by the EU are interesting examples of this policy production effort on a mega scale, even if the adoption of such proposals at a national level has been questioned by several authors (cf. Field 2006; Antunes 2008, among others).

On a second level, the guidelines produced by the EU for lifelong learning have been appropriated by the various nations according to historical development trends and to the characteristics of the adult education systems and projects in each country. It seems that a reinterpretation of lifelong learning has taken place in the framework of the processes by which national public policies are produced (cf. Antunes 2008; Lima and Guimarães 2011).

On a third level, much research has shown that the adoption of national public policies for adult education has involved a reinterpretation by local actors such as the promoters of forms of provision. In this case, quite often several conceptions of adult education run through the reproduction and the giving of new meaning when devising and understanding a public policy. It is at this stage that a public policy may reveal ambiguities and contradictory trends due to conflicts between goals set at supranational and national levels and outcomes actually accomplished (cf. Sá 2009; Alves 2010; Guimarães 2011; Lima and Guimarães 2012).

On the one hand, these various reinterpretations have led to several lifelong learning developments in the different countries, owing to the national or regional realities of adult education. On the other hand, according to the EU the diversity of national interpretations has led to inadequate outcomes, with respect to the goals established by the Lisbon Strategy (2000), for instance (cf. Commission of the European Communities 2005). In fact, in some cases, including that of Portugal, lifelong learning seems to be achieved locally under an inconsistent policy that is in need of new educational approaches such as that of critical education. Adult education in our country is based on priorities that barely express national aspirations and realities, focused on raising school participation (basic and secondary certification) rates in line with European guidelines for competitiveness and employability. Thus, the outcomes achieved do not go beyond convincing adults that lifelong learning is important. Furthermore, the results are not translated into effective changes in people's lives and the way they perceive their intervention in Portuguese society and the economy.

The European and Portuguese Agendas for Basic Skills: National Aspirations and Reinterpretation

The chronology of the *relaunch* of a public adult education policy and system in Portugal (cf. Melo et al. 2001b) is in tune with some important supranational developments. The programme Project of Society: To Know+ (in Portuguese *Projecto de Sociedade: S@ber+*) was part of the 1998 National Plan for Employment,[1] the Portuguese government's answer to the European Employment Strategy (1997). This programme also concerned the lifelong learning strategy that was formulated for the first time to supplement the 2001 National Plan for Employment. On the one hand, the strength of the European Employment Strategy and the Lisbon Strategy was unavoidable given the adoption of lifelong learning as a crucial policy for the priorities of competitiveness and social cohesion; likewise, the Education and Training 2010 Programme and the basic skills for lifelong learning framework must be considered (cf. Hozjan 2009). On the other hand, the first movements and programmatic documents for the mentioned *relaunch* stemmed from the devastating diagnosis on adult education sector (made public during the electoral campaign before the elections of 1995, in which the low schooling levels of the Portuguese population were stressed), from the European Year of Lifelong Learning events of 1996, as well as from the participation of the Portuguese delegation at the V CONFINTEA in Hamburg in 1997 (cf. Melo et al. 2001b). Additionally, the *Referential of Key Competences* (Alonso et al. 2000; Gomes 2006), the conceptual and procedural frameworks that have underpinned adult education forms of provision, was the basis for major innovations and forms of provision of adult education policy – the recognition, validation and certification of competences and adult education and training courses (AET courses). These two forms of provision were initially run as experimental pilot projects in 2000. This establishment was simultaneous with (and not just a derivative of) the debate on *A Memorandum on Lifelong Learning* (2000), the *Communication of the European Commission on Lifelong Learning* (2001) and the *Strategic Framework for European Cooperation in Education and Training* 2010 that was framed by the Lisbon Strategy. Therefore, several connections between supranational agendas, especially the EU one, within the adoption of lifelong learning guidelines and the building of the framework of

---

[1] Adult education is probably the educational domain in which the Portuguese democracy has done less and most weakly since 1974. An adult education public policy and system were never built, although some trials were made in the last decades. This is very well expressed by the idea that adult education has had in Portugal (and this is all the more true today, August 2012) 'a sinuous process' and is 'a blocked project', as argued by Melo et al. (2001b). In 1998, this so-called relaunch promised to be a serious effort to build such a policy and system, as we shall see further. For more details, see 'Relaunch of the programme 'Project of Society: To Know+' for adult education and training for lifelong learning' (cf. Resolução do Conselho de Ministros 59/98, April 8th 1998). http://www.igf.min-financas.pt/inflegal/bd_igf/bd_legis_geral/Leg_geral_docs/RCM_059_98.htm. (Accessed 28 February 2012).

basic skills became clear. These guidelines were essential both for the European political priorities that were directed at the education systems of member states and for economic and employment policies. It is also evident that the definition of an adult education policy was driven by deep-rooted social and historical experiences and aspirations, through relations and structural processes, institutional resources, social actors, interest groups and communities and their interpretations of the Portuguese realities[2] (cf. Antunes 2008, 2011).

We can thus argue that the emphasis on basic skills since the 1990s made room for two decisive and interrelated thrusts in adult education policy. The first one involves the development of only three (formal) dimensions from the multifaceted universe of adult education and training. The second thrust involved the adoption of *Referential of Key Competences*, frameworks that were technical and political instruments of regulation of adult education forms of provision.

So, in accordance with the first option, it has been fostered: (1) the *educational recovery* of large numbers of Portuguese who had not being offered access to the system of formal education for several decades, apart from compulsory education; (2) *vocational training* directed at supporting the conversion of the Portuguese economy towards a progressive opening to global markets; and (3) the *recognition of prior learning*, as it was considered that knowledge possessed by adults, specifically those adults who were already in the labour market, ought to be formally validated and valued.

The focus of the three aims mentioned assembled, in a quite unbalanced and inconsistent way, concerns with social justice, human resource management principles and attributing a more humanistic meaning to adult education policy. Following this reasoning, the appropriation of the lifelong learning strategy proposed by the EU since the mid-1990s and the definition of the adult education policy in Portugal were based on a discourse that emphasised an 'unacceptable educational deficit' for democracy. Education was a social right to which the adult population had repeatedly been denied access by the elites (Melo 2004). The most evident outcome was a significant variance between the patterns of

---

[2] This expression underlines an effort to understand the density of the sociohistorical and political Portuguese context, which makes this country the poorest country among the richest ones, in Europe and the world. This reality includes several aspects such as: (1) a democratic regime and a welfare State built after the 1970s within the economic crisis, when other welfare States were already in crisis; (2) around 1/3 of the population (five million) spread throughout the world as emigrants and which nowadays has half a million immigrants, mostly from former Portuguese colonies in Africa and Eastern European countries; (3) some health standards (e.g. child mortality) at the top of the richest and most developed countries in Europe and the world, with a public universal health system built after the 1980s; (4) the highest inequality indicators in wealth distribution in the EU; (5) one of the highest poverty rates of Europe; (6) the participation rates in higher education consistent with the EU average; and (7) an absolutely isolated negative situation in Europe on adult population rates, namely, people that completed secondary education, and young people's secondary schooling attendance rates. That expression was consecrated in seminal works on educational policies by Stephen Stoer (1982, 1986), one of the most prominent Portuguese sociologists that for around 30 years (1978–2005) studied the *Portuguese realities*, specifically in what concerned education and social change.

education in Portugal and those in other European countries. Moreover, the so-called return[3] of lifelong education took place in the EU and in Portugal during the second half of the 1990s, at a time when the sociopolitical climate was favourable, both in terms of turning back to education as a human and social right pertaining to the development of individuals and communities, as well as its classification as a private and individual consumer product which is subject to the terms of trade (Afonso 1998). These two strands have been in action through conflicts, defeats and compromises between different protagonists, proposals and courses of action. In fact, the idea of an 'ambivalent policy dynamic' expresses the unbalanced presence and influence of those tendencies.

After that, an ambivalent policy dynamic has been under development. At first the adult education policy adopted after 1999 was seen as a global proposal for the building of a public basic education and training system within a multidimensional social programme, overcoming some managerialistic barriers imposed by EU guidelines. But providing more without having to build up a public system of adult education seemed to have been the decision, when in 1999 the 'To Know+Programme for the Development and Expansion of Adult Education and Training 1999–2006' (Melo et al. 2001a) was developed (cf. Antunes 2008, 2011; Sá 2009). In fact, the development of this programme had progressively moved away from humanistic proposals that had been proposed both in the mentioned document and previously in 'An Educational Commitment in Participation of All: Strategy Document for the Development of Adult Education' (Melo et al. 1998). Still, adult education came across as a State policy, which gave it visibility to a sector that until then was not known in Portugal (cf. Guimarães 2011).

Since then, this sector was referenced in political programmes by succeeding Governments; it became more and more an object of political marketing, highly politicised and increasingly relevant in the context of modernisation, the conversion of a globalised economy and the qualification of the workforce. It became clear that the growing importance of adult education was undertaken by the Portuguese government in the framework of lifelong learning, mostly according to human resources management interpretations advocated by the EU. So, proposals aimed at adults benefited from funding through the European Social Fund. If this policy was deemed to have an educational value, as was the perspective of the Strategy Document and To Know+Programme, it was thus seen as a social, economic and employment policy, as was evident in the New Opportunities Initiative adopted after 2005 (Iniciativa Novas Oportunidades 2005). Therefore, in recent years, this policy was mainly framed by modernisation and managerial aims, within a national strategy of human resources management and social control orientation. In political discourses the focus on competitiveness and social cohesion led to an emphasis on qualification and pedagogism (cf. Lima 2007; Guimarães 2011; Lima and Guimarães 2011).

---

[3] This 'return', in the EU context, concerned new meanings given to ideas preferred by the UNESCO in the 1970s, such as lifelong education and learning; in the Portuguese context, it referred to a political pattern of intermittent adult education plans developed since 1974, when the Democratic Revolution occurred, whose programmes were abandoned almost as soon as they were implemented.

Methodology and Research Techniques

Within this framework, this chapter aims to value the meanings of the strong social visibility and priority given to lifelong learning in the last decade and to adult education. The reasons for this focus include the discussion of the reinterpretation of lifelong learning made by the adult education policy locally, namely, the analysis of ideas expressed by learners concerning their recent educational pathways when most of them were not traditional participants in adult education activities. Following this perspective the analysis of similar trends as outcomes of the EU orientations is considered, as well as the policy recontextualisation, made by the Portuguese State and socio-educational actors, as a result of national educational specificities. Therefore, this debate allows us to ask if and how the Portuguese realities and the ambivalent political dynamics (between a multidimensional social policy and an economically driven policy) are expressed by learners in what refers to lifelong learning (specifically when learners involved in adult education and training courses were considered).

We have opted for a discussion based on the opinions of adults who had joined AET courses (one of the two main forms of provision being promoted in the last decade[4]) and which we based on the question:

– What conceptual understandings of adult education policy were at stake when courses that involved mainly long-term unemployed adults were considered?

The empirical data analysed came from qualitative research, and the central methodological strategy was based on a *case study of adult education policy* (cf. Guimarães 2011). The aim was to investigate the way that a public policy, which was legally defined and which consisted of certain educational processes and official procedures, could influence the modes of thinking and acting of local participants. For this reason, semi-structured interviews were conducted with ten individuals who attended these courses in a non-governmental organisation. These interviews focused on various aspects. The data presented here concern the representations of these individuals regarding these provisions – in essence, the reinterpretation or local appropriation given to that public policy. In this chapter, we highlight adults' motivation for following these courses, as well as their expectations concerning the impact of learning on their lives.

Lifelong Learning as an Investment

The AET courses can be attended by adults who have not completed basic and secondary education (equivalent to 4, 6, 9 and 12 years of schooling). In this way

---

[4]Apart from these courses other provisions include the recognition, validation and certification of competences and modular training courses (cf. http://www.anq.gov.pt. Accessed 2 November 2011).

such courses allow those who attend to gain a school certificate.[5] This is in line with the aims of remedying the low rates of school education recorded by the Portuguese population and improving basic skills, as sought by the EU (cf. Council of the European Union 2003).

In certain situations, these courses can lead to a professional qualification, in the case of basic training and technological training courses allowing people to get a vocational qualification level 1, 2, 3 or 4, in accordance with the current typology to date adopted by the EU. Therefore, the main aim of the latter courses is 'the (re) integration or progression in the labour market'.[6] The vocational component of this provision represents an innovation in public adult education policies in Portugal, which, in the past, was mostly about giving a second opportunity within the formal education (cf. Lima 2008; Guimarães 2011, among others). Additionally, these courses are based on a modular training model and draw on guidelines for key competences (such as the Memorandum on Lifelong Learning) and training standards that are part of the National Catalogue of Qualifications and thus the European Qualifications Framework. The vocational dimension of these courses accomplishes the aim of enhancing the vocational qualifications of the population, a fundamental concern for the country in the context of converting the economy and for the priorities established by the EU under the Lisbon Strategy.

Moreover, with these courses the aim is to develop a type of training based on a reflexive process and competences acquisition.[7] This achieves the purpose of recognising prior learning and valuing education and individual training paths, according to EU guidelines, but it also concerns more humanistic approaches in adult education. Therefore, the *Referential of Key Competences* embodies the aim of considering knowledge acquired through experience as a basis for formal recognition and at the same time gives a useful answer to longstanding demands from pedagogues and educational activists. At the same time, the *Referential of Key Competences* is a technical and political instrument that regulates different forms of provision (recognition, validation and certification of competences; AET courses; and Modular Training Actions, recently established). It is, in fact, directed at the dissemination of basic skills for lifelong learning towards economic growth and employment in the EU (as stated in the Lisbon Strategy).

According to data collected, based on a qualitative approach of how adults themselves discuss the issue in the interviews, these aspects made the combination of school certification and professional qualification within AET courses quite

---

[5] Those over 18 years of age can attend these courses equivalent to years 4, 6, 9 and 12 of schooling. These courses provide a school certificate and in some cases a professional qualification and last for a minimum of 100 h and a maximum of 2,390 h (cf. http://www.anq.gov.pt. Accessed 2 November 2011).

[6] For more information see http://www.anq.gov.pt. Accessed 11 February 2011.

[7] This can be achieved by means of the module entitled *Learn Autonomously* (basic education level – 4, 6 or 9 years of schooling and in some cases a professional qualification) or by means of a *Reflective Learning Portfolio* (secondary education level and in some cases a professional qualification).

attractive for the adults involved.[8] The vocational training component consisted of a training module in a real work situation context. On the one hand, this module enabled them to have (renewed) contact with the world of work, in a more protected environment, as it was framed by a contract guaranteed by local promoters and by an educational and training relationship. On the other hand, because these courses highlighted the education, training and learning dimension, as well as the discussion of what was learned, which, in an actual work situation (with little or no qualification), would probably be given little value.

These circumstances contributed to the dual appreciation given by respondents to justify their attending this course. Following the aims of professional qualifications and school certification, the reasons identified were, firstly, those which related to the exercise of a profession and after that, reasons connected with an educational certification. The urgency of entering the job market was highlighted. In a context in which they felt increasingly less prepared, the growing importance of a (stronger professional) *curriculum vitae* represented an important goal. These reasons resulted in the very utilitarian nature that these trainees gave to adult education, emphasising a 'culture of work'[9] (Imaginário et al. 2002). They also show the social recognition of the school certificate, which takes on a profoundly instrumental and localised character (cf. Ávila 2008).

Adult Education Unquestioned

Interviewees were individuals of working age who were unemployed at the time of enrolling in the AET courses.[10] In this way and with all the ensuing economic and social problems as well as the disappointment, they felt towards education and training as being opportunities to break the cycle of poverty and social exclusion that many of them found themselves part of, led them to feel deeply unmotivated at the beginning of the course. However, the vast majority of adults already had work experience. For many of them, contact with the world of work had taken place in their adolescence and was characterised:

1. By the intermittent nature of *irregular periods* of work and unemployment, usually after doing seasonal or occasional jobs, often in sectors where higher levels of schooling and professional qualification were not required
2. By *diversity*, in areas where they worked and the types of tasks performed – in this scenario, the idea of a professional career was simply not appropriate

---

[8] This model was based on both a technical component which favoured the acquisition of a professional qualification as well as another that would lead to a school certificate. These components came about as 'means to obtain essential requisites for a more successful integration in the workplace and in subsequent training opportunities' (Decree Law n° 1083/2000, 20 November).

[9] As opposed to a 'school culture' that had school as a learning environment that was valued by society.

[10] Most of those interviewed had been out of work for over a year.

3. By job *insecurity*, owing to the absence of contractual agreement or to the existence of short-term contracts

Therefore, associated to the benefits of the diploma, many trainees stated that 'it was always good to have a qualification' that 'it was better to have completed a course of study than not to have', even if they were not always able to expound on the reasons for such a belief:

> There is a girl who is working with me, who is only doing weekends. She is a single mother and is going through a divorce. And it is very difficult to find a job, isn't it? And I told her: 'why don't you go to [the local association] and see if there is an EFA Course which you can get onto?' – because she has only done the 6th year – 'and you can get a good foundation for your future'. And then she came; actually there wasn't a course, but at least she tried. But I always advise this, because I think this is one of the best things there is. [Amanda][11]

The evidence that 'everything changed in society' and that it was important 'to have foundations for the future' in order to have another vision of hope in life, such as the symbolic recognition of a certificate or diploma, contributed highly towards getting back a personal sense of achievement and an increase in self-esteem. In addition, when questioned about the effects of training (achieved or expected), the new concepts of self-awareness were constantly being transformed into life-changing possibilities that, in the absence of other economic and employment policies to back them up, more often than not turned into life opportunities which were not fulfilled.[12] The following extract from an interview highlights this attitude:

> I have already had the occasion to say (to friends), and even to people who have a job, that they should, absolutely, get more training, do a course and develop more skills. Because there it is, there's an age-old idea that 'knowledge does not take up extra place' and 'the greater the range of knowledge, the more doors can open', isn't that true? If we have this experience and we can pick up a few ideas, we can then certainly compete and have more opportunities. [Helena][13]

Interestingly, there was an uncritical acceptance of the benefits that education and training of adults could bring to the most disadvantaged social groups and individuals. Once special importance was given to 'finding a job'. Moreover, work seemed vital for an effective change in the lives of these individuals, and, in this articulation between the types of knowledge developed and adult education, the latter materialised as a complementary aspect to employment. Thus, respondents seemed to be examples of people who 'had been left behind', who were irrelevant to economic development, who seemed to be incapable of reflection and were unwanted either on a cyclical or permanent basis (Bélanger and Federighi 2001;

---

[11] Alias name for learner interviewee 1.

[12] Following a similar line of thought, recent studies into the New Opportunities Initiative (cf. Valente et al. 2011) point to the fact that 'career progress or employment prospects did not occur' in the case of those who had been granted certificates by the above-mentioned forms of educational provision. Moreover, this idea has already been referred to in previous studies (CIDEC 2007, among others).

[13] Alias name for learner interviewee 4.

Field 2006). For many of these people, unemployment was not just a 'temporary anomaly' (being temporarily out of a job) but a permanent state. For this reason, they were regarded (and often saw themselves) as a problem for contemporary societies and for the taxpayers (Bauman 2005). In this context, adult education had a weak role within social and economic development. Therefore, we believe that for adults, these courses were a missed opportunity in terms of the flowering of educational courses aimed at promoting civic participation and social emancipation and in initiatives in which they actually took a leading role.

Final Thoughts

In this chapter we have discussed the ways in which the EU's lifelong learning agenda, specifically the guidelines for basic skills, has been interpreted according to the Portuguese realities. This reinterpretation involved an ambivalent policy dynamic, where different strands and understandings about adult education and lifelong learning conflict and compromise with an unbalanced presence and influence, since 1998; so, particularly since 2001,[14] we witnessed the adoption of aims that stressed remedying the low school education rates of large segments of the population, the rise of vocational qualifications in the context of economic conversion and the recognition of prior learning. At a local level, the way specific actors, such as adults involved in public provision, understood and intervened in adult education were consistent with EU guidelines and national policy aims. However, none of the EU guidelines nor any of the aims established by the Portuguese state contained any critical meanings and intentions to effectively transform the living conditions of peoples, which were affected by drastic economic and social changes and faced difficult and precarious situations.

The interviewed adults saw adult education through the acquisition of basic skills as a promise of a better life. Thus, as we intended to suggest and show, fulfilling this promise is hard given the inconsistency of the lifelong learning policy, on officially established goals, forms of provision developed and outcomes achieved. It is therefore important to question lifelong learning and adult education in light of humanistic and critical education concerns. It is not just lifelong learning (and adult education) that fails to achieve the outcomes established under the Lisbon Strategy. Apart from promises related to economic growth, employment and social cohesion, goals such as the promotion of civic participation and social emancipation are non-existent, although in fact they would make more consistent supranational and national policies for adult education. We argue that the paramount societal challenges brought by complex fast-changing, multicultural

---

[14]After the June 2011 elections and after the external *troika* (International Monetary Fund, European Central Bank and European Commission) intervention initiated in May 2011, adult education and lifelong learning have been given an ostensive denial from the newly elected Portuguese government in charge.

and *knowledge* societies (and economies) ask for more (not less) democratic and empowering European social policies and education. So we have a serious problem, when European political elites take their decisions in favour of an economy and social policies that fabricate and turn their back to the growing millions of unemployed and poor people in rich Europe. Of course the need for an integrated and global public policy, that may include goals devoted to economic growth and human resources development but also others of a humanistic nature, of personal and social development and of social emancipation and change, becomes an essential issue for the Portuguese (and European) context.

References

Afonso, A. J. (1998). *Políticas educativas e avaliação educacional. Para uma análise sociológica da reforma educativa em Portugal (1985–1995)*. Braga: Universidade do Minho/IEP/CIEP.

Alonso, L., Magalhães, J., Imaginário, L., Barros, G., Castro, J. M., Osório, A., & Sequeira, F. (2000). *Educação e formação de adultos. Referencial de competências-chave*. Lisboa: Agência Nacional de Educação e Formação de Adultos/Ministério do Trabalho e da Solidariedade and Ministério da Educação.

Alves, M. G. (Ed.). (2010). *Aprendizagem ao longo da vida e políticas educativas Europeias: tensões e ambiguidades nos discursos e nas práticas de estados, instituições e indivíduos*. Lisboa: Unidade de Investigação, Educação e Desenvolvimento/Faculdade de Ciências e Tecnologia.

Antunes, F. (2008). *A nova ordem educacional. Espaço europeu de educação e aprendizagem ao longo da vida*. Coimbra: Almedina.

Antunes, F. (2011). Governação, reformas do Estado e políticas de educação de adultos em Portugal: pressões globais e especificidades nacionais, tensões e ambivalências. *Revista Crítica de Ciências Sociais, 92*, 3–29.

Ávila, P. (2008). *A literacia dos adultos. Competências-chave na Sociedade do Conhecimento*. Lisboa: CIES-ISCTE/Celta Editora.

Bauman, Z. (2005). *Vidas desperdiçadas*. Rio de Janeiro: Jorge Zahar Editor.

Bélanger, P., & Federighi, P. (2001). *Analyse transnationale des politiques d'éducation et de formation des adultes*. Paris: UNESCO-L'Harmattan.

CIDEC. (2007). *O impacto do reconhecimento e certificação de competências adquiridas ao longo da vida. Actualização e aperfeiçoamento*. Lisboa: Direcção-Geral de Formação Vocacional.

Commission of the European Communities. (2005). *Modernising education and training: A vital contribution to prosperity and social cohesion in Europe*. Draft 2006 joint progress report of the Council and Commission on the implementation of the "Education and Training 2010 work programme" (SEC(2005) 1415. Brussels, 30 November. COM(2005) 549 final/2).

Council of the European Union. (2003). *Council conclusions on reference levels of European average performance in education and training (benchmarks)*. Brussels: Council of the European Union.

Field, J. (2006). *Lifelong learning and the educational order*. Stoke on Trent: Trentham Books.

Gomes, M. C. (Coord.). (2006). *Referencial de competências-chave para a educação e formação de adultos – nível secundário*. Lisboa: Direcção-Geral de Formação Vocacional.

Guimarães, P. (2011). *Políticas de educação de adultos em Portugal (1999–2006). A emergência da educação e formação para a competitividade*. Braga: Universidade do Minho/Cied.

Hozjan, D. (2009). Key competences for the development of lifelong learning in the European Union. *European Journal of Vocational Training, 46*(1), 196–207.

Imaginário, L., Carimbo, S., Duarte, I., & Araújo, S. S. (2002). *A aprendizagem dos adultos em Portugal: exame temático no âmbito da OCDE*. Lisboa: Agência Nacional de Educação e Formação de Adultos.

Iniciativa Novas Oportunidades. (2005). http//novasoportunidades.gov.pt/np4/9.html. Accessed 30 Nov 2011.

Lima, L. C. (2007). *Educação ao longo da vida. Entre a mão direita e a mão esquerda de Miró*. São Paulo: Cortez.

Lima, L. C. (2008). A Educação de Adultos em Portugal (1974–2004). In R. Canário & B. Cabrito (Orgs.), *Educação e formação de Adultos. Mutações e convergências* (pp. 31–60). Lisboa: EDUCA.

Lima, L. C., & Guimarães, P. (2011). *European strategies of lifelong learning: A critical introduction*. Opladen/Farmington Hills: Barbara Budrich Publishers.

Lima, L. C., & Guimarães, P. (2012). *Percursos educativos e vidas dos adultos. O reconhecimento, certificação e validação de competências numa associação de desenvolvimento local*. Vila Verde: ATAHCA/Universidade do Minho/Unidade de Educação de Adultos.

Melo, A. (2004). The absence of an adult education policy as a form of social control and some processes of resistance. In L. C. Lima & P. Guimarães (Eds.), *Perspectives on adult education in Portugal* (pp. 39–63). Braga: Universidade do Minho/Unidade de Educação de Adultos.

Melo, A., Queirós, A. M., Silva, A. S., Rothes, L., & Ribeiro, M. (1998). *Uma aposta educativa na participação de todos. Documento de estratégia para o desenvolvimento da educação de adultos*. Lisboa: Ministério da Educação.

Melo, A. (Coord.), Matos, L., & Silva, O. S. (2001a). S@ber+. *Programa para o desenvolvimento e expansão da educação de adultos (1999–2006)*. Lisboa: Agência Nacional de Educação e Formação de Adultos.

Melo, A., Lima, L. C., & Almeida, M. (2001b). *Novas políticas de educação e formação de adultos. O contexto internacional e a situação portuguesa*. Lisboa: ANEFA.

Sá, R. (2009). *Políticas para a educação de adultos em Portugal – a governação pluriescalar da «nova educação e formação de adultos» (1996–2006)*. Ph.D. thesis, Universidade do Minho/ Instituto de Educação e Psicologia, Braga.

Stoer, S. R. (1982). *Educação, estado e desenvolvimento em Portugal*. Lisboa: Livros Horizonte.

Stoer, S. R. (1986). *Educação e mudança social em Portugal*. Porto: Afrontamento.

Valente, A. C., Carvalho, L. X., & Carvalho, A. X. (2011). Bringing lifelong learning to low-skilled adults: The new opportunities initiative. In R. Carneiro (Dir and Ed.), *Accreditation of prior learning as a lever for lifelong learning. Lessons learnt from the new opportunities initiative, Portugal* (pp. 145–181). Braga: UNESCO/MENON Network/CEPCEP – Centro de Estudos dos Povos e Culturas de Expressão Portuguesa.

Chapter 8
Vocational Education: The Tension Between Educational Flexibility and Predictability

Eva Andersson and Gun-Britt Wärvik

Introduction

Vocational education in Sweden has been the subject of several changes in recent years. In 2011, the upper secondary school was reformed, and there are now two separate qualifications, one preparing for higher education and the other for vocational work. Further, apprenticeship education at the upper secondary level has been introduced, which implies that all vocational programmes are provided either as school-based education or as workplace-based apprenticeship education. The responsibility for both alternatives lies, however, with the upper secondary schools. In addition, a new form of education at the post-upper-secondary level (higher vocational education – HVE in the following text) has been established.

For almost half a century, education policy has been intertwined with discourses on lifelong learning. This chapter aims to analyse and problematise the new picture of vocational education in Sweden in the light of the European policies on lifelong learning. The chapter discusses two issues. In what ways does the new picture match or not match the ambitions outlined in the European lifelong learning policy and what tensions and contradictions can be identified as permeating the new educational reform? These issues relate to the motives behind the recent Swedish reform interpreted from the directives, official reports and government bills preceding the reform. Our main argument is that the new reform implies a return to a previous school form with two tracks, one preparing for higher education and one for vocational work. Further, that the organisation of upper secondary education in Sweden is moving away from the European lifelong learning policy where vocational education is concerned. This is, for instance, manifested in the reduction of

E. Andersson (✉) • G.-B. Wärvik, Ph.D.
Department of Education and Special Education, University of Gothenburg,
Gothenburg, Sweden
e-mail: eva.andersson@ped.gu.se

G.K. Zarifis and M.N. Gravani (eds.), *Challenging the 'European Area
of Lifelong Learning': A Critical Response*, Lifelong Learning Book Series 19,
DOI 10.1007/978-94-007-7299-1_8, © Springer Science+Business Media Dordrecht 2014

study hours in subjects close to the key competences related to democratic and civic issues, for instance, the Swedish language. The educational life courses for those who have chosen a vocational programme risk being less flexible and more predictable.

Before discussing our analysis, we will present a brief overview of vocational education in Sweden and its historical development.

The Development of Vocational Education in Sweden

Vocational education has its roots in the guild system, principally organised in the form of apprenticeships. A few technical schools and handicraft schools were started up in the nineteenth century, but it was not until the 1918 school reform that Sweden got an integrated vocational education system consisting of apprenticeship schools, workshop schools and vocational continuation schools (Lindberg 2003). Vocational education was, however, separated from general upper secondary academic education.

The 1970 upper secondary school reform marked a transition in the development of the Swedish vocational education. The existing school forms were now integrated in one organisation, a unified upper secondary school. However, a division between the general academic programmes and the vocational programmes remained. The vocational programmes lasted for 2 years in contrast to the general programmes that lasted for 3 or 4 years. A few general subjects were added to the vocational programmes, but there were no common courses for the two tracks. In fact, an extensive reformation of the whole school system took place, including the introduction of the 9-year compulsory school in 1962. These reforms should be seen against the backdrop of a political debate that started as early as in the 1940s and was embedded in ideas of an expansion of the welfare state. After the 1970 reform, vocational education became an educational policy issue rather than an issue for labour market policy (Lundgren 2007).

In 1994, yet another new upper secondary school reform was launched. The reform stipulated that all programmes should be 3 years long, and that all vocational programmes should include general subjects parallel with the vocational subjects. All upper secondary school students studied the general subjects.[1] At the same time, all study programmes, vocational as well as general, qualified for higher education. The idea was to make the educational system accessible to students from different social backgrounds in order to realise potential of lifelong learning for all (Lundahl et al. 2010). A new curriculum, the same for both the vocational and the general

---

[1] The common subjects for all the study programmes were mathematics, natural science, religious instruction, Swedish, English, civics, sport, aesthetics, courses chosen by the individual and a larger project assignment.

programmes, specified an ethical and democratic foundation on which the whole school system should be based. This reform can also be framed by periods of economic decline in the 1970s and early 1990s with rising unemployment, and thus education offered meaningful activities. However, general education was explicitly included in the discourses of the growing knowledge economy, the multicultural society and technological developments that fuelled the demand for highly competent and flexible workers. The schools were also encouraged to provide programmes adapted to local needs in order to increase flexibility for the individuals as well as for the local communities.

The right-wing alliance that came into power in 2006 launched the most recent upper secondary school reform, implemented in 2011. The reform reintroduced apprenticeship education and once again made a distinction between general programmes leading to higher education and vocational programmes that do not.[2] As we will discuss later, in many respects this reform is a return to the situation before 1994 (Lundahl et al. 2010). However, according to the Education Act (SFS 2010:800, ch. 20, § 19), the students who have graduated from a vocational programme have a legal right to complete their studies in municipal adult education (*komvux*)[3] in order to qualify for higher education studies. Short-term initiatives in the form of extra places for vocational education for adults, both school-based and in the form of apprenticeships, have also been introduced by the government, motivated by the labour market's need for skilled workers (Government Bill 2009:43; Government Bill 2010:2016).

A new post-upper-secondary education (HVE) was launched in 2009 (Government Bill 2008/09:68). This educational form is not a part of the higher education system, despite its name. It is a school form in its own right, under the authority of The Swedish National Agency for HVE. The length of the courses varies from 6 months and up, and the content is specific to the current labour market demands. The idea is that the students should quickly establish themselves in the labour market.[4] All upper secondary school programmes, general as well as vocational, qualify for HVE.

Figure 8.1 summarises changes in the Swedish school system from 1970 and onwards.

---

[2] It is worth mentioning that there is also a new teacher education system in Sweden, launched in the autumn of 2011. Students studying to be teachers in vocational subjects no longer study together with students who will be teachers in general subjects. Furthermore, the vocational teacher education no longer leads to a bachelor's degree as it did before. The new teacher education programme strengthens the division between vocational and general upper secondary school programmes.

[3] The municipalities are responsible for the organisation of komvux, but most often these education programmes are provided by private contractors.

[4] HVE was preceded by advanced vocational education, a similar form of education that started as a pilot project in 1993.

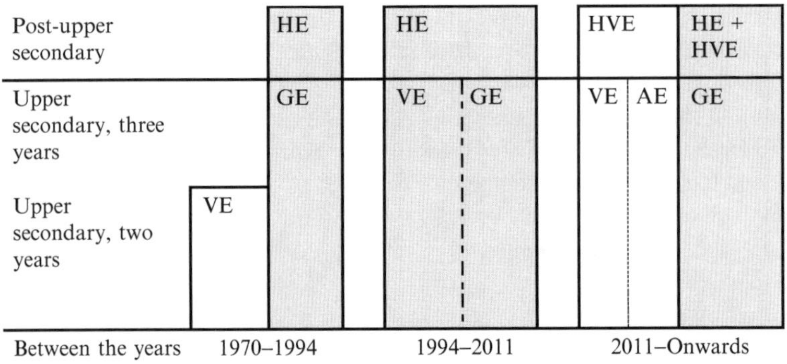

	Between the years 1970–1994	1994–2011	2011–Onwards
Post-upper secondary	HE	HE	HVE / HE + HVE
Upper secondary, three years	GE	VE / GE	VE / AE / GE
Upper secondary, two years	VE		

Fig. 8.1 Changes in the Swedish school system at the upper secondary and post-upper-secondary level (*VE* vocational education, *AE* apprenticeship education, *GE* general education, *HE* higher education at universities and university colleges, *HVE* higher vocational education)

Vocational Education in the Light of Education Policy and Labour Market Policy

Education policy often has the features of a "world movement" (Meyer et al. 1992). However, no matter how compelling and forceful this policy may be, it is always "refracted" in national education policies. Refraction is a metaphor that indicates that a policy idea in the shape of a similar globalised initiative can end up in a number of dissimilar national directions (Goodson and Lindblad 2011). Thus, to understand tensions and contradictions in the 2011 Swedish upper secondary school reform, it must be situated in a policy context of the national development of vocational education.

Education policy has been intertwined with discourses on lifelong learning for more than 50 years. Rubenson (2009) sees this period as a tension between two competing paradigms, humanism represented by the UNESCO and economy or global capitalism represented by the OECD. Documents from the European Union (EU) contain both paradigms, but not presented as conflicting. In the *Memorandum on Lifelong Learning* (European Commission 2000, p. 5), the European Commission points out "two equally important aims for lifelong learning: promoting active citizenship and promoting employability". There is also an assumption that employability will lead to full employment, which, in turn, will lead to active citizens since "…having paid work underpins independence, self-respect and well-being, and is therefore a key to people's overall quality of life" (European Commission 2000, p. 5). This is a far-reaching goal. In a later EU document, *On the new skills for new jobs* (European Union 2007), there is, however, no doubt that the function of education and education policy is to serve the labour market. Thus, it is clear that education policy and labour market policy have become fully intertwined in the European lifelong learning policy.

A European Union argument is that the objectives of full employment, job quality, labour productivity and social cohesion can better be achieved if they are reflected in clear priorities: to attract and retain more people in employment, to increase labour supply, to improve the adaptability of workers and enterprises and to increase investment in human capital through better education and the development of skills and competences (European Union 2007). The EU documents identify eight categories of key competences: (1) communication in the mother tongue, (2) communication in foreign languages, (3) mathematical competence and basic competences in science and technology, (4) digital competence, (5) learning to learn, (6) social and civic competences, (7) sense of initiative and entrepreneurship and (8) cultural awareness and expression (European Commission 2007; European Union 2006, 2011a). According to the EU recommendations, the key competences "... provide added value for the labour market, social cohesion and active citizenship by offering flexibility and adaptability, satisfaction and motivation" (European Union 2011b, p. 1). Strengthening the key competences is expected to result in flexible individuals who can move between branches and workplaces and therefore are more employable in the labour market and also better prepared to become active citizens in the knowledge society.

The development of the Swedish upper secondary school system from 1994 was in many respects in line with what was later recommended in the lifelong learning documents from the EU. The common core of general subjects for all upper secondary school students, and that all programmes should provide qualifications for higher education, involved an educational flexibility for the young people. We could argue that the Swedish school system in many ways was ahead of the EU recommendations. However, the most recent school reform in 2011 goes in the very opposite direction. The number of general subjects is reduced and as is the number of teaching hours. The content of general subjects has been considerable reduced, and, for instance, mathematics is oriented towards the specific vocation (Lindberg 2011). Less time is also given for elective courses and for the Swedish language. Vocational education has once again turned towards narrower competences, further strengthened by the fact that it only qualifies students for HVE. The vocational programmes on both levels are focused on explicit labour market demands in narrowly specified fields. The latest reform means that the students have to choose a vocational track at a young age, thereby narrowing their educational opportunities later in life. Educational flexibility is no longer a salient feature. This break in the organisation and content of vocational education has not (so far) been followed by a break in the lifelong learning policy documents.

Educational Life Transitions: From Flexibility to Predictability?

The European lifelong learning policies can be seen as a tool to push national governments and authorities to create activities that make it easier for individuals to flexibly change their life courses in order to adapt to different changes in society. Research on life transitions also shows that people's life courses have gone from being socially based, predictable and linear in modern society to be more individually based, diverse and non-linear in the postmodern era (Field 2009; Ecclestone et al. 2009). Historically, life transitions were few and predictable, from being a child to starting working, getting married, having a family and finally retiring. With reference to theorists such as Giddens, Bauman and Beck, Field (2009) argues that transitions nowadays are the defining characteristics of everyday life, and that this development has been supported by international organisations such as the OECD in order to make the workforce more flexible and mobile. Life courses have also become increasingly elective and fragmented. In recent decades, being flexible, mobile and equipped to constantly make individual choices has been seen as a way for individuals – as well as governments – to adapt to a rapidly changing global labour market. Education has played a central role in this development. Ecclestone et al. (2009) investigate the main characteristics of transitions depicted in policy, practice and research. They argue that there have been political attempts to manage transitions more effectively in the form of "de-standardisation and increasing non-linearity of youth transitions, together with the individualisation and complexity of many life course transitions for adults" (ibid, p. 3). With reference to Colley et al. (2003), Ecclestone et al. (2009, p. 4) point to some critical aspects of the policies in this field, i.e. tensions between "images of flexible, self-managing, self-aware 'portfolio' workers and people's ability to deal with transitions without professional help".

The development of people's life courses matches in many respects the formulations of what is desirable according to the EU documents on lifelong learning. According to the research on transitions, individuals have become more flexible and mobile, and their non-linear life courses should suit the labour market's needs as emphasised by the European Commission. But if this is the case, how can we then understand the recent changes in the Swedish school system?

The aim of the new upper secondary school is to provide a good foundation for work and continued studies as well as for personal development and active citizenship (SFS 2010:800). The new upper secondary school reform was preceded by an official report from the Swedish government (SOU 2008, p. 27). Two problems were presented in the report. One was the problem of national equivalence in a decentralised school system. The other was the problem of dropouts. The numbers of students graduating with a pass credit were too low. As recently as in 2001, the former government appointed a commission in order to broaden the recruitment to higher education and increase the diversity of students in higher education in relation to social background, gender and ethnicity and to facilitate the transition from upper secondary school to the universities and university colleges (Government Bill 2001:935). The recent reform contradicts these intensions by dividing the students into two separate tracks.

The new education system in Sweden seems rather to be a tool to control the students' educational life courses and make them more predictable. This is a labour market policy developed with the ambition to satisfy the unpredictable conditions created by the global economy. This is done in terms of flexibility for the individuals, but the more narrow educational tracks, laid down by the state, might make their life courses more predictable.

In a study of transitions from vocational education and training to higher education in the UK, Hoelscher et al. (2009, p. 88) argue that the new labour policy sees employees as "actors striving to make themselves marketable in a more flexible labour market". Further, they claim that the role of the state has changed from regulating the labour market to ensuring that individuals develop human capital. But in their empirical study of students with a vocational background studying in higher education, they found that these students were "…tracked institutionally into less prestigious HEIs" (ibid, p. 91). The new HVE in Sweden is at risk of becoming that less prestigious educational form to which the students from vocational programmes will be tracked.

Tensions Permeating the Education System

We will now discuss three tensions, related to the motives behind the new upper secondary school reform, and the other educational changes discussed above, as these can be interpreted by reading the directives, official reports and government bills. These are as follows: (a) the tension between keeping general and vocational programmes together or separate, (b) the tension between "general and generic competences" and "work-specific" competences and (c) the tension between flexibility and predictability. The tensions identified are in many ways intertwined. Nevertheless, we think it is constructive to discuss them one by one.

Keeping All Programmes Together Versus Separating the Vocational Programmes in Their Own Track

Keeping general and vocational education separated is a break in the trend of Swedish educational development (Nylund and Rosvall 2011). This is also true of the post-upper-secondary level. One explicit reason for this change is to prevent too many dropouts and to improve the students' performance. But why did the government choose to create two separate tracks in order to achieve this?

Going deeper into the government bill (2008/09:199, pp. 36–37, our translation) on the new upper secondary school, the changes are motivated by the arguments that "the vocational programmes are too theoretical and many students have a hard time completing their education"; therefore, "the upper secondary school must be designed so that it appears meaningful for all young people and motivate them to make an effort". The same kinds of reasons are also behind vocational education and apprenticeship education for adults (Andersson and Wärvik 2012). These statements can be interpreted in two ways. Either the government believes that not all students have the mental ability (intelligence) to reach the goals in the general subjects at a certain level, irrespective of how much help they get from school, or that some students will not be able to reach those goals with the help they can get within the budgetary framework.

The government also seems to believe that all students having difficulties in reaching the goals in the general subjects prefer vocational subjects and find those subjects more meaningful. This can also be interpreted in two ways: either the government thinks that students are either theoretically or practically oriented or it believes that the vocational subjects are easier in every respect. This is, however, not further elaborated in the bill.

It also lies reasonable to believe that other, more hidden, reasons have been considered. Keeping vocational and general education apart can, for instance, be legitimised in a discourse on the necessity of creating elite universities in order to compete in the international comparisons. To screen out those students not interested in competing on this level at an early stage can be rational from such a perspective. Since it is easier to be eligible for a vocational programme, one can expect students with low grades to choose such a programme and thereby sort themselves away from the universities. Differentiating between students at an early age has also traditionally been proposed by the conservative parties (Lundgren 2012). It is, however, interesting to notice that fewer students applied for a vocational programme in 2012, after the reform had been launched, than was the case in the earlier upper secondary school.

Values Connected to Citizenship Versus Work-Specific Competences

All the programmes at upper secondary level aim to give a good foundation for work and continued studies as well as for personal development and active citizenship (SFS 2010:800). Examples of values are democracy, human rights and equality between the sexes. These values should, according to the curriculum, permeate all the programmes and all subjects; but how the values are to be implemented is not formulated. However, the values are not repeated in the goals of the different programmes; nor are they repeated in the goals of the subjects or in the description of the courses within the subjects. This means that the teachers have to be aware of these values so that they will be taken into account in the designs of the courses and the individual lessons. One can be specifically concerned about the position of these values in the apprenticeship form where most of the education is mediated by working life supervisors without a proper teacher training. In many respects, it seems as the responsibility for the less motivated students is handed over to working life and the trade and industry.

As mentioned above, the time and content of general school subjects have been largely reduced in the vocational programmes since these are adapted to the vocation in question. The government argues that the changes will motivate the students and make them more employable in the labour market (Government Bill 2008/09:199). It is clear that the government believes that vocational subjects are more motivating than general subjects and apprenticeship education is the most motivating for those students at risk of dropping out or leaving upper secondary school without the grades required for graduating. The government also hopes that the workplaces will "take care of" those students who are in the weakest position on the labour market, almost a social function. According to the Swedish independent public service debate, the upper secondary schools, private as well as municipal, have had great difficulties in finding apprenticeship work placements for the students (svt.se 2011).

Nylund (2010) argues that the aim of vocational education as it appears in the official report (SOU 2008:27) is to reproduce existing power relations in society and make them more effective by producing employable, ready-to-work workers with competences that match the needs of the labour market. His argument is supported by a large survey conducted by the Confederation of Swedish Enterprises in 2007. Seven of ten enterprises answered that they have had difficulties in recruiting new employees due to the applicants' shortage of work experience (Svenskt Näringsliv 2010). Six of ten enterprises mentioned shortage of people with the "right" education. However, the report does not say anything about what is meant by "right", for instance, what kind of skills and competences the enterprises are looking for. Small enterprises stated more often than large ones that they failed to recruit due to lack of competent applicants. One explanation might be that narrow work-specific competences are more highly valued by those employers since they cannot afford to pay for too much staff training or to provide workers with in-service training.

Flexibility Versus Predictability

One of the problems with the previous upper secondary school, pointed to by the government, was the large number of local programmes and courses. As a result, students, parents and employers have difficulties in understanding the different types of education (Government Bill 2008/09:199). However, the government also stresses the importance of keeping the upper secondary school flexible and taking into account local and regional needs. This contradiction is close to that of general and specific competences. Too general and flexible workers may be less loyal to their employers and may move to other enterprises if they do not feel sufficiently challenged. On the other hand, these employees can be expected to work more independently and have the ability to grasp large working processes. However, this dilemma is probably more problematic for the representatives of the labour market than for the government.

Viewed from the government's point of view, an education system with relatively stable programmes in the long term may be easier to understand than an open course-based system. Short-term initiatives, like the ones offered by adult education, provide, on the other hand, more flexibility to adapt to changes in the (local) labour market. The short-term vocational adult education initiatives can also be seen as a lack of trust in the municipalities' ability to prioritise between their different areas of responsibility and their ability to decide what education programmes to arrange and when. These initiatives are thus a way for the state to regain some control over how tax money is spent. It is, however, too early to say if a break in the trend towards decentralisation has taken place.

Concluding Remarks

In this chapter, we have discussed how the Swedish education system at upper secondary and post-upper-secondary level has changed in the last 10 years. From having been an education system with a large number of general subjects, the system has now been divided into two types of qualifications, targeting two different student groups: the highly motivated who are supposed to choose a general programme and the less motivated who are expected to choose a vocational programme. This can be related to the government's challenging task of coping with conflicting problems and interests. The government seems to stress that what is needed by the labour market is more vocational subjects. As we discussed earlier, the European Commission instead points in the opposite direction and stresses the key competences as important for an efficient labour market and, in the long run, for lowering the unemployment figures. In this respect, Sweden is moving away from the lifelong learning policy. This is being done with the intention of keeping students from dropping out of school and increasing the number of students graduating from the upper secondary school.

References

Andersson, E., & Wärvik, G.-B. (2012). Swedish adult education in transition? Implications of the work first principle. *Journal of Adult and Continuing Education, 18*(1), 90–103.

Colley, H., James, D., Diment, K., & Tedder, M. (2003). Learning as becoming in vocational education and training: Class, gender and the role of vocational habitus. *Journal of Vocational Education and Training, 55*(4), 471–498.

Ecclestone, K., Biesta, G., & Hughes, M, (2009). Transitions in the lifecourse. The role of identity, agency and structure. In K. Ecclestone, G. Biesta, & M. Hughes (Eds.), *Transitions and learning through the lifecourse* (pp. 1–15). Hoboken: Routledge.

European Commission. (2000). *A memorandum on lifelong learning*. Brussels: European Commission.

European Commission. (2007). *Action plan on adult learning. It is always a good time to learn*. Brussels: European Commission.

European Union. (2006). *Recommendation of the European Parliament and of the Council of 18 December 2006 on key competencies for lifelong learning*. Brussels: Official Journal of the European Union.

European Union. (2007). *On the new skills for new jobs* (2007/C 290/01). Brussels: Official Journal of the European Union.

European Union. (2011a). *Council conclusions on the role of education and training in the implementation of the 'Europe 2020' strategy*. Brussels: Official Journal of the European Union.

European Union. (2011b). *Key competencies for lifelong learning.* Summaries of the EU legislation at the official EU website. http://europa.eu/legislation_summaries/education_training_youth/lifelong_learning/c11090_en.htm. Accessed 26 Aug 2012.

Field, J. (2009). Preface. In K. Ecclestone, G. Biesta, & M. Hughes (Eds.), *Transitions and learning through the lifecourse* (pp. xvii–xxiv). Hoboken: Routledge.

Goodson, I. F., & Lindblad, S. (Eds.). (2011). *Professional knowledge and educational restructuring in Europe.* Rotterdam: Sense Publishers.

Government Bill. (2001:935). *Förordningen om statligt stöd för att främja rekryteringen till universitet och högskolor* (Government bill on state funding for promoting the recruitment to universities and university colleges). Stockholm: The Ministry of Education and Research.

Government Bill. (2008/09:68). *Yrkeshögskolan* (Higher vocational education). Stockholm: The Ministry of Education and Research.

Government Bill. (2008/09:199). *Högre krav och kvalitet i den nya gymnasieskolan* (Higher standards and quality in the new secondary school). Stockholm: The Ministry of Education and Research.

Government Bill. (2009:43). *Om statsbidrag för yrkesinriktad gymnasial vuxenutbildning och yrkesinriktad gymnasial vuxenutbildning för utvecklingsstörda mm* (Government bill on state funding for vocational adult education and vocational adult education for mentally disabled etc.). Stockholm: The Ministry of Education and Research.

Government Bill. (2010:2016). *Förordning om statsbidrag för lärlingsutbildning för vuxna* (Government bill on state funding of apprenticeship education for adults). Stockholm: The Ministry of Education and Research.

Hoelscher, M., Haywaard, G., Ertl, H., & Dunbar-Goddet, H. (2009). The transition from vocational education and training to higher education. A successful pathway? In K. Ecclestone, G. Biesta, & M. Hughes (Eds.), *Transitions and learning through the lifecourse* (pp. 87–102). Hoboken: Routledge.

Lindberg, V. (2003). *Yrkesutbildning i omvandling* (Vocational education in transition). Stockholm: SU förlag.

Lindberg, L. (2011). *The role of mathematics in the future VET programmes in Sweden compared to the previous.* Paper presented at ECER 2011, Berlin.

Lundahl, L., Erixon Arreman, I., Lundström, U., & Rönnberg, L. (2010). Setting things right? Swedish upper secondary school reform in a 40-year perspective. *European Journal of Education, 45*(1), 46–59.

Lundgren, U. P. (2007). *Vocational education. The case of Sweden in a historical and international context.* Washington, DC: World Bank.

Lundgren, U. P. (2012). En gemensam skola. Utbildning blir en nödvändighet för alla (A comprehensive school. Education becomes a necessity for all). In U. P. Lundgren, R. Säljö, & C. Liberg (Eds.), *Lärande, skola, bildning. Grundbok för lärare* (pp. 77–99). Stockholm: Natur & Kultur.

Meyer, J. W., Ramirez, F. O., & Soysal, Y. N. (1992). World expansion of mass education, 1870–1980. *Sociology of Education, 65*(2), 128–149.

Nylund, M. (2010). Framtidsvägen. Vägen till vilken framtid för eleverna på gymnasieskolans yrkesprogram? (The road to the future. The road to which future for the pupils at the vocational programmes on upper secondary level?). *Pedagogisk Forskning i Sverige, 15*(1), 33–52.

Nylund, M., & Rosvall, P.-Å. (2011). Gymnasiereformens konsekvenser för den sociala fördelningen av kunskaper i de yrkesorienterade utbildningarna (The consequences of the upper secondary school reform for the social distribution of knowledge in the vocational programmes). *Pedagogisk Forskning i Sverige, 16*(2), 81–99.

Rubenson, K. (2009). Lifelong learning. Between humanism and global capitalism. In P. Jarvis (Ed.), *The Routledge international handbook of lifelong learning* (pp. 411–422). London/New York: Routledge.

SFS. (2010:800). *Skollagen* (Education act). Stockholm: Ministry of Education and Research.

SOU. (2008:27). *Framtidsvägen – en reformerad gymnasieskola* (The road to the future – A reformed upper secondary school). Stockholm: Fritzes. (Official report from the Swedish Government).

Svenskt Näringsliv. (2010). *Att söka men inte finna* (Seeking but not finding). Stockholm. (report).

Svt.se. (2011). *Var sjätte elev får ingen praktikplats* (Every sixth student do not get work placement). http://www.svt.se. Published 9 May 2011; Accessed 10 Sept 2012.

Chapter 9
Lifelong Learning and Employability

Andreas Fejes

Introduction

Lifelong learning has emerged as a policy area and a policy concept during the last two decades. In Europe, lifelong learning is especially connected to the *Memorandum on Lifelong Learning*, published by the European Commission (2001), which positions lifelong learning as a central policy concept in the realisation of the commission's strategies. As a concept, lifelong learning partly replaces former concepts such as adult education (Lindeman 1926), and lifelong education. Lifelong learning have become the dominant manner in which to speak about the education and learning of adults in policy terms. The shift from speaking about education to speaking about learning signifies a shift in how citizens are construed. For example, during the late 1960s and early 1970s, the concept of lifelong education attained a central position within policy discourse. The catchword was, according to Rubenson (2004), personal development where people were to 'make themselves' instead of 'being made'. This concept was a humanistic definition of education and was, for example, produced through the Faure report, *Learning to Be*, published by UNESCO (Faure 1972). In the report, we can see how lifelong education is related to a positive humanistic notion of progress and personal development. Individual development was by Faure seen as good for society. This type of discourse construes a public concern for education, and education is seen as a way in which to meet and manage the changing future. As Rubenson (2004) argued, the idea was that lifelong education would enable people to control and adapt to change.

During the 1990s, we can see how the concept of lifelong education was replaced by lifelong learning within the policy texts. Lifelong learning was used by UNESCO in 1994 as a midterm strategy for the coming years, and the OECD (1996) published

A. Fejes (✉)
Department of Behavioural Sciences and Learning, Division for Education
and Adult Learning, Linköping University, Linköping, Sweden
e-mail: andreas.fejes@liu.se

G.K. Zarifis and M.N. Gravani (eds.), *Challenging the 'European Area
of Lifelong Learning': A Critical Response*, Lifelong Learning Book Series 19,
DOI 10.1007/978-94-007-7299-1_9, © Springer Science+Business Media Dordrecht 2014

the report *Making Lifelong Learning a Reality for All*. Lifelong learning also became a cornerstone in Jacques Delors' white paper on competitiveness and economic growth within the European Union in 1994, and the European Commission then declared 1996 as the European year of lifelong learning. In 2001, the European Commission (2001) published their *Memorandum on Lifelong Learning* (The Lisbon Strategy), which positioned lifelong learning as a central policy concept in the realisation of the commission's strategies, which had the goal of shaping Europe into a knowledge-based society. The policy indicated a shift from a humanistic to an economic discourse (cf. Fejes and Nicoll 2008; Rubenson 2004). In 2010, the Lisbon Strategy was replaced by a new policy agenda (European Commission 2010) that further outlined a long-term strategy for lifelong learning that included an initiative aiming to integrate work and education as a lifelong learning process. At the same time, talk about lifelong learning and a 'research, education and innovation' triangle in European policy (European Commission 2009, p. 2) suggested that there was a new emphasis on the relationship between knowledge production and lifelong leaning in the contemporary discourses of governing. This new emphasis suggests a shift from positioning lifelong learning as a support for creating a knowledge-based economy to positioning lifelong learning as an integral part of the work and knowledge production processes (Nicoll and Fejes 2011).

The shift from speaking about education to speaking about learning can be seen as problematics of governing which is a situation in which the issues regarding government are problematised (cf. Fejes and Nicoll 2008). Today, learning is discursively inserted into practices that were not previously construed as practices of learning. Learning is related to not only formal schooling, such as adult education institutions or universities, but also, for example, the workplace, family life, media, crime prevention and health promotion. Thus, in a Foucauldian-inspired reading of these changes, there has been a reconfiguration of the relations of power, which has effects in terms of what type of subject is defined as desirable and the type of governance that is operating (cf. Fejes and Nicoll 2008).

While education often refers to a relationship between the educator and the student (a relational concept), learning refers to an activity that a person can do by herself/himself (cf. Biesta 2006). This relational aspect can also be seen in the use of the term 'adult learner' (cf. Fejes 2006). Therefore, the argument here is that learning becomes an individualised and all-embracing activity at the same time that it becomes the responsibility of the individual. Learning is something that is always taking place, and each and every citizen needs to take responsibility for learning and for acquiring knowledge that will be helpful in directing one's life towards self-fulfilment and towards the good of society. Life has been colonised to become a life of learning.

This discursive shift from education to learning is related to a reconfiguration of the relationship between the public and the private. Instead of a public concern for education as a way in which to control and plan the future, there is now a concern for learning as a way in which to manage a future that we know nothing about except that it is constantly changing (Fejes 2006). A society that is construed as constantly changing does not need to rule governed citizens but rather flexible and adaptable citizens. The management of learning is conducted by constantly encouraging the citizens to make their own individual choices (concerning learning); thus, the citizens are shaped to become 'free' and active subjects (Fejes and Dahlstedt 2012; Fejes and Nicoll 2008). This encouragement is conducted through numerous practices. As argued by Biesta (2006), these shifts in discourse have transformed lifelong learning from a right to a duty and responsibility. All of the citizens who participate in learning activities accept that they are indeed learners and, as such, that they are in constant need of learning. What is needed is citizens who develop a constant 'will' to learn. The shift, thus, not only brings with it a focus on learning but also on the learner. More than previously, educational policy positions the learner as responsible for her/his own learning (cf. Fejes 2010).

Closely connected to discourses on lifelong learning and the repositioning of the learner in terms of responsibility are discourses on employability. A couple of decades ago, employability emerged as discourse, which replaced the previous way of describing the workforce (cf. Clarke and Patrickson 2008; McQuaid and Lindsay 2005). Instead of speaking about a shortage of employment and describing the citizen as employed or unemployed, policy now spoke about a lack of employability and the citizen came to be described as employable or not employable (Garsten and Jacobsson 2004) or in need of employability skills. Employability is currently used as an explanation, and to some extent a legitimation, of unemployment (cf. Fejes 2010). This kind of discourse positions the citizen as responsible for her/his own employment, and less emphasis is placed on structural inequalities and problems in the labour market. Thus, discourses on employability and lifelong learning seem to signify a shift in terms of how government is conducted and how the citizen is positioned as a subject of government. The aim of this chapter is to analyse how governing operates in the present time through discourses on lifelong learning and employability. A special interest is directed at what kind of citizen is being shaped through such discourses and how such discourses is taken up and shaped by those who are their target.

Theorising and Analysis Government

As my interest is in analysing how governing operates within discourses on lifelong learning and employability, the analysis was conducted drawing on a governmentality perspective (cf. Foucault 2007; Fejes and Nicoll 2008). Governmentality emerged in Foucault's (2007) later writings. Here, government is analysed as something more complex than the government of the nation state: it involves the government of ourselves, the government of others and the government of the state. Further, there is a focus on liberal mentalities of governing. Liberalism is not seen as an ideology that can be related to a specific political party. Instead, liberalism is seen here as a mode of governing or ideas about how governing should be conducted.

Foucault (2007) argues that during the last few centuries, there has been a shift in rationalities of government and how governing operates in society – from a situation in which society was planned through legislation and repression to a situation where governing is conducted by the citizens themselves. Here, the notion of freedom is important. The governmentality of today is dependent on the freedom of the citizen. The starting point within such rationality of governing is that the freedom of the citizen is both a prerequisite and an effect of governing. Without the freedom to choose, there is only a situation of constraint, and thus there is no governing.

There is a different notion of the state related to such a perspective – a decentred state. The state is not an a priori actor who does things. Instead, it is seen here as an epistemological pattern of assumptions of how governing should operate (cf. Fejes and Nicoll 2008). In his writing, Rose (1999) has called the contemporary state the 'enabling state'. An important aspect of such a state is providing the opportunity (enabling) for citizens to make choices in accordance with her/his wishes and desires; thus, the political ambition to govern coincides with individual dreams and aspirations. Here, freedom is both the prerequisite and the output of governing.

Based on the above, this chapter will draw on a governmentality perspective to analyse how discourses on lifelong learning and employability are mobilised in the wider discursive terrain of governance. How does governance operate, what subject is produced and, more specifically, how are these discourses taken up by those who are their target?

The chapter is part of a wider project on how the learning adult is being shaped and fostered through discourses and practices of lifelong learning. The argument pursued connects to prior policy analyses of policies on lifelong learning (e.g. Fejes 2005, 2006, 2008a; Fejes and Nicoll 2008) and analyses of interviews and observations within elderly care work (Fejes 2008b, 2010, 2011, 2012; Fejes and Andersson 2009; Fejes and Nicoll 2010, 2011; Fejes and Dahlstedt 2012). The latter empirical material is related to an in-service training programme for workers in elderly care (health-care workers, HCA) who were provided the opportunity to, during work hours, have their prior learning recognised in order to receive a certificate from the health-care programme on upper secondary school level. Previously, working as an HCA required either no formal competencies or a 10-week course in care work. Although people with little or no education are still employed, employers (municipalities and private companies) increasingly advertise for licensed practical nurses (LPNs) instead of HCAs. Employment as an LPN normally requires a health-care certificate or equivalent. The increasing demand on formal education means people already employed as HCAs do not meet present-day requirements for new employees, leaving them unemployable if they decide to change employers (Fejes 2010), thus excluding them from the labour market. Thus, the in-service training programme provided some HCAs with the opportunity to meet the present-day qualification requirements.

As the specific focus of this chapter is on how transnational discourses on lifelong learning and employability are shaped and taken up by those who are their target, an analysis of both policy documents and interviews has been conducted. In order to identify transnational discourses on lifelong learning and employability, policy papers written by the EC and the OECD on those topics were analysed

(EC 2001, 2007; OECD 1998, 2005). Interviews with 14 care workers, working at 6 different nursing homes, were analysed in order to identify how discourses on employability and lifelong learning were taken up and shaped by those who are their target (for more elaboration on the entire empirical material, see, e.g. Fejes and Andersson 2009).

Policy papers and interviews have been analysed as text, drawing on a discourse perspective (Foucault 2007; Fejes 2006). By analysing texts and focusing on statements, it is possible to see how the world is constituted in the specific practice analysed. More precisely, the analyses have focused on what is being stated, how it is being stated and what is being constituted through such statements.

Travelling Discourses

If we turn to policymaking in the EU, we can see how a more flexible labour market and measures for making work pay are seen as response to the challenges of globalisation. Such measures should be combined with employment security and investment in human capital as a way to improve employability (EC 2007, p. 11). Citizens should be offered the opportunity to participate in training, thus becoming better prepared to get a job. Similar ideas are raised by the OECD, which argues for the need of investment in human capital to manage ourselves in the knowledge-based economy. Human capital is proposed as a solution to present and future problems within the knowledge-based economies. A truth is constructed about the future, which needs to be managed by creating citizens who are flexible, adaptable and constant learners; thus, there is an emphasis on the responsibility of the individual to become such a subject (OECD 1998, p. 3).

We can also see how the EU documents construe a more flexible labour market as a solution to unemployment. Further, human capital and lifelong learning are advanced as a way to face the uncertain future. However, there is a noticeable difference in the focus of the EU as compared to the OECD. The OECD (1998) discourse on employability is more economically driven than the EU discourse. For example, the focus of the OECD is on the knowledge-based economy, instead of the knowledge-based society promoted by the EU (2001). Further, according to the OECD (1998, p. 9) human capital is foremost an investment in skills that can be utilised to increase economic prosperity and employability. However, it is also recognised that social issues such as equal distribution of skills are important (OECD 2005, p. 1).

However, even though aspects of equality are raised, the framing for such discussions is within an economically driven discourse where the main goal is an overall good economic performance. The economic discourse is present in the EU policy texts. However, such a discourse is also closely related to ideas about social cohesion. Social inclusion and personal fulfilment are emphasised as important goals in connection with employability and lifelong learning. Even though economic goals are important, learning for personal or civic purposes is stressed as a 'good' goal in itself (EC 2001, p. 9).

Despite the differences between the OECD and the EU discourses on employability, we can see how subjects are positioned in a similar way in terms of responsibility for their employability. Flexibility and adaptability are emphasised in the OECD texts as something that should be an individual characteristic. Adaptability signifies a subject who is responsible for being adaptable to new and changing circumstances in the labour market. The citizen needs to train and retrain, to be mobile and flexible as a way to be able to keep herself/himself employable. Such a connection between adaptability and employability is also clearly emphasised by the EU where 'the employability and adaptability of citizens is vital for Europe to maintain its commitment to becoming the most competitive and dynamic knowledge based society in the world' (EC 2001, p. 6).

To sum up so far, discourses on lifelong learning and employability operating in the EU and OECD documents include ideas about economic prosperity and development, social cohesion and equality and flexibility and adaptability of the citizen. Even though there seem to be a consensus perspective promoted via these documents where the state, the employer and the individual are all positioned as being jointly responsible for creating the 'good' future, where lifelong learning and investment in human capital are central, it is still the individual who is positioned as responsible for becoming adaptable and flexible as a way to become/remain employable. One could say that there is a responsibilisation of the individual (Rose 1999). The individual needs to take responsibility for using the opportunities for lifelong learning, by means of education and in-service training, offered by the state and the market, thus transforming herself/himself into an employable person. The role of the state is then more distanced than was previously the case (Fejes and Nicoll 2008; Fejes 2006). Now, structures for supporting the individual in her/his own choice are created instead of collectively planning the future by means of legislative measures and regulations.

Turning to the interviews with those working in elderly care, we can see how a statement repeated in the interview transcripts is the idea that the municipality and the private companies (where the interviewees are employed) have changed their demands on their employees. Now, they are demanding that all their personnel should have the higher qualification of the two levels most common among the employees. The new requirements create a future threat, which needs to be tackled by means of more education and learning. In the following statement by one care worker, we can see how such an idea is created when she describes why she participates in the programme.

> Foremost to secure your job…To secure your job in the future, to avoid being kicked out when one becomes…, I am 44 years old. If this home were privatised, I might feel that I don't want to stay here. I want to be employed by the municipality, and then I wouldn't stand a chance of getting a job in the municipality, I think, only with [the lower level qualification]. (Sofie)

Such statement constructs a strong individual responsibility. The individual herself construes future threats in terms of not being able to continue as an employee in the future. Such threats should be faced by updating one's qualification. Such statements can also be interpreted as a way of handling future risks within the framework of which competencies need to be increased as a way of participating in the competition for new jobs. Here there is a risk of the nursing home being privatised (operated by a company instead of the municipality) and the risk of not having the right qualifications. Other statements support the idea about risk. For example, as expressed by one care worker:

> Because I…now I believe, now I'm this old. But I think in this way, you never know with the municipality. Without notice – poff, and then we are privatised. And it will probably not get better now when we have a right-wing government because then every nursing home should be privately run. And I believe this will lead to them saying that they only want LPNs. And I mean, it's not…it's a requirement, I understand that the requirement should be an LPN. So, partly, and then I wanted to study to become an LPN. Yes, I think it's fun! Very hard, but fun. You are happy every time you have taken an exam. (Jasmine)

Here, we can see how the care worker identifies risks of not being qualified as an LPN, something she relates to the politics of the conservative government. On the other hand, she construes the qualification of LPNs as an ideal sought after by herself. In other words, these statements construct an idea of risk and self-responsibility. The handling of risk is the responsibility of the individual. Each person should make their own calculation of risks in the future, and education and in-service training can be a tool to counter those risks.

Despite the role of self-responsibility, there is also to some extent a responsibilisation of the municipality and the state. They are the ones positioned as responsible to make possible participation in in-service training. Several statements in the interviews with the care workers concern the necessity of financial support as a condition for participation in in-service training. If the in-service training for the care workers had not taken place during paid workdays financed by the municipality and the state, participation would have been limited, according to the interview participants. For example, as expressed by Beverly:

> Yes, I can honestly say that I wouldn't have participated if it hadn't taken place during working hours. It was about seizing the opportunity when offered. To participate in the education. Otherwise I wouldn't have taken the initiative to apply for participation in a regular programme, thus having to take time off work to be able to study. I wouldn't have done that. (Beverly)

Through such statements there is a responsibilisation of the individual, at the same time as the individual is positioned in relation to the employer and the state. The latter two are constructed as enablers making it possible for the individuals to realise their wishes – in this case, to increase their employability and to make something interesting and fun.

Final Remarks

In the last 30 years, there has been a shift from speaking about employment to speaking about employability (Garsten and Jacobsson 2004). The discourses on lifelong learning and employability have been taken up in several areas such as education and labour market policies. In this chapter I have argued that an individual responsibility of the citizen to become and stay employable is constructed through transnational policymaking on lifelong learning and employability. Further, I have illustrated how those working in elderly care themselves take up and produce similar discourses by positioning themselves as responsible for their own employability.

In one way, the responsibilisation of the individual can be seen as illustrating how a different mode of governing has emerged than was previously the case. One could say that the role of the state is redefined from being a distributor of resources to offering services (Garsten and Jacobsson 2004), or as Rose (1999) argues, there has been a shift from a social state to an enabling state, where the state should make it possible for the citizen to make active choices. The employer is partly positioned in the same way – making it possible for the individual to stay employable in relation to the workplace in which she/he works. Thus, the individual is positioned as responsible for making use of the opportunities offered as a way of transforming herself/himself into an employable citizen.

Another way to phrase these changes is that the state has become distanced from the governing practice. Governing should now be conducted via each citizen's 'free' choices. This is particularly visible in the statements analysed from the interviews with health-care workers. Here, participation in in-service training is construed as desirable in relation to the future even though it is voluntarily to participate. In this way, we can see how there is no need for governing to operate through legislative measures. Instead, governing can operate powerfully through discourses on lifelong learning and employability by enabling active choices.

Acknowledgements The research on which this chapter is based was made possible by a grant from the Swedish Research Council.

References

Biesta, G. (2006). What's the point of lifelong learning if lifelong learning has no point? On the democratic deficit of policies for lifelong learning. *European Educational Research Journal, 5*(2–3), 169–180.

Clarke, M., & Patrickson, M. (2008). The new covenant of employability. *Employee Relations, 30*(2), 121–141.

European Commission (EC). (2001). *Communication from the commission: Making a European area of lifelong learning a reality*. Brussels: European Commission, Directorate-general for Education and Culture and Directorate-general for Employment and Social Affairs.

European Commission (EC). (2007). *Communication of the commission to the spring European Council: Integrated guidelines for growth and jobs (2008–2010)*. Brussels: European Commission.

European Commission (EC). (2009). Developing the role of education in a fully-functioning knowledge triangle'. *Notices from European Union Institutions and Bodies: Official Journal of the European Union. Council Conclusions 2009*. Brussels: European Commission.

European Commission (EC). (2010). *Strategic framework for education and training*. Brussels: European Commission.

Faure, E. (1972). *Learning to be*. Paris: UNESCO.

Fejes, A. (2005). New wine in old skins: Changing patterns in the governing of the adult learner in Sweden. *International Journal of Lifelong Education, 24*(1), 71–86.

Fejes, A. (2006). The planetspeak discourse of lifelong learning in Sweden: What is an educable adult? *Journal of Education Policy, 21*(6), 697–716.

Fejes, A. (2008a). To be one's own confessor: Educational guidance and governmentality. *British Journal of Sociology of Education, 29*(6), 653–664.

Fejes, A. (2008b). Governing nursing through reflection: A discourse analysis of reflective practices. *Journal of Advanced Nursing, 64*(3), 243–250.

Fejes, A. (2010). Discourses on employability: Constituting the responsible citizen. *Studies in Continuing Education, 32*(2), 89–102.

Fejes, A. (2011). Confession, in-service training and reflective practices. *British Educational Research Journal, 37*(5), 797–812.

Fejes, A. (2012). Knowledge at play: Positioning care workers as professionals through scientific rationality and caring dispositions. In A. Kamp & H. Hvid (Eds.), *Elderly care in transition: Management, meaning and identity at work – A Scandinavian perspective* (pp. 83–105). Copenhagen: Copenhagen Business School Press.

Fejes, A., & Andersson, P. (2009). Recognising prior learning. Understanding the relations among experience, learning and recognition from a constructivist perspective. *Vocations and Learning: Studies in Vocational and Professional Education, 2*(1), 37–55.

Fejes, A., & Dahlstedt, M. (2012). *The confessing society: Foucault, confession and practices of lifelong learning*. London: Routledge.

Fejes, A., & Nicoll, K. (Eds.). (2008). *Foucault and lifelong learning: Governing the subject*. London: Routledge.

Fejes, A., & Nicoll, K. (2010). A vocational calling: Exploring a caring technology in elderly care. *Pedagogy, Culture & Society, 18*(3), 353–370.

Fejes, A., & Nicoll, K. (2011). Activating the worker in elderly care: A technique and tactics of invitation. *Studies in Continuing Education, 33*(3), 235–249.

Foucault, M. (2007). *Security, territory, population: Lectures at the Collège de France 1977–1978*. Houndmills: Palgrave Macmillan.

Garsten, C., & Jacobsson, K. (Eds.). (2004). *Learning to be employable: New agendas on work, responsibility and learning in a globalized world*. New York: Palgrave Macmillan.

Lindeman, E. C. (1926). *The meaning of adult education*. New York: New Republic.

McQuaid, R. W., & Lindsay, C. (2005). The concept of employability. *Urban Studies, 42*(2), 197–219.

Nicoll, K., & Fejes, A. (2011). Lifelong learning: A pacification of "know how". *Studies in Philosophy and Education, 30*(4), 403–417.

OECD. (1996). *Lifelong learning for all*. Paris: OECD.

OECD. (1998). *Human capital investment: An international comparison*. Paris: OECD.

OECD. (2005). *Promoting adult learning. Executive summary*. Paris: OECD.

Rose, N. (1999). *Powers of freedom: Reframing political thought*. Cambridge: Cambridge University Press.

Rubenson, K. (2004). Lifelong learning: A critical assessment of the political project. In P. Alheit, R. Becker-Schmidt, T. Gitz-Johansen, L. Ploug, H. Salling Olesen, & K. Rubenson (Eds.), *Shaping an emerging reality – Researching lifelong learning* (pp. 28–47). Roskilde: Roskilde University Press.

Chapter 10
Human Capital and Human Action in Lifelong Learning: Questions Concerning the Revival of a Seemingly Obvious Theory

Despina Tsakiris

Introduction

The financial crisis plaguing EU countries today is an occasion to analyse the functioning of its underlying economic, political and social institutions. The member states' recessional economies seem to lead – openly or not – to a questioning of the whole undertaking of uniting Europe and primarily of the legislative, political, economic and social institutions upon which it was founded.[1] People thus find themselves before a political situation where uncertainty and the unpredictability of how things will develop leave them helpless and frightened of the declaration of economic catastrophe.

In view of these circumstances, this chapter seeks to explore the tenacious influence of certain capitalist economic ideologies, which find application in the educational policies of lifelong learning. More specifically, interest is focused on the idea of human capital as it is presented in education policy texts, as an economic theory that seeks to explain human action in the work activity. In these texts, emphasis is placed on the way this theory is interwoven with the mission and the role of lifelong learning. The theory of human capital, which was formulated by the two Nobel prize-winning economists Theodore Schultz (1961) and Gary Becker (1964), has returned to the discourse of supranational bodies (the EU and the OECD), aiming at laying down policies concerning the mission, role and organization of education in general and of lifelong learning in specific.

---

[1] I am referring to the statements made by the European Heads of national and supranational authorities in Greece in the spring of 2012 during the pre-election campaign, aiming at creating a government able to deal with the "financial crisis" the country is experiencing. These statements concerned the hypothetical political scenario of Greece exiting the Eurozone.

D. Tsakiris (✉)
Department of Social and Educational Policy, University of Peloponnese, Korinthos, Greece
e-mail: dtsakiri@uop.gr

G.K. Zarifis and M.N. Gravani (eds.), *Challenging the 'European Area of Lifelong Learning': A Critical Response*, Lifelong Learning Book Series 19, DOI 10.1007/978-94-007-7299-1_10, © Springer Science+Business Media Dordrecht 2014

In this chapter, I attempt to shed light on the social significations of lifelong learning promoted through this particular economic theory in order to highlight the way meaning is given to human action and to elucidate the organizational elements, which triggers the motivation of human resources and potential. In this context, I provide a general overview of the basic institutional texts that establish lifelong learning as an economic strategy, and I refer to the basic principles on which the theory of human capital is founded. I then present the social critical approaches levelled at this theory. Finally, I highlight the social significations of the economic rationalism that the theory of human capital proposes, illuminating the imaginary dimensions the logic of "capital", which has been promoted as the uncontested regulator of human action.

Lifelong Learning as an Economic Strategy

The value of lifelong learning is nowadays undisputed. A series of official documents bear witness to its acceptance and establishment as an institution.[2] This paper focuses on the EU *Memorandum on Lifelong Learning* (2000), precisely because this text is used as a springboard for further discussion and action since it states that lifelong learning is no longer merely one aspect of education and learning, but is the guiding principle of all actions over the whole spectrum of education. In the Memorandum one may ascertain not only the institutional recognition and establishment of lifelong learning but its primacy in dealing with recessional economies as well as with their political, social and cultural repercussions.

However, statistics reveal that only one-third of the EU population aged 25–64 participates in lifelong learning and formal, non-formal or informal training, mainly motivated by the option of choosing a better career or advancing its career. For the remaining two-thirds of the population, family obligations and heavy workloads do not foster their involvement in the learning process (Alison 2012).[3] At the same time, over the last 20 years, there has been a considerable reduction in vocational training as state-subsidized programmes have seen a corresponding decrease. The same applies to further training budgets in the business sector.

With the onset of the financial crisis, the economic upheaval in public spending drove EU members to slash lifelong learning budgets and mainly to weaken further education programmes targeting employability, given that these types of programmes are not easily transferable and, as such, are unprofitable.

---

[2] Also see:
- Lisbon Treaty (European Council 2000)
- Lifelong Guidance Expert Group-LGEG, 2000
- EU Official Journal C 295 05/12/2003
- Keeley (2007)
- EU Official Journal C 119 28/05/2009

[3] Eurostat statistics. See: http://epp.eurostata.ec.europa.eu/statistics_explained/index.php/lifelong_learning_statistics

In the midst of the crisis, there is a dearth of data (qualitative and quantitative) allowing for a review of the selected strategies' repercussions in the field of life-long learning. Nonetheless, the emerging trends beg the question of how far the advocated rationalistic strategies for lifelong learning (EU Commission 2000), such as that of human capital, express a form of rationalist thinking that truly serves the stated aims or is simply a construction that conceals certain goals that are incompatible with those openly advocated. This can be ascertained primarily in the EU Commission's six key messages contained in the Memorandum on lifelong learning, which refer to (a) the announced aims in education for the active involvement of citizens in learning and society as well as the boosting of employability and (b) the means of achieving these aims, where it is mentioned that "education and training systems should adapt to individual needs and demands rather than the other way round" (p. 8). It is in this context that we need to understand "what counts as investment" (p. 12) in human resources and the way "to ensure the replenishment of the skills pool" (p. 12). More specifically, while it seems that on the rhetorical level the reference to knowledge capital contained the various fields of knowledge necessary for the citizens' active participation in society as well as the improvement of employability and reduction of unemployment, in fact the subject of capital investment knowledge become those skills meet requirements just labour market. Apparently, the problem is not promoting employability through investment in learning, but it is basing learning on the rationale of human capital, which, despite not being expressed as such, is, nonetheless, implied by the claims this approach makes.

Governing Principles of the "Theory of Human Capital" and Critical Approaches

The theory of human capital has undoubtedly enjoyed particular success in the past and present. With the Lisbon Treaty, the concept of "capital" defines the aspirations of educational policy.

The ruling educational doctrine clearly mentioned in Brian Keeley's book, *Human Capital: How What You Know Shapes Your Life* (Keeley 2007), is based on the concept of human capital. This plays a crucial role in the pursuit of strategic goals because it gathers together the knowledge, skills, competencies and personal qualities that facilitate the creation of personal, social and economic prosperity (OCDE 2001, p. 18).

According to Laval (2003), the success of this theory in supranational organizations is due to the fact that it advocates "long-term development" on the other hand, but mostly because it is an economic rationalization of education expenses that was acceptable to national and supranational decision-makers.

The return of human capital to the fore of economic theories is of particular importance in this chapter not so that we can juxtapose it with other economic theories[4] but so as to illuminate the significations of the reappearance of the specific conceptual context, which holds a prominent place in institutional discourse. As Poulain (2001) mentions, human capital is acknowledged as a category of practice and a commonly accepted interpretation of the relation between humans and their work and remuneration. It is from this perspective that we place particular emphasis on the way in which human activities take on meaning through the theory of human capital with the ultimate aim of illuminating its influence on the social signification of lifelong learning.

As the contemporary proponent of this neoclassical theory, Schultz (1977) defined human capital as all the skills, knowledge and competencies that allow for improvement in human production. Developing this notion further, Becker (1993) placed emphasis on the relationship between educational level and income productivity as well as on the relation between the amassment of human capital and economic development.

The theorists of human capital (Becker 1975; Willis 1986) view the productivity of education as a working theory that is formulated not to explain salary differences but to clarify the gap between real economic development and that which arises from production factors. According to human capital theorists, this difference is explained by the qualitative development of the work factor, which is attributed to education and experience.

Based on the above, one may ascertain that in this neoclassical theory there is a cause and effect relationship between education and remuneration. However, this relationship raises the issue of its validity concerning economic reality because, as Poulain (2001) mentions, any remunerative differences amongst earners are mainly due to the size of the capital stocks (Knowledge) and not to "rental fee" paid by employers per unit of stocks.

The critical approaches levelled at the theory of human capital is not only limited to the economic issues this theory raises but also concerns issues raised by the sociology of education, which are related to the theory of selection. The proponents of the selection theory (Bourdieu and Passeron 1964, 1970; Baudelot and Establet 1971; Bowles and Gintis 1976) dispute the fact that education increases the productivity of the earners. This dispute is linked with the view that education aims not at producing suitable competencies and skills but at spotting and selecting those earners who already possess these skills. The sociologists of education maintain that by employing the rhetoric of equal opportunities, schools propagate social inequalities, thus serving its selective function.

Laval (2003), on the other hand, holds that economists define human capital as that stock of knowledge which is of economic value and is embedded within the individual. The term "human capital" includes many privileges that the individual can take advantage of in the work market and can be recognized by employers as potential sources of value, such as physical appearance, manners and the health of the individual. More specifically, this term possesses the

---

[4] Such as the theory of distribution regarding the functions of profits or the theory of development emphasizing domestic development and the economy of development. See Poulain (2001).

advantage of translating and rationalizing the shortcomings of the equation between the school diploma and employment at a time when there is an inflationary increase in the number of degrees, thus justifying employers' selections when the assessment of earners' employability is based on unofficial criteria, such as social background (Laval 2003).

From an economic standpoint, of course, this view comes under question given that school is proven to be a very costly mechanism if its role is limited only to pinpointing those who possess suitable skills and businesses do not shape the hierarchy of salaries in accordance with the hierarchy of the educational system. We can therefore assume that through schools there is a reward regarding the payback of the skills produced by the educational system (Poulain 2001). The question is how the individual gains this reward and through which manipulations the state ends up managing it.

Analysis of the Conceptual Context of the Theory of Human Capital

The concept of human capital and specifically its theoretical construct appeared in the 1960s when economic development was linked not only to production factors but also to the quality of manual labour, which was attributed to workers' educational level.

In this socio-economic context, the idea of investing in capital is highlighted, an idea that Schultz maintains is that the formation of a human model, which can be perceived by observed phenomena, can be explained as a component of the individual's action. The same applies to the construction of cognitive concepts, which should agree with categories of practice, such as that of human capital.

At first glance, Schultz's reappearance in institutional discourse seems to occur in order to emphasize the quality aspect of labour and to stress the role of the individual in relation to the education/productivity/remuneration triad at the foundation of the neoclassical theory. Acknowledging something like this on the part of the political and economic powers, however, constituted in essence the legitimization of an individualistic perception[5] and by extension the neo-liberal theory with which the individualistic perception finds itself in full agreement. It is worth noting that its legitimization was not solely the result of political and economic powers but also of other groups, which, theoretically at least, counterbalance the above powers, such as labour unions, which adopted the conceptual context of human capital in their phraseology and practices (Laval 2003).

The term "human capital" is essentially a metaphor for the idea of investing in knowledge. As a metaphor, however, it creates a misleading translation of the idea of investing in knowledge precisely because its semantic core is exclusively linked

---

[5] We see this mainly in Becker, who maintains that human capital is a private commodity that yields profit to the person who owns it.

to productivity profits. In brief, we might say that the semantic content of the above concept implies that individuals possess those potentialities that they must cultivate and develop throughout the course of their lives in order to increase their productivity and by extension their financial gains and social privileges. Hence, acquiring this capital is to the benefit of the individual, a benefit which is based on a rationale of utility. Precisely this utilitarianism presupposes that the choice of occupation as well as development or reconversion is one dimensional; ergo the sole motivation in the choice of occupation is financial. In other words, according to the above rationale, what is pushed aside and ignored is the projection of the individual into the future through representations formed in relation to circumstantial social conditions and values, but mostly in relation to the way individuals comprehend their actions by means of their personal and social history. When this rationale of utility finds application in lifelong learning, it implies that individuals opt for and become involved in the learning process as a rationalistic effort to acquire higher financial gains. The intensity of the effort seems to be defined by the reward expected from the investment in question. In a similar way, the funding of the training procedure is also dependent on the expected profits and the utility of the acquired skills (Laval 2003).

These utilitarian views of education have a major influence on dominant representations. They create a double standard in the field of education for those who are acknowledged as cost-efficient and those who do not perform well. This rationale also defines lifelong learning, where those who benefit from training are the executives and not the simple employees. Hence, the rhetoric concerning equal opportunities seems to be refuted as well because it contradicts the defence of the rationale of utility.

The Imaginary Significations of the Return of the "Capital" Rationale to Lifelong Learning

By calling upon the theory of human capital, economic organizations laid the ideological foundations of a new order of things in education, an approach that essentially depersonalized the individual because it took it for a rationalistic and unbiased being. Despite the fact that in 1993 Becker himself condemned the claim according to which people are regarded as machines from the point of the human capital theory, in reality what Becker maintains is that according to this theory, the immaterial wealth of individuals, that is, their intelligence and their skills, are transplanted into the heart of economic and social progress.

We have already mentioned numerous times that the concept of human capital is based on a utilitarian rationale. There is, however, the question of how this school of thought came into being and which imaginary significations shaped its content.

In the nineteenth century, Bentham formulated his utilitarian philosophy, maintaining that happiness is the only thing people can aspire to (Liechti 2007). Utility is defined as pleasure and satisfying desire. In this sense, utility constitutes from this point on a unit of measurement that allows for the assessment of pleasures.

The cardinal rule of utility is proven to be his famous "felicific calculus", the algorithm Bentham formulated to show that any amount of pleasure corresponds to a level of happiness. These "elements", as Bentham called them, are the database for calculating one's personal well-being.

This theory was later developed by Mill, who, through the prism of morality, defined two concepts to provide the basis for utilitarianism: pleasure and the absence of pain (Liechti 2007). According to utilitarianism, the concepts of pleasure and the absence of pain are not purely sensory manifestations and thus are not part of an intuitive approach. On the contrary, as part of the Epicurean tradition, they are considered the expression of intelligence and, as such, fall within the jurisdiction of rational thinking, that is, they are considered rationalistic skills that can be defined in relation to the utility they provide (Sen 2000, p. 32).

In addition, the choices (be they beneficial or not) individuals make, they do so in connection to the environment to which they belong or have access, in relation to their preferences, which reflect a myriad of various and different social influences and are more or less random from an economic perspective (Castoriadis 1997).

Based on the above, we can see that in utilitarianism, the individual ceases to exist as a subject, that is, a psychical being with representations, intentionalities, desires and emotions; the individual is seen as a being of idealized rationalism and makes his/her decisions based on financial motives. What is curious about the theory of human capital and especially about decision-makers who have revived it in politics is that they seem to disregard History, Sociology, as well as Psychology, Psychoanalysis and the Psycho-sociology of Groups and Organizations, the sciences, that is, that showed that no one functions as a unit in order to judge what is useful or not. The individual is born, brought up and dies within an organizational context. The theories of organization precisely demonstrated the mutual influences of humans and organizations, each theory expressing in this way a different ideological perception of humans and organization.[6]

Ever since 1913, Sigmund Freud proved in his work *The Claims of Psycho-Analysis to Scientific Interest* the significance of the unconscious not only for the individual but for society as a whole (Freud 1953). In his works *Totem and Taboo* (1912–1913) and *Moses and Monotheism* (1939), he highlights how the unconscious plays a definitive role in the whole spectrum of human behaviour and in the way social bonds are forged either in the context of a whole society or of an organization or group (Freud 1955, 1964). As Enriquez (2003) indicatively mentions, Freud's contribution allowed us to comprehend the evolution of the social bond when he describes that individuals do not exist outside the social milieu and are constantly torn between the expression of their personal desires (recognition of their desires) and the need to identify with others (i.e. the desire for recognition).

Based on the above we are led to a series of questions: Why has this instrumental rationalism become dominant as compared to any other form of thought? Why is it covertly and through unconscious mechanisms plaguing the individual and social strategies as well as decision-making procedures concerned with education and

---

[6]For an analytical description of the theories, see: Petit (1979).

particularly lifelong learning? What are the conscious or unconscious intentions underlying human action so that it is lent meaning by the theory of human capital? How can we put up a strong resistance to the infiltration of an economic rationale of human action in area of lifelong learning?

According to Castoriadis (1997), the boundless expansion of faith in a rationalistic mastery of social and economic processes led political theory to a backslide in the field of economics, which in this phase is embodied in the neo-liberal and monetary dictates of capitalism. A context is being formed within which the meaning of work is being destroyed, the role of humans in the production process of work and knowledge is being obliterated and the role of the state is becoming dismantled.

Perhaps it is strange to be speaking still of "rationalistic economy" at a time when the rate of unemployment in Greece is near the 21 % mark and the only solution suggested is the reduction in inflation and budget deficits. Even more curious is the ideological regression plaguing Western societies for one to three decades now. As Castoriadis mentions, the criticism made between 1930 and 1965 by the scholars of economic policy of the Cambridge school of thought have either been hushed up or forgotten, while the reintroduction of certain political views, such as that of human capital, appears on the scene as self-evident and well-meaning.

For Castoriadis, the capitalist system is the only social system that produces an ideology according to which it is self-proclaimed as a rationalistic social system. In other words, capitalism has not only legitimized rationalism but elevated it to an institution.[7] This becomes even more interesting when the legitimization and inclusion of this rationalistic approach in institutional discourse is established as non-negotiable, that is, self-evident.

It is not possible to answer the question why this form of rationalism dominated the existing system because, according to Castoriadis, this trend cannot be inferred from any historical or economic analysis. We can, however, link it to another dominant trend: that of mastery. Capitalism's propensity for mastery differs from other similar trends one finds in other social systems whose primary aspiration was to conquer others. This particular trend of capitalism concerns society as a whole and not just the economy. It extends to education, justice and politics, for example, and it makes use of rationalized extremes (Castoriadis 1997, p. 37). This is why Castoriadis maintains that this impulsion towards an endless expansion of rationalistic mastery is of core significations in the capitalistic system.

The dominant social imaginary significations that governs the theory of human capital and the utilitarian rationale on which it is founded are the continual effort to present the economic system in the applied field of lifelong learning as a field of "*scientificity*" that is both inevitable and the best. Castoriadis (1997) says indicatively that it is impossible even if one did map exercises in order to go from the reality of oligopolistic markets to general equilibriums, improving something other than the profits of the oligopolies or, more specifically, of the groups that rule them.

---

[7] Castoriadis says that every society legitimizes and lays down its institutions. The question is to which degree each society allows for a questioning of its institutions and hence their potential contestation.

Of course, in the existing system all activities are defined as economic and the results of these activities are regarded as "products" whose assigned value is given only in economic terms. Even when the existing system displays interest in other noneconomic activities – such as civic duty, interest and participation in public affairs, social justice and solidarity – not only do they not overshadow the dominance of the individual's economic interests, but they constitute a rationalization or an excuse in order to conceal the submission of all human activities to economy. An indicative example is the labelling of lifelong learning as an economic and cultural strategy, initially adopted by the Lisbon Treaty and established by the *Memorandum on Lifelong Learning*. More specifically, by claiming that through investing in human resources enables people to "manage their own 'time-life portfolios'", the memorandum promotes an individualistic perspective and attempts to rationalize the involvement of industrial corporations in lifelong learning by calling on moralistic motives such as "introducing a European award for particularly progressive companies" (Memorandum, Key message 2, p. 12) and "progressive employers" (Memorandum, Key message 2, p. 13). This attempted social simplification cancels out the specific ideological superstructure for "investment in knowledge". The text in question essentially presents the individual as able "to contribute to the cost of their own learning through special savings and deposits" (Memorandum, Key Message 2, p. 12). In other words, the text places the individual in an economic, social and political setting where prosperity and a balanced distribution of incomes prevail. This scenario, however, is in stark contrast with the recessional economic state of many countries plagued by unemployment, part-time employment, unequal opportunities for accessing (quality) education, the low quality of general education and training as well as people who display passivity and a lack of interest in civic life (Memorandum, p. 4–5), features which were, in fact, the springboard for the drafting of this Memorandum.

This, therefore, is how one might explain that, despite all the rhetoric in defence of personal desires and aspirations and social needs, what the question ultimately boils down to is:

> How can investment in learning be made more tangible and transparent for the individual and for the employer or enterprise, in particular by strengthening financial incentives and removing disincentives? What are promising ways to encourage and enable individuals to co-fund and take control of their own learning? (Memorandum, p. 13)

In the face of this pecuniary approach to lifelong learning and in spite of these difficult times, a plethora of training programmes whose topic is the discontent of professionals (educators, psychologists, social workers, therapists, etc.), who are occupied with human relations. These are programmes through which the participants attempt to deal with the complex professional daily reality, be it educational, therapeutic, advisory or supportive, without promoting or seeking profit (Blanchard-Laville 2001; Giust-Desprairies 1997, 2005; Cifali and Giust-Desprairies 2006; Tsakiris 2010).

Of course, the criteria that will define the "product" of training (which sectors it will pertain to, which aims it will serve, what its content will be, by which organizational methods it will be implemented and what the cost will amount to) generally depend on the social imaginary significations that society itself has set (Castoriadis 1975). The social imaginary significations on which the economic rationalism proposed by the theory of human capital is based show that all human action must or should serve the idea of capital, which is considered either self-evident or imperative even if reality contradicts it. It is, in other words, a fabrication and ultimately an irrational contrivance. Of course, the question is whether this irrational contrivance can be deconstructed in the social consciences of people and consequently delegitimized as a dominant policy.

In conclusion, the analysis of the Memorandum on lifelong learning showed that the strategy of defending human capital as a form of rationality is an imaginary social construction which both in the project level and in the level of facts seems to invalidate the defended form of rationality. The analysis revealed that the same text as the hub contains certain opposing or contradictory goals that are incompatible with those openly advocated. In this sense, the Memorandum is a social example of how it is understood in the project of human action in work activity specifically and in the social activity generally. As such it highlights the contradictions of the project of human action known at this time which seems to motivate human action.

We are experiencing a sociohistorical conjuncture where there is a pronounced imbalance of social dynamics. On one hand, we have the bankruptcy of left-wing parties with the resulting loss of the influence once exercised by labour unions and their transmutation into corporations; we have all levels of social life being bombarded by client relations; we have the "privatization of the state" by these client systems and we have a bureaucratic state. On the other hand, a conservative anti-revolution is taking place, resulting in the revival of a savage and blind neo-liberalism (Castoriadis 1997), where capitalist imaginary triumph in their most repugnant forms. It would be absurd to claim that any economic memorandum could bring those countries diverging from the initial criteria back to where they were or to a state of a harmonious division of labour on the international level. It would also be absurd for one to defend the rationalism of any economic theory, such as that of human capital. Yet, however absurd the defence of this theory's rationalism may seem, even more difficult is it to undertake to delegitimize it. And this is not because it warrants such specialized knowledge in order to carry out the necessary analyses, but because it demands a social project, which will allow individuals to "summing" their volunteered scientific (with or without quotes) analyses, based on the criterion of a value system that advocates the emancipation of human action through personal and social autonomy.

References

Alison, M. (2012). *Education et formation tout au long de la vie – un capital humain* in fr.jobs.lu/ Education Learning.htm/
Baudelot, C., & Establet, R. (1971). *L'école capitaliste en France*. Paris: Maspero.
Becker, G. (1964). *Human capital. A theoretical and empirical analysis with special references to education*. Chicago: University of Chicago Press.
Becker, G. S. (1975). *Human capital* (2nd ed.). Chicago: University Press.

Becker, G. S. (1993). *Human capital: A theoretical and empirical analysis with special reference to education*. Chicago: N.B.E.R.

Blanchard-Laville, C. (2001). *Les enseignants entre plaisir et souffrance*. Paris: PUF.

Bourdieu, P., & Passeron, J.-C. (1964). *Les héritiers: les étudiants et la culture*. Paris: Minuit.

Bourdieu, P., & Passeron, J.-C. (1970). *La reproduction: éléments pour une théorie du système d' enseignement*. Paris: Minuit.

Bowles, S., & Gintis, H. (1976). *Schooling in Capitalist America*. New York: Basic Books.

Castoriadis, C. (1975). *L' institution imaginaire de la société*. Paris: Seoul.

Castoriadis, C. (1997). La «rationalité» du capitalisme. *Revue Internationale de Psychosociologie, 8*, 31–51.

Cifali, M., & Giust-Desprairies, F. (2006). (ssd) *De la clinique. Un enseignement pour la formation et la recherche*. Brussels: De Boeck Université.

Enriquez, E. (2003). *L' organisation en analyse*. Paris: PUF.

EU Official Journal C 119 28/05/2009, Council Conclusions of 12 May 2009 on a strategic framework for European cooperation in education and training (ET 2020).

EU Official Journal C 295 05/12/2003.

European Council. (2000). *Presidency conclusions*, Lisbon (23-24/3/2000, Brussels, 2000, paragraph 5[a]).

European Parliament Commission. (2000). *Memorandum on lifelong learning*, SEC (2000) 1832, Brussels, 30/10/2000.

Freud, S. (1953). The claims of psycho-analysis to scientific interest. In J. Strachey (Ed.), *The standard edition of the complete psychological works of Sigmund Freud* (Vol. 13). London: Hogarth Press. (Original work published 1913)

Freud, S. (1955). Totem and taboo. In J. Strachey (Ed. & Trans.), *The standard edition of the complete psychological works of Sigmund Freud* (Vol. 13). London: Hogarth Press. (Original work published 1913)

Freud, S. (1964). Moses and monotheism. In J. Strachey (Ed.), *The standard edition of the complete psychological works of Sigmund Freud* (Vol. 23). London: Hogarth Press. (Original work published 1939)

Giust-Desprairies, F. (1997). La rationalité comme défense dans la relation educative. *Revue Internationale de Psychologie, 8*(3), 81–92.

Giust-Desprairies, F. (2005). (ssd) *Analyser ses pratiques professionnelles en formation*. Créteil: CRDP Académie de Créteil.

Keeley, B. (2007). *Human capital: How what you know shapes your life*. Paris: OECD.

Laval, C. (2003). *L' école n' est pas une enterprise*. Paris: La Découverte/Poche.

Liechti, V. (2007). *Du capital humain au droit de l' éducation. Analyse théorique et empirique d' une capacité*. Doctoral thesis for the Department of Economic and Social Sciences University of Fribourg (Switzerland) under the tutelage of Professors Dr Jean-Jacques Friboulet and Madame Dr Marie-France Lange.

OCDE. (2001). *Du bien–être des nations, le rôle du capital humain et social*. Paris: OCDE.

Petit, F. (1979). *Introduction à la psychosociologie des organisations*. Paris: Privat.

Poulain, E. (2001). Le capital humain, d'une conception substantielle à un modèle représentationnel. *Revue économique, 52*, 91–116.

Schultz, W. T. (1961). Investment in human capital. *American Economic Review, 51*(1), 1–17.

Schultz, T. W. (1977). Investment in human capital. In J. Karabel & A. H. Halsey (Eds.), *Power and ideology in education* (pp. 313–324). New York: Oxford University Press.

Sen, A. (2000). *Un nouveau modèle économique: développement, justice, liberté*. Paris: Editions Odile Jacob.

Tsakiris, D. (2010). Prescriptive orderliness and pedagogical practices in the institution of school. In B. Koulaides & A. Tsatsaroni (Eds.), *Pedagogical practices: Research and educational policies* (pp. 225–269). Athens: Metechmio.

Willis, R. (1986). Wage determinants: A survey and reinterpretation of human capital earnings functions. In O. Ashenfelter & F. Layard (Eds.), *Handbook of labor economics*. New York: Elsevier Sc Pub.

Part III
Lifelong Learning, Innovative Teaching and Learning, and Rethinking Guidance and Counselling

Chapter 11
Re-representing Education's Image and Status: In the 'Interest' of Pedagogical Innovation

Stephen O'Brien

Introduction

The European Commission's *A Memorandum on Lifelong Learning* (2000, p. 3) sets out the vision for 'a successful transition to a knowledge-based economy and society'. Six key messages suggest 'a comprehensive and coherent lifelong learning strategy for Europe' (European Commission 2000, p. 4). This paper focuses on the third message, namely, the strategy's goal 'to develop effective teaching and learning methods and contexts for the continuum of lifelong and life-wide learning' (ibid.). Such a focus does not preclude a relational critique of the other five messages since, at their core, all share assumptions regarding the value of the following: 'skills-based' knowledge, investment in the principle of 'human capital', the efficacy of 'learning outcomes', a focus on equal 'opportunity' over-and-above equal 'conditions' and equal 'effects' and the (intended) appeal to an inclusive range of learners. The overall strategy was to have been, by now, fully implemented (European Commission 2000, p. 3). This paper proffers an implicit assessment of this profligate target. With specific attention to the message on teaching and learning, it argues that the strategy connects with neo-liberal meanings, standpoints and practices that oversee an incomplete educational representation. Despite inadequate representation, productive power is ideologically, structurally and culturally secured via loose connectivity at various supranational, nation state, political interest, academic, media and wider societal levels. These levels cohere at some point to cast education's dominant image and status and enunciate new ways to 'innovate' teaching and learning.

There are aspects to this *Memorandum* that are to be welcomed, not least the commendable goals to: build an inclusive society with equal access to quality

S. O'Brien (✉)
School of Education, University College Cork, Cork, Ireland
e-mail: s.obrien@ucc.ie

G.K. Zarifis and M.N. Gravani (eds.), *Challenging the 'European Area of Lifelong Learning': A Critical Response*, Lifelong Learning Book Series 19, DOI 10.1007/978-94-007-7299-1_11, © Springer Science+Business Media Dordrecht 2014

learning; adjust the ways in which education and training is provided (including how paid working life is organised); set out objectives for higher overall levels of education and qualification; and seek and facilitate deeper forms of active citizenship (European Commission 2000, pp. 4, 5). Such worthy goals are chiefly diluted, however, by the strategy's insubstantial analysis of education as a field of power – specifically, the concern that education reflects and produces diverse interests and effects (e.g. Bourdieu 1984, 1988, 1998). Here, education's image and status – how it is unremittingly interest-led and powerfully contested – is of primary concern for this paper. Thus, whilst it is welcome to observe 'questions for debate' accompanying each strategy message in the European Commission's *A Memorandum on Lifelong Learning*, this paper argues for further, wider enquiries. Ultimately, if there is to be *innovation* in teaching and learning, the paper concludes; this is best served, and can only be effectively engaged, via a more complex and authentic representation.

A Vision of Lifelong Learning: Questions for Further Debate

Crucially, the *Memorandum* presents 'two equally important aims for lifelong learning – promoting active citizenship and promoting employability' (European Commission 2000, p. 5). Little is said about their relationship other than indicating that the latter provides a 'core dimension' of the former and is 'decisive' in developing European-wide 'prosperity':

> For much of most people's lives, having paid work underpins independence, self-respect and well-being, and is therefore a key to people's overall quality of life. Employability – the capacity to secure and keep employment – is not only a core dimension of active citizenship, but it is equally a decisive condition for reaching full employment and for improving European competitiveness and prosperity in the 'new economy'. (European Commission 2000, p. 5)

The primacy of education's 'economic' value is assumed here. This, in turn, obscures other important (sociopolitical) questions that speak directly to the challenges of active citizenship. These questions include: How can dynamic economic growth *and* social cohesion be strengthened? What and whose 'knowledge, skills and competence' are being represented? Beyond 'skills gaps' recognition, how are diverse educational opportunities, conditions and effects addressed? Is the economic revelation 'to raise demand for learning as well as its supply' an adequate response 'for those who have benefitted least from education?' (ibid., p. 8). Do proposed 'public-private initiatives' and 'new user-oriented learning systems' include the interest of marginalised learner groups? (ibid., p. 8). There is intimation in the *Memorandum* that education is not all about employability:

> Employability is obviously a key outcome of successful learning, but social inclusion rests on more than having paid work. Learning opens the door to building a satisfying and productive life, quite apart from a person's employment status and prospects. (European Commission 2000, p. 9)

Notwithstanding this (fleeting) recognition, 'obvious' economic value connections are still securely established. Moreover, whilst there is no hesitation in revealing that 'learning opens the door', the 'door that opens learning' (i.e. the portal of access) remains firmly closed from view.

Similarly, when it extols the message of innovation in teaching and learning, the *Memorandum* stresses the 'obvious' economic value of education. There are commendable objectives that need *not* be imbued with such value, such as the need to: challenge traditional systems of learning; reform initial and continuing teacher professionalism; extend and practise open and participatory teaching and learning methods; and encourage meaningful *qualitative* standards of practice (European Commission 2000, pp. 13, 14).[1] But these objectives overlap with those of clearer economic purpose that endorse the following: more user-oriented learning systems; outcome-based learning approaches; and the 'added value' of applied educational research (European Commission 2000, pp. 13–15). Moreover, all these objectives, including those directed towards 'innovation in teaching and learning', coalesce around an economic 'sign value' (Brancaleone and O'Brien 2011). In this way, the primary focus is on teaching and learning as technical, skills-based activities, where *innovation* implies effective *methods* of service delivery (e.g. ICT-based pedagogies) and functional *outcomes* (e.g. qualifications exchange in the marketplace). Challenging such pedagogical representation remains key to challenging the lifelong learning vision presented in the *Memorandum*.

Power Interest in Education's Image and Status

Contestation around pedagogical representation speaks to the prevalence of *power interest* in education's image and status. Image here concerns itself with both semiotics (e.g. how one imagines education; attaches meaning to it) *and* modus operandi (e.g. how one practises teaching and learning). Status concerns itself with distinction (e.g. Bourdieu 1984), particularly the prominence afforded to certain educational positions (e.g. dominant perspectives on educational 'effectiveness'). Whilst image and status do not *directly* form practice, they can be hugely influential – particularly if they garner structural support and cultural endorsement. Accordingly, education may be viewed as a field of power that is contested both symbolically and effectually. Emissary voices are ever-present, sometimes cohering, other times contradicting each other's evocative claims.

---

[1] In making this point, I have deliberately chosen to alter certain terminology. The *Memorandum* stresses the phrase 'teacher training'. I have replaced this with 'teacher professionalism' to emphasise the importance of 'craft', in addition to/over, 'skills-based' knowledge forms. The *Memorandum* also uses the term 'qualitative benchmarks'. I use 'qualitative standards' in its stead to demonstrate that such measures are intrinsically valuable and are ultimately irreducible to *transferability*. It is clear that language is key to any declaration of power interest in education.

Their resonating power interest may be more apparent or hidden from view.[2] Notwithstanding their transparency, diverse interest groups powerfully invest in education's image and status and its associated pedagogical relations. Accordingly, 'innovation' in teaching and learning is shown to have different meanings, purposes, parameters and actions. This paper examines some 'innovation' messages, notably those that relate to Irish university education. Critical analysis centres on unveiling and articulating the power interests that lie within these messages.

The *Memorandum* concludes that an investment in people ('Europe's main assets') is best achieved by adapting (read synchronising) 'education and training systems' (European Commission 2000, p. 6). Such supranational authority, so bound up in the 'lifelong learning' message, has greatly shaped national policy agendas on education. Changes have duly followed. The European Credit Transfer System (ECTS) movement and the subsequent establishment of national qualifications frameworks provide for a paradigmatic shift towards the measurability, transfer and progression of outcome-based skills, knowledge and competences.[3] In agreement with Gleeson (2011, p. 3), the focus of such a shift has been on 'curriculum as content' and the mutual recognition of technical systems and award qualifications in different jurisdictions, rather than on learning processes, teaching methodologies and student-centred forms of assessment. The introduction of outcomes-based education, in particular, complements regulatory approaches to teacher 'competence' and development (e.g. European Commission 2004; OECD 2005; Tuning Project 2010). Such a focus shift has largely resulted from neo-liberal pressures for increased ('contractual' forms of) accountability, alongside greater 'quality' control systems and the expansion of 'performance-based' indicators (e.g. Sleeter 2007; Roberts 2007; Beck 2010). Gleeson and O'Donnabhain (2009) point to the Department of Education and Skills' *Customer Service Action Plan* as a good exemplar of an Irish policy response to such pressures.

Education's image and status increasingly reflect this select supranational interest. Concomitantly, a particular pedagogical representation is produced. Standardised forms of assessment bear strong emblematic and concrete influence. To illustrate, international tests such as PISA (Programme for International Student Assessment), PIRLS (Progress in International Reading Literacy Survey) and TIMMS (Trends in International Mathematics and Science Study) comparatively 'rank' national test scores. From 'common sense' and 'reasonable' perspectives, these international tests present a renewed focus on education with improved opportunities for innovative ('benchmark') practices.[4] 'Commonsense' assumes that the 'outcomes' of education

---

[2] The forces that shape education's image and status are difficult to fully articulate since they assemble at a myriad of power-knowledge, structural and sociocultural levels. Such forces may become more articulate at a point of some convergence between these levels.

[3] In contradistinction to note 1 above, I have deliberately chosen to leave unchanged the language terminology presented here. These terms resonate with a particular, managerialist/neo-liberal, image of education (e.g. O'Brien 2012).

[4] Of course 'benchmarking' is hugely problematic. For example, does one follow Finland or South Korea for exemplar educational policies and practices? Both nations appear to perform well in

systems are pre-eminent, capable of being effectively measured and readily adopted (O'Brien and Brancaleone 2011). A 'reasonable' perspective assumes that comparative tests are unproblematic, or at least have the capacity to overcome their (inherent) limitations.[5] Whilst a more exhaustive critique of comparative standardised testing is beyond this paper's remit, it is clear that both assumptions are highly contentious. Hitherto, however, they remain largely uncontested at official policy levels. The power effects of standardised testing are especially neglected vis-à-vis their consequences for how education is inexorably signified and positioned. The impact on teaching and learning, including pedagogical 'innovation', is likewise neglected. Despite this, structural authority continues to support the image and status production of 'tests' and, concurrently, new pedagogical 'truths'. Whilst the levels and powers of structural authority vary, they may coalesce at some mutual educational position. Further, as a loosely interconnected set of forces, structural authority may not always be transparent. To illustrate, those with a particular power interest in assessment are often presented as discrete/disconnected when, in reality, they have (an equivalent or greater) power interest in education's image and status, including its constituent pedagogical character. Thus, it is possible (indeed necessary, from a critical perspective) to identify test sponsors, designers and administrators as 'interested' power groups, e.g. the role of *The Indicators and Analysis Division Directorate for Education at the OECD* in PISA and the function of *The International Association for the Evaluation of Educational Achievement* with respect to PIRLS and TIMMS. In this way, ideological, structural and cultural connectivity is exemplified in the European Commission's explicit position on 'lifelong learning' and the ongoing work of international assessment organisations.

'Change', states the *Memorandum*, 'can only come about in and through the impetus of the member states' (European Commission 2000, p. 5). In an Irish context, the 'connected' state has advanced its response with the introduction of the *National Strategy for Literacy and Numeracy among Children and Young People* (DES 2011). This emphasises the primacy of outcomes-based education and its regular test functions.[6] The Educational Research Centre, established on the campus of St. Patrick's College of Education in Dublin, has positively welcomed this shift to 'national testing' (Educational Research Centre 2011). Whilst it 'officially' recognises the importance of 'classroom-based' assessment (ibid.), as espoused by the National Council for Curriculum and Assessment (e.g. NCCA 2007), the interrelationship between this formative/developmental model of assessment and more

---

international tests (as evaluated by 'exam scores'), but they could not be any different in terms of their philosophical, methodological and sociocultural construction!

[5] To illustrate, comparative tests may overcome their (inherent) limitations via the cyclic improvement of their apparatus, including the moderation of 'hard' statistics (e.g. introducing '*ranges* of rank order positions' and *schools like ours* data), the use of provisional statements (e.g. encompassing such phrases as 'all other variables being equal') and an engagement with some qualitative measures (e.g. 'student motivation' levels, 'reading enjoyment' indicators place etc.,).

[6] Among its proposals for primary (elementary) schools is the compulsory requirement to implement, from 2012 onwards, standardised testing in reading and mathematics for all students in 2nd, 4th and 6th classes (i.e. ages 7–8, 9–10 and 11–12).

standardised forms, is not adequately engaged.[7] The main 'work' of the Educational Research Centre continues to be the development of standardised, diagnostic and profile test systems. To illustrate, the centre analyses the results of state examinations, monitors the 'outcomes' of education in areas of literacy and mathematics ('connecting' with PISA, PIRLS and TIMMS) and develops new assessment instruments. The authenticity of this work is not questioned here. But, crucially, the limitations of standardised testing are largely neglected, including their potentially negative impact on education's image and status. Of course the work of the centre is upheld by those (e.g. government, various schools and parents) who claim that the system is made more measurable and visibly accountable. There is obviously some basis to this argument and there are apparent benefits to various groups that uphold such a position. But it is important to stress that 'accountability' takes on specific meaning here, allied as it is to the understanding that a range of 'output' indicators echoes comparable degrees of 'performance'. Furthermore, the (oft unforeseen) consequences of this association are manifest in individual schools and teachers being increasingly orientated towards these outcomes. Likewise, 'innovation' in teaching and learning is progressively framed by such values.

The Bologna process and Lisbon strategy exemplify the European Union's commitment to become the most competitive 'knowledge society' in the world (Lisbon European Council 2006). The role of the university is core to this objective as it captures the so-called knowledge triangle of research, education and innovation. Universities are thus seen as valued research and pedagogical environments that produce, accredit and transmit innovative knowledge, ultimately serving the expansion of Europe's competitive global status. This value position is frequently championed by the European University Association (e.g. EUA 2004). Moreover, the European Commission (2006) sees universities' specific association with industry as key to the production of a European knowledge economy. The OECD's recent *Economic Survey of Ireland 2009* similarly stresses advanced coordination with industry in the interests of increasing 'innovation and wealth'. Irish politicians have readily borrowed and adopted this position on higher education. Increasingly, they perceive their role as being 'hands-on' in directing and managing the purpose and function of the university:

> Our universities have a critical role to play as a dynamo energising our Smart Economy with new ideas and creativity. Increased collaboration among our universities – joining forces – greatly helps us to up our game in the intense ongoing global competition to come up with new ideas, new products and new services. (Former Taoiseach/Prime Minister Brian Cowen, *Education Matters* 2010, Feb 20)

Symbolic, and real, links between education and the economy are unambiguous in the state's habitual (and 'imitative') use of the phrase 'smart economy'. Yet, a

---

[7] The 'two types of assessment' are said to 'share several features' (The Educational Research Centre 2011, p. 6), though this is not explicated further. The following is also presented: 'The immediate introduction of standards-based classroom assessments, without first establishing a strong underlying knowledge base about classroom assessment strategies among teachers, may not be successful' (ibid.). This initial 'problematising' is welcome, but further elaboration on, and investigation into, the statement's conclusion is (regretfully) not provided.

fundamental contradiction persists in the state's accommodation of the autonomous role of the university (as secured in *The Universities Act*, 1997) and its verification of the university's (contingent) economic purpose:

> I have no hesitation in firmly endorsing the need for our institutions to enjoy strong levels of autonomy [...] In terms of graduate education, we must ensure that our Doctoral graduates have not only in-depth knowledge of their chosen research area but also the broad range of 'workplace' skills and competencies required by industry [...] [We need] to maximise the impact of our research results in terms of the commercialisation of that research and its conversion into real sustainable jobs. (Minister for Education and Skills Ruairi Quinn, *Education Matters* 2011, Nov 22)

Politicisation presents as a particular power interest in education. At a concrete level, the financial dependence of universities on the exchequer 'has given politicians and civil servants the power to bend them to their own purpose' (Fitzgerald 2010, p. 1). Actual current spending on higher education has reduced by almost two-thirds between 2001 and 2005 (ibid.). Despite a 15 % increase in student numbers over the past 3 years, universities have 10 % fewer academic staff than 2 years ago and government grant funding has been reduced by 9 % in that same period (Murray 2011 statistics). Economic austerity and new public sector reforms are presented as the 'rationalising rationale' for this diminution of resources. Such rationale has given rise to ideologically informed policy decisions that subvert the role of education to the needs of business/industry, whilst promoting state dynamism in facilitating people 'back to work'. Whilst present resource reductions are undoubtedly arduous, the exhortation to 'do more with less' precedes more straitened economic times. Ireland has always operated an underfunded education system.[8] Looking outside for policy direction appears, in 'good times and bad', to consolidate the nation state's compact fiscal position. The European Commission has long argued for the efficient management of resources and the 'rolling back' of state investment in education to include 'higher private spending' and 'incentives for more and sustained investment from enterprises and individuals' (European Commission 2003, pp. 3–4). A parallel position is to be found in the World Bank's promotion of the global market economy (including the educational market economy) and the liberalisation/privatisation of education services through the World Trade Organisation's General Agreement on Trade in Services (GATs) (Robertson 2008). Shaped by this politicised discourse, the 'knowledge industry' encapsulates an ever-expansive network of 'learning services'. This encourages increased HE privatisation (e.g. Hibernia College in Ireland) and 'performance-based' comparisons amongst educational providers (e.g. the Russell Group in the UK). Moreover, an economic value for education is greater secured via 'fee' payments and the depiction of students/learners as 'consumers'. This is exemplified by the Minister for Education and Skills' recent encouragement to university students to be 'critical consumers' of the education they receive:

---

[8] On an OECD scale ranking overall education spending in relation to wealth or gross domestic product, Ireland lies 27th of 31 countries surveyed. To illustrate how resource constraints operate in practice, Ireland has already the second most overcrowded primary classrooms in the EU. Further, Irish universities are operating at approximately 60 % of the funding available to their counterparts in Britain and the rest of the EU. (all statistics from Flynn in *The Irish Times*, Feb 08, 2012a).

A bad restaurant doesn't get repeat business. I think there has to be some response from the user of the service provided in an open market economy like ours. People can exercise their choice by moving to another supplier of the service. (Minister for Education and Skills Ruairi Quinn, in Duggan, *Sunday Independent* 2012, Feb 5, p. 6)

The above sentiments by an Irish (Labour education) minister appear acutely rooted in the neo-liberal zeitgeist. This ideological outlook is ever-more culturally inscribed into civic arenas of society, including public education. Moreover, it increasingly permeates individuals' 'life-world perspectives' (Shutz and Luckmann 1973), fashioning for them particular possibilities and choices (Rose 1999).[9] Emissary voices for greater 'innovation' in education are saturated in, what Stephen Ball might call, the 'discourse of business sensibility' (e.g. Ball 2007, 2009). This is clearly evident in a recent edition of 'Innovation', *The Irish Times Business Magazine* (November, 2011), specially entitled 'Saving Our Education System: The reforms needed to make us competitive again'. As a compendium of articles and commercials affirming the education-economy relation, they provide a curious role for business/enterprise (particularly science and technology) in the drive to 'innovate' a (supposed) moribund education system. One such article is written by an academic so disposed to this 'innovative' task (Walsh 2011). As a former President of the University of Limerick, Dr. Ed Walsh believes that 'competition in the knowledge economy is a global race for talent' (Walsh 2011, p. 24). Citing PISA test scores, he maintains that Ireland's 'international rankings [...] have been plummeting' (ibid.). There is an impending need to 'innovate' education (and pedagogical relations therein). Exhortations are thus made to, inter alia (Walsh 2011, p. 25):

- 'Upgrade the performance of existing teachers by boosting in-service [...] linking outcomes to award of annual increments'
- Reform governance structures – particularly at National Council for Curriculum and Assessment (NCCA) and university levels – to comprise a majority of board members from the private sector
- Introduce a graduation tax system to enable the full introduction of university fees
- 'Permit universities to compete in the market for international talent by removing limits on individual salary offers, while imposing strict limits on average salary levels within the university'[10]

The above 'innovations' are highly contentious. Crucially, they disregard the recent signs and consequences of market failure. They also disregard extensive research critiquing the impact of neo-liberal change on educational institutions and the teaching profession (e.g. Clark and Newman 1997; Ball 2003; Olsen and Peters 2005; Harris

---

[9] Of course 'choice' (e.g. school choice) is central to neo-liberal lexicon and conceptual thought. It is unsurprising, therefore, to see 'choice' being named (and therefore legitimated) in the minister's quotation above.

[10] Interestingly, the government's recent finance bill (Feb 2012) ensures, under its 'Special Assignee Relief Programme' (SARP), that highly skilled workers can be exempt from income tax (up to 5 years) on 30 % of salaries between 75,000 and 500,000 euro. Worker competition and attracting 'the best human capital' (key tenets of neo-liberal thinking) appear central to parallel 'innovation' messages.

2006; Clegg 2008). Moreover, the arguments presented are both paradoxical and incomplete. To illustrate the former, Walsh (2011, p. 24) cites PISA as the rationale for drastic innovation whilst, at the same time, decrying the 'narrowness' of the final summative state school examination and the 'tyranny' of [test score] appraisal for entry to university (Walsh 2011, p. 24). Also, Finland, South Korea, Singapore and Canada are jointly presented as 'the world's best school systems' (Walsh 2011, p. 25), without due regard for variation in philosophical, structural, sociocultural and methodological substances. These distinctions are key to any attempt to establish equivalent 'innovation' lessons for Ireland. Finland's education system, for example, is characterised by more: professional trust in teachers, extensive network supports, critical peer accountability systems and non-prescriptive approaches to school-based curriculum development (e.g. Gleeson 2011). Finland is frequently presented as the 'leader to follow' in terms of its productive 'outputs' but is hardly ever presented in terms of its qualitative 'inputs'. Walsh's arguments are incomplete too. As exhortations, they appeal to a demand for 'teaching excellence', a system that does not permit 'any student to fall behind',[11] an 'upgrade [of] the skills of those that teach', 'rigorous teacher assessment', etc. (Walsh 2011, p. 25). These exhortations are short on methodological details, vague in their proposals for 'how' innovation is to be achieved. Moreover, they mask vested power interests that seek to shape education's image and status in a particular, neo-liberal, direction.

It is important to acknowledge that not all business/enterprise perspectives are captured by Taylorist forms of managerialism and crude 'outcome' approaches to education. At the very least, 'innovation' necessitates creative independence, not blind imitation, and professional trust/engagement, not suspicion/control. The proliferation of interest groups in education is such that, even within one power base, 'innovation' messages frequently present as ambiguous and contradictory. Even so, policy paradigms rely on social context for some coherence – specifically the 'intersubjective level' of social formations for 'shared thought, language systems or discourses' – to become identifiable and embodied (O'Sullivan 2005, p. 66). In this way, a circuitous intertextual quality is prevalent in Irish education's diverse power interest base. Recent addresses by university leaders to some of Ireland's business leaders illustrate this point well, with frequent cross-referencing to the primacy of the education-economy relation (Barry 2011; Murphy 2011). Here, 'innovation' is captured by the 'enterprising' character of university-industry partnerships[12] (ibid.). The education-economy relation is further consolidated by the national strategy for Irish higher education (Hunt Report 2010) and by those seeking a new 'technological university' status (Neavyn 2012). A 'technological university' is characterised

---

[11] The language used here resonates with a particular *authoritative* stance on school and teacher effectiveness (e.g. High Reliability Schooling and *No Child Left Behind* in the US; the work of Ofsted and the Training and Development Agency for Schools in the UK).

[12] To illustrate further, University College Cork now holds an annual Innovation Week (Innov8). In the 2012 calendar, a 'Bright Ideas Competition' was organised. Guest speakers were invited from business enterprises; an 'entrepreneur of the year university lecture series' was launched and 'celebrity' entrepreneurs (from the TV show *Dragons' Den*) gave keynote presentations.

by the 'professional readiness of its graduates and proximity to the world of work' and the focus of its research and innovation 'on application and enterprise' (O'Cathain 2012, Feb 7). Whilst there are power divisions on the question of this 'new' university (Flynn 2012b), somewhat paradoxically all higher education institutions appear eager to contest for business/industry partnerships. Beyond symbolic alliance, practical gains are to be made from sourcing much needed funds from agencies like Science Foundation Ireland and Enterprise Ireland. Higher level institutions themselves have become culturally inscribed by this ideological/pragmatic rationale, to the point where academics' work (some more than others) has been increasingly occupied by partnership/sponsorship concerns (e.g. Maguire 2011). Of course all academics are affected in some way by new managerial structures and power relations in the university (e.g. O'Brien 2012). This pervasive impact would not be possible but for certain academics' 'buy-in' to paradigmatic change. In an Irish context, it is possible to imagine some manifestation of 'free-floating intellectuals' (Mannheim 1949 cited in O'Sullivan, 2005, p. 66) positioning themselves strategically and shifting allegiances in line with hegemonic constituencies. In this way, various academics may actively participate in the types of politicisation and business/enterprise perspectives that sustain the dominant paradigm.

Thus, whilst a proliferation of power interest groups exist, a circuitous intertextual quality prevails with respect to the dominant education-economy relation. As above discussions demonstrate, there is loose connectivity here at various supranational, nation state, political interest and academic levels. Whilst this connectivity may occasionally falter, through what Foucault calls 'slippage', it nevertheless possesses an intrinsic (economic) 'rationality' (Foucault 1978, 1997). Moreover, connectivity popularly expands to the media via various public presentations, policy statements, television, radio and newspaper coverage. What is produced is a general 'acceptance' that education (with particular focus on the STEM[13] disciplines) 'forms and informs our path to economic recovery'[14] (*Education Matters*, Feb 12, 2012). This 'innovation' message very clearly ties education to jobs. Parents are given an assumed responsibility for 'steering' their children towards sectors where jobs are available:

> The mammies and daddies of Ireland need to move away from the notion that future secure employment is in the traditional professions such as medicine, law and teaching [...] The real opportunities for Irish graduates will be in technology, science and engineering, and students with an interest in these areas must be encouraged to pursue courses in those fields. (John Hennessy chairperson of the Higher Education Authority and former managing director of Ericsson Ireland, in Donnelly, the Irish Independent 2012, Dec 30)

---

[13] STEM denotes the collective disciplinary sphere of Science, Technology, Engineering and Mathematics. These subjects are popularly related to 'innovation' and 'enterprise' concepts.

[14] This quote is attributed to the EU Commissioner for Research, Innovation and Science (Maire Geoghegan-Quinn) on the occasion of her speech at a Science Foundation of Ireland (SFI) board meeting on Feb 9, 2012. Ms. Quinn (who has helped develop a new 80 billion euro EU funding programme called *Horizon 2020*) was invited by the chairperson of the SFI (a significant funder of STEM disciplines in universities), Professor Pat Fottrell. Professor Fottrell is also chairperson of the strategic planning group associated with the lead and development of 'technology universities'.

Concomitantly, teachers and learners are given an assumed ('contractual') responsibility to co-operate and secure a successful learning 'product'. This pedagogical relation is thus shaped by 'innovation' messages circumscribed by couched 'interest' in such concepts as 'accountability', 'performativity' and 'success'. The 'internalisation of [the] externality' of these messages, as Bourdieu (1977, p. 72) might put it, leads to a type of (Foucauldian) 'self surveillance' whereby 'the student acts the good student, the teacher acts the good teacher, the school acts the good school' (Youdell 2006, p. 36). Wider media remains largely complicit in the enunciation of this message, even fuelling its open broadcast. This it does via, inter alia: insubstantial debate on the real purpose of education; the presentation of league tables; acritical commentary on connected elements of educational policy and practice; decontextualised 'celebrations' of parental, student[15] and school 'successes' and general disinterest in 'interested' educational perspectives. Thus, the power effects of the media, in loose connectivity with other aforementioned 'interests', largely inauthenticate the image and status of education.

Re-representing Education's Image and Status: In the 'Interest' of Pedagogical Innovation

This paper suggests that 'innovation' messages (such as those that relate to teaching and learning in *A Memorandum on Lifelong Learning* 2000) need to be seriously questioned. This is easier said than done. Part of their 'connectivity' is contradictory, much is tacit and hard to identify. Moreover, the greatest expression of their reception manifests itself in their wide cultural endorsement in society. Though 'interested' power groups can never fully determine education's image and status, this paper demonstrates how loosely connected forces convene to shape 'real' practice.[16] A range of individuals, perhaps unwittingly, reproduce (and sometimes realign) this practice.

Of course, I write this paper with a particular 'interest' in how education's image and status is cast. As a professional educator and critical social researcher, I am interested in questioning/challenging the representative scope of 'innovation' messages. This paper responds to a professed need to interrogate the *educational sensibility* of particular power 'interests' in education. The evidence presented indicates

---

[15] To illustrate, one student (Cillian Fahey) who achieved straight 'A' grades in his final state examination (The Leaving Certificate), made headlines when he sold his exam notes on eBay for 3,000 euro. He subsequently wrote a series of articles for the *Irish Times* (entitled 'Secrets of My Success') outlining to ('interested') readers how to achieve top grades in different subject disciplines. He also began to work for a team of entrepreneurs who provide 'comprehensive' notes for postprimary students via their website mocks.ie. On the 27 January 2012, Cillian Fahey appeared on *The Late Late* – a popular Irish TV chat show that airs to (a weekly population average of approximately) three-quarters of a million viewers.

[16] An inauthentic representation, or 'simulacrum' (Baudrillard 1994), still produces 'real' educational effects (Brancaleone and O'Brien 2011).

an over-representation of the education-economy relation that obviates against education being seen as a moral and social practice (e.g. Biesta 2012). Consequently, this paper's evidence indicates the need to establish a stronger intellectual and teacher-professional presence at the educational 'partnership' table. Intellectuals and teacher-professionals have a (critically informed) role to play in challenging consensual forms of partnership. Crucially, they are well placed to confront the crude, inauthentic, order of education's prevailing status and image.

Calls for an extensive public debate on the purpose of education, such as that proposed by Tim Rudd at the Department of Education in the University of Brighton, are now timely. In recognition of the state's 'interested' position, he is calling for an independent body to arbitrate diverse educational perspectives and disseminate balanced findings in the wider public arena. The role of government is designed to act upon these results. Such a worthy proposal transcends the educational sphere. As Ireland's President Dr. Michael D. Higgins reminds, there exists 'an intellectual crisis in society' (Flynn, the *Irish Times*, Jan 26, 2012c). Intellectuals are now challenged to 'a moral choice, to drift into, be part of, a consensus that accepts a failed paradigm of life and economy or to offer, or seek to recover, the possibility of alternative futures…' (Higgins, Feb 21, 2012). This brings great responsibility to bear on those that enunciate 'innovation' messages. *A Memorandum on Lifelong Learning* (2000) undoubtedly exercises its power to represent education along these lines. But where education's image and status falls short, re-representation is required, not least in the 'interest' of pedagogical innovation.

Acknowledgements I would like to acknowledge the valuable contributions of Karl Kitching and Tim Rudd who helped to critically review the substance of this paper.

References

Ball, S. J. (2003). The teacher's soul and the terrors of performativity. *Journal of Education Policy, 18*(2), 215–228.

Ball, S. J. (2007). *Education plc: Understanding private sector participation in public sector education*. London: Routledge.

Ball, S. J. (2009). Privatising education, privatising education policy, privatising educational research: Network governance and the 'competition state'. *Journal of Education Policy, 24*(1), 83–99.

Barry, D. (2011, December 20). Skills shortages can be addressed. *Irish Times*. Retrieved from http://www.irishtimes.com/newspaper/education/2011/1220/1224309289199_pf.html

Baudrillard, J. (1994). *Simulacra and simulation*. Michigan: The University of Michigan Press.

Beck, J. (2010). Makeover or takeover? The strange death of educational autonomy in neo-liberal England. *British Journal of Sociology of Education, 20*(2), 223–238.

Biesta, G. (2012). *Professional work and the interference of evidence: Why evidence-based practice is not really a good idea*. Presentation at the Cohort PhD School of Education Lecture Series. Cork: University College Cork.

Bourdieu, P. (1977). *Outline of a theory of practice*. Cambridge/New York: Cambridge University Press.

Bourdieu, P. (1984). *Distinction*. London: Routledge and Kegan Paul.

Bourdieu, P. (1988). *Homo academicus*. London: Polity Press.

Bourdieu, P. (1998). *Acts of resistance: Against the new myths of our time*. London: Polity Press.

Brancaleone, D., & O'Brien, S. (2011). Educational commodification and the (economic) sign value of learning outcomes. *British Journal of Sociology of Education, 32*(4), 501–519.

Clarke, J., & Newman, J. (1997). *The managerialist state – Power, politics and ideology in the remaking of social welfare*. London/Thousand Oaks/New Delhi: Sage.

Clegg, S. (2008). Academic identities under threat? *British Educational Research Journal, 34*(3), 329–345.

Department of Education and Skills. (2011). *National strategy for literacy and numeracy among children and young people*. Dublin: Stationery Office.

Donnelly, K. (2012, December 30). Steer children to science, parents urged. *Irish Independent*. Retrieved from http://www.independent.ie/lifestyle/education/latest-news/steer-children-to-science-parents-urged-2976208.html

Duggan, B. (2012, February 6). I haven't a clue if lecturers are doing their jobs, says minister. *Sunday Independent*, p. 6.

Education Matters. (2010, February 20). *Two universities forge 'strategic alliance'*. Retrieved from http://www.educationmatters.ie/2010/02/20/two-universities-forge-strategic-alliance/

Education Matters. (2011, November 22). *Minister in interview with Dr. Tony Hall*. Retrieved from http://www.educationmatters.ie/2011/11/22/minister-in-interview-with-dr-tony-hall/

Education Matters. (2012, February 12). *Science forms and informs our path to economic recovery*. Retrieved from http://www.educationmatters.ie/2012/02/12/science-forms-and-informs-our-path-to-economic-recovery/

European Commission. (2000). *A memorandum on lifelong learning*. Brussels: EU Publication.

European Commission. (2003). Communication from the commission. In *Investing efficiently in education and training: An imperative for Europe*. Brussels: EU Publication.

European Commission. (2004). *Common European principles for teacher competences and qualifications*. Brussels: EU Publication.

European Commission. (2006). *Delivering on the modernisation agenda for universities: Education, research and innovation*. Brussels: European Commission online publication. Retrieved from http://ec.europa.eu/education/higher-education/doc1324_en.htm

European University Association. (2004). *Statement on the research role of Europe's universities*. Prepared for the Europe of knowledge 2020: A vision for university-based research and innovation conference. Liege 26–28 April, 2004. Retrieved from http://www.eua.be/eua/jsp/en/upload/Research_Liege_conf_23042004.1083058845634.pdf

Fitzgerald, G. (2010, May 1). Independence would enhance role of universities in society. *Irish Times*. Retrieved from http://www.irishtimes.com/newspaper/opinion/2010/0501/1224269476058_pf.html

Flynn, S. (2012a, February 8). Back to prefabs and leaky roofs? *Irish Times*. Retrieved from http://www.irishtimes.com/newspaper/Ireland/2012/0208/1224311460422_pf.html

Flynn, S. (2012b, January 23). Third-level presidents oppose new university. *Irish Times*. Retrieved from http://www.irishtimes.com/newspapaer/ireland/2012/0123/1224310627145_pf.html

Flynn, S. (2012c, January 26). *President calls for response to 'intellectual crisis' in society*. Retrieved from http://www.irishtimes.com/newspaper/ireland/2012/0126/1224310758999_pf.html

Foucault, M. (1978). Governmentality. Lecture at the College de France, Feb 1, 1978. In G. Burchell, C. Gordon, & P. Miller (Eds.), *The Foucault effect: Studies in governmentality* (1991, pp. 87–104). Hemel Hempstead: Harvester Wheatsheaf.

Foucault, M. (1997). The birth of biopolitics. In P. Rabinow (Ed.), *Michel Foucault, ethics: Subjectivity and truth* (pp. 73–79). New York: The New Press.

Gleeson, J. (2011). The European Credit Transfer System and curriculum design: Product before process? *Studies in Higher Education*, 1–18, iFirst Article.

Gleeson, J., & O'Donnabhain, D. (2009). Strategic planning and accountability in Irish education: Strategy statements and the adoption and use of performance indicators. *Irish Educational Studies, 28*(1), 27–46.

Harris, S. (2006). Rethinking academic identities in neo-liberal times. *Teaching in Higher Education, 10*(4), 421–433.

Higgins, M. D. (2012, February 21). *Public intellectuals, universities, and a democratic crisis. Speech at the London School of Economics and Political Science.* Retrieved from http://www.president.ie/index.php?section=5&speech=1068&lang=eng

Hunt Report. (2010). *National strategy for higher education: Draft report of the strategy group.* Dublin: DES Publication.

Maguire, A. (2011, November 8). Macro, micro and neutrino. *Irish Times.* Retrieved from http://www.irishtimes.com/newspaper/education/2011/1108/1224307200100_pf.html

Mannheim, K. (1949). *Ideology and utopia.* London: Routledge and Kegan Paul. Cited in O'Sullivan, D. (2005). *Cultural politics and Irish education since the 1950s: Policy paradigms and power.* Dublin: Institute of Public Administration Publication.

Murphy, M. (2011, December 20). *Address by President of University College Cork at the Cork Chamber Business Breakfast. Speech in the News @ UCC.* Retrieved from http://www.ucc.ie/en/news/fullstory-144045-en.html

Murray, N. (2011, December 21). Pressure on college resources sees flight of talent. *Irish Examiner.* Retrieved from http://www.irishexaminer.ie/ireland/pressure-on-college-resources-sees-flight-of-talent

National Council for Curriculum and Assessment. (2007). *Assessment in the primary school curriculum – Guidelines for schools.* Dublin: NCCA Publication.

Neavyn, R. (2012, February 3). New president sets out vision for WIT. *Education Matters.* Retrieved from http://www.educationmatters.ie/2012/02/03/new-president-sets-out-vision-for-wit/

O'Brien, S. (2012). Cultural regulation and the reshaping of the university. *Globalisation, Societies and Education, 10*(4), 539–562.

O'Brien, S., & Brancaleone, D. (2011). Evaluating learning outcomes: In search of lost knowledge. *Irish Educational Studies, 30*(1), 5–21.

O'Cathain, C. (2012, February 7). A strong case for a new university. *Irish Times.* Retrieved from http://www.irishtimes.com/newspaper/education/2012/0207/1224311389704_pf.html

O'Sullivan, D. (2005). *Cultural politics and Irish education since the 1950s: Policy paradigms and power.* Dublin: Institute of Public Administration Publication.

Olssen, M., & Peters, M. A. (2005). Neoliberalism, higher education and the knowledge economy: From the free market to knowledge capitalism. *Journal of Education Policy, 20*(3), 313–345.

Organisation for Economic Cooperation and Development. (2005). *Teachers matter: Attracting, retaining and developing teachers.* Paris: OECD Publication.

Roberts, P. (2007). Neoliberalism, performativity and research. *International Review of Education, 53*(4), 349–365.

Robertson, S. (2008). *The Bologna process goes global: A model, market mobility, brain power or state building strategy?* Invitational paper to ANPED's annual conference, October 2008, Recife.

Rose, N. (1999). *Governing the soul: Shaping of the private self.* London: Free Association Books.

Shutz, A., & Luckmann, T. (1973). *The structures of the life-world* (Vol. 1). Evanston: Northwestern University Press.

Sleeter, C. (2007). *Facing accountability in education: Democracy and equity at risk.* New York: Teachers College Press.

The Educational Research Centre. (2011). A response to chapter 6 of the Department of Education and Skills Document. *Better literacy and numeracy for children and young people: A draft national plan to improve literacy and numeracy in schools.* Dublin: St. Patrick's College.

Tuning Project. (2010). *Reference points for the design and delivery of degree programmes in education.* Retrieved from http://www.tuning.unideusto.org/tuningeu/

Walsh, E. (2011, November). 13 lessons we need to learn. *Irish Times Business Magazine,* 'Innovation', pp. 24–25.

Youdell, D. (2006). *Impossible bodies, impossible selves: Exclusions and student subjectivities.* Dordrecht: Springer Publication.

Chapter 12
Teaching Methods and Professional Teaching in Adult Education: Questioning the Memorandum's Understanding of Professional Teaching

Regina Egetenmeyer and Patrick Bettinger

Introduction

In its *Memorandum on Lifelong Learning* (Commission of the European Communities 2000), the European Commission presented a strategy for lifelong learning at the beginning of the twenty-first century, which heavily focuses on the individual learner and on methods of self-directed learning. This focus coincides with the lifelong learning strategies of other international organisations such as the OECD and UNESCO. It sees learning as an activity that ultimately remains the responsibility of individual learners:

> In practice, the achievements of these [education and training, RE & PB] systems are dependent … not least upon the efforts of individuals themselves, who, in the last instance, are responsible for pursuing their own learning. (ibid., p. 5)

It sees "individual motivation to learning and a variety of learning opportunities" (ibid., p. 8) as "ultimate keys to implementing lifelong learning successfully" (ibid., p. 5).

The *Memorandum* seems to consider the role of teachers and trainers as marginal. They appear within "Key Message 3: Innovation in teaching and learning" with the objective to "develop effective teaching and learning methods and contexts for the continuum of lifelong and lifewide learning" (ibid., p. 13). The *Memorandum* emphasises self-directed learning and a new role for learning professionals:

> Teaching as a professional role faces decisive change in the coming decades: teachers and trainers become guides, mentors and mediators. Their role – and it is a crucially important

R. Egetenmeyer (✉)
Julius-Maximilians-University Würzburg, Faculty of Arts II, Institute for Education,
Professorship for Adult and Continuing Education, Oswald-Külpe-Weg 82,
97074 Würzburg, Germany
e-mail: regina.egetenmeyer@uni-wuerzburg.de

P. Bettinger
University of Augsburg, Faculty of Philosophy and Social Sciences, Institut of Media and
Communication Science, Media Didactis, Universitätsstraße 10, 86159 Augsburg, Germany
e-mail: patrick.bettinger@phil.uni-augsburg.de

G.K. Zarifis and M.N. Gravani (eds.), *Challenging the 'European Area of Lifelong Learning': A Critical Response*, Lifelong Learning Book Series 19,
DOI 10.1007/978-94-007-7299-1_12, © Springer Science+Business Media Dordrecht 2014

one – is to help and support learners who, as far as possible, take charge of their own learning. The capacity and the confidence to develop and practise open and participatory teaching and learning methods should therefore become an essential professional skill for educators and trainers, in both formal and non-formal settings. (ibid., p. 14)

This demand goes hand in hand with the requirement for innovative teaching and learning methods. Therefore, the *Memorandum* sees high potential in ICT-based learning technologies. To bring these new teaching and learning methods into practice, the *Memorandum* requests teachers and trainers "to adapt, upgrade and sustain" (ibid., p. 14) their skills. This is requested from all education and training practitioners:

> … whether as paid professionals, as volunteers or as those for whom teaching activities are a secondary or ancillary function (for example, experienced skilled tradespeople in the workplace or community development workers). (ibid., p. 14)

Under the perspective of professional teaching, the main focus of the *Memorandum* is on skills to develop and practise innovative teaching and learning methods. This paper questions the close link between teaching and learning methods on the one hand and professional teaching on the other. Thereby the paper focuses on teachers and trainers in adult education: under the perspective of professionalisation, the paper questions the role of teaching and learning methods within the professionalisation of teachers and trainers in adult education. Subsequently, the complexity of learning processes is scrutinised under the perspective of teaching and learning research. Under the perspective of evaluation studies, the paper also highlights empirical findings that deal with the effects of innovative teaching. These perspectives end in the conclusion, which summarises the position of teaching and learning methods within professional teaching in adult education.

Perspectives of Professionalisation of Adult Teachers and Trainers

In the transnational European context, one can find diverse competence models for adult learning professionals. Especially within European projects, diverse European experts and stakeholders have developed competence models aimed, for example, at the validation and/or development of competences of teachers and trainers in adult education.

The projects "Learning 4 Sharing" (Carlsen and Irons 2003) and "A good adult educator in Europe (AGADE)" (Jääger et al. 2006) identify 4 roles and 16 criteria, which teachers and trainers in adult education should fulfil. As roles for teachers and trainers in adult education, the projects formulate "teacher", "guide", "facilitator" and "trainer". The listed 16 criteria are grouped into two areas: (1) personal development, which is understood as the ethical dimension, and (2) professional development, which is subdivided into the three dimensions of (a) knowledge, (b) skills and (c) organisation. These three dimensions are attributed to the organisational stage, the performance stage and the evaluation stage of learning processes. In this model, "knowledge of methods in adult education (AE) and learning" (ibid., p. 18) could be found as one criterion within the organisational stage of learning processes: "knowledge and ability to choose different ways of teaching and learning according to the content of learning and participants' interests, abilities and experiences". However, you can also find indirect hints towards teaching and learning methods within the performance stage: the "ability to motivate for learning", the "development of learning environment" and "skills to activate learners" also require expertise in using teaching and learning methods. In this model, teaching and learning methods are integrated into a complex competence setting of teachers and trainers in adult education.

The project "Learning 4 Sharing" refers to necessary variations in the use of teaching and learning methods as well as its manipulative potential:

> There is no one and only "salvation method" or "best for everything" method. The key word we should bear in mind is – variation! The more methods you master, the more you are able to vary. … In some way all of the methods are about manipulation. However, some of them are more manipulative than others. The adult educator has to be sure to have his/her "ethical compass" turned on. (Carlsen and Irons 2003)

The transnational project "VINEPAC" (Sava et al. 2008) developed a validation instrument for teachers and trainers in adult and continuing education. This model distinguishes between five competence clusters. It contains teaching and learning methods within the competence "training programme delivery" in the competence cluster "training management". Within this competence, the validation instrument considers the "… use suitable teaching strategies" as a performance criterion. Within the entire concept of the validation instrument, using teaching and learning methods seems to be only one small competence within a complex cluster of competences. The instrument includes a knowledge base focused on adult learners and group dynamics. It demands competences concerning needs analysis, the preparation of training programmes, training programme delivery and the use of technology and resources. Furthermore, the model validates competences concerning the assessment and validation of learning, motivation and counselling, as well as personal and professional development.

The study "Key competences for adult learning professionals" (Research voor Beleid 2010) was carried out on behalf of the European Commission. The study developed a competence model for adult educators. The basis of the model was the analysis of academic and policy-related documents, job descriptions, job advertisements, competence profiles and the learning outcomes of educational programmes. These were accompanied by several expert workshops. As a result, the model formulates seven generic and 12 specific competences. While the seven generic competences should be fulfilled by all professionals working in adult education, the 12 specific competences focus on requirements that an adult education organisation should fulfil. Teaching and learning methods can be found within the generic competences as "didactical competences", which should be fulfilled by all professionals "involved in the learning process or supportive in a managerial, administrative way" (ibid., p. 11). This competence focuses on:

> Making use of different learning methods, styles and techniques including new media and awareness of new possibilities, including e-skills and ability to assess them critically: being able to deploy different learning methods, styles and techniques in working with adults. (ibid., p. 50)

Compared to the other models, this model has the greatest tendency to see teaching and learning methods as a technique that should only be used within learning settings.

In contrast to these competence models, you can find, especially in the German context, an approach that is strongly influenced by a professionalisation discussion in an educational context. Based on this background, professionalism of adult educators is seen as a hermeneutic issue (cf. Egetenmeyer and Schüßler 2012). Based on the assumption of a "technology deficit"[1] of educational action, learning professionals are requested to challenge dubiety (Luhmann and Schorr 1982). Due to the complexity of education and learning processes, professionals cannot act according to a recipe or behaviour guidelines. There are no linear solutions for educational demands. Rather, educational situations have to be interpreted by teachers and trainers. Hereby, the ability to approach cases hermeneutically is the basic requirement for professional action.

Professionalism of adult educators consequently means "the ability to use broad, scientifically based and diverse abstract knowledge which is adequate in concrete situations. Or contrariwise: to acknowledge in just these situations which parts of the knowledge could be relevant"[2] (Tietgens 1988, p. 38). Gieseke (2010, p. 386) defines professionalism as "differentiated handling of research results of the discipline, together with interdisciplinary knowledge for the interpretation of an actor's situation in a specific practical field".[3]

But there is another dimension within educational action, which has to be handled by professionals in adult education: contradictions and antinomies (von Hippel 2011; von Hippel and Schmidt-Lauff 2012). Teachers and trainers in adult education have to deal with situations that are characterised by unsolvable contradictions on the level of knowledge, action and relationship. Therefore, the interpretation of these situations can be understood as a core competence. Professional action is thereby only possible on the basis of these interpretations.

From the perspective of professionalisation in adult education, the adaptation of innovative teaching and learning methods is missing. Besides, the reflection of the role of teachers and trainers in adult education, which is also mentioned in the *Memorandum* as a complex understanding of the competences, is missing. Furthermore, the *Memorandum* seems to have a technical understanding of the adaptation of teaching and learning methods. From the background of the characteristic of educational settings, this understanding ignores the complex needs of educational settings.

---

[1] Translated by the authors. Original in German, "Technologiedefizit".

[2] Translation from Egetenmeyer and Käpplinger (2011). Original in German, "Professionalität heißt, auf die Kurzformel gebracht, die Fähigkeit nutzen zu können, breit gelagerte, wissenschaftlich vertiefte und damit vielfältig abstrahierte Kenntnisse in konkreten Situationen angemessen anwenden zu können" (Tietgens 1988, p. 38).

[3] Translation from Egetenmeyer and Käpplinger (2011). Original in German, "sondern den differenzierten Umgang mit Forschungsbefunden aus der Disziplin und mit interdisziplinarem Wissen zur Deutung von Handlungssituationen mit Handlungsanspruch in einem bestimmten Praxisfeld" (Gieseke 2010, p. 386).

Perspectives of Teaching and Learning Research

If we take a closer and more sophisticated look at the aspects of successful teaching, we find a variety of factors. In the field of adult education, the range of tasks is quite widespread. Applying innovative teaching methods is only one aspect of professional teaching and training. Also important for a sustainable learning success is the quality of the relationship between teachers and learners (Wolf 2006) as well as the influences of the learning community (Mandl et al. 2004), the correct fit of the learning environment and the learners (Reinmann and Mandl 2006) and the teacher's ability to consider various aspects linked to learning processes (Kraft 2006; Illeris 2006).

By defining all personal relationships as depending on a specific history of interaction, Wolf (2006) states that these relationships always touch the present, the future and the past. The author concludes that it is a crucial aspect in the educational context of professional teaching to remember the history of interaction in order to build a fruitful relationship between teachers and learners. In this perspective, professional teaching increasingly depends on the teacher's ability to adapt his or her methods to the individual learning biography and learning experience. Consequently, social bonding is the main factor affecting all future learning experiences. It is the key to enduring educational productivity.

A similar statement is made by Mandl et al. (2004). The authors conclude that learning always takes place in a community. This implies certain cultural and social variables that influence the way we learn. Here, expertise is distributed in a specific way among the different persons to whom learners are connected. These communities can vary according to structural indicators (aims, microculture, interaction, organisational growth, life span and life cycles) and forms (learning communities, communities of practice, online communities and communities that enable continuing further education). If we follow the authors and assume that communities have a great influence on the learning process, we should question whether and in which way innovative teaching methods have an impact on the learning process.

Kraft (2006) takes a closer look at the meaning of learning in adult education and finds that a broader understanding of the concept, including "personal and social conditions of teaching and learning" (p. 212), has to be considered. In particular, self-directed learning demands a lot more than just the application of innovative teaching methods. Teachers and trainers are asked to support learners and keep in mind that they are dealing with different and individual ways of learning. A stable base of knowledge about adult learning and the ability to transfer this knowledge into practice seem to be more important than simply testing new didactical methods (cf. ibid.).

Reinmann and Mandl (2006) come to the conclusion that adapting teaching methods to the learners is the most promising way for a functioning learning environment. This adaptation can be realised in different manners, for example, by varying chronological interspaces, the way of adaptation or the purpose of adaptation. Such a procedure is supposed to enhance the learning output.

If we change our perspective from teaching to learning and consider theories related to the constructivist paradigm, some of these theories point towards a more or less humble influence of teachers on their learners. A constructivist view on learning considers the acquisition of knowledge to be an individual and internal process (cf. Pätzold 2011). It could thus be questioned how much those aspects that ostensibly do not deal with concrete teaching and learning situations (e.g. setting the right framework of the learning environment or the organisation and preparation of courses) gain a greater role in the learning process. These factors appear increasingly important in a constructivist view of learning. Looking at the *Memorandum*'s recommendations, innovative teaching has to consider this in order to be effective. In conclusion, the teacher's ability of context-based abstraction and reflection is considered to be an essential aspect for a fertile learning environment (cf. Faulstich 2003). These basic skills are a necessary foundation to foster teaching that adequately enhances individual learning processes.

In conclusion, innovation as a key to successful learning should not only be thought of in terms of teaching methods. Instead, a broader understanding of innovation implying different aspects of learning appears to be helpful. Facing the lack of empirical research in the field of innovative teaching, Mandl et al. (2004) propose design-based research or use inspired research studies. These approaches appear to give further insight into "how, when and why innovation in education can also in practice show positive effects" (ibid., p. 74). In researching learning with consideration to the close connection between theory and practice, the complexity of the phenomenon can be handled appropriately and innovative teaching is constantly evaluated and improved.

By defining three dimensions of learning, Illeris (2006) offers another perspective on the complexity of the phenomenon. Besides the interaction between individuals and their environment, learning occurs between the poles of recognition and emotion. In this framework, the dimensions recognition, emotion and environment are included in every kind of learning. Illeris, quite similarly to the community aspect mentioned by Mandl et al. (2004), adds that his model of a learning triangle is always embedded within a certain society. Here the question can be raised as to how innovative teaching can influence the different dimensions. It appears, for example, that emotional aspects of learning are most likely to defy direct methodological control.

The findings of teaching and learning research thus show the multiplicity of aspects linked to the success of learning. Regarding the professionalisation of adult teachers and trainers, they also show that it seems to be necessary to further discuss the idea of what the application of innovative methods can – and especially cannot – achieve.

Perspectives of Evaluation Studies

Further insight into the connection of innovative teaching methods and professional teaching can be found by taking a look at evaluation studies. Kehoe et al. (2004) found that it is not necessarily an improvement for learners if they have the choice between alternative types of courses. Even if some of the students in this study seem to benefit from new forms of teaching and assessment, the authors point out that innovative teaching can lead to inferior learning results in other cases. Especially when the didactical design involves ICT, it is important to keep in mind the individual premises of the learners and their ability to engage in self-directed learning.

Further research indicates that, for example, the target group of elderly people can be put off by the implementation of ICT in the learning context – even if they are generally interested in learning with new media (cf. Gehrke 2008). As a result, they withdraw from learning. In order to prevent such a distortion, a fundamental role is seen in the preparation of courses, especially regarding the analysis of the target group. This should also be considered when new media are going to be implemented in learning contexts (cf. Weidenmann 2006). Professional adult educators need to critically analyse the application of ICT in order to avoid an inconsiderate following of trends. Particularly when it comes to the implementation of ICT, it is a challenge for every professional to keep the diversity of the target group in mind to really benefit from the potential.

In the course itself, empathy of teachers has proved to be a promising basis for adapting teaching methods to the skills of their learners (cf. Tippelt and Schmidt 2009). For example, elderly learners can then integrate their own expertise and life experience into the course. On the one hand, this serves as a valuable source for a whole course; on the other, the learners gain confidence and feel esteemed.

Rindermann (2003) analyses a variety of national and international evaluation studies in the context of higher education and refers to the question of which traits characterise good lecturers and good lectures. He points out that structuring and clarification are the main factors to be considered. In his multidimensional model of successful learning, Rindermann underlines the multitude of influences. Referring to higher education, the author states that "the quality of teaching in higher education exceeds the quality of courses. It covers content aspects as well as target, process and framework requirements ..."[4] (ibid., p. 237). In this respect, "good teaching is not only achievable by particular didactically successful courses. Moreover, it has to be integrated into an appropriate subject-related environment, a university and adjuvant framework"[5] (ibid., p. 237).

Evaluation research thus confirms that successful learning depends on a multitude of impact factors. Innovative teaching can therefore be regarded as one aspect among many that can influence our learning in a positive way. It is essential to remember that it takes more than developing and applying new methods to obtain a sustainable basis for successful learning. Innovation is only useful when

---

[4] Translated by the authors. Original in German, "Die Qualität der Lehre an Hochschulen geht über die der Veranstaltungen hin- aus. Sie umfasst inhaltliche sowie formale Ziel-, Prozess- und Bedingungsgrößen ..." (Rindermann 2003, p. 237).

[5] Translated by the authors. Original in German, "Gute Lehre ist nicht nur durch einzelne didaktisch erfolgreiche Lehrveranstaltungen erreichbar, sondern muss in ein entsprechendes Umfeld eines Faches, einer Universität und förderlicher gesellschaftlicher Rahmenbedingungen eingebettet sein" (Rindermann 2003, p. 237).

there is a clear improvement – in this case for the learners in adult education and training – and it takes a further deepening of the professionalisation debate as well as more empirical research on the subject to get a more profound picture of the ways innovative teaching and learning success are connected. The argumentation of the *Memorandum* falls short in suggesting a clear link between these statements.

Conclusion

From the perspective of professionalisation, the application of methods for teaching and learning only serves as one of many competences. A complex cluster of competences is necessary to provide professional teaching for adults. Research shows that innovative teaching methods are less relevant than the appropriate adaptation of methods. Teaching methods cannot be applied in a universal way; they have to be adjusted to the target group, the topic, the framework and the situation to promote success in the learning process.

The adoption of ICT-based teaching methods requires particular attention. There are target groups that can be put off by such a learning scenario. This causes learning barriers that prevent an enhancement of learning.

Finally, the term "effectiveness" of methods does not seem to be the appropriate choice in the context of innovative methods and professional teaching. Rather, "adequacy" appears to be a helpful concept. Teaching and learning situations cannot be planned in a technological manner but require individual adjustment to the particular situation. Thus, teaching and training methods can be seen as one condition among others that have to be considered.

We therefore see a need for the further development of the issue of the *Memorandum*'s understanding of professional teaching. It needs to go beyond teaching methods and the role of professionals in teaching and learning scenarios. Adult education plays a central role in the realisation of lifelong learning in Europe. As adult education has various target groups, a fixed set of teaching methods is neither appropriate nor sufficient. To cope with the demands in adult education, this paper shows that a complex competence set is necessary for professional teaching.

References

Carlsen, A., & Irons, J. (Eds.). (2003). *Learning 4 sharing: Manual for adult education practitioners*. Vilnius. http://www.kansanopistot.fi/nvl/learning4sharing/contents.html

Commission of the European Communities. (2000). *A memorandum on lifelong learning*. Brussels. http://www.bologna-berlin2003.de/pdf/MemorandumEng.pdf

Egetenmeyer, R., & Käpplinger, B. (2011). Professionalisation and quality management: Struggles, boundaries and bridges between two approaches. *European Journal for Research* on the Education and Learning of Adults, 2(1), 21–35. http://www.rela.ep.liu.se/issues/10.3384_rela.2000-7426.201121/rela0058/10.3384rela.2000-7426.rela0058.pdf

Egetenmeyer, R., & Schüßler, I. (2012). Zur akademischen Professionalisierung in der Erwachsenenbildung/Weiterbildung. In R. Egetenmeyer & I. Schüßler (Eds.), Akademische Professionalisierung in der Erwachsenenbildung/Weiterbildung (pp. 7–25). Hohengehren: Schneider.

Faulstich, P. (2003). "Selbstbestimmtes Lernen" – vermittelt durch die Professionalität der Lehrenden. In U. Witthaus, W. Wittwer, & E. Clemens (Eds.), Selbstgesteuertes Lernen. Theoretische und praktische Bezüge (pp. 91–101). Bielefeld: Bertelsmann.

Gehrke, B. (2008). Ältere Menschen und Neue Medien. Entwicklungschancen für künftige Medienprojekte für Frauen und Männer mit Lebenserfahrung in Nordrhein-Westfalen. www. ecmc.de/teedrei/uploads/media/expertise_deutsch.pdf

Gieseke, W. (2010). Was ist erwachsenenpädagogische Professionalität? In H. U. Otto, T. Rauschenbach, & P. Vogel (Eds.), Erziehungswissenschaft: Professionalität und Kompetenz (pp. 197–208). Opladen: Leske u Budrich.

Illeris, K. (2006). Das "Lerndreieck". Rahmenkonzept für ein übergreifendes Verständnis vom menschlichen Lernen. In E. Nuissl (Ed.), Vom Lernen zum Lehren. Lern- und Lehrforschung für die Weiterbildung (pp. 29–41). Bielefeld: Bertelsmann.

Jääger, T., Irons, J., & Varga, K. (Eds.). (2006). Agade. Towards becoming a good adult educator. Course book. http://www.nordvux.net/download/1740/manual_for_ae_prac.pdf.

Kehoe, J., Tennet, B., & Windknecht, K. (2004). The challenge of flexible and non-traditional learning and teaching methods: Best practice in every situation? Studies in Learning, Evaluation, Innovation and Development, 1(1), 56–63.

Kraft, S. (2006). Die Lehre lebt. "Lehrforschung" und Fachdidaktiken für die Weiterbildung – Resümee und Forschungsbedarfe. In E. Nuissl (Ed.), Vom Lernen zum Lehren. Lern- und Lehrforschung für die Weiterbildung (pp. 29–41). Bielefeld: Bertelsmann.

Luhmann, N., & Schorr, E. (1982). Zwischen Technologie und Selbstreferenz. Frankfurt am Main: Suhrkamp.

Mandl, H., Kopp, B., & Dvorak, S. (2004). Aktuelle theoretische Ansätze und empirische Befunde im Bereich der Lehr-Lern-Forschung. Schwerpunkt Erwachsenenbildung. http://www.die-bonn.de/esprid/dokumente/doc-2004/mandl04_01.pdf

Pätzold, H. (2011). Learning and teaching in adult education. Contemporary theories. Opladen/Farmington Hills: Barbara Budrich Publishers.

Reinmann, G., & Mandl, H. (2006). Unterrichten und Lernumgebungen gestalten. In A. Krapp & B. Weidenmann (Eds.), Pädagogische Psychologie. Ein Lehrbuch (5th ed., pp. 613–658). Weinheim und Basel: Beltz.

Research voor Beleid. (2010). Key competences for adult learning professionals. Contribution to the development of a reference framework of key competences for adult learning professionals (Final report). Zoetermeer. http://ec.europa.eu/education/moreinformation/doc/2010/keycomp.pdf

Rindermann, H. (2003). Lehrevaluation an Hochschulen: Schlussfolgerungen aus Forschung und Anwendung für Hochschulunterricht und seine Evaluation. Zeitschrift für Evaluation, 2, 233–256.

Sava, S., et al. (2008). Handbook for the use of Validpack: For the validation of psycho-pedagogical adult-educator's competences. Timisoara: Ortpm.

Tietgens, H. (1988). Professionalität für die Erwachsenenbildung. In W. Gieseke (Ed.), Professionalität und Professionalisierung (pp. 37–41). Bad Heilbrunn: Klinkhard.

Tippelt, R., & Schmidt, B. (2009). Handlungsempfehlungen und Forschungsdesiderate. In R. Tippelt, B. Schmidt, S. Schnurr, & C. Theisen (Eds.), Bildung Älterer: Chancen im demographischen Wandel (pp. 198–206). Bielefeld: Bertelsmann.

von Hippel, A. (2011). Programmplanungshandeln im Spannungsfeld heterogener Erwartungen: ein Ansatz zur Differenzierung von Widerspruchskonstellationen und professionellen Antinomien. REPORT – Zeitschrift für Weiterbildungsforschung, 34(1), 45–57.

von Hippel, A., & Schmidt-Lauff, S. (2012). Antinomien akademischer Professionalisierung. Studienmotive und Erwartungen von Erwachsenenbildungsstudierenden. In R. Egetenmeyer &

I. Schüßler (Eds.), *Akademische Professionalisierung in der Erwachsenenbildung/ Weiterbildung* (pp. 81–93). Hohengehren: Schneider.

Weidenmann, B. (2006). Lernen mit Medien. In A. Krapp & B. Weidenmann (Eds.), *Pädagogische Psychologie. Ein Lehrbuch* (5th ed., pp. 423–476). Weinheim und Basel: Beltz.

Wolf, G. (2006). Der Beziehungsaspekt in der Dozent-Teilnehmer-Beziehung als Ressource und Detminante lebenslangen Lernens. *REPORT -Zeitschrift für Weiterbildungsforschung, 29*(1), 27–36.

Chapter 13
From 'Innovation' to 'Quality': The Topic of Professionalisation for Adult Learning Staff in Selected European Policy Documents

Simona Sava

Introduction

Education plays an important role in European policymaking, as it is relevant not only for the common labour market but also for the ambitious goal of developing the most competitive knowledge society in a global perspective.

To achieve this goal by means of improving the competencies of the European population and labour force, the European Commission has been active since the Maastricht Treaty (1992) by launching programmes, organising debates and discourses and structuring the field in papers, communications, action plans and comparative and monitoring studies and reports. For this purpose, the professionals in education are important conditioning factors, facilitating the competence acquisition.

My interest is related to the European policymaking for the professionals in adult education, and I am trying to identify which aspects of 'professionalisation' can be found in the relevant European documents and to what extent they are stressed. In order to understand the principles and to be able to put the measures of the EU in a certain framework, I will look at the relevant documents following more specific the questions: which importance is put on the professionals and is there a change over the years? To do so, my article will focus on the period between 2000 and 2010: this period starts with the Lisbon Goals and *A Memorandum on Lifelong Learning* which sets certain goals for 2010, and it ends with a summary of the achievements, the new goals and the guidelines until 2020. Thus, it is also from the point of view of the policymakers a defined decade which begins and ends, as the set goals are for such period (see 'Lisbon 2010', 'Europe 2020').

S. Sava (✉)
Department of Education Sciences, Faculty of Sociology and Psychology,
West University of Timisoara, Timisoara, Romania
e-mail: ssava@socio.uvt.ro

G.K. Zarifis and M.N. Gravani (eds.), *Challenging the 'European Area of Lifelong Learning': A Critical Response*, Lifelong Learning Book Series 19, DOI 10.1007/978-94-007-7299-1_13, © Springer Science+Business Media Dordrecht 2014

The selection of the documents to be analysed is based on three criteria: the range of documents has to cover all members states, but also candidate states, the character has to be summarising, aim-oriented towards promoting and stimulating lifelong learning, and the concept has to be related to developing practice and to initiating activities. According to these criteria, the content analysis will cover five documents:

1. *A Memorandum on Lifelong Learning* (2000)
2. *Making a European Area of Lifelong Learning a Reality* (2001)
3. *Adult Learning: It Is Never Too Late to Learn* – Communication from the Commission on Adult Learning (2006)
4. *Action Plan on Adult Learning: It Is Always a Good Time to Learn* (2007)
5. *Renewed European Agenda for Adult Learning* (2011)

The frame of interpretation will be to put the documents briefly in their historical context, pointing out the main purpose of the documents and identifying the paragraphs which are directly oriented to the professionals and the staff in adult education, irrespective of their name (i.e. 'facilitators'). As it will be pointed out later on, in the documents from the beginning of the decade, the staff working in adult education was mainly seen as trainers, teachers, mentors and facilitators; from the second part of the decade, however, they are called 'professionals' or 'adult learning staff' in a broader way highlighting the fact that the policy messages cover all staff, not only the trainers, and that this staff should be professionalised or at least considered as a professional group.

A Memorandum on Lifelong Learning

A Memorandum on Lifelong Learning (2000) had the explicit purpose to 'launch a European-wide debate on a comprehensive strategy for implementing lifelong learning at individual and institutional levels, and in all spheres of public and private life' (European Commission 2000, p.3). The character of the Memorandum was unique at that time as an important means of policymaking in the field of education, which is – since Maastricht – part of the political agenda of the EU but only in form of a so-called soft and open method of coordination. The member states kept their autonomy in this crucial field so that it is not compulsory for them any decision of any body of the EU in regard with education. The form of common discourse to replace political decisions was not new, but very innovative in this dimension and in the procedure: launching a paper with a certain aim, relaunching it 1 year later with a supposed stronger message to be followed as it is including the feedback of all the participating member states and it has the form of a common compromise/agreement.

The *Memorandum* contains six 'messages' to ensure lifelong learning as a guiding principle of provision and participation at education and training (E&T). One of them was 'the innovation in teaching and learning' (message 3). The other one, which is closely related to the work of the staff in adult education (AE), is message number five 'rethinking guidance and counseling'. Both messages describe the role and the tasks of the people working in the field.

The new teaching role and methods are considered to be new and represent a paradigmatic 'shift' from 'the traditional way of teaching in the at least half a century' (European Commission 2000, p.14); it is also meant for user-oriented learning systems, with the independent learner in the centre and teachers with a more supportive and facilitating role. In empirical and theoretical works related to the educational systems, this 'shift' of paradigm is indeed considered to have happened in the mid-1990s (Nuissl 2010). Since the document sees this development as a new one, it calls for 'innovations' in teaching role, methods and integration of counselling. The big innovation is seen in relation with the ICT use and related new teaching methods, the collaboration of ICT technicians and teachers and databases and the increase of counselling opportunities.

In order to sustain innovation, 'applied educational research' effort should be raised so as to inform the practice about the missing knowledge on 'how to generate productive self-directed learning, […] how senior citizens best learn, how to adjust learning environments' (European Commission 2000, pp.14–15). It is interesting that this idea of educational research is left out in further policy documents.

Besides 'innovation', two other terms are used as aims to be reached in relation with the teaching and learning methods and contexts: the (improving) *quality* and the *effective* performance. In this respect, '*significant investment* by Member States to adapt, upgrade and sustain the skills of those working in formal and non-formal learning environments, whether as paid professionals, as volunteers or as those for whom teaching activities are secondary or ancillary function' (European Commission 2000, p.14) should be undertaken. These desiderata can be found as ideas in the further policy documents from the middle and the end of the decade (see the ones analysed later on); the direct link to the Memorandum is not even mentioned. Since an aim of the Memorandum was 'to debate on a comprehensive strategy for implementing lifelong learning', it is highly important to research to what extent the member states can report such investment and such priority action, mainly that such message comes again in all the analysed documents, as direct solution for ensuring the needed quality.

But when it comes further to the qualifications of the teachers and trainers, they are mentioned as follows: 'Training courses and qualifications for education and training practitioners in non-formal sectors […], in adult education or in continuing training are under-developed everywhere in Europe. What can be done to improve this situation, including through European co-operation?' (ibid., p.15). 'What can be done to modernize and improve initial and in-service training for guidance and counseling practitioners? Where are the most urgent needs for enriched training?' (ibid., p.18).

The openness of these questions shows that there is hardly any concrete idea about the specific lack of competences and the appropriate ways to solve the given underdevelopment. It is mentioned, in a rather vague way, that something should be done. Unfortunately, this vague way is kept in the further documents, possible reasons for such situation being either the lack of research in this area to feed the content and suitable practices or the lack of reliable experiences which have been proven efficient and, therefore, might be extended to a large scale or the missing concrete point of view and the determinate willingness to act from the policymakers.

Taking a look at the priorities of the messages, the *Memorandum* puts the innovation in teaching and learning in the third place and the improvement and fostering of counselling in the fifth. This will change after the feedback of the discussions in the member states. This changed priority might be indirectly foreseen from the wording used in the Memorandum as the appellative attached to the counsellors is 'professionals', but teachers and trainers are seen only as practitioners who need to upgrade their skills and knowledge. Such different naming can be understood also because of a long period of practice in teaching and learning, but a rather limited one in counselling, a new complex service to be set up in a systematic way and performed therefore by specialised people, specially prepared in this respect.

Making a European Area of Lifelong Learning a Reality (2001)

This document has been completed and published 1 year after the Memorandum, only a short period if we were to take into consideration the large consultation process (over 12,000 stakeholders from around Europe; see European Commission 2001, p.8). It unites the revisions done by the member states to the Memorandum. The order of the messages is now changed: information, guidance and counselling are on the second place (behind 'valuing learning'), whereas 'innovative pedagogy' comes at the end as the sixth message. Obviously the national debates prioritised the messages differently compared to the original Memorandum.

The consultation feedback confirms the shift from 'knowledge' to 'competence' and from teaching to learning (ibid., p.23), as well as the growing importance of guidance and counselling in a system of education, in which learners find their own individual pathways.

The information, counselling and guidance (ICG) are seen as an integrative part of at least three building blocks of the lifelong learning strategy, the 'facilitating access to learning opportunities', 'creating a learning culture' and 'partnership working'. ICG as support service accompanying the individuals amongst the education and training system needs to develop and enhance its quality, concrete actions being pointed out in this respect in the document. But the counsellors are mentioned only indirectly, in relation to the quality of the service, as 'guidance workers' who need a training (ibid., p.18). There is no mentioning about their competencies or about the professionals to run these services, but only about the fact that the envisaged European Guidance Forum will reflect on the 'quality of guidance provision, with a view to developing common guidelines and quality standards for guidance services and products' (ibid., p.18).

Concerning the 'innovative pedagogy' priority of action, the innovation is very much related to the ICT potential for supporting learning. This aspect is stressed further in the document (ibid., p.27) while listing the indicators for measuring progress in lifelong learning: 'innovative pedagogy (e-Learning is particularly relevant in this priority)'. The innovation comes also from the paradigmatic shift from teacher to learner, from the changed roles of the teachers, seen as 'learning facilitators' (see the glossary in Annex 2, p.33), and requires different competencies for teachers, as well as further training. This time the term 'competence' is used as such, and, in order to master it, concrete fields of needed training (i.e. in 'multicultural competences' – p.24) or exchange of experience are mentioned. In this respect, not only the financial resources of the Socrates or Leonardo da Vinci programmes are put in place by the Commission but also the Commission commits itself to 'contribute to the construction of a common framework of reference for the competencies and qualifications of teachers and trainers' (ibid., p.24), pointing out that the member states should make 'development opportunities accessible to learning facilitators', mainly to the ones in non-formal adult education, where the formal training is not a requirement, but an improved quality of training is needed. Later on, it can be noticed that the commitment of the European Commission was partly fulfilled, with the study done in 2010 under the coordination of Research voor Beleid, '*Key competences for adult learning professionals – Contribution to the development of a reference framework of key competences for adult learning professionals*', complementing more specific for the adult educators the general development of the 'European Framework of Qualifications' (EQF). But the structure of qualifications is not set up yet, and neither is the way of how this may be done. The later documents are just mentioning generally that the member states should set up effective systems of initial and continuing professional development.

Also, the financial resources are made available for researching the way adults learn and for developing 'efficient and effective pedagogic approaches for various groups of learners' (ibid., p.30), in the first Annex, with the research proposals until the end of 2003 the ones sustaining the innovative pedagogy being amongst the first ones.

The document is more concrete than the *Memorandum* on good reasons: it is no longer oriented to structure a discussion, but to structure real activities in the member states, based on their feedback. That is why the document mentions concrete divisions of roles in this agenda, both of the Commission and of the actors from state/regional/local level. The document shows a rather clear view of the reality in the field and the variety of stakeholders to be involved, pointing out in a more direct manner, on one hand the gaps (i.e. lack of training (opportunities), lack of enough research input for developing innovative pedagogy and enabling teachers and trainers in this respect) and on the other hand the responsibilities and the roles each (institutional) actor should play in the attempt to improve the practice of fostering adult's learning.

It Is Never Too Late to Learn (2006)

This document follows the activities in the field of adult education which have been realised in the years after the *Making a European Area of Lifelong Learning a Reality*, which was actually the first 'action plan' in lifelong learning. It points out the achievements made in the last 5 years and gives perspectives for the remaining 5 years until the end of the decade in 2010.

Amongst the messages of the document, the question of staff and professionals gained a higher priority than before (part of the 2nd message), and it is much more concrete in pointing out the needs of this professional group, both for career prospects and for professional development. They are seen as determinant of quality and emphasised as focus in relation to adult learning (see the title of the second message, 'Ensuring quality of the adult learning').

The role of the system of education is pointed out much stronger than in the earlier documents, and the paradigmatic shift from teacher to learner is reconsidered, as it is noticed that 'poor quality of provision of adult learning leads to poor quality of learning outcomes' (European Commission 2006, p.6). Therefore, ensuring quality in adult learning is discussed more differentiated from the teaching methods and the didactic setting until the quality of providers and of the delivery, the quality of staff being a distinct factor. Above all there is pointed out the strong relation between staff competences and the aim of higher quality of teaching and learning: 'The professional development of people working in adult learning is a vital determinant of the quality of adult learning' (ibid., p.7).

In the didactic setting, the ICT disappeared totally, and it is not talked anymore about innovation, but about learning outcomes, and how to ensure them. In order to make 'explicit' the 'intended learning outcomes' (ibid., p.6), a concrete stipulation is made in the document, showing the need of the politicians for tangible and measurable results and concrete mentioning of what teachers provide to the public and to the learners. Furthermore, concrete learning support resources are to be made available to the learners, meaning that the work of the teachers and trainers should be better documented and made visible and more easily measurable/controlled. So, one might argue that such stipulations are not meant to only support the learner or to guide him/her but to ensure a better control on the quality of provision and professional behaviour of teacher in the classroom.

Compared with the former documents, not only the need for training and competence development is pointed out here, but the heterogeneity of the group is also described and the challenges for a system of training as different professional pathways are undertaken and are to be recognised, valorised and integrated. In this Communication the other categories of 'adult learning staff', not only the teachers and trainers, are acknowledged, and all the 'adult learning personnel' is taken into consideration. The counsellors are not mentioned anymore distinctly, and the counselling as a whole is less stressed, being pointed out only at the end of message one.

The ways to become a professional, as well as the career perspectives, are seen as elements of a system which has to allow a status and working condition of a higher quality. Concern is expressed therefore not only about more in depth analysis of the work done by them and on the different routes to becoming practitioner in this field but about the needed training and qualification, as 'little attention has been paid to defining the content and processes for initial training of adult learning staff, and... the profession is not always recognized within formal career structures. ... Member States should... put in place initial and continuing professional development measures to qualify and up-skill people working in adult learning' (ibid., p.7).

Arguing at this macro-system level, the needed research is not related anymore to didactical innovation but to providing the needed data for evidence policy-making (ibid., p.9), like 'defining the content and processes for the training of adult learning staff' or describing the needs for continuing professional development and upskill, for instance. Also, benchmarks, frames of competencies and instruments are needed to recognise and integrate the different professional paths into 'formal career structures'.

Financial resources, concludes the second message, should be used for improving the teaching materials and for qualifying and up-skill people working in adult learning' (ibid., p.8), as preconditions for the quality of learning. However, better quality assurance mechanisms are also demanded, for a better checking of the provision.

It could be foreseen that these concrete contributions to the discussion, which have been already running in some member states at this time, would have some follow-ups in the action plan that has been launched on the basis of this document 1 year later.

It Is Always a Good Time to Learn (2007)

In this *Action Plan on Adult Learning*, concrete actions are drawn (for 2008–2010) at the policy, governance and delivery levels, in order to implement the messages launched in the *Communication on Adult Learning* in 2006.

The topic of quality of teaching and learning is in this document, the main point of the argumentation. Even more, the paradigmatic shift is moving back to teaching, as the role of the teacher in supporting and stimulating adults to learn is recognised (mainly of the ones with limited study skills): 'the quality of staff is crucial in motivating adult learners to participate' (European Commission 2007, p.9). Such consideration is to be seen, however, not only as a recognition of the importance of the teacher in the relation teacher-learner but also as a demand for the teacher moving the responsibility on the teacher's shoulders to attract adults to learning, as the figures show that adults do not participate in lifelong learning by themselves.

In order to 'improve the quality of provision in adult learning sector' (the title of the third priority of action), the main concern is represented by the quality of the staff which is seen as the most important conditioning factor. If in the *Communication* from 2006 ensuring quality of adult learning on four different coordinates (*teaching methods, quality of staff, quality of providers, quality of delivery*) was discussed, in the *Action Plan*, the didactic settings and teaching methods are left out, and the concern is moved towards the institutional aspects ensuring the quality of provision. The provision is seen in a wider way (not only of courses), and, therefore, the staff ensuring it is distinctly mentioned: 'management, guidance personnel, mentors and administration' (ibid., p.9). Thus, the former wording of 'teachers and trainers' is changed with 'adult learning staff', being explicitly mentioned who they are, beside the teachers and trainers, as all of them have their role in provision. As wording 'adult learning professionals' is also used, suggesting not only the need for the better understanding of this group of professions but also its more systematic regulation, once it is aimed to set professional standards for the personnel performing them (at a certain qualitative level).

For improving the quality of provision, concrete actions are foreseen for 2008 (comparative studies), for 2009 (standards for adult learning professionals) and for 2010 (research on the development of quality standards for providers).

The study on *Adult Learning Professions in Europe* (*ALPINE*) (see Research voor Beleid 2008) shows on one hand the need to map the landscape of existing occupations fostering the learning of adults (distinctly enumerated here), as still too little is known in a systematic way, and, on the other hand, points out the solution of promoting the learning from each other and capitalising on existing good practices. The comparative analysis on adult learning professions covers not only the systems of training and qualification but also their status and payment, meaning that deeper understanding of the system and context of their work as well should be provided.

In this way, more coherent basis for policymaking can be ensured, and also the building up on existing positive developments, without neglecting them by 'innovations', paradigmatic shifts and so on, now left out.

Two of the three distinct actions to be undertaken in this period concern the adult learning staff, showing the importance attached to them in the quality of provision frame, but also the need for a better understanding and also standardisation of the profession. However, the attempt of the Commission to develop standards for adult learning professional until 2009 is one of concern, taking into account the heterogeneity of this professional group and the specificity, for instance, of those working in liberal adult education, compared to the ones working in vocational education. Not only the variety and specificity of the work the professionals perform in different sectors of adult education make such attempts difficult, but also one can question to what extent it is needed: can everything be standardised? Who defines a professional and by what standards? With what authority does the Commission decides upon the professional profile of a particular group?

Although it is difficult to put standards, the main effort carried in these 3 years was spent on developing standards and the research on the development of quality standards. This is a cautious way of acting, but irrespective of the sensitivity of this aspect, the coherence of acting at all levels of policy circle, including the evaluation and monitoring, in order to ensure the aimed quality, can be noticed.

Renewed European Agenda for Adult Learning (2011)

This document resumes the performances of the previous decade, welcoming the fact that 'quality assurance has been raised as an important issue in adult learning and strides are being made in developing the professional profile and training of adult learning professionals' (European Council 2011, p.5). Coherent and complementary to the actions undertaken in the previous action plan, for the period 2012–2014, the priorities of acting are very much comparable, with the *Improving the quality and efficiency of education and training* in the second place (ibid., p.15).

Amongst the next steps are strong desires for the quality of teaching staff; therefore, effective systems of initial and continuing professional development (CPD) are to be put into place. The further training is not meant to be an arbitrary one, but one done against a competency profile to be set and with carefully established career steps and levels of expertise which a coherent system of CPD should include. As policy measure, the mobility of adult education staff is mentioned.

The group of professionals is now not anymore the prerequisite for the quality of provisions and learning; they have the need of quality for their own learning, the right to have a qualified training, etc. Actually now the professionals are considered to play an important role in building up the lifelong learning.

Conclusions

The analysis of the documents launched at European level in this decade concerning the adult learning professionals pointed out different positions stressed towards this group of professionals having the role to sustain adult learning. Thus, it can be noticed that in the last part of the decade, there is more emphasis on the need to professionalise adult learning staff, considering that the quality of professional behaviour is seen as determinant for the quality of learning. This need comes as a solution to failing to attract 12 % of adult population to lifelong learning, thus better qualified staff being needed in this respect. Therefore, the last three documents emphasise more the needed steps towards a professional way of acting and for ensuring the competent adult learning staff.

This paper itself focused only on these documents, mapping in a wider way the efforts spent at European level for adult learning professionals, directly or indirectly. One can say that the actions cover all the policy circle, from the studies aimed to ground the policymaking (see 'ALPINE Report' 2008, and the consecutive one done by both Research voor Beleid in 2010 and 'Key competences for adult learning professionals'), formulating visions and setting policy agenda in different policy documents (as in the documents analysed) and putting in place tools and instruments for implementation (i.e. Europass, European Qualification Framework) and financial measures (see the grants available within the Lifelong Learning Programme) (Ferreira-Lourenco 2009), undertaking a close monitoring within the Progress reports or evaluation and impact studies (see the study on 'Achievements and results of implementing the Action Plan' or the one of 'West Scotland Colleges' in 2011). However, it is not clear to what extent such studies are used in further policy documents, neither if we can talk about a coherent evolution, as far as even the previous documents are mentioned, it cannot be derived that the new policy documents are built on lessons learnt, and impact analysis.

Nevertheless, in spite of all these efforts and developments, the questions launched as debate in Memorandum 'What can be done to modernize and improve initial and in-service training for ...practitioners? Where are the most urgent needs for enriched training?' are still not answered in a convincing way, and it is not clear how the 'effective' initial and CPD systems to be established by the member states might look like. Instead, the solution recommended is learning from each other with the help of staff mobility. The vague mentioning can be a reason for which the member states did not put in place such systems, and neither a wider training resources system for (up)skilling the adult learning professionals (see Sava 2011; Nuissl and Lattke 2008). It is to be seen if at the end of 2014 more concrete steps will be taken.

References

Commission of the European Communities. (2000). *A memorandum on lifelong learning*. Brussels: SEC(2000) 1832. http://ec.europa.eu/education/lifelong-learning-policy/doc/policy/memo_en.pdf

Commission of the European Communities. (2001). *Making a European area of lifelong learning a reality*. Brussels: COM(2001) 678. http://eur-lex.europa.eu/LexUriServ/LexUriServ.do?uri= COM:2001:0678:FIN:EN:PDF

Commission of the European Communities. (2006). *Adult learning: It is never too late to learn – Communication from the commission on adult learning*. Brussels: COM(2006) 614 final. http:// eur-lex.europa.eu/LexUriServ/site/en/com/2006/com2006_0614en01.pdf

Commission of the European Communities. (2007). *Action plan on adult learning: It is always a good time to learn – Communication from the commission on adult learning*. Brussels: COM(2007) 558. http://ec.europa.eu/education/policies/adult/com558_en.pdf

Commission of the European Communities. (2011). *Action plan on adult learning: Achievements and results 2008–2010*. Retrieved from http://ec.europa.eu/education/lifelong-learning-policy/ doc1288_en.htm

Ferreira-Lourenco, M. (2009). Achievements and challenges for adult education in Europe in the last decade. *Journal of Educational Sciences, 2*(20), 10–15. Timisoara: Ed. Universitatii de Vest; interview done by Simona Sava; www.resjournal.uvt.ro

Nuissl, E. (2010). From teaching to learning and back. In S. Sava (coord.). *10 ani de dezvoltare europeana in educatia adultilor – Realizari si provocari in atingerea obiectivelor "Lisabona 2010", volumul celei de-a treia Conferinte nationale de educaţie a adultilor [10 years of European development in adult education – Achievements and challenges in reaching the ai Member States of "Lisabona 2010" – the volume of the 3rd national conference on adult education]* (pp. 33–38). Timişoara: Ed. Eurostampa.

Nuissl, E., & Lattke, S. (Eds.). (2008). *Qualifying adult learning professionals in Europe*. Bielefeld: W. Bertelsmann Verlag.

Research voor Beleid. (2008). *ALPINE – Adult Learning Professionals in Europe. A study of the current situation, trends and issues*. Zoetermeei. http://ec.europa.eu/education/more-information/doc/ adultprofreport_en.pdf

Research voor Beleid. (2010). *Key competences for adult learning professionals. Contribution to the development of a reference framework of key competences for adult learning professionals*. Zoetermer. http://ec.europa.eu/education/more-information/doc/2010/keycomp.pdf

Sava, S. (2011, November). Towards the Professionalization of Adult Educators. *Andragogical Studies, Journal for the Study of Adult Education and Learning, 2*. Belgrade: Cigoja Stampa.

The Council of the European Union. (2011, November 17). *Council Resolution on a renewed European agenda for adult learning*. Brussels 16743/11. http://register.consilium.europa.eu/ pdf/en/11/st16/st16743.en11.pdf

Treaty on European Union (92/C 191/01), Maastricht, 1992. http://eur-lex.europa.eu/en/treaties/ dat/11992M/htm/11992M.html

West Scotland Colleges. (2011). *Grundtvig study: In-service training; analysis of provision of and participation in Grundtvig in-service training activities*. Glasgow. http://eacea.ec.europa.eu/ llp/studies/analysis_exploitation_results_grundtvig%20_lot2_en.php

Chapter 14
Being an Adult Learner and Learning Through Life

Larissa Jõgi

Introduction

Lifelong learning has been extensively researched and discussed in different contexts. The concept of learning also is a central issue to the lifelong learning policy context. Numerous discussions and studies, articles, books and reports have been published all contributing to the discussion, interpretation, development, analysis, reports and suggestions in regard to learning. My intention as a researcher is to write a chapter for this book in order to value and respect adults and their learning by presenting their *voice* as learners. Having a voice – a presence, power and agency – means having the opportunity to speak one's mind, be heard and counted by others and, perhaps, to have an influence on the processes and outcomes (Cook-Sather 2006, 364). Research by Fielding (2001) highlights that by eliciting the learner's voice, learners will feel that their views are being taken more seriously. Listening to adult voices as learners means that we recognise, respect and understand them also as the main stakeholders in lifelong learning and educational policy. An increased sense of respect will in turn make them more inclined to reflect and discuss their learning and provide the tools to influence what, why, how, where and when they learn.

Based on studies conducted in Estonia, I can state that there are tensions between the understandings of learning among educational policymakers and experts and adult learners (Aava 2010; Jõgi et al. 2007, 2008a, b). As the different counterparts understand learning, they often do not hear and understand each other's. And in turn, this tension brings misunderstanding and confusion in the educational policy discussions.

L. Jõgi, Ph.D. (✉)
Department of Adult Education, Institute of Educational Science,
Tallinn University, Tallinn, Estonia
e-mail: larj@tlu.ee

G.K. Zarifis and M.N. Gravani (eds.), *Challenging the 'European Area
of Lifelong Learning': A Critical Response*, Lifelong Learning Book Series 19,
DOI 10.1007/978-94-007-7299-1_14, © Springer Science+Business Media Dordrecht 2014

Educational policymakers and experts understand "learning as a tool for economic change and development" and talk about "learning for future work and competitive economy". A individual is phrased "as a kind of capital" (Aava 2010, 6) and "learning support is important because adult learners are not prepared for lifelong learning" (Jõgi et al. 2007, 127). The understandings of learning among educational experts are narrow, limited by their professional practice and legitimised through policy. However, adult learners experience learning in a broader manner (Jõgi et al. 2008a, 36), which is significantly different from the kind of lifelong learning that is central in current lifelong policies (Biesta 2008).

I concur with Peter Jarvis and Mads Hermansen that there will be no future development, consensus and constructive relationships without dialogue, conversation and social interaction between these two counterparts – adult learners and adult learning policymakers (Jarvis 1992, 2011; Hermansen 2005).

In this chapter, I will present some meaningful findings from the study "*Andragogical, social and psychological factors that co-influence the readiness for learning and activeness in training in the context of lifelong learning in Estonia*"[1] by discussing how adults as learners understand learning and how understandings of learning differ throughout generations in the life-course context. Some results from the study were originally presented in the *5th ESREA international conference "Adult Learning and the Challenges of Social and Cultural Diversity: Diverse Lives, Cultures, Learnings and Literacies"* in order to present ongoing research (Jõgi et al. 2007, 104–119).

By writing this chapter, I would like to encourage educational policymakers, experts and adult educators to listen and value adults as learners. This kind of study also helps us as researchers and educators to understand the entity of the life of adult learners, their learning experience as well as their era and generation and learn from them. This chapter focuses on understandings of learning and adult learner experiences of learning in the life-course context.

Empirical data for the study was collected between 2004 and 2006 using semi-structured interviews and analysed between 2006 and 2011. The interviews were based on a semi-structured open-ended questionnaire and open conversations.

Fifty-five interviews were conducted with 41 women and 14 men of different ages and educational levels from 9 Estonian counties and 5 cities. It was important that different generations from different counties were represented. For empirical analysis, five interviewees were chosen from seven age groups (*21–30, 31–40, 41–50, 51–60, 61–70, 71–80, 81–90*). The youngest interviewee was a 20-year-old woman and the oldest, a 99-year-old man. All interviews were analysed separately in the context of the individual life course in order to understand the differences and uniqueness in understandings of learning. The interpretation of the empirical data was based on a hermeneutic-phenomenographic approach, holistic perspectives and inductive analysis (Marton and Booth 1997; van Manen 2001). The phenomenographic approach

[1] Research project "*Andragogical, social and psychological factors that co-influence the readiness for learning and activeness in training in the context of lifelong learning in Estonia*" was granted by the Estonian Ministry of Education and Research (2004–2006). Research was conducted at the Department of Adult Education (Institute of Educational Science, Tallinn University).

sees learning comprehension as a social construction and interpretation (McLeod 2002; van Manen 2001). Subjective comprehensions make it possible to analyse and understand the essence of learning, the development understandings of learning and the attitudes towards learning (Alheit 1994). The analyses of the interviews involved a process in which we were looking for structurally significant differences or a structural individual nexus in understandings of learning, which belongs to a particular lived experience, which becomes part of contextually related experiences (van Manen 2001, 37).

For this chapter, empirical examples from 11 interviews were chosen from age groups 21–30, 31–40, 51–60, 61–70, 71–80 and 81–90 in order to illustrate understandings of learning.

Learning in the Context of the Life Course

Our understanding of how adults from different generations experience learning is based on the following theoretical views (Alheit 1994; Hermansen 2005; Field et al. 2008; Miller and Boud 1996; MacKeracher 2004):

- Learning is a holistic process; there is continuity between life and experience.
- Learning is connected with time, life and experiencing self.
- Learning is socially, emotionally and culturally constructed.
- Experience is a foundation for learning.
- Life experience, life course and learning experiences form understandings of learning.

Any learning has its starting point in something that has to do with existence and life (Hermansen 2005, 29). Learning takes place in the context of the life course and is seen as social and a personal development process, which occurs throughout sociohistorical time.

The life course can be defined as the sequence of positions of a particular person in the course of time and provides a framework for studying and understanding learning as phenomena at the nexus of social pathways, developmental trajectories and social change (Elder et al. 2003, 10).

The life-course perspective is based on the following set of principles (Elder 2002):

- Personal development and ageing are lifelong processes.
- People are actors with choices that construct their lives.
- The timing of events and roles, whether early or late, affects their impact.
- Lives are embedded in relationships with other people and are influenced by them.
- Changing historical times and places profoundly influence people's experiences.

The life course is stage-like; each person experiences a number of transitions, events and turning points in life. Adults accumulate experience and learning over their lifetime; therefore, learning is a socially determined life-wide and lifelong process including socialisation. The life-wide dimension of learning makes it possible to understand learning more extensively – individuals learn in different fields of life and also learn to be themselves (Jarvis 1992, 32).

We proceed from the viewpoint that a person and generation is influenced by events, social changes and life transformations connected to social roles, social positions, age, relations, life experience and processes in society, which in turn influence the development of learning experiences.

Through an adult's experiences about their learning, it is possible to understand the entity of learners and the essence of the development understandings of learning during the life course and in social and educational contexts (Jõgi and Karu 2004; Field et al. 2008).

Understandings of Learning

Based on findings, it is possible to point out one typical pattern in development of understandings of learning. The younger generation (21–30-year-old interviewees) associate learning with knowledge and skills, practical things and acquiring something.

> Learning is acquiring new knowledge, that I can connect and use in my work. (Riina, 28)
> Learning is acquiring knowledge, but the understanding of learning also changes as studies become more practical, and the older the person gets, the more conscious learning becomes. (Laura, 20)

It is important to this generation that whatever they learn is useful. Their life experience is too short for reflecting, remembering and analysing. They have not experienced so much life or work experiences, transformational events, and do not have enough personal resources and learning skills. Their comprehension of learning is normative, habitual and has no meaning yet.

Later generations (31–40-, 51–60-, 61–70-, 71–80-year-olds) perceive learning in a broader sense as development, relationships, discovering, creating as well as personal growth and life opportunities.

> Learning is definitely discovering your own individuality followed by strengthening and perfection. During the last two years I have discovered that I have found the courage to challenge myself. (Katrin, 30)
> I am like an oak tree. Oak is a strong tree, grows slowly and doesn't break easily. I have tested myself many times in life – will I break or not? Can I handle it? (Regina, 74)

Learning is integrated into everyday life; it is life wide. Learning is life; learning is a way of life which influences apprehensions, values, beliefs, life course, education, work and professional career.

> I have learnt that everything is temporary…life itself, new relationships, new situations have all required me to move from one work place to another and required me to learn. (Vaike, 56)
> Learning makes you to stay in society/…/. Being constantly knowledgeable of what's going on in society; it is an attitude. (Mare, 67)

The support of parents, home and family is very important when choosing study and learning opportunities.

> When I was a child, my FATHER was very important to me, I didn't see much of my mother. She only told me to decide by myself…. Now, my partner has supported my studies which is very important to me. I just don't want to be a housewife or identified only as a mother of three children. (Liina, 36)

School and high school remind people of a place where learning and studies were not very meaningful. School is perceived as being important for life and the development of self, but school is not a place where people see themselves as conscious learners. They remember a couple of teachers, who influenced their apprehensions and the development of their world view. School is seen and talked about as something negative, compulsory; teachers are associated with negative emotions. All this is remembered and talked about in later years.

> I was afraid of my high school Estonian language teacher. I was good at Estonian language, but I was constantly terrified because of her screaming and yelling. When the class was over, the feeling of relief was amazing. Until the next day of course. (Rita, 31).
> Unbelievable, yes. The better I felt, the better the results I got. In elementary school, I studied a lot, but the teachers there were very strict and even a bit abusive. I wish they had been a little bit more humane and friendly. I remember that in physics class nobody new much and the teacher just yelled out our family names: "Sokk, Sütt, stand, sit, F". You couldn't think, you just listened and hoped that your name wouldn't come up. (Elvi, 56)

Study and continuing learning supports individual development, self-actualisation and managing life and work.

> People participate in training programmes to make a better life for themselves. I have understood that I haven't had a big career and I won't ever have it. I want to have a job which offers satisfaction and so I can manage my life. (Vaike, 56)
> I once understood that the teacher is the one who knows and tells how things really are. Now I have a different understanding. I have reached the conclusion that the result is not as important as the process. The process of… did I reach the result and how we explain our opinions. (Raivo, 66)

The more experienced the person is, the more she/he senses or values learning opportunities in informal situations and in life itself without defining themselves as learners.

Uniqueness of Understandings of Learning

How we conceptualise the self is foundational to how we conceptualise learning (Clark and Dirkx 2000). The examples from two different generations (Heleri, 22 years old, and Arno, 99 years old) present generational differences: (1) in the positioning of the self as learner and (2) in understandings of learning. The meanings of learning were extracted from the empirical data and classified according to types under categories of meaning. The following categories were set in the two interviews with Heleri and Arno: learning as self-reliance and capability, understanding of self as a learner.

Heleri's (student, 22 years old during the interview) and Arno's (former farmer and blacksmith, 99 years old during the interview, died in 2005) understandings of learning were different, unique and were interpreted accordingly. Differences in understandings of learning are influenced by experience, differences in a person's life course and the social framework of situations in life.

Arno was born in 1907 (1907–2005), experienced more than four periods of radical political, economic and social change in Estonia: first the Estonian independent republic (1918), World War II (1941–1945), two deportations to Soviet labour camps in Siberia (1941, 1949) and the restoration of the Republic of Estonia in 1991. The most meaningful and transformational events for him were experiencing the Soviet labour camps and the restoration of the Estonian Republic. *Arno* experienced learning as life, as a life experience and a social process, where there are a lot of changes, difficulties and learning. *Arno* learned to be and feel free.

Arno's learning experience is influenced by the life he has led and by finding his place in that life. For Arno, learning is connected to life, learning is lifelong, life is learning.

> Life is learning. Learning starts from childhood, when a child starts to learn, he learns for life and learns it throughout his life until he dies. A person learns until he dies; to death, yes, it is important that you stay calm. That you don't have so many prejudices…I am happy with everything./../(Arno, 99)

Arno has experienced dispositional barriers. Simply existing is difficult at his age, but it is more important than knowing.

> I don't have learning obstacles, but may be they don't show./…/, but my memory isn't good and walking is difficult, I would be more active, it's difficult being like this… I am not capable of much any more, I don't have a good memory any more. I put something in one place, it is there for some time, but when you turn around, it's not there any more (laughs). I haven't thought about it that much. (Arno, 99)

For Arno learning gives strength to live and learn. He uses words like "teacher", "treasure" and "wealth" as metaphors for learning.

> Life experience is a teacher, a treasure and wealth… I am a learner that learns from life and experience. (Arno, 99)

Heleri was born in 1984. Since Heleri was born after 1980, she grew up with new information technology and social media. She has experienced two meaningful events: graduation from high school and her first job. Heleri sees the need to acquire knowledge; she is used to learning like she did at school.

> I can't really vocalise it, this job I have, I have to learn new things all the time. When I came, I could only do so much with the computer. (Heleri, 22)

Learning is acquiring knowledge and she is the one who acquires the knowledge, knowing is important.

> It's when I don't know anything, but I want to know and then I acquire that knowledge. When you decide that you know about a lot of things, it is a very powerful feeling. I think that people who know a lot of things are very interesting to listen to and then I think what kind of a feeling it is to look down on people in terms of knowledge. Looking down not in

a negative context, but they see things more broadly. I think it must be a great feeling. (Heleri, 22)

For Heleri, learning is tiring, learning is a burden. She uses the word sickness as a metaphor for learning. Heleri's experience of learning is influenced by the experience of school studies, which was "difficult, frustrating and tiring".

...I have this nature that I like to learn, but when it gets too much, I get tired. Now, for example, I don't want to study. I flee from it now and I fight with myself. (Heleri, 22)

Heleri's and Arno's apprehensions of learning are based on life events, episodes, life course and learning experiences and are influenced by interpretations of experiences during their childhood, work and studies (Heleri) and adulthood, transformational events, social situations and life itself (Arno). Heleri's apprehensions of learning are knowledge centred and influenced by normative beliefs and little challenges. Arno does not connect learning with knowledge or studies, but with life, experiences and himself. Arno's apprehensions differ because of his "life wisdom", his unique set of values and life experience.

Conclusion

It is vital to understand adults as learners and value their learning experiences in their life course. Learning in the context of the life course can be understood as life based and a constant process connected to life; learning is personally meaningful and significantly different from "economised" learning. Learning is understood and talked about differently by different generations. Understandings of learning are constantly changing during life, intertwined with life, where one of the dimensions that is not dependent on the life course is understanding learning as acquiring skills and knowledge:

- Understandings of learning are always subjectively unique, non-recurring, meaningful and socially designated in the context of the life course (Krueger et al. 2006).
- Understandings of learning are influenced by interpretations of events experienced during childhood, school years, work, transformational events and through interpretations of life and the person herself/himself.
- Understandings of learning develop through life.
- Changes in understandings about learning last throughout life.
- Self-reliance and an understanding of one's self as a learner increases as life experiences increase.

Influences from the social environment and the support of home and family are crucial in life. People, who have experienced success and support in their lives, their studies and their learning, including support from home and family, their employer and their organisations, wish to continue and do continue their studies actively.

The younger generation perceives learning as knowledge and acquiring knowledge. However, with more experience and a deeper understanding of self, the more life wide and complex a person's experiences of education and work become. The more people have life experiences, more significant events and transformative learning experiences in their life, the more they understand and value learning possibilities and learning. Hence, they learn more, want to learn more and are more active in life.

The generational differences associated with positioning self as learner and understandings of learning help us to reflect how different is personal learning experience and how different are understandings and expectations of learning, which adults as learners bring to educational and social process.

Acknowledgements I would like to acknowledge with much appreciation all interviewees and my colleagues Katrin Karu and Kristiina Krabi from the Department of Adult Education at Tallinn University for significant discussions and continuing cooperation. The all have my sincerest gratitude.

References

Aava, K. (2010). *Eesti haridusdiskursuse analüüs (The analysis of Estonian educational discourse)*. Tallinn: Tallinna Ülikooli Kirjastus.

Alheit, P. (1994). *Taking the knocks. Youth unemployment and biography-qualitative analysis*. London: Cassell.

Biesta, G. (2008). Learning lives: Learning, identity and agency in the life-course: Full Research report ESRC end of award report, RES-139-25-0111. Swindon: ESRC. http://www.leeds.ac. uk/educol/documents/190224.pdf. Accessed 30 Aug 2012.

Clark, M., & Dirkx, J. (2000). Moving beyond a unitary self: A reflective dialogue. In A. Wilson & E. Hayes (Eds.), *Handbook of adult and continuing education* (pp. 101–116). San Francisco: Jossey-Bass.

Cook-Sather, A. (2006). Sound, presence, and power: "Student voice" in educational research and reform. *Curriculum Inquiry, 36*(4), 359–390.

Elder, G. H. (2002, November 11). *The life course and aging: Some accomplishments, unfinished tasks, and new directions*. Paper presented at the annual meeting of the Gerontological Society of America, Boston, Massachusetts. http://www.unc.edu/~elder/presentations/Life_Course_ and Aging.html. Accessed 10 Aug 2012.

Elder, G., Johnson, M., & Crosnoe, R. (2003). The emergence and development of life course theory. In J. Mortimer & M. Shanahan (Eds.), *Handbook of the life course* (pp. 3–19). New York: Kluwer/Plenum Publishers.

Field, J., Lynch, H., & Malcolm, I. (2008). *Generations, the life-course and lifelong learning. Learning lives summative paper nr 3*. University of Stirling. http://www.ioe.stir.ac.uk/staff/ documents/Generationsandthelifecourse.pdf. Accessed 19 Aug 2012.

Fielding, M. (2001). Students as radical agents of change. *Journal of Educational Change, 2*(2), 123–141.

Hermansen, M. (2005). *Relearning*. Copenhagen: Danish University of Educational Press/CBS Press.

Jarvis, P. (1992). *Paradoxes of learning. On becoming an individual in society*. San Francisco: Jossey – Bass.

Jarvis, P. (2011). Learning: The experience of a lifetime. In L. Jõgi & K. Krabi (Eds.), *Raamat õppimisest. Õppides täiskasvanuks-õppimine erinevates perspektiivides (Book about learning. Learning from different perspectives)* (pp. 28–48). Tallinn: TLÜ.

Jõgi, L., & Karu, K. (2004). Täiskasvanu õppimine kui koolituse problem (Adult learning as educational problem). In *Õppimine mitmest vaatenurgast* (*Learning from different views*) (pp. 130–139). Humaniora 24. Acta Universitatis Scientiarium Socialium et Artis Educandi Talliensis. Tallinn: Tallinna Pedagoogika Ülikooli Kirjastus.

Jõgi, L., Karu, K., & Krabi, K. (2007). Understandings lifelong learning in Estonia-voices from experts, decision makers and adult learners. In E. Lucio-Villegas & M. del Carmen Martinz (Eds.), *Proceedings of the 5th ESREA research conference "adult learning and the challenges of social and cultural diversity: Diverse lives, cultures, learnings and literacies* (pp. 119–134). Sevilla: University of Sevilla.

Jõgi, L., Karu, K., & Krabi, K. (2008a). Comprehensions of learning and learners-understanding experiences of adults and experts in adult education. *Studies for Learning Society, Nr 1*, 23–38.

Jõgi, L., Jääger, T., Leppänen, R., & Rinne, R. (Eds.). (2008b). *Eesti ja Soome haridus ning muutused EL-i hariduspoliitikas 1990–2000 (Education in Estonia and Finland and changes in European Union education policy 1990–2000)*. Tallinn: Tallinna Ülikooli Kirjastus.

Krueger, J., Alicke, M., & Dunning, D. (2006). Self as source and constraint of social knowledge. In M. Alicke, D. Dunning, & J. Krueger (Eds.), *The self in social judgement. Studies in self and identity* (pp. 3–17). New York: Psychology Press.

MacKeracher, D. (2004). *Making sense of adult learning*. Toronto/Buffalo/London: University of Toronto Press.

Marton, F., & Booth, S. (1997). The idea of phenomenography. In R. Sternberg (Ed.), *Learning and awareness* (pp. 110–136). Mahwah: Lawrence Erlbaum Associates Publishers.

McLeod, J. (2002). *Qualitative research in counselling and psychotherapy*. London: Sage Publications.

Miller, N., & Boud, D. (1996). Animation learning from experience. In D. Boud & N. Miller (Eds.), *Working with experience. Animating learning* (pp. 4–14). London/New York: Routledge.

Van Manen, M. (2001). *Researching life-experience*. London: The Althouse Press.

Chapter 15
Perspectives on Guidance and Counselling as Strategic Tools to Improve Lifelong Learning in Portugal

Maria Paula Paixão, José Tomás da Silva, and Albertina L. Oliveira

Introduction

This chapter focuses on guidance and counselling services and their coordination in Portugal, in the light of the lifelong learning policies that are fostered in Europe and, in particular, the Commission's *Memorandum* as part of the broader initiative for the development of an European area of lifelong learning. Although we embrace the need to provide to all citizens with access to 'good quality information and advice about learning opportunities throughout Europe and throughout their lives', as stated in the *Memorandum* (p. 16), we will show that this objective is far from being fulfilled in Portugal. This can be partially explained by the services' different origins and also by the traditions of the two more relevant disciplines (psychology and education) that informed their creation, as well as by the current political and ideological context prevailing in Europe.

Guidance and counselling are umbrella concepts which have different meanings in diverse life and political contexts. Following Gysbers' (2008) suggestion, after his thorough analysis of specialised literature on this topic, we will use the words *guidance and counselling* combined in order to encompass all the terms currently used in documents discussing lifelong learning policies (e.g., vocational guidance; vocational counselling; information, advice and guidance; career development).

For the purposes of this chapter, we will refer to guidance as 'a range of activities that enables citizens of any age and at any point in their lives (lifelong) to identify their capacities, competences and interests, to make meaningful educational,

Albertina L. Oliveira contributed equally to this chapter.

M.P. Paixão • J.T. da Silva • A.L. Oliveira (✉)
Faculty of Psychology and Educational Sciences, University of Coimbra,
Coimbra, Portugal
e-mail: mppaixao@fpce.uc.pt; jtsilva@fpce.uc.pt; aolima@fpce.uc.pt

G.K. Zarifis and M.N. Gravani (eds.), *Challenging the 'European Area
of Lifelong Learning': A Critical Response*, Lifelong Learning Book Series 19,
DOI 10.1007/978-94-007-7299-1_15, © Springer Science+Business Media Dordrecht 2014

training and occupational decisions and to manage their individual life paths in learning, work and other settings in which these capacities and competences are learned and/or used (lifewide)' (CEDEFOP 2005, p. 11). Likewise, counselling 'is a generic term that refers to a relationship between two or more people in which one person facilitates the growth and development of others in order to help them deal with their problems more effectively' (Glasser and Fine 2004, p. 519).

Guidance and counselling policies have a tremendous impact on individuals' ability to adjust to both voluntary and involuntary transitions which citizens face throughout their entire lifespan. As Fouad and Bynner (2008) have pointed out, involuntary transitions are often accompanied not only by personal obstacles and difficulties but also by obstacles in the form of opportunities as well as by institutional obstacles. Thus, guidance and counselling services are expected not only to support citizens in their lifelong voluntary transitions but clearly to help reinforce their internal and external resources during involuntary transitions, particularly in target underprivileged groups.

This chapter is organised in three main sections: we start by addressing the history of guidance and counselling services in Portugal, then we will discuss the implementation of lifelong learning and guidance structures and services within adult education in Portugal, and finally we will take a critical stance on a recent proposal addressing the creation of a comprehensive system of lifelong education and guidance policy.

Notes on the Context of Guidance and Counselling Services in Educational Institutions and Public Employment Services in Portugal

The history of guidance and counselling in Portugal can be viewed taking into account two separate levels of analysis. If, from the theoretical point of view, the developments in Portugal were comparable to those of other international contexts, the established political power, from the mid-1920s until the late 1970s, never created the favourable conditions for the emergence of a sound practice encompassing the needs of both children and adults (Duarte et al. 2007). In fact the roots of guidance and counselling services can be found in a historical period that ranged from the mid-1800s to the beginning of the First World War. However, the events that occurred from the 1920s onwards were critical for the development of the guidance and counselling practice in Portugal, and especially of its career strand (Abreu 2003), since it had a bright start during the 1920s, in close connection with the creation of experimental psychology units within the higher education institutions of Coimbra and Lisbon.

In the field of vocational guidance, the most important fact was that, in 1925, a professor of general psychology at the University of Lisbon, Faria de Vasconcelos

(1880–1939), founded the Portuguese Institute for Career Guidance and Counselling (IOP) following the widespread theoretical and methodological movement of psychological testing.[1]

In the period following the Second World War, there was a progressive delay of Portugal relative to other European countries and the United States of America. Career guidance and counselling in school contexts didn't exist until the late 1960s. It was not until the early 1960s that the political authorities started to foresee the need to provide guidance and career interventions, via the implementation of two political measures: training of former school teachers, during a brief period, to deliver vocational guidance services to pupils attending the third cycle of basic education, and the creation, in 1965, of the National Employment Service under the auspices of the Ministry of Labour.

During the 1970s and early 1980's, these measures were further strengthened through two initiatives: (1) the creation, in 1979, of the Institute of Employment and Vocational Training (IEFP, PES) by the Ministry of Labour and (2) the reintroduction of technical-vocational studies in the educational system, (1982–1983). In this new system, Occupational Guidance Counsellors (COPs) began to carry out their activities, predominantly for the purposes of increasing vocational training and occupational opportunities among adults, as well as the production, classification and dissemination of occupational information for prospective career deciders and workers. These counsellors were mostly psychologists and others with major studies in social sciences. Later on, they focused predominantly on unemployed adults and young people seeking first employment.

It was in the mid-1980s that school psychologists with a specialised training in career guidance and counselling entered the regular school system in Portugal for the first time. Following the publication in 1986 of a new law redesigning an educational system adapted to a democratic ideology (Lei de Bases do Sistema Educativo) which extended compulsory education until the age of 15, *Psychological and Guidance Services* (PGSs) were created, in 1991, under the Ministry of Education in order to provide information and advice to students facing critical decision points for their future educational path. In 1997, the career of PGS psychologist was finally institutionalised in schools.

---

[1] During Vasconcelos' leadership a number of important activities were undertaken, in accordance with the theoretical and methodological tenets of the vocational guidance, then dominant, namely, (1) the publication of a large series of occupational monographs and (2) psychological assessment and guidance of pupils attending formal education whenever required, mainly within a research focus.

In fact, his model of career guidance and counselling was similar to the one operationalised by Parsons (1909) in its Vocational Bureau: "Knowing the skills that characterize an occupation and the aptitudes that an individual has, it must be determined whether this individual is suited for the job he wishes to follow, and if not, what profession he should pursue instead. Therefore, the problem lies in the knowledge that we have about an individual and in what is known about occupations and the labour market" (Pinho 1986, p. 8, quoting Vasconcelos, 1928).

In the last years of the twentieth century, there was a huge increase in the recruitment of guidance experts. As Abreu (2003) commented, 'these quantitative changes were not without influence on qualitative improvements in educational practice also relevant to many schools, in which psychologists could collaborate as catalysts of work teams, in developing projects of renovation of educational practice in schools and its relations with the surrounding community' (p. 155).

However, the staffing of PGSs in schools slowed down in the first decade of the twenty-first century, and, consequently, the counsellor-student ratio is still very high and uneven, especially considering that compulsory education has been extended until the 12th grade, as a result of the *New Opportunities Initiative*,[2] having as target population students in secondary education and the adult population without certification equivalent to that level.

Considering more specifically guidance and counselling services for the adult population in education and training in Portugal, solid roots seemed to be planted when the National Agency for the Education and Training of Adults (*Agência Nacional para a Educação e Formação de Adultos*, ANEFA) launched the first network of Centres for the Recognition, Validation and Certification of Competences (CRVCC) in 2001. As we will see later, what looked like a bright beginning, at least in the field of Adult Education, has disappeared, a prisoner of a functionalist orientation that increasingly took place. The changes were very similar to those that happened in the European and international contexts concerning the increasing importance given to the concept of lifelong learning. As we know, although established as a priority by the European Commission (2001) to achieve the Lisbon political aim of a knowledge-based society, the concept of lifelong learning is not new. However, since the beginning of the 1990s, a change in the meaning of this concept started to emerge. As is recognised in the Global Report of Adult Learning and Education (UNESCO 2009), the Delors Report (1996), addressing the challenges posed by education and training policies, 'marked the shift from the use of the term 'lifelong education' in the Faure Report to 'lifelong learning'' (p. 22), which was reinforced by several events and initiatives such as the meeting of the Ministers of Education of OECD countries, in 1996, under the theme *Making Lifelong Learning a Reality for All*. However, this shift, framed within the notion of human capital, has been developed and maintained 'on principles of instrumental rationality that consider the outcomes of learning primarily in terms of use-value' (UNESCO 2009, p. 22), reflecting a narrow and functionalist interpretation of the human being, certainly not oriented towards human liberation and critical awareness and reflection.

In Portugal, precisely in the 1970s, the perspective of lifelong education was conceptualised as a framework to guide the transformation of the educational and training systems, encompassing several dimensions, including guidance. Simões' model (1979) envisioned education as continuously accessible to every human being across their lifespan and at the same time oriented towards the promotion of personal autonomy and empowerment. Such a system was conceived as integrating

----

[2] This initiative was launched in 2005 by the Ministry of Education and the Ministry of Labour and Social Security.

the following four key elements: the permanence of education, equal opportunities, guidance and self-direction. Therefore, some of the dimensions mentioned in the model have been considered by the European policies of this new century (CEC 2000), like the emphasis on valuing non-formal and informal learning by its formal accreditation; others are still in need of being further developed and implemented either in Europe or in Portugal.

Implementation of Lifelong Learning and Guidance Structures and Services Within Adult Education in Portugal

A huge step towards the implementation of lifelong education and guidance in Portugal happened in the domain of adult education when, in 1997, the Secretary of State for Education and Innovation asked for the creation of a task force of Portuguese specialists to present a 'strategy document for the development of adult education' (Melo et al. 1998). This valuable paper recommended that the State must take on various responsibilities, and among several proposals it strongly highlighted the creation of an organisational structure specifically for adult education – ANEFA. Among other tasks assigned to ANEFA was the setting up of a system of formal validation of prior learning for adults that was meant to be a truly innovative public structure in Portugal, which had been lacking for a long time. Indeed, in 2001 the National System for the Recognition, Validation and Accreditation of prior learning (NSRVCC) was created by the Ministry of Education and the Ministry of Labour and Social Security under the coordination of ANEFA, giving rise to the first network of Centres (CRVCC).

Despite the dissolution of ANEFA in 2002, with the corresponding dilution of the adult education identity, the NSRVCC has been maintained and enlarged and it continued to function from 2007 onwards under the responsibility of a new agency (National Agency for Qualification, ANQ) in the context of the *New Opportunities Initiative*. Launched in December of 2005, this initiative presented a strategy for national education and training in Portugal aiming to increase the qualification level of the population based on two goals: (1) to strengthen vocational and technical paths as realistic options for young people and (2) to develop basic and secondary education and vocational training for the active population. However, the sound principle stressed by ANEFA of cooperating and establishing strategic liaison with several partners and institutions at different levels has been maintained. For instance, the activities developed by the ANQ have been organised in strong cooperation with social partners and organisations from the civil society as well as with the Institute of Employment and Vocational Training.

Thus, from 2005 onwards, a process of vast reforms took place in Portugal covering basic, secondary and higher levels of education and training. One of the main components of this ongoing process is the National Qualifications System (NQS) which has reorganised vocational training within the educational system and the labour market to give rise to the national qualifications framework, following the

European Qualifications Framework principles. The NQS intends to 'ensure that all Portuguese citizens will achieve education at 12th grade level' and its purpose is 'to integrate all qualification systems and all sectors, and to establish a national qualifications framework to improve access to qualifications and progression, in order to respond to the needs of civil society and the labour market' (Pires 2011, p. 3).

One of the main axes of the NQS is the New Opportunities Centres (*Centros Novas Oportunidades*, NOCs), which replaced the previous NSRVCC. In 2005 there were only 98, and in order to implement the government goal of qualifying one million adults up to 2010, they expanded rapidly, reaching in April 2010 a total of 454 centres scattered throughout the country. As will be seen later, this expansive movement has represented an important step towards making guidance services continuously and locally accessible to NOCs adult target population, as recommended in the Memorandum. Thus, in terms of basic and secondary education and training and regarding validation processes serving the adult population, NOCs are still the national structures that provide guidance and counselling services as well as skills assessment and certification at a local level for adults, although another transition is taking place just now to replace them with Centres for Qualification and Professional Training at the end of 2012.

In spite of the recent extinction of many NOCs, it should be stressed that the work of the technical teams in these structures is developed in an integrated manner: all the centres are using a digital platform which enables information to be constantly updated regarding education and training offers, the validation processes at national level and the situation of each adult benefiting from the Cemtres' activity. Thus, the Integrated System of Information and Management of Education and Training Offer SIGO is the current political device developed to support information, advice and guidance networks. Therefore, in the context of the NOCs, guidance staff provide advice and guidance locally to all adults who want to reach a certification of basic or secondary education. They aim 'to establish the candidate's profile and to determine adequate follow-up steps as part of the intervention' (Pires 2011, p. 8). The possible paths are twofold: guidance towards further education and training or towards a process of accreditation of prior learning. However, concerning the first path the problem arises when the legal regulations emphasise the orientation to a course of qualification achievable at a local level, but the education and training offerings are not sufficient to address the interests, characteristics and expectations of adults, resulting in an inadequate orientation to the second path (process of accreditation).

Also from a critical standpoint, it should be stressed that the qualification requirements for counselling and guidance staff are very general. The regulations establish that guidance staff should have, in addition to a degree in higher education, knowledge about educational and training on offer to the adult population and about techniques and strategies for diagnostic evaluation and guidance. In the case of validation practitioners, the regulations vaguely require that they have knowledge about methodologies appropriate for adults as well as experience in the adult and training domain. Although many of these professionals have a degree in psychology or in educational sciences, it should be highlighted that in most cases the specific training in guidance and counselling principles and techniques is clearly insufficient, since there are no formal requirements beyond any higher education degree.

Concerning access to guidance and counselling services for all in a perspective of lifelong learning, Portugal is far from having reached the necessary articulation or integration of its various structures and services. Although for the active population without a formal certification, the structure and services were well developed at national, regional and local levels; the qualification requirements of the counselling professionals, as was said above, are inadequate; and the adults in need of a deeper psychological counselling support have not been adequately guided to suitable services, since the system was not meant for that purpose. Furthermore, since we are now facing a step back with the significant reduction of the CNOs as a consequence of the recent political changes, we may say that not only are the professionals' qualifications inadequate but also that they are indeed very few.

In the case of higher education, each institution is completely autonomous concerning the creation and organisation of guidance and counselling interventions, as well as in their definition, meaning that liaison with other structures at different levels of education is very poor or even absent.

Regarding guidance and counselling services for older people, including those entering retirement, there are also no official structures under the lifelong and lifewide framework to give them support, which compromises the accessibility of guidance and counselling services for everyone as stated in the Memorandum. 'Senior Universities'[3] and 'Universities for Older People' have been in a process of expansion in the last decade in Portugal and still are growing. However, the initiatives came out of the grounding in the civil society, and the seniors that benefit from them are mainly those in more favourable positions in society, better educated and with a good socioeconomic position and status. Thus, an effective dimension of guidance and counselling services should be available, safeguarding equal opportunities for all, supporting the process of growing and learning beyond the retirement frontier up to the end of life, in a perspective of a lifelong integrated education system. Such a system would considerably improve the opportunities for an active, wise and fulfilled ageing process but still needs to be constructed.

Towards a System of Lifelong Education and Guidance Policy in Portugal

According to Watts (2005), a need is evident in many countries for stronger mechanisms to provide coordination and leadership in articulating a vision and developing a strategy for delivering lifelong access to guidance and counselling.

---

[3] These institutions have as their target population people over 50 years old and are usually created, managed and organised by seniors. The topics studied are very diverse depending upon the seniors' interests and the teachers are volunteers. Currently there are 175 in the entire country comprising 30,000 senior learners.

That is clearly the case for Portugal, where responsibility for guidance and counselling services is often fragmented across a number of ministries and governmental entities, some of which are created and dissolved according to strictly political and governmental (and not expert) views.

As a matter of fact, regarding our national guidance and counselling services, we are currently faced with distinct services, operating in different ways, as mentioned above, with almost no intercommunication (ANQ 2011a, b). To overcome this situation, the ANQ presented a proposal of a Lifelong Guidance System (LLGS) to a panel of guidance and counselling experts (Van Esbroeck et al. 2011).

This proposal, although quite innovative, has some serious limitations in its scope, once it is quite ambiguous in relation to the main objectives as well as to the preferential target groups of the guidance and counselling services (Guichard 2003), namely, to what social questions these services will mainly respond and also who formulates them (politicians, employers, educators). As is stated in the experts' report,' the goals and frame of reference acknowledge both sides of the two alternative visions for guidance, one focused on humanistic sensitivities and the other focused on economic/technological realities. However, it should be noted that the documents lean toward emphasizing the economic needs of the state over a humanistic vision of the individual' (p. 5). As a matter of fact, if we carefully analyse both the content and the language used in the proposal, it becomes quite evident that the supply-side approach clearly dominates the demand-side approach of the LLGS to be created: the importance ascribed to the construction of a more realistic view of the labour market in Portuguese society is overemphasised in relation to other relevant societal goals, such as the reduction of existing social barriers and forms of discrimination, the reinforcement of social cohesion and citizenship education and personal development promotion.

We should also underline the fact that tensions between the experts operating within different sys.ems are quite visible in the presentation of the above-mentioned proposal, since it integrates three distinct and mutually exclusive organisational models (integration, articulation and coordination), each directly linked to the dominant views and presumptions of the different guidance and counselling providers. Nevertheless, it represents the first comprehensive and consistent effort to create a National System of LLGS not directly focused on specific transitions and their short-term outcomes, with a common competence framework allowing intercommunication among subsystems.

However, issues and aspects to be improved are, for instance, stronger recognition of the diversity of career challenges across the lifespan; the competence framework, which needs further elaboration; and the consideration of ethical issues. The intentional and systematic incorporation of ICT in guidance and counselling services, as recommended in the Memorandum, although widely considered a relevant and mandatory tool to provide good quality and timely career information and to assist citizens in the decision-making process, is not sufficiently addressed in the proposal. Concerning terminology, the panel proposed the term guidance to be replaced by a more comprehensive term such as *career services*. This new term would also improve communication and networking among specialists to achieve an integrated perspective and functioning of coordinated career services at a national level. An ambiguous issue, already alluded to, concerned the specific training that should be provided to the career professionals operating at different intervention levels. Also, the question of quality assurance mechanisms was not mentioned in the proposal.

Very recently, in February 2012, the National Government restructured the ANQ, creating the ANQEP, whose mission is to coordinate vocational training for both young people and adults with the accreditation of prior experiential learning procedures. One of the main attributions of this Agency is, once again, to assure the management and articulation of the network of providers of career information and guidance services. Taking into account the political developments that have been lately taking place in Portugal as well as the European Union, it is not surprising that of the two main aims for lifelong learning envisioned in the Memorandum – promoting active citizenship and employability – this newly created Agency has clearly privileged the latter (in a supply-side logic, as explained above), precisely via the creation of new formal learning structures in big and concentrated school groupings, sometimes encompassing more than 20 different schools which are almost always located in medium-sized cities. Gradual osmosis between structures of guidance provision, as advocated in many guidance and counselling policymaking documents (and in the Memorandum itself), is far from being a reality. In many ways, the successive scattered measures which the last governmental offices have been inclined to implement show the state of confusion caused by the recent paradigmatic changes, both in terms of how the policies are adapted and the structures developed and also on how language is used to create new realities in the already existing ones. This current state of affairs, where reaching towards satisfying the guidance needs of large groups of citizens is becoming more difficult, can, in the long run, undermine access to guidance and counselling services to potential clients, in general, and to underprivileged groups, in particular. Looking back to main achievements regarding guidance and counselling in Portugal in the last decade, we realise that there is a long way to go in order to implement the innovative ideas presented in the Memorandum. We are currently facing many political and structural challenges, and uncertainty prevails on the horizon. We hope (but are also very sceptical!) that the measures adopted to solve the pressing problems in the short term (e.g., very high unemployment rates) do not blind political decision-makers in their commitment to strengthen lifelong guidance services for all.

References

Abreu, M. V. (2003). Principais marcos e linhas de evolução da Orientação Escolar e Profissional em Portugal. In S. N. Jesús (org.), *A psicologia em Portugal/Psychology in Portugal* (pp. 117–180). Coimbra: Quarteto.

Agência Nacional para a Qualificação (ANQ). (2011a). *Working paper: National system for lifelong guidance. Organisation and operation of a lifelong guidance service (LLGS)*. Lisboa: ANQ.

Agência Nacional para a Qualificação (ANQ). (2011b). *Working paper: National system of lifelong guidance (LLGS). Guidance qualification frame of reference*. Lisboa: ANQ.

CEDEFOP. (2005). *Improving lifelong guidance policies and systems: Using common European reference tools*. Luxembourg: Office for Official Publications of the European Communities.

Commission of the European Communities. (2000). *A memorandum on lifelong learning*. Brussels: European Commission.

Delors, J., et al. (1996). *Educação, um tesouro a descobrir*. Porto: Edições ASA.

Duarte, M. E., Paixão, M. P., & Lima, M. R. (2007). Perspectives on counseling psychology: Portugal at a glance. *Applied Psychology: An International Review, 56*(1), 119–130.

European Commission. (2001). *Communication from the commission: Making a European area of lifelong learning a reality*. Brussels: Commission of the European Communities.

Fouad, N., & Bynner, J. (2008). Work transitions. *American Psychologist, 63*(4), 241–251.

Glasser, P. H., & Fine, S. F. (2004). Counseling interview. In C. Spielberger (Ed.), *Encyclopedia of applied psychology* (pp. 519–525). New York: Academic.

Guichard, J. (2003). Career counselling for human development: An international perspective. *The Career Guidance Quarterly, 51*(4), 306–321.

Gysbers, N. C. (2008). Career guidance and counselling in primary and secondary educational settings. In J. A. Athanasou & R. V. Esbroeck (Eds.), *International handbook of career guidance* (pp. 249–263). Dordrecht: Springer Science Business Media B.V.

Melo, A., et al. (1998). *Uma aposta educativa na participação de todos: Documento de estratégia para o desenvolvimento da educação de adultos*. Lisboa: Ministério da Educação.

Parsons, F. (1909). *Choosing a vocation*. Boston: Houghton Mifflin.

Pinho, P. B. (1986). Faria de Vasconcelos e a introdução da orientação vocacional em Portugal. *Jornal de Psicologia, 5*, 3–15.

Pires, A. L. (2011). *European inventory on validation of non-formal and informal learning 2010 – Country report: Portugal*. European Commission, Brussels: DG Education and Culture.

Simões, A. (1979). *Educação permanente e formação de professores*. Coimbra: Livraria Almedina.

UNESCO. (2009). *Global report on adult learning and education*. Hamburg: UNESCO Institute for Lifelong Learning.

Van Esbroeck, R., Guichard, J., Janeiro, I., Paixão, M. P., Savickas, M., & Taveira, M. C. (2011). *Seminar report. Lifelong guidance: Discussions, reflections and considerations*. Lisboa: Instituto de Orientação Profissional.

Watts, A. (2005). Career guidance policy: An international review. *The Career Development Quarterly, 54*(1), 66–76.

Part IV
Lifelong Learning and Valuing Learning

Chapter 16
Contradicting Values in the Policy Discourse on Lifelong Learning

Nils Bernhardsson

Introduction

In the countries of Europe, a system of lifelong learning is under construction (Brödel 2011). This is reflected in recent developments: The professionalisation of staff working in adult and continuing education is ongoing and currently realised in different research projects all over Europe (Bernhardsson and Lattke 2010); skills that learners have acquired outside of educational institutions are being certified through the use of so-called learning portfolios (Harp et al. 2010), and new learning places are being created to extend the opportunities to support learning far beyond the existing educational institutions (Stang and Hesse 2006; Tippelt and Reich-Claassen 2010). These developments are significantly influenced by *A Memorandum on Lifelong Learning*, which was published by the European Commission in 2000. The *Memorandum* was initiated to encourage the member states to operationalise lifelong learning within their political agenda. It led to a series of subsequent documents and actions, which aimed to facilitate the proposed operationalisation. In retrospect, 11 years after the *Memorandum* was published, Europe is still far from realising this relatively long-awaited *Area of Lifelong Learning* (European Council 2010). It is bemoaned that the six key messages of the *Memorandum* can be implemented only with great difficulty by the individual countries. As reasons for this, different political interests and social issues within individual member states have so far been cited as the main determining factors for success where lifelong learning policy is concerned (BMBF 2001; European Council 2004).

It seems to be a consensus that lifelong learning has so far been implemented insufficiently. I assume that the main reasons for this are contradicting values which are inherent in the concept of lifelong learning. The aim of this paper is to analyse

N. Bernhardsson (✉)
German Institute for Adult Education, Leibniz Centre for Lifelong Learning, Bonn, Germany
e-mail: bernhardsson@die-bonn.de

G.K. Zarifis and M.N. Gravani (eds.), *Challenging the 'European Area of Lifelong Learning': A Critical Response*, Lifelong Learning Book Series 19, DOI 10.1007/978-94-007-7299-1_16, © Springer Science+Business Media Dordrecht 2014

exactly these contradictions. I will argue that lifelong learning is a concept which is at the centre of a "policy of values" [Politik der Werte] (Joas 1999, p. 16). This policy seeks to combine community-based values such as solidarity and tolerance with more liberal values, such as utility orientation, flexibility and self-realisation. In this paper I will show how lifelong learning in the course of its development became a concept that carries with it a certain brand of policy, and my main argument is that there are fundamental contradictions between the values of the original idea of lifelong learning and the values inherent to the concept currently in use. The way in which these contradictions do exactly hamper the construction of a sustainable lifelong learning system requires a more comprehensive analysis and can only be lightly touched upon in this chapter.

In order to describe the development of lifelong learning, I will firstly outline the concept of Social Imaginaries developed by Charles Taylor (2002, 2004). Based on the concept I will then proceed with a description of the development of lifelong learning in terms of the political discourse from the 1970s until today. This development took place in a first phase in the 1970s, in an intermediate phase in the 1980s, where no extensive discussion on lifelong learning took place, and in a second phase, which began in the mid-1990s and lasts until today (Ioannidou 2010; Kraus 2007).

Approaching Values

For the following approach to values, a pragmatist understanding becomes relevant: Pragmatism is a philosophical school which stands for a certain understanding of the way in which humans acquire knowledge (Biesta and Burbules 2003). A basic pragmatist precondition is that knowledge is always connected to action. The main focus of pragmatism lies on the interaction of humans with their environment and in connection to this, the acquirement of knowledge. According to Joas (1999), also values and the commitment to certain values evolve out of actions. For grounding the evolvement of values in an action theory perspective, Joas refers to the works of Charles Taylor (1989a, 1991) who describes how personal identities are shaped through the confrontation with society. In accordance with Joas' interpretation of Taylor's work, I am using the concept of "Social Imaginaries" (Taylor 2002, 2004), for identifying the values that are in the policy discourse on lifelong learning.[1]

Using Social Imaginaries it is possible to reconstruct values that are implicit in discourses. Social Imaginaries are broader objectives summarising certain ways of thinking that are shared within society. They are composed of complex and unstructured processes, based on experience, as well as emotion. This creates no fully articulated "understanding of the whole situation within which particular features of our world become evident" (Taylor 2002, p. 107). Social Imaginaries are never fully

---

[1] For Social Imaginaries and lifelong learning, see also Rizvi (2007).

articulated and therefore have the potential to give sense and legitimacy to everyday activities. Furthermore, Social Imaginaries are implicit and normative; implicit, because they are embedded in theories, practices and events, and normative because they convey basic normative notions and images that are constitutive for society. Consequently, Social Imaginaries have more depth and are much broader than mere scientific, political and intellectual patterns and models, which are examples used in presentations and publications to depict the social reality (Taylor 2004, p. 23). These Social Imaginaries are therefore designed to hide values that should be realised by the introduction of certain norms. Only in this way, the norms have the necessary potential to structure everyday life. This allows revoking the intended values of official descriptions and critics.

This contradictory logic of values is also inherent in the discourse of lifelong learning. In the following, the concept of Social Imaginaries will be used for a detailed description of this value question. It serves as a concept for reconstructing the broad objectives which have been underlying education policy on lifelong learning since the 1970s and how they have evolved.

The Political Discourse on Lifelong Learning: First Wave (1970s)

In international education policy debates the topic of lifelong learning first emerged in the 1970s, through the terms "Permanent Education" and "Recurrent Education".[2] Both concepts called for a massive reform of the educational system and strove for a new, more humane society (Kallen 1996). The aim was to raise the social participation in broad parts of the world, especially in developing countries. The Social Imaginary was characterised by creating a more humane society through increasing the investment in education and was mainly based on two assumptions. The first assumption was a social humanistic view, with humankind's innate desire to learn at the centre (ibid.), and the second one was a particular assumption about the opportunities of political influence on economic issues.

The concepts of Education Permanente and Recurrent Education which emerged in the early 1970s were based on fundamental ideas which evolved in the 1960s (ibid.). The 1960s was mainly characterised by the understanding applied that the state acts as an economic actor through providing goods and services and thus takes care of the social welfare of its population. The theoretical structure of this central pillar of the Social Imaginary was provided by the political economics of John Maynard Keynes. According to his economic philosophy, the right

---

[2] The expression Permanent Education was introduced by UNESCO on whose behalf the so-called Faure-Report "Learning to Be – The World of Education Today and Tomorrow" was released in 1972 (Faure et al. 1972). Recurrent Education has been introduced by the OECD through the report: "Recurrent Education: A Strategy for Lifelong Learning" (1973).

conditions for growth and employment could be created through a good management of demands.[3]

Both assumptions, the targeted management of demands as well as the politically progressive ideal of humanism shaped a Social Imaginary in which it seemed possible to extend social participation and to create a more human society through a targeted reform of the educational systems. This Social Imaginary of the 1960s represents the values of both original concepts of lifelong learning – Education Permanente and Recurrent Education.

The idealistic spirit of both concepts, however, had little effect on the actual educational policy of UNESCO and OECD. The objective of the humanisation of society through education and training was replaced by "more realistic" objectives,[4] which had very little in common with the originally required radical changes in society (ibid.). With the onset of the economic crises in the 1970s and the resulting rise of unemployment in the 1980s, the required radical social changes seemed to be too utopian and no longer feasible. Supposedly solid cornerstones of society, the national priority of full employment had to be increasingly abandoned, because the reasons for unemployment could not be seen only in economic cycles, but in other factors such as the inflexible structure of the labour market which now moved to the centre of political attention (Garsten and Jacobbson 2004).

In summary it can be emphasised that it came to a contradiction between ambition and reality. This conflict between the ethical issues of the two original concepts of lifelong learning (Education Permanente and Recurrent Education) and the requirements of reality was resolved by dropping lifelong learning from the political agenda. In the following "intermediate phase", however, issues that had considerable influence on the way in which lifelong learning was reactivated in the mid-1990s were discussed.

The Political Discourse on Lifelong Learning: Intermediate Phase (1980s)

In the late 1970s, it became obvious that contradicting ethical issues can't be solved by leaving out conflicting topics like lifelong learning: Increasing political frustration and problems of social cohesion were observed. This provided the impetus for the so-called liberal-communitarian debate in which the moral foundations of modern society were basically tested and discussed by many philosophers (e.g. Gutmann 1985; MacIntyre 1984; Rawls 1971, 1985; Sandel 1982, 1984; Taylor 1985, 1989b).

---

[3] For a critical discussion of the so-called time of Keynesianism, see Skidelsky (2009). Skidelsky argues that the fundamental concepts of Keynes have only been applied in a very reduced and shortened manner in this time.

[4] This concerns the understanding that lifelong learning should be aimed on solving more specific social problems like the drastically increasing unemployment in the 1970s and 1980s.

In the liberal-communitarian debate which was triggered by John Rawls' *Theory of Justice* (1971), it was intensively discussed which set of values was suitable for maintaining moral institutions that guaranteed freedom (Honneth 1993). In order to keep the order of democratic societies, it was debated whether more community-based, so-called communitarian values, or more liberal values, such as benefits orientation, flexibility and self-realisation should have normative priority. During the discussion, however, both positions were approaching each other. It was recognised that for the preservation of liberal-democratic societies, a shared horizon of values is needed that links the liberal principle of equality and freedom with a collective good (ibid.). "Communitarians" and "liberals" agreed that the liberal principles of freedom and equality can only be realised in connection with community-based values. The change in direction that Rawls gave his liberal theory of justice can be seen as the core of the process of rapprochement between the two positions and the development of a common horizon of values. Rawls no longer attributes maximum freedom and economic equality as principles of justice that are based on an original contract situation within which socially prejudiced subjects negotiate a contract (ibid.). Within his new interpretation, Rawls replaces the original contract situation by a real situation, in which actual citizens of Western democracies, who already acquired common value commitments, participate. Therefore, the normative enabling of contract-based individual experiences of justice requires the prerequisite of commonly shared values (Rawls 1985).

The idea of merging communitarian and liberal values has influenced European politics immensely and transported the promotion of a particular Social Imaginary: "a balance between the logic of competition and globalization on the one hand and the production of meaning, solidarity and belonging as the preconditions of social and political stability on the other hand" (Vorländer 2001, p. 8). This Social Imaginary was expressed through the politics of the so-called third way (Giddens 1998).[5] The biggest challenge of this "politics of values" (Joas 1999, p. 16) consists in finding the "right balance between competition and solidarity" (Larsson 1996, p. 724). The difficulty is that this balance cannot be universally defined with validity for all social contexts. However, as a point of reference for finding the right balance within specific contexts, the issue of employability resulted from liberal-communitarian debate (Vorländer 2001).

In the first half of the 1990s, the OECD (Organization for Economic Cooperation and Development 1994) as well as the EU (European Commission 1993) published strategy papers whose objective was to increase employability in the member states. The OECD first relied on the deregulation of existing structures (Jacobsson 2004). The recommendations included, for example, the reduction of wage costs for the creation of jobs and the introduction of performance-related pay systems to make it possible to increase the employability, by providing a "pricing of productivity" for the individual employees (Garsten and Jacobsson 2004, p. 9). The EU argued, however, that a mere deregulation of the structures in the market sense was not enough,

---

[5] In the UK Tony Blair started the so-called third way strategy, and in Germany Gerhard Schröder launched the policy "der neuen Mitte".

but should go hand in hand with targeted promotion of professional training and development of human resources over the entire working life of individuals (Jacobsson 2004). Within the EU, the ability and willingness of people to learn anew and relearning are seen as prerequisites for the improvement of employability. As a consequence, the OECD extended their political strategy to enhance employability through acknowledging that learning and knowledge management play an important role next to the deregulatory measures (ibid.). In this way, the topic of lifelong learning came back on the agenda. However, this time lifelong learning had a different objective. Instead of the humanisation of society through the reform of educational systems, it was now used to preserve the liberal-democratic societies through a skilful mediation between competition and solidarity between people. Since the mid-1990s, international organisations have been trying to achieve this Social Imaginary through the operationalisation of lifelong learning in educational programmes.

The Political Discourse on Lifelong Learning: Second Wave (Mid-1990s Until Today)

After the academic discussion of contradictions between different fundamental ethical issues of modern societies in the intermediate phase, lifelong learning came back on the political agenda. This time the political organisations based lifelong learning mainly on liberal and economic issues, without reflecting the emerging contradiction to the original humanistic version of the concept: Lifelong learning was (re)discovered with the aim to implement new employment concepts (European Council 2001). The OECD presented its development of the Recurrent Education concept with the report *Lifelong Learning for All* (OECD 1996), and the European Union published the *Memorandum on Lifelong Learning* (European Commission 2000). A central feature of both documents is the increased focus on informal learning processes that occur outside the educational institutions, e.g. within the workplace. Learning and working are no longer clearly held in separate areas as previously but come together in one action (Kraus 2001). Therefore, in this second phase, a shifting occurs from the concept of education as organised learning in educational institutions towards the concept of learning as individual learning processes (Kraus 2007). Another important feature is the strong focus on employment and the so-called job skills (Kraus 2006). By the notion of employability, lifelong learning becomes a new objective. An instrumental rationality is inscribed to lifelong learning, which is functionalising the learning. The Social Imaginary of an amalgamation of competition and interpersonal solidarity which was established within the intermediate phase was further operationalised through assigning this functionality to lifelong learning.

Rizvi (2007, p.126) describes that, here, a Social Imaginary of "social efficiency" has prevailed. The central pillar of the original versions of lifelong learning, the demand-driven competition and the humanistic view of people characterised as studious were replaced by other economic assumptions and a different view of human beings. In order to respond to the crisis of western democracies in the 1970s, OECD and EU changed their priorities towards low inflation and budget discipline, as well as towards structural reforms. The demand-driven economic policy has been replaced by a supply-oriented economic policy which prefers a state that stays as far as possible out of welfare funding and that focuses on instrumental values such as competition and economic efficiency. The central idea of such a policy is global competition (Jacobsson 2004). Even when it comes to the image of humanity, social efficiency is now central. According to Bröckling (2007, p.143) the upcoming image of humanity can be described as "anthropology of the homo contractualis". This anthropology argues that humans have a contractual nature and regulate the exchange with others on mutually binding agreements. The actions of humans are thus always negotiations. The negotiation is the key aspect that distinguishes humans as social beings. A corresponding rhetoric of contracts is mainly determining the discourse on learning and employability in companies. It tends to combine the demands of the market with the demands of social security through introducing concepts like the "New Social Contract" (Lombriser and Uepping 2001). Another approach which aims on reconciling market issues with security issues is the flexicurity approach which has mainly achieved success in Denmark and the Netherlands (Kronauer and Linne 2005).

Conclusion

In summary, it can be stated that it is being attempted to establish lifelong learning as a means to increase social efficiency. As a result, learning in itself is not at the centre of educational policy; instead it becomes only relevant in a particular and limited purpose. This intended form of learning serves the purpose to create economically meaningful active persons, who feel responsible for their own employability. Furthermore, we must distinguish between a propagated and an actually realised Social Imaginary. The propagated goal aims on identifying a balance between liberal (more economy related) values and communitarian values for all the social contexts of society. Conversely, the Social Imaginary, which has been realised within education policy, excludes questions of social cohesion. Paradoxically, however, it views them as essential for economic productivity.

The description of the development of lifelong learning and the reconstruction of the Social Imaginaries which emerged in the policy discourse show that all political attempts of developing a comprehensive system of lifelong learning cannot overlook anymore the fact that the core of values which could carry or prevent such a system is being shaped by social discourses and learning processes of individuals. This creates issues for the field of educational sciences and adult education. Lifelong learning has an ethical dimension which requires an increased attention to ethical learning processes and their methodical framing, organisation and monitoring which are the key elements of all teaching, learning and counselling interaction (Fuhr 2011).

References

Bernhardsson, N., & Lattke, S. (2010). Initial stages towards adult educational professional development in a European perspective – Some project examples. In A. Strauch, M. Radtke, & R. Lupou (Eds.), *Flexible pathways towards professionalization – Senior adult educators in Europe* (pp. 21–35). Bielefeld: Bertelsmann.

Biesta, G. J. J., & Burbules, N. C. (2003). *Pragmatism and educational research*. Lanham: Rowman & Littlefield.

Bröckling, U. (2007). *Das unternehmerische Selbst. Soziologie einer Subjektivierungsform.* Frankfurt a. M.: Suhrkamp.

Brödel, R. (2011). Lebenslanges Lernen. In T. Fuhr, P. Gonon, & C. Hof (Eds.), *Erwachsenenbildung – Weiterbildung. Handbuch der Erziehungswissenschaft 4* (pp. 235–246). Paderborn: Leske & Budrich.

Bundesministerium für Bildung und Forschung (BMBF). (2001). *Deutsche Stellungnahme zum Memorandum der EU-Kommission über lebenslanges Lernen.* Bonn: BMBF.

European Commission. (1993). *Growth, competitiveness, employment: The challenges and ways forward into 21st century – White paper.* Brussels: European Commission.

European Commission. (2000). *A memorandum on lifelong learning.* Brussels: European Commission.

European Council. (2001, January 24). Council decision of 19 January 2001 on guidelines for member states' employment policies for the year 2001. *Official Journal of the European Communities, OJ L/22*, 27–37, Brussels.

European Council. (2004). *Education and training 2010 – The success of the Lisbon Strategy – Hinges on urgent reforms.* Joint interim report of the Council and the Commission on the implementation of the detailed work programme on the follow-up of the objectives of education and training systems in Europe. Brussels.

European Council. (2010, January). *Joint progress report of the council and the commission on the implementation of the education and training 2010 work programme, "Key competences for a changing world".* Brussels: European Council.

Faure, E., Herrera, F., & Kaddoura, A.-R. (1972). *Learning to be. The world of education today and tomorrow.* Paris: UNESCO.

Fuhr, T. (2011). Ethik der Erwachsenenbildung/Weiterbildung. In T. Fuhr, P. Gonon, & C. Hof (Eds.), *Erwachsenenbildung – Weiterbildung. Handbuch der Erziehungswissenschaft 4* (pp. 505–518). Paderborn: Leske und Budrich.

Garsten, C., & Jacobsson, K. (2004). An introduction. In C. Garsten & K. Jacobsson (Eds.), *Learning to be employable. New agendas on work, responsibility and learning in a globalizing world* (pp. 1–22). New York: Plagrave McMillan.

Giddens, A. (1998). *The third way. The renewal of the social democratic.* Cambridge: Polity Press.

Gutmann, A. (1985). Communitarian critics of liberalism. *Philosophy and Public Affairs, 14*(3), 308–322.

Harp, S., Pielorz, M., Seidel, S., & Seusing, B. (2010). *Praxisbuch ProfilPASS. Ressourcenorientierte Beratung für Bildung und Beschäftigung.* Bielefeld: Bertelsmann.

Honneth, A. (1993). *Kommunitarismus. Eine Debatte über die moralischen Grundlagen moderner Gesellschaften.* Frankfurt/New York: Campus.

Ioannidou, A. (2010). *Steuerung im Europäischen Bildungsraum. Internationales Bildungsmonitoring zum Lebenslangen Lernen.* Bielefeld: Bertelsmann.

Jacobsson, K. (2004). A European politics for employability: The political discourse on employability of the EU and the OECD. In C. Garsten & K. Jacobsson (Eds.), *Learning to be employable. New agendas on work, responsibility and learning in a globalizing world* (pp. 42–62). New York: Plagrave McMillan.

Joas, H. (1999). *Die Entstehung der Werte.* Frankfurt a.M: Suhrkamp.

Kallen, D. (1996). Lebenslanges Lernen in der Retrospektive. *Berufsbildung, Europäische Zeitschrift*, CEDEFOP 8/9, 17–24.

Kraus, K. (2001). *Lebenslanges Lernen – Karriere einer Leitidee*. Bielefeld: Bertelsmann.

Kraus, K. (2006). *Vom Beruf zur Employability? Zur Theorie einer Pädagogik des Erwerbs*. Wiesbaden: VS-Verlag.

Kraus, K. (2007). Lebenslanges Lernen – Eine bildungspolitische Programmatik in der Retrospektive. *Education Permanente, 3*(3), 18–19.

Kronauer, M., & Linne, G. (Eds.). (2005). *Flexicurity. Die Suche nach Sicherheit in der Flexibilität*. Berlin: Trauner.

Larsson, A. (1996). Social policy: Past, present and future. *Transfer, 2*(4), 724–737.

Lombriser, R., & Uepping, H. (Eds.). (2001). *Employability statt Jobsicherheit. Personalmanagement für eine neue Partnerschaft zwischen Unternehmen und Mitarbeitern*. Neuwied: Luchterhand.

MacIntyre, A. (1984). *Is patriotism a virtue? The Lindley lecture* (pp. 3–20). Lawrence: University of Kansas.

Organization for Economic Cooperation and Development. (1973). *Recurrent education: A strategy for lifelong learning*. Paris: OECD.

Organization for Economic Cooperation and Development. (1994). *European jobs study. Facts, analysis, strategies*. Paris: OECD.

Organization for Economic Cooperation and Development. (1996). *Lifelong learning for all*. Paris: OECD.

Rawls, J. (1971). *A theory of justice*. Cambridge: Harvard University Press.

Rawls, J. (1985). Justice as fairness: Political not metaphysical. *Philosophy and Public Affairs, 14*(3), 223–251.

Rizvi, F. (2007). Lifelong learning: Beyond neoliberal imaginary. In D. Aspin (Ed.), *Philosophical perspectives on lifelong learning* (pp. 114–130). Dordrecht: Springer.

Sandel, M. J. (1982). *Liberalism and the limits of justice*. Cambridge: Harvard University Press.

Sandel, M. J. (1984). The procedural republic and the unencumbered self. *Political Theory, 12*(1), 81–96.

Skidelsky, R. (2009). *Keynes: The return of the master*. London: Penguin.

Stang, R., & Hesse, C. (2006). *Learning Centres. Neue Organisationskonzepte zum lebenslangen Lernen in Europa*. Bielefeld: Bertelsmann.

Taylor, C. (1985). Atomism. In C. Taylor (Ed.), *Philosophy and the human sciences: Philosophical papers 2* (pp. 187–210). Cambridge: Harvard University Press.

Taylor, C. (1989a). *Sources of the self: The making of the modern identity*. Cambridge: Harvard University Press.

Taylor, C. (1989b). Cross-purposes: The liberal-communitarian debate. In N. L. Rosenblum (Ed.), *Liberalism and the moral life* (pp. 159–182). Cambridge: Harvard University Press.

Taylor, C. (1991). *The malaise of modernity*. Concord: Anansi Press.

Taylor, C. (2002). Modern social imaginaries. *Public Culture, 14*(1), 91–124.

Taylor, C. (2004). *Modern social imaginaries*. Durham: Duke University Press.

Tippelt, R., & Reich-Claassen, J. (2010). Lernorte. Organisationale und lebensweltbezogene Perspektiven. *REPORT – Zeitschrift für Weiterbildungsforschung, 33*(2), 11–22.

Vorländer, H. (2001). Dritter Weg und Kommunitarismus. *Aus Politik und Zeitgeschichte, B16–17*, 16–23.

Chapter 17
Quality in Adult Learning: EU Policies and Shifting Paradigms?

Bert-Jan Buiskool and Simon Broek

Introduction: Increasing Attention for Quality in Adult Learning

Improving the quality of Adult Learning provision is included as a key priority in European documents published since the *Memorandum on Lifelong Learning* in 2000. By studying the work done by the European Commission on quality in lifelong learning since 2000, an assessment is made on the development of European Commission's thinking on, conceptualisation of and approach towards quality in Adult Learning. This chapter identifies a shift in the interpretation what quality in Adult Learning means and how policy-makers approach quality. Hence, this chapter does not depart from a theoretical, academic conceptualisation of quality, but tracks the way in which the concept of quality is used in relation to Adult Learning. In doing so, the *Memorandum* (European Commission 2000a) will be considered as the baseline, the 2007 Action Plan (European Commission 2007) as the intermediate result and the renewed European Agenda for Adult Learning published in December 2011 (Council of the European Union 2011) as the current stage of thinking. By discussing these three official documents and relevant additional work (such as European studies published, peer learning activities and consultations organised in this policy-making context), this chapter sketches the developments in quality thinking in Adult Learning since the publication of the *Memorandum*.

The 2000 *Memorandum on Lifelong Learning* emphasises the importance of lifelong learning for building an inclusive society where quality learning is accessible for all. In addition, lifelong learning is regarded essential for achieving higher overall levels of education and qualifications in all sectors, to ensure high-quality provision of education and training and at the same time to ensure that people's

B.-J. Buiskool (✉) • S. Broek
Ockham - Institute for Policy Support, Utrecht, The Netherlands
e-mail: b.buiskool@ockham-ips.nl

G.K. Zarifis and M.N. Gravani (eds.), *Challenging the 'European Area of Lifelong Learning': A Critical Response*, Lifelong Learning Book Series 19, DOI 10.1007/978-94-007-7299-1_17, © Springer Science+Business Media Dordrecht 2014

knowledge and skills match the changing demands of jobs and occupations, workplace organisation and working methods. This means that lifelong learning should underlie all educational sectors, not only strictly Adult Learning offering equal opportunities for access to quality learning throughout life to all people, and in which education and training provision is based first and foremost on the needs and demands of individuals (European Commission 2000a).

The importance of high-quality provision is mentioned several times in the *Memorandum*. Firstly, it is mentioned in relation to *basic education*: 'High quality basic education for all, from a child's youngest days forward, is the essential foundation. Basic education followed by initial vocational education and training, should equip all young people with the new basic skills required in a knowledge-based economy. It should also ensure that they have "learnt to learn" and that they have a positive attitude towards learning' (European Commission 2000a, p. 7). Secondly, it is mentioned in relation to *basic skills*: 'Member States' formal education and training systems – whether initial, further/higher or adult/continuing – are responsible for ensuring that each and every individual acquires, updates and sustains an agreed skills threshold. Non-formal learning domains also have a very important role to play in these respects. This all requires the assurance of high quality learning experience and outcome for as many people as possible' (European Commission 2000a, p. 11). Thirdly, it is mentioned in relation to *innovation in teaching and learning*. Here it is stated that 'Quality of learning experience and outcome is the touchstone, including in the eyes of learners themselves' (European Commission 2000a, p. 13). On top of that, 'improving the quality of teaching and learning methods and contexts will mean significant investment by Member States to adapt, upgrade and sustain the skills of those working in formal and non-formal learning environments, whether as paid professionals, as volunteers or as those for whom teaching activities are a secondary or ancillary function' (European Commission 2000a, p. 14). Fourthly, quality in provision is mentioned in relation to *guidance and counselling*.

The 2006 Communication *It Is Never Too Late to Learn* emphasised the importance of ensuring the quality of provision by suggesting that Member States should invest in improving teaching methods and materials adapted to adult learners and put in place initial and continuing professional development measures to qualify and upskill people working in Adult Learning. It further recommends the introduction of quality assurance mechanisms and the improvement of delivery (European Commission 2006). According to the 2006 Communication, poor quality provision of Adult Learning leads to poor quality learning outcomes addressing the need for policy action improving the quality of Adult Learning provision. However, this Communication also indicated that quality is a multifaceted concept, which makes it difficult to provide a common approach and policy answer to it. Improving quality of provision includes action on information and guidance; needs analysis; relevant learning content matching actual needs and demands; delivery; learning support; assessment approaches; and recognition, validation and certification of competencies (European Commission 2006).

The 2007 Action Plan on Adult Learning *It Is Always a Good Time to Learn*, in implementing the key messages of the 2006 Communication, goes a step further and indicates that although quality of provision is affected by policy, resources, accommodation and a host of other factors, the key factor for quality Adult Learning is the quality of the staff involved in delivery (European Commission 2007). Whether it concerns teachers, counsellors, managers or supporting staff, they are all crucial in motivating adult learners to participate (Research voor Beleid/PLATO 2008; Buiskool et al. 2009). The importance of working on the quality of Adult Learning provision is reaffirmed by the 2008 Council Conclusions (Council of the European Union 2008). The Council recognises that there is a need to 'ensure the efficiency, effectiveness and quality of Adult Learning, with the aim of increasing active participation in such learning, especially among disadvantaged groups, of attracting sufficient public and private investment to this area, and of encouraging the private sector to consider such learning as a key component of workplace and business development' (p. 11). In addition, the Education and Training strategic framework 2020 (Council of the European Union 2009) includes a strategic objective for improving the quality and efficiency of education and training (Objective number two (p. 3)).

Finally, the Council Resolution on a Renewed Agenda for Adult Learning 2012–2014 sets out priorities for action in the period 2012–2014 including actions with regard to improving the quality and efficiency of education and training (Council of the European Union 2011). The title of 'priority area 2' puts together 'quality' and 'efficiency' ('improving the quality and efficiency of education and training'). It is suggested that Member States need to focus on developing quality assurance systems for providers, improve the quality of staff, look into the issue of viable and transparent financing of learning, develop systems so that learning provision better reflects labour market needs and finally intensify cooperation amongst different stakeholders. Although shifts might be noticeable already, before clearly identifying them, first additional material concerning Commission thinking on quality in Adult Learning will be examined.

Commission Studies and Policy Documents in the Field of Adult Learning

Within the framework of the Action Plan on Adult Learning, various initiatives have been taken to boost quality of provision and to stimulate Member States to take action. Quality has been the subject of various studies, workshops and working groups of the Commission, of which the most relevant are summarised below.

– The Commission study on Adult Learning Professions in Europe (Research voor Beleid and PLATO 2008) studied Adult Learning professions in Europe (in the non-vocational Adult Learning sector) on a number of issues such as their employment situation, the tasks they carry out and the educational background they have.[1]

- The study Key competences for Adult Learning professionals (Research voor Beleid 2010; Buiskool and Broek 2011) builds further on the Adult Learning Professions study and made a European-wide inventory of competence profiles, competence requirements and educational programmes for becoming an Adult Learning professional.[2]

- The study on enabling low skilled to take their qualifications 'one step up' (University of Florence 2010) identified key factors underpinning good practices in this area, emphasising the need to attune systems and didactics, counselling and guidance to the specific target group to deliver quality Adult Learning.[3]

- Quality comes along with monitoring and evaluation as well. Without knowledge about effects of policy measures, it remains difficult to see what works and what does not work. The study Assessment of the Impact of Ongoing Reforms in Education and Training on Adult Learning (PPMI 2010) laid down methods to measure the impact of reforms.[4]

- The study on European Terminology in Adult Learning for a common language and common understanding and monitoring of the sector (NRDC 2010) examined key concepts in relation to quality in Adult Learning and mapped available data sources to monitor the sector.[5]

---

[1] It was concluded that Adult Learning staff conduct a variety of tasks and that there is a variety of educational pathways leading to the profession; there is no clear view on standard competences or skills needed to fulfil the professional tasks in non-vocational Adult Learning (NVAL), partly due the diversity of the field, and that a large group works under precarious employment conditions. Recommendations on the basis of the study included amongst others: developing (European) competence profiles for staff working in the sector, focus more on in-service training since people often start working in the sector 10–15 years after their initial educational training, pay more attention to continuous professional development (internal and external) evaluation and set up an independent body for quality standards (national and European level).

[2] Based on this inventory a set of key competences was identified taking into account the variety of contexts in which Adult Learning professionals work and the variety of tasks they conduct.

[3] The findings and recommendations of this study and the results of a number of peer learning activities and a workshop on Priority Action 3 of the Action Plan (increase the possibilities for adults to achieve a qualification at least one level higher than before ('go one step-up'): European Commission 2007) were incorporated in a set of concrete policy and practical guidelines for organising quality Adult Learning provision facilitating basic skills development of adults (see www.kslll.net/Documents/Basic%20skills%20guidelines.pdf).

[4] The follow-up study on Ongoing Reforms II (Research voor Beleid 2011) subsequently reviewed reforms from the perspective of what are effective ways to mobilise adults to participate in learning. Quality of provision (in all its dimensions) was considered to be one of the six major 'mobilisation strategies'. Research shows that not only more flexible forms of provision but also the enhanced quality of provision and staff can lead to decreased numbers of dropouts in Adult Learning (Schuller and Watson 2009).

[5] The study identified four subfields of quality, namely, validation of learning; accreditation and evaluation of provision; professional development of teachers and trainers; and finally, innovative pedagogy.

Other studies and reports drawn up outside the scope of the framework of the Action Plan portray a particular emphasis on quality as well. For instance, the CONFINTEA VI regional report (Keogh 2009) emphasises that public authorities play a crucial role in the governance of Adult Learning and assessing the accountability of systems and providers through establishing regulatory frameworks, setting quality standards, certifying adherence to these standards and making information on providers' performance against explicit indicators available to service users. Also it concludes that in general, public authorities are more interested in the quality of provision when public funding is involved, but that they also have a role to play – in the interests of effectiveness and consumer rights – where Adult Learning is privately provided, often with multisource funding.

Furthermore, the *Belém Framework for Action* (UNESCO 2009a), the final document of the international conference of CONFINTEA VI adopted on 4 December 2009 in Belém, declares that 'Fostering a culture of quality in Adult Learning requires relevant content and modes of delivery, learner centred needs assessment, the acquisition of multiple competences and knowledge, the professionalisation of educators, the enrichment of learning environments and the empowerment of individuals and communities' (p. 6). Delegates to the conference committed themselves to the development of these quality requirements in their respective countries.

In addition, one Commission study prior to the implementation of the Action Plan is particularly relevant, namely, the study on Local Learning Centers and Learning Partnerships (Research voor Beleid and PLATO 2005). This study analyses successful learning centres and the conditions for qualitative partnerships. It analysed what constitutes a quality learning environment (it should be motivative, rich and reflexive), and it studied in depth the conditions for organising this quality learning environment (quality content, financial resources, quality of staff, public relations and, finally, partnerships). Quality staff brings continuity, flexibility, a balance between a core team and incidental staff and a balance between content expertise and process expertise. In addition, the staff composition should mirror the target group, meaning that it is of a similar cultural, ethnic, language and work domain composition. Furthermore, besides quality of staff also, funding is mentioned as an important element or determinant of quality and continuity.

Finally, a study conducted in the Nordic countries on 'Systematic quality assurance in Adult Learning, Nordic tiles in a mosaic' (Faurschou 2008) established a framework for assessing quality in Adult Learning and took as reference point the Quality Assurance Model – The Common Quality Assurance Framework for VET (see European Commission 2010). The framework provides a number of steps and related questions that can be asked at all levels (ministries, study and educational organisations as well as schools, departments, individuals and lectures), to rationalise processes with the aim to improve the quality.

Besides these studies, a number of workshops and conferences, as well as many other initiatives in the area of quality, have been initiated in recent years by the Member States. In some cases these initiatives have been supported by

European programmes, such as European Social Funds (ESF)[6] and the Lifelong Learning Programme (LLP).[7] Another interesting development with regard to quality in Adult Learning is the establishment of the European Lifelong Guidance Policy Network (ELGPN)[8] on quality of guidance. This network addresses the development of quality assurance systems for guidance services from a user perspective and the need for an evidence base for developing policies for guidance provision. The network gathers good practices, initiatives and developments from across Europe and aims at developing a proposal for a common EU framework for quality assurance from a lifelong guidance perspective.

All in all, the studies conducted and meetings organised support National and European level policy makers to further develop their thinking on quality in Adult Learning. In addition, they look closely to what happens in other educational sectors.

Developments of Quality Initiatives in Educational Fields Other Than Adult Learning

As has been mentioned already in the *Memorandum* on lifelong learning, lifelong learning should enclose all educational sectors (Field 2006). In addition to this, it appears to be very difficult to clearly demarcate the 'Adult Learning field' from other educational fields, since a lot of Adult Learning takes place in other sectors, such as higher education (HE), vocational education and training (VET, including both in-service and continuing VET) and general education (see Research voor Beleid 2011; Van Dellen and van der Kamp 2008). As a consequence, the issue of quality crosses sectoral borders and therefore potential measures should take account of initiatives in other sectors. At European level major steps have been

---

[6] See, for instance, governmental programmes in Portugal to increase participation in Adult Learning and to increase educational attainment (New Opportunity Initiative). Also, in the new Member States (Poland, Romania, Hungary), ESF is used to build better Adult Learning structures, for instance, to target disadvantaged groups (e.g. Roma).

[7] With regard to the latter, both the Leonardo da Vinci and the Grundtvig sub-programme contributed to developing tools and measures to improve quality. Interesting projects are, e.g. Validating Mentoring 2 (Project Number: LLP-LDV-TOI-07-BG-166007), i2i – Internship to industry (Project Number: LLP-LdV/TOI/2007/SE/1291), Assessment, Visibility and Exploitation of non/in-formally acquired competencies of EXperienced EMPLOyees in Enterprises (Project Number: LLP-LdV-TOI-2007-TR-051). Development of a validation framework for mentoring: evaluating the achievements of disabled and disadvantaged people (Project Number: BG/05/C/F/TH-83300), European Fundraising Accreditation and Training (Project Number: EUR/05/C/F/PP-84711), and Quality management of Peer Production of eLearning (Project Number: 134009-LLP-1-2007-1-FI-LEONARDO-LMP). A selection of best practices are analysed and presented (2012) in the QALL project.

[8] http://ktl.jyu.fi/ktl/elgpn

taken in the last few years establishing quality standards and guidelines within HE and a quality reference framework in VET.[9] In addition, also with regard to quality in school education, developments have been initiated. In discussing the developments in the three sectors, the most relevant to Adult Learning are discussed first:

The *European Quality Assurance Reference Framework for VET* (*EQARF*) was approved in 2009 (see European Parliament and the European Council 2009). EQARF provides a European-wide system to help Member States and stakeholders to document, develop, monitor, evaluate and improve the effectiveness of their vocational education and training (VET) provision and quality management practices.[10] The EQARF framework consists of a quality circle consisting of four parts – (1) planning, (2) implementation, (3) evaluation and (4) review – and contains ten guidelines for working on quality, such as rules for deciding who offers VET provision, the roles and responsibilities for different parts of the VET system, the information and data, the role of a communication strategy, to pilot initiatives and value success, use feedback to improve VET, provide clarity over funding, ensuring quality assurance covers all aspects of VET provision and ensure VET is founded on a strong involvement of external and internal partners and relevant stakeholders.

In its *Standards and Guidelines for Quality Assurance in the European Higher Education Area* (ENQA 2009), the ENQA in cooperation with EUA, EURASHE and ESIB[11] and endorsed by the ministers of education of the Bologna signatory[12] makes a distinction between (1) internal quality assurance within HEI, (2) the external

---

[9] The Education and Training 2010 work programme launched in 2001 and its follow-up, the strategic framework for European cooperation in education and training ("ET 2020") adopted by the Council in May 2009 are the European strategy and co-operation in education and training. The first phase of the development of a Reference Framework focused during 2001–2003 on developing common principles and tools. This was organised in the European Forum on Quality in VET (2001–2002) and in a Technical Working Group on Quality in VET (2003–2004). A common quality assurance framework (CQAF) was presented in Maastricht in 2004. The second phase of the work focused on consolidation and further development of tools. ENQAVET was founded in October 2005 and continued to December 2009, where the activities were continued in the EQARF and in the ECVET Recommendation. Developed by Member States in cooperation with the European Commission, the Reference Framework has in 2009 been adopted by the European Parliament and the Council. It is a key element in the follow-up of the Copenhagen Declaration and the ongoing work in renewing Europe's education and training systems. The adoption and implementation of the Framework in the participating countries is voluntary. The name EQAVET has been used since 1.1.2010.

[10] The EQARF builds on the European Qualifications Framework (EQF), the European Credit for VET (ECVET) system and previous European quality assurance systems (such as the Common Quality Assurance Framework – CQAF).

[11] ENQA, the European Association for Quality Assurance in Higher Education; EUA, Association of European institutions of higher education; EURASHE, European Association of Institutions in Higher Education; and ESIB, European Students' Union

[12] See European Ministers of Education meeting in Bergen in May 2005.

quality assurance of higher education and (3) finally the quality assurance of external quality assurance agencies.[13]

In 2000, *indicators for measuring quality of school education* have been developed. The indicators can be used to identify issues which should be examined in greater detail, and they give Member States the opportunity to learn from one another by comparing the results achieved. Indicators on attainment include issues such as progress in mathematic skills, reading competences and ICT. Indicators on success and transition include school dropout rates and completion of upper secondary education. Indicators on monitoring of education include evaluation and steering of school education. Finally, indicators on resources and structures include indicators such as participation in pre-primary education (European Commission 2000b).

In comparing quality assurance in VET, HE and school education, it can be noticed that all three initiatives contain a degree of freedom in determining how quality is measured. Foremost, existing initiatives should not be replaced, but the guidelines for both VET and HE should improve existing practices. Also, the guidelines include a general quality cycle and improvement perspective, based on a general evaluation perspective: (1) setting clear goals and rules and defining roles and responsibilities, (2) implementing measures to improve and monitor quality of provision (e.g. quality of staff, resources, support structures), (3) evaluating results of the provision (e.g. assessment of students, collecting feedback) and (4) reviewing the evaluation and drawing conclusions towards improving the practices.

Quality assurance in Adult Learning sector could take into account these above-mentioned developments. This is in line with the outcomes of the European Commission Workshop on Quality (European Commission 2010) that concluded that cooperation with other education and training sectors could provide good learning experiences about what can be considered as quality structures and processes, such as the higher education sector and the VET sector. Structures, such as the EQARF and ESGs, could be further developed going beyond sector models and transferred into an integrated learner-focussed model for quality assurance. On the other hand, the distinct characteristics of the Adult Learning sector should be kept in mind while accessing the quality in the sector. Providers should have the opportunity to choose processes and tools that are best suitable with their specific situation. Moreover, the role of stakeholders, such as social partners, is stressed in order to ensure confidence in the outcomes of Adult Learning. In addition to this, quality monitoring is required to review progress in the sector.

---

[13] *Internal quality* guidelines include (1) policy and procedures for quality assurance; (2) approval, monitoring and periodic review of programmes and awards; (3) assessment of students; (4) quality assurance of teaching staff; (5) learning resources and student support; (6) information systems; and (7) public information. The *external quality assurance* emphasises the importance of reporting, periodic reviewing, follow-up procedures and system-wide analyses. Furthermore, *external quality assurance agencies* should have an official status, have the resources necessary, should be independent and should be accountable.

In addition to the quality frameworks as developed for HE and VET, an even more important development in recent years is the implementation of the *European Qualifications Framework* (*EQF*)[14] and subsequent National Qualifications Framework in the Member States.[15] According to the updated monitoring study of CEDEFOP (2011), approximately 17 countries have completed their referencing reports, linking national qualifications to the eight levels of the EQF. The EQF initiative is built upon the following key elements: qualifications are described in learning outcomes; qualifications are issued by competent bodies; and qualifications can be regarded as 'currency' in which people, institutions and employers should have trust. Given this conception of qualification, the institutions offering qualifications, diplomas or certificates (either through initial education or validation of non-formal and informal learning) should be trustworthy and hence have mechanisms for quality assurance. This counts for all institutions where learning takes place and even more when it concerns the learning of adults.

Quality Developments at Member State Level

When reviewing the developments at national level, it is still true that there is a wide diversity of quality management systems and procedures. This amongst else due to the wide variety of Adult Learning settings and providers ranging from upper secondary, vocational, higher and liberal education provided by different stakeholders, leading to a fragmentation of quality approaches. In general, quality assurance is regulated at system level when public money is involved and when the learning results in a formal qualification. In these cases Adult Learning is, if not always, regulated by legal frameworks and has accreditation systems and institutions and monitoring or evaluation instruments. In addition, in the formal sectors staff requirements are more often legally determined (Eurydice 2011). When it concerns nonpublicly financed Adult Learning providing non-formal and informal learning,

---

[14] The European Qualifications Framework (EQF) aims to relate different countries' national qualification systems to a common European reference framework. One of the main ideas behind the EQF is that individuals and employers will be able to use the EQF to better understand and compare the qualification levels of different countries and different education and training systems. This leads to increased labour mobility between countries, mobility between education systems and increased opportunities for lifelong learning (see: European Parliament and the European Council 2008).

[15] The European Parliament and the European Council (2008) suggests that the Member States (MS) relate their national qualification systems to the European Qualifications Framework by 2010, either by referencing, in a transparent manner, their qualification levels to the EQF levels, or, where appropriate, by developing national qualifications frameworks; by 2012, all new qualification certificates, diplomas and Europass documents contain a reference to the appropriate EQF level; the Member States designate national co-ordination points, in order to support the relationship between national qualifications systems and the European Qualifications Framework.

it is mostly up to the sector, provider or client to define the standards. General frameworks, either national or European, play only a minor role.

When quality procedures are in place within higher, vocational and second chance education, in most cases no distinction is made between initial and continuous learning. The key question in this respect is to what extent do the quality procedures take into account some basic principles for Adult Learning, often linked to the quality of the learning process, such as making use of experience adults bring in, identifying their specific learning needs, make learning relevant for their context, using specific didactic methods and having a flexible offer taking into account adults responsibilities and time schedule (Research voor Beleid 2011; Broek and Buiskool 2012).

Nevertheless, in a number of countries, such as Austria and Switzerland, there is specific legislation ensuring quality of Adult Learning (such as Ö-Cert and eduQua). Moreover, there is ample evidence that European initiatives, such as the Grundtvig programme, EQARF, EQF, the Action Plan on Adult Learning and the European emphasis on lifelong learning strategies, influence developments in quality assurance related to Adult Learning. For instance, to be eligible for Grundtvig in Austria, Adult Learning providers need to have quality assurance systems in place. A current issue that plays a role is the implementation of National qualifications frameworks and the role of learning outcomes in describing qualifications (Cedefop 2011). In relation to this, additional requirements could be set for (private) providers wishing to link their qualifications in an NQF, such as in the Netherlands.

Discussion

So far we discussed developments on quality thinking at EU level and examined in this regard what happens in the Member States. From this point, it is interesting to further explore how these developments at European level relate to the policy discourse globally. In doing this, some shifts in thinking are identified, which are confronted with developments in Adult Learning practices.

A shift in focus is noticeable in Commission thinking on quality. This shift can be illustrated by taking into account the four key principles of quality in Adult Learning, developed by UNESCO in the framework of the CONFINTEA VI. These principles include firstly, *equity*, which relates to equitable access to and participation at all levels of education and training. Secondly, *efficiency*, which relates to levels and distribution of resources and to economical investment of resources to achieve specified aims under given conditions, that is, the ratio of costs to benefits. Thirdly, *effectiveness*, which generally expresses means-end relationships in terms of educational outcomes for learners and the time needed to achieve programme aims. Completion rates and achievement levels are hard indicators of effectiveness. Finally, *relevance*, which the CONTINTEA VI report considers the most important dimension of quality in adult education and training and which means that provision must represent an effective route to and support for personal and social change and must engender and sustain motivation to participate and support persistence in learning to the achievement of individual goals (UNESCO 2009b). Given these four principles, one could argue that there is a shift noticeable in the last decade on Commission thinking on quality, moving from quality primarily related to the issue of equity to quality primarily related to effectiveness and efficiency and relevance. This entails as well a shift from quality thinking at system, or input level, to quality thinking at provider, or process/outcome level. This shift fits well with broader shifts identified for instance in the framework of higher education from quality as accountability (Kells 1992; Vroeijenstijn 1995) to consumer protection and transparency (Weusthof and Frederiks 1997). Providing transparency and validation are key principles behind the establishment of the European Qualifications Framework and National Qualifications Frameworks (European Parliament and the European Council 2008; Research voor Beleid 2012).

Although, as identifying shifts in the near past is difficult, in this section some illustrative evidence will be provided to support our claim. In the *Memorandum* quality was mainly discussed in the light of improving accessibility for all to learning opportunities. Also, the issue of quality is considered first an issue concerning the quality of the system as such. Moreover, quality should be reviewed through the eyes of the learner. At that time, minor emphasis was given to quality of staff working in (adult) learning. The 2007 Action Plan and accompanying documents show that the so-called UNESCO focus on quality lifelong learning systems in terms of equal accessibility is replaced by more pragmatic messages on staff continuous development and the quality of delivery. The 2011 Renewed Agenda further developed this thinking into a focus where quality and efficiency are closely linked and where relevance of learning outcomes is emphasised. This is illustrated in Table 17.1.

Given this shift in thinking about quality, it does not necessarily mean that the issue of equitable access to learning provision is forgotten; it is however not anymore considered a constituent of the quality of the systems, but as an issue that needs to be dealt with in addition to organising Adult Learning in an efficient and effective way. It is covered by its own priority area, namely, priority area 3: promoting equity, social cohesion and active citizenship through Adult Learning (the Council of the European Union 2011, p. 5).

Despite shifting paradigms at Commission policy level from the more equity-driven perspective (education accessible for all) to the more effectiveness and relevance-driven perspective (programmes better reflect labour market needs) on quality, it is not clear whether much progress can be seen at Member States' level, in the years since the *Memorandum*. The analysis of quality developments in Europe is seriously hampered by the fact that until this moment no European-wide overview is available on national and regional policies in a comparative perspective, including frameworks, legislation and standards, with regard to quality approaches in the field

Table 17.1 Focus in Commission publications on quality 2000, 2006, 2007, 2008 and 2011

2000 Memorandum	2006 Communication/2007 Action plan/2008 Conclusions	2011 Renewed Agenda
"Lifelong learning for building an inclusive society where quality learning is **accessible for all**" "Member States' formal education and training systems – whether initial, further/higher or adult/ continuing – are responsible for ensuring that **each and every individual** acquires, updates and sustains an agreed skills threshold. Non-formal learning domains also have a very important role to play in these respects. This all requires the assurance of high quality learning experience and **outcome for as many people as possible**"	"Member States should invest in improving teaching methods and materials adapted to adult learners" (2006) "introduce quality assurance mechanisms and improve delivery" (2006) "poor quality provision of Adult Learning leads to poor quality learning outcomes" (2006) "that the key factor is the quality of the staff involved in delivery" (2007) "ensure the efficiency, effectiveness and quality of Adult Learning, with the aim of increasing active participation in such learning" (2008)	"Improving the quality and efficiency of education and training" "developing quality assurance systems for providers" "look into the issue of viable and transparent financing of learning" "develop systems so that learning provision better reflects labour market needs"
Focus on UNESCO principle of equity	Focus on UNESCO principle of effectiveness	Focus on UNESCO principles efficiency and relevance

of Adult Learning. Moreover, a critical reflection is lacking on the issues and challenges that are specific to the Adult Learning sector in relation to assuring quality of its providers and provision. In addition, less information is available on processes and mechanisms for quality assurance in the Adult Learning sector. Finally, one could discuss what the differences and common characteristics are in the non-vocational Adult Learning sector compared with the development of quality assurance systems in VET and Higher Education and whether there is a need to have a common framework on quality in lifelong learning, including all educational sectors.[16]

---

[16] These issues are addressed in an ongoing study of the European Commission on quality in Adult Learning for which the results are foreseen in the beginning of 2013 (European Commission 2011). This study should feed the work of the Thematic Working Group in Quality in Adult Learning, established in 2011, by the European Commission to work further on quality issues in Adult Learning in the context of the Open Method of Coordination.

References

Broek, S. D., & Buiskool, B. J. (2012). Mapping and comparing mobilisation strategies throughout Europe: Towards making lifelong learning a reality. *Journal of Adult and Continuing Education, 18*, 1.

Buiskool, B. J., & Broek, S. D. (2011). Identifying a common set of key competences for adult learning staff: An inventory of European practices. *Journal of Adult and Continuing Education, 17*(1), 40–62.

Buiskool, B. J., Broek, S. D., & van Lakerveld, J. (2009). Educators at work in two sectors of adult and vocational education: An overview of two European research projects. *European Journal of Education, 44*(2), 64–82.

CEDEFOP. (2011). *The development of national qualifications frameworks in Europe.* Luxembourg: Publications Office of the European Union.

Council of the European Union. (2008). OJ C140/10, Council conclusions of 22 May 2008 on Adult Learning (2008/C 140/09).

Council of the European Union. (2009, May 28). Council conclusions of 12 May 2009 on a strategic framework for European cooperation in education and training (ET 2020). *Official Journal, C* 119/2.

Council of the European Union. (2011). OJ C 372/5, Council Resolution on a renewed European agenda for Adult Learning (2011/C 372/01).

ENQA. (2009). *Standards and guidelines for quality assurance in the European higher education area.* Helsinki: ENQA.

European Commission. (2000a). *A memorandum on Lifelong Learning*, 30.10.2000, SEC(2000) 1832. Brussels: European Commission.

European Commission. (2000b). *European report of May 2000 on the quality of school education: Sixteen quality indicators.* Report based on the work of the Working Committee on Quality Indicators.

European Commission. (2006). *Communication: Adult Learning: It is never too late to learn*, 3.10.2006 COM(2006) 614 final. Brussels: European Commission.

European Commission. (2007). *Communication: Action plan on adult learning, it is always a good time to learn*, 27.9.2007 COM(2007) 558 final. Brussels: European Commission.

European Commission. (2010). *Workshop on quality*,30th of June – 1st of July 2010, background report. Brussels: European Commission.

European Commission. (2011). Terms of reference developing the adult learning sector – Lot 1: Quality in the adult learning sector, Lot 2: Financing the adult learning sector, Lot 3: Opening higher education to adults 2011/S 158–261567.

European Parliament and the European Council. (2008). OJ C111/1 6.5.2008, Recommendation of the European Parliament and of the Council of 23 April 2008 on the establishment of the European Qualifications Framework for lifelong learning (Text with EEA relevance) (2008/C 111/01).

European Parliament and the European Council. (2009). OJ C 155/1 8.7.2009, Recommendation of the European Parliament and of the Council of 18 June 2009 on the establishment of a European Quality Assurance Reference Framework for Vocational Education and Training (Text with EEA relevance) (2009/C 155/01).

Eurydice. (2011). *Adults is formal education: Policies and practice in Europe.* Brussels: EACEA.

Faurschou, K. (2008). *Systematic quality assurance in Adult Learning, Nordic tiles in a mosaic.* Nordic Network Quality in Adult Learning.

Field, J. (2006). *Lifelong learning and the new educational order.* Stoke on Trent: Trentham Books.

Kells, H. R. (1992). *Self-regulation in higher education. A multi-national perspective on collaborative systems of quality assurance and control.* London: Jessica Kinsley Publishers.

Keogh, H. (2009). *The state and development of adult learning and education in Europe, North America and Israel: Regional synthesis report*. Hamburg: UNESCO Institute for Lifelong Learning.

NRDC. (2010). *Study on European terminology in adult learning for a common language and common understanding and monitoring of the sector*. London: NRDC.

PPMI. (2010). *Assessment of the impact of ongoing reforms in education and training on adult learning*. Vilnius: PPMI.

Research voor Beleid. (2010). *Key competences for adult learning professionals*. Zoetermeer: Research voor Beleid.

Research voor Beleid. (2011). *Impact of ongoing reforms in education and training on the adult learning sector (2nd phase)*. Zoetermeer: Research voor Beleid.

Research voor Beleid. (2012). *State of play of the European qualifications framework implementation*. Brussels: European Parliament.

Research voor Beleid and PLATO. (2005). *Developing local learning centres and learning partnerships as part of member states' targets for reaching the Lisbon goals in the field of education and training: A study of the current situation*. Leiden: Research voor Beleid/PLATO.

Research voor Beleid/PLATO. (2008). *Adult learning professionals is Europe (ALPINE)*. Leiden: Research voor Beleid/PLATO.

Schuller, T., & Watson, D. (2009). *Learning through life, inquiry into the future for lifelong learning, summary*. Leicester: NIACE.

UNESCO Institute for Lifelong Learning. (2009a). *Harnessing the power and potential of adult learning and education for a viable future, Belém framework for action*. Hamburg: UIL.

UNESCO Institute for Lifelong Learning. (2009b). *Global report on adult learning*. Hamburg: UIL.

University of Florence. (2010). *Enabling the low skilled to take their qualifications 'one step up'*. Florence: University of Florence.

van Dellen, T., & van der Kamp, M. (2008). Work domains and competences of the European adult and continuing educator. In S. Lattke & E. Nuissl (Eds.), *Qualifying adult learning professionals in Europe*. Bielefeld: W. Bertelsmann Verlag.

Vroeijenstijn, A. I. (1995). *Improvement and accountability, navigating between Scylla and Charybdis, guide for quality assessment in higher education*. London: Jessica Kingsley Publishers.

Weusthof, P. J. M., & Frederiks, M. M. H. (1997). De functies van het stelsel van kwaliteitsverzorg heroverwogen. *Tijdschrift voor Hoger Onderwijs, 15*(4), 318–338.

Chapter 18
The Adoption of an International Education Policy Agenda at National Level: Conceptual and Governance Issues

Alexandra Ioannidou

Introduction

Since the mid-1990s, there have been a raising number of policy documents, journal articles, and books dealing with the concept of lifelong learning from different perspectives. OECD's publication *Lifelong Learning for All* (1996), UNESCO's Report *Leaning – The Treasure Within* (1996), and Commission's *Memorandum on Lifelong Learning* (2000) are major policy documents that launched a worldwide debate on lifelong learning. When researchers study lifelong learning, they often point to the education policy dimension, or to historical, social, and economical aspects (cf. Istance et al. 2002; Field 2006; Hake 2008). However, matters concerning the worldwide dissemination of lifelong learning and the influence of supra- and international organizations on the governance of lifelong learning have not been sufficiently examined.

Questions regarding the impact of international organizations on educational policy making in general and on the governance of lifelong learning in particular are of paramount importance. In the long run of modern states' history, education and education policy have been run under the control of the nation-state and were a core element of its sovereignty and autonomy. The analytical perspective on issues concerning political steering and governance of education systems was for a long time state centered and normative. Even if this is still true to a varying extent in many countries, recently there is a shift in the examination of issues concerning educational governance.

With an international comparative study at the University of Tuebingen, Germany, we sought to answer questions regarding educational governance and the impact of

A. Ioannidou (✉)
Open University of Cyprus, Faculty of Humanities and Social Sciences, Nicosia, Cyprus
e-mail: alexa.ioannidou@gmail.com

G.K. Zarifis and M.N. Gravani (eds.), *Challenging the 'European Area of Lifelong Learning': A Critical Response*, Lifelong Learning Book Series 19, DOI 10.1007/978-94-007-7299-1_18, © Springer Science+Business Media Dordrecht 2014

the EU and OECD in this field taking as a case the concept of lifelong learning.[1] The project goals were to reconstruct the concept of lifelong learning with respect to its political and empirical aspects and to examine its implementation at a national level. The research questions were triggered by three striking developments: (a) the global spread of the concept of lifelong learning in the education policy (cf. Jakobi 2009), (b) the emergence of a "transnational educational space" (Lawn and Lingard 2002) beyond the nation-state, and (c) the appearance of new steering mechanisms and instruments in education based on a new management philosophy: the output-oriented steering (cf. Ioannidou 2007).

The study explored issues of educational governance and pursued questions concerning the adoption of an international education policy agenda at a national level taking as a case the concept of lifelong learning. To do so the following questions have been addressed: What are the characteristics of the post-national educational space? Who are the key actors in this field? What are their action orientations? What kind of resources do they use? What is the impact of their actions? What are the implications for the nation-state?

In order to explore these phenomena, three EU countries were selected Germany, Finland, and Greece, one supranational organization, the European Union, and one international, the Organization for Economic Cooperation and Development.

In the pages that follow, first I will outline the new analytical perspective of educational governance and define the terms as used in this chapter. Then I will present the theoretical framework and the empirical research design of the study. Building on that, I will highlight selected empirical findings of the study regarding (a) the adoption of the concept of lifelong learning at national level and (b) governance lifelong learning. Emphasis is given on the identification of influential actors in the European area of lifelong learning, their resources and modes of interaction as well as on the presentation of the impacts of their actions. In conclusion some reflecting remarks on the adoption patterns of an international education policy agenda at national level are provided.

A New Analytical Perspective: Educational Governance

Analytical perspectives on issues concerning regulation and control of education systems were from the very beginning and for a long time state centered. There was much faith both in the capacity of the nation-state to manage, regulate, guide, and control functional systems such as the economic or the educational system as well as in the feasibility of the functional systems to be efficiently managed, regulated,

---

[1] The international comparative project was funded by the Hans-Böckler-Foundation and the University of Tübingen (Germany). The project was based on the theoretical approaches of path-dependent development and actor-centered institutionalism both emanating from political science. The methods applied were document analysis, expert interviews, and comparative analysis of educational monitoring and reporting systems.

guided, and controlled by the nation-state.[2] However, during the late 1960s and particularly in the 1970s, many sociologists and political scientists argued vigorously against these propositions drawing on a number of empirical policy analyses and on the growing influence of systems theory (Mayntz 1997, 2004). Policy making was seen as increasingly involving, partially cooperative, partially conflictive exchanges and interactions between the state and a range of private public and voluntary organizations. The term "governance"[3] was proposed in the political sciences to replace the traditional term "controlling" (Mayntz 1997, p. 278). The latter, it was argued, no longer reflected the patterns that emerged as a result of mutual interactions and interdependencies among actors from various levels, of which the state was only one.

The term "governance" has been widely disseminated and stimulated scientific discussions in a range of academic disciplines. In the last years it has been extensively used in political sciences, in political economy, in sociology, and also in different connotations, analytical or normative (e.g., "good governance") (cf. Benz 2004). The term has been recently introduced in the educational sciences as well. Questions concerning the coordination and management of mutual interdependencies of various actors of the education system have been examined under the generic term "educational governance" (cf. Altrichter et al. 2007). The new term clearly recognizes the dynamics that arose from the emergence of policy actors at various levels (local, regional, national, transnational) and emphasizes a variety of patterns of interaction (networks, coalitions, majority rule, negotiations) among them. These policy actors operate as a nonhierarchical, multilevel governance system with no clear sovereign authority, but still with capacity of policy shaping (cf. Mayntz and Scharpf 1995).

The emergence of "new arenas of education governance" (Martens et al. 2007) makes it evident that new concepts are necessary for the analysis of the governance capacity and governance practices of the main actors involved in education policy beyond the nation-state.

Adopting an International Education Policy Agenda at National Level: Theoretical Reflections

It seems undisputed nowadays that the primary driving forces behind current policy reforms in national education systems are actually external to the national systems themselves: global labor markets, modernization and transformation processes,

---

[2] The current economic crisis dramatically confirms the dynamics and mutual interdependencies of various actors and the immanent difficulties of sufficient management and control of the economic system by the political system.

[3] The origin of the term governance comes from Greek (*"kybernein"*) and it initially meant the steering of ships. The Latin term *"gubernare"* was used both for steering of ships and governing a state.

regional integration processes – primarily within Europe – demographic trends and changing working patterns, common societal problems, and the "diffusion of world cultural principles" (Meyer and Ramirez 2003). Moreover, despite the fact that official European discourse insists that education will remain a national policy domain, a gradual strengthening movement toward supranational policy formation in Europe has become visible. The ambitious policy objectives of the Lisbon Strategy of "making the European Union the most competitive and knowledge-based economy in the world" as well as the "Europa 2020 Strategy" place education in the center of policy interest and lead to a post-national, transnational educational space.

This is a new policy arena that brings forth a host of actors from different levels who influence policy formation at the international as well as at the national level. The transnational educational space shows characteristics of a multilayered system with horizontal and vertical policy linkages, with network-like structures from state and non-state actors, and with interaction patterns that are based more on coalitions, negotiations, and mutual adjustment rather than on hierarchical regulation. New and emerging policy actors such as international and supranational bodies like the OECD, UNESCO, or the EU along with local authorities and organizations of the civil society and the market interact with old and established ones (nation-states) concerning the mandate, the capacity, and the governance of education. As Dale states, the mandate of education refers to "what is desirable for the education system to achieve; its capacity – what is considered feasible for it to achieve; and its governance – how those objectives are realized" (2003, p. 102).

The aforementioned developments have given rise to a range of complex issues relating to the future of nation-states, their relation to international and supranational bodies, and their capacity to control and govern their own policy destinies and set their own agendas.

The concept of lifelong learning exceeds the narrow national and geographical boundaries and has become a global norm. EU and OECD as supra- and international organizations play an important role both at the level of widely spreading the message globally as well as at the policy formulation at national level. In addition, the spatial characteristics of the transnational educational space indicate a multilayer structure with a variety of actors from different levels (supranational, national, and regional) who may endorse or reject the adoption or implementation of lifelong learning. In a multilayer structure, the various actors come into different constellations and create interdependent relationships with each other demanding high coordination in order to enforce decisions.

The theoretical framework of the study presented is built on the approaches of path-dependence and actor-centered institutionalism, both emanating from political sciences. With reference to Scharpf (2006, p. 17), the adoption of the concept of lifelong learning and its implementation in Greece, Germany, and Finland can be considered as "the product of interactions between intentionally acting actors – individual, collective or corporate."

The identification of key actors, their action orientations, their material and immaterial resources, and their interaction are crucial in this theoretical context. Both the EU and the OECD are, according to Scharpf, complex actors who purposefully and strategically act to achieve their goals. Their ability in strategic action depends firstly on the convergence or divergence of the action orientations between their members and secondly upon the institutional conditions that make an internal conflict resolution more difficult or easier (ibid., p. 108). According to the approach of actor-centered institutionalism, the institutional context within the EU and OECD favors political decisions taking place in the mode of negotiation or by majority decision rather than being determined by unilateral action or by hierarchical decisions.

In this action-theoretical context, institutional structures, culture-specific diversification, and path-dependent development patterns might be underestimated. The notion of path dependence, despite different uses in diverse disciplines, is linked to the idea that "history matters" in the interpretation of phenomena (cf. Bassanini and Dosi 1999). According to the theorem of path dependence, the reception and implementation of a global educational policy concept such as lifelong learning at a national level can be enforced or prohibited according to historical paths or institutional organizational forms and the cultural traditions or conventions of a country. National path dependencies exist in every country. Empirical findings to education policy borrowing and to internationalization of education point out that there exists "an antagonistic tension between, the transnational diffusion of modern models and rules and the self-evolutive continuation or even revival of culture-specific semantic traditions" (Schriewer and Martinez 2004, pp. 36–37, cf. also Mayer 2001).

A Comparative Research Design

As a consequence of the assumptions and reflections discussed in the previous section, a comparative research design was chosen including a combination of methods. In order to explore the intentions, interests, and interactions of major stakeholders, expert interviews were conducted with key stakeholders from the educational policy administration and the educational research.

Eighteen experts were interviewed in individual structured interviews. The interviewed experts belong to the functional elites of their organizations. Some of them are in an advisory or executive position in the administration of national ministries of education in the areas of adult education and lifelong learning, or they work in the education directorates of the EU and the OECD. Others are educational researchers at universities or other research institutions with long experience in the field of monitoring and reporting on education.

The data analysis was based on the evaluation strategy of Meuser and Nagel (2005) who proposed an interpretive model for structured expert interviews (ibid., p. 81). The expert interviews were fully transcribed and qualitatively analyzed using computer-aided data analysis (cf. Kuckartz 2005).

Complementary, in terms of contextualization and validation of the experts' views, education policy documents such as programmatic texts, memoranda, guidelines, communications, recommendations, reports, conference papers, and legal acts between 1996 and 2008 were analyzed in order to manifest the political discourse, to reveal culture-specific semantic traditions, and to identify path-dependent development patterns.

Finally, a comparative analysis of educational monitoring instruments was used in order to analyze the empirical approach to the concept of lifelong learning. The examination focused on how the theoretical concept of lifelong learning has been translated into empirical research. In order to do so, definitions, concepts, and tools of measuring lifelong learning, European and national surveys, and studies were compared. In addition, background documents, e.g., conceptual and strategy papers used to measure lifelong learning, methodological texts, as well as pilot tests were analyzed.

For investigating the adoption of the lifelong learning agenda at national level in the European area, three European countries have been identified as suitable cases for the comparative research design: Germany, Finland, and Greece. EU and OECD have been selected as a supranational and an international organization with major influence and agenda-setting capacity in the field of lifelong learning.

The selection of the countries was based on the principle of maximal variation on the basis of selected structural features (including the structure of the education and training sector and the type of governance in education) and on the basis of quantitative indicators (including participation in continuing education and lifelong learning). Finland, Greece, and Germany have differently organized education and training systems that are historically rooted and have a great heterogeneity in the structuring of the education sector. Their training systems have different legal requirements and funding arrangements that result from their particular course of history and special characteristics. In addition, the actual importance of lifelong learning in the selected countries varies greatly, as the use of quantitative indicators shows.

However, all three countries belong to the European geographical and cultural territory, and they are members of the EU and the OECD; thus, they lay under the direct influence of these organizations. Through their membership in the European multilayer system, they accept a common policy framework which enables specific developments at national level. Their membership in the OECD also promotes convergent developments in these countries, although the degrees of freedom are greater in this case.

Highlights of the Study[4]

Lifelong Learning and Its Adoption Within National Education Policy Agenda

Regarding the concept of lifelong learning and its adoption within national education policy, the findings of the study confirm that lifelong learning has become the new "master narrative" in all three countries under examination.

---

[4] For more information, see Ioannidou (2010).

Lifelong learning has been considered as an important part of the EU Lisbon Strategy according to which the European Union should become by 2010, the most competitive and dynamic knowledge-based economic area in the world, as well as a more cohesive and inclusive society. Acquiring and continuously updating and upgrading skills and competences are considered a prerequisite for the personal development of all citizens and for participation in all aspects of society in the three countries.

The *Memorandum* recognizes lifelong learning as an essential policy for the development of citizenship, social cohesion, and employment (p. 6). The following definition was adopted as a working definition for subsequent discussion and action in the Member States: Lifelong learning encompasses all purposeful learning activity, undertaken on an ongoing basis with the aim of improving knowledge, skills, and competence (ibid., p. 3).

The findings of the document analysis as well as of the experts' interviews point out that at the level of political rhetoric the national debate is almost entirely determined by the rhetoric of the EU and the OECD. In the political rhetoric in all three countries, lifelong learning is considered as a vehicle for the promotion of both active citizenship and employability. Nevertheless, the findings illustrate how different is the notion of lifelong learning in Germany, Finland, and Greece even though the political rhetoric is identical. The connotations of the term "lifelong learning," the driving forces for promoting this idea, and the priorities given in each country seem to be different.

In Germany, the idea of lifelong learning is mainly linked to employability and is considered as a vehicle for maintaining the competitiveness of the German economy with an emphasis on continuing professional education and training and on promoting diverse forms of learning, validation, and certification. In Finland, whose educational system is characterized by excellent permeability between the different levels of education and an integrated system of validation and certification of informal learning, the contribution of lifelong learning both to maintain social cohesion and remain competitive is highlighted. In Greece, due to the lack of a widespread tradition in adult education and lack of structures and mechanisms for validation and certification of informal learning, the connotation of lifelong learning indicates a strong link to institutionalized adult education.

The findings clearly point out that the concept of lifelong learning seems to become an educational norm and part of the educational narrative in all three countries. A concept that was initially developed at the international level and formulated by international organizations (Council of Europe, UNESCO, OECD, EU) gradually became part of the educational discourse at national level. Its inclusion in the official discourse in Greece, Germany, and Finland initially took place on a declarative level by the national authorities before it was broken down, depending on the type of governance in education (centralized for Greece, regionally in Germany, local to Finland) to the regional and local level. Nevertheless, there is empirical evidence that the adoption and implementation of lifelong learning in the three countries is significantly path dependent, i.e., it is infiltrated by national traditions and culture-specific patterns of meaning.

The way educational policy and administration in Greece, Germany, and Finland adapt and interpret the concept of lifelong learning seems to depend on a number of factors: the actual importance of education and lifelong learning in every country, the social climate that may promote learning outside the formal educational system, the degree of institutionalization of adult education in the respective countries, and the national educational and culture-specific semantic traditions in each country.

Governance Lifelong Learning

Regarding the governance of lifelong learning, the empirical findings confirm the emergence of a transnational educational space in which powerful actors interact with each other on a variety of settings, i.e., public, private, and nongovernmental, and at various levels, i.e., local, regional, national, and supranational.

These findings tend to be in line with the *Memorandum's* appeal to systematically integrate social partners in the development and implementation process, in conjunction with public-private initiatives, and to actively involve local and regional bodies and civil society organizations (pp. 9–10).

The comparative examination of the experts' interviews shows both similarities and differences in the perceptions of experts regarding the influence of the EU and OECD on national education policy. Almost unanimously, the experts confirm the impact of both organizations. However, they are far apart in their assessments of the degree of influence. First, there are some country-specific differences: The interviewed Greek experts confirm a major influence of the European Union on the national education policy. The same is also true for the interviewed Finnish experts who consider a high impact of the EU on the national education policy. They both assign to the Commission its ability for policy formation due to the supranational power of the EU and its financial mechanisms. On the contrary, the German experts expressed skepticism in this regard. This might be explained through the federal structure of Germany. For education policy, the federal states ("Länder") are responsible; it is the "heart" of their policy and an issue that can cause tension among the federal and regional level.

With respect to the impact of the OECD on a national level, country-specific differences appear. In Finland the OECD enjoys the greatest recognition. For the Finnish experts, the impact of the OECD on national education policy is as powerful as the one of the EU. For Greece, the OECD plays an important role, but compared to the influence of the EU, it can be considered as modest. The German respondents seem to be divided regarding their assessment of the OECD's influence. While the representatives of educational administration at federal and state level affirm reluctantly the question of the influence of the OECD on national education policy, at the same time, however, they make this effect relative with reference to the "opportune moment" and the "coincidence" of national priorities and international recommendations. On the contrary, for the experts from the

German educational research, the influence of the organization, since the publication of the PISA results, is undisputed.

When comparing the instruments of governance regarding lifelong learning of both organizations, the EU and OECD, the interviewed experts recognize both similarities and distinct differences. The EU is classified as a supranational authority,[5] whose decisions and regulations are almost binding to the member states. This organizational structure allows promoting and enforcing certain decisions using EU law. The OECD, however, as an international organization,[6] cannot affect the sovereignty of its member states or bring out binding decisions for its members. The experts agree that the EU mainly works with funding mechanisms and where the treaties allow it, with legislation that is with "hard" instruments (money, power). Since the introduction of the open method of coordination in education in 2000, the European Commission is also working increasingly with processes such as peer review or monitoring and evaluation. At that time (2000) the *Memorandum* claims lack of appropriate targets and meaningful benchmarks in relation to lifelong learning and highlights the importance of indicators that reflect "the full meaning of lifelong learning" for a coherent policy development (p. 20).

The OECD, in turn, works mainly with recommendations, evaluations, large-scale studies, and peer reviews, in other words, using rather "soft" instruments which are based more on knowledge and expertise.

When asking for key actors in the field of lifelong learning, the verdict of the interviewed experts is astonishingly uniform. EU and OECD are unanimously identified by the experts as influential collective actors. The identified key actors are facilitated by institutional resources. According to Scharpf (2006) material resources and institutional rules belong to institutional resources. The institutional resources include both tangible means such as money, technology, and privileged access to information as well as institutional rules – that means rules by which relations among the actors are regulated, such as collective decision-making process or prohibitions. It is evident that not all actors have equal access to resources. The steering media of money, power, and knowledge are unevenly distributed, creating dependencies and interdependencies between the actors (cf. Ioannidou 2007).

The OECD, for example, using its surveys, international comparative reports, and evaluations, can spread good practice or use "the name and shame" strategy (e.g., PISA). The European Commission emphatically asks for regular education monitoring and reporting from its member states in the framework of the open

---

[5] Supranational organizations such as the European Union (EU) have due to their constituting treaties legal power to shape national policy in some fields (e.g., economics, labor market). The EU has no legislative competencies in the education field, as stated in the Treaties of Maastricht (Article 126 & 127) and of Amsterdam (Article 149 & 150), but it can strongly influence national education policy through policy formation in other fields.

[6] International organizations such as the United Nations Educational Scientific and Cultural Organization (UNESCO) or the Organization for Economic Cooperation and Development (OECD) are influential actors even if, due to their intergovernmental structure, they have no regulative capacities upon their member states. Their power derives from their agenda-setting capacity and their existence as policy-making arenas.

method of coordination or even through legislation (e.g., EU-Adult Education Survey). Furthermore, by means of their publications, the EU and the OECD circulate concepts, norms, and models and generate normative pressure upon their members.

In addition to the collective actors, policy officers at European and national level as well as consultants, experts, and researchers are identified as individual actors who can influence with their decisions the adoption and implementation of lifelong learning. The findings show very clearly that, besides the institutional resources, their influence derives mostly from their personal characteristics. It turns out that experience, knowledge, communication skills, and openness constitute the intellectual resources which are at the disposal of the relevant actors in varying degrees. Furthermore, the findings indicate that they form a kind of closed elite circle who work together and decisively influence the discourse about lifelong learning.

These experts show convergences in their cognitive, normative, and evaluative orientations that result from their specific role within an institutional context. For example, they all consider systematic and evidence-based knowledge as essential for rational decision making. These shared values and common standards facilitate the decision-making process and increase the capacity for strategic action in nonhierarchical contexts.

The findings also support the assumption that the institutional context enables decisions that take place through negotiations rather than by majority rules or unilateral actions or hierarchical order. Thus, it favors the work in networks and working groups, since decisions there take place on the basis of negotiations. In the EU context, the coordination of action usually takes place in the form of negotiations or as a majority decision. For example, the adopted indicators and benchmarks for lifelong learning are the product of continuing negotiations between Member States and Commission. Nevertheless, unilateral actions cannot be excluded because of the bureaucratic and hierarchical organizational structure of the EU. In the OECD context, due to its constitution, decisions derive from negotiations, sometimes even as a majority decision, but never in the form of hierarchical order.

As far-reaching impact of the influence of EU and OECD is the establishment of a particular research paradigm. Both the EU and the OECD enforce the quantitative paradigm with studies and comparative reports based on quantitative indicators. This research paradigm is increasingly shaping evidence-based policy not only at an international but also at a national level (cf. Landesinstitut 2008). In alliance with this research paradigm, a new form of knowledge and a new management philosophy in education seem to have prevailed. The findings suggest that a shift from the input- to output-oriented management takes place all over Europe. The output, the result of the learning effort, moves into the foreground, while input and process aspects that had traditionally served as reference levels gradually lose their significance. This shift requires the generation of relevant knowledge to enable evaluation so that the new form of knowledge and the new management philosophy assist and strengthen one another: The evidence-based policy requires knowledge that is quantifiable and explicit and can be translated in the logic of the educational planners.

Conclusion

This chapter has focused on conceptual and governance issues with regard to the adoption of lifelong learning as an international education policy agenda at national level. The analysis highlighted the emergence of a post-national, transnational educational space that enables and accelerates the dissemination of global educational ideas, such as the concept of lifelong learning at national level. Furthermore, it became evident that national path dependencies and culture-specific semantic traditions decisively influence the reception and implementation of these concepts in the respective country-specific reality.

More particularly, regarding the adoption of the concept of lifelong learning in Greece, Germany, and Finland, the findings point out that there are country-specific reinterpretations of the concept and confirm the results of international comparative educational research. Concepts such as lifelong learning, knowledge, economy, and learning society are discursive and ideological products which create within a given historical and sociocultural context their own importance (cf. Robertson 2008; Robertson and Dale 2009).

Hence, the detected differences in Germany, Greece, and Finland are more gradual than they are principal. In all three countries, the influence of the EU and the OECD is well recognized, as well as the impact of their initiatives regarding lifelong learning. All three countries use the definition of lifelong learning as proposed in the *Memorandum*, adopt lifelong learning in national legislation, and promote its implementation. Moreover, their educational administration increasingly adopts new management tools and output-oriented models of governance as proposed by the EU and OECD.

Regarding the governance of lifelong learning, the empirical findings support the emergence of a transnational educational space in which influential actors interact with each other on a variety of settings. The emergence of a transnational educational space undermines the long-term development of purely national education policies and weakens the role of the nation-state in shaping educational policy. Supranational and intergovernmental bodies like the EU and the OECD emerge as major centers of influence in shaping educational policies. These organizations promote new educational tools and practices of governance. The shift to empirical models of educational governance (evidence-based policy) and the shift in focus from input- to output-driven models promote the dominance of specific educational governance instruments based on knowledge and mutual learning such as monitoring and evaluation on the assumption that indicators and comparative reports support autonomy and accountability.

The attention that was paid already with the *Memorandum*, and particularly in recent years, to the construction and further development of indicators leads to increasingly elaborated and composed indicators in this field. Since 2000, impressive progress has been done by the European Commission in cooperation with the OECD in the field of indicators development and benchmarks setting in relation to lifelong learning. The European Lifelong Learning Index (ELLI) is the next step for country-level assessment of lifelong learning in the EU Member States.[7] In this context, indicators play an important role as appropriate and effective tools for evidence-based policy. However, the assumption that informed decisions are good decisions suggests also that the quality of decisions rises together with the accumulation of statistical data and information (cf. Keiner 2005). However, the example of the PISA reception in Germany reveals that educational planners interpret the findings from the PISA study according to their interests and mainly use them for the stabilization and legitimacy of their political decision making (cf. Tillmann et al. 2008).

References

Altrichter, H., Brüsemeister, T., & Wissinger, J. (Hrsg.). (2007). *Educational governance. Handlungskoordination und Steuerung im Bildungswesen*. Wiesbaden: VS Verlag für Sozialwissenschaften.

Bassanini, A., & Dosi, G. (1999). When and how chance and human will can twist the arms of Clio. First draft. *Laboratory of economics and management. Sant'Anna school of advanced studies* (LEM Working Papers, Laboratory of Economics and Management Sant'Anna School of Advanced Studies, Pisa 5, pp. 1–33). http://www.lem.sssup.it/WPLem/files/1999-05.pdf

Benz, A. (2004). *Governance – Regieren in komplexen Regelsystemen. Eine Einführung*. Wiesbaden: VS Verlag.

Commission of the European Communities. (2000). *A memorandum on lifelong learning. Commission staff working document* (30.10.2000 SEC(2000) 1832). Brussels: Commission of the European Communities.

Dale, R. (2003). Globalization: A new world for comparative education? In J. Schriewer (Hrsg), *Discourse formation in comparative education* (pp. 87–109). Bern: Peter Lang.

Delors, J., et al. (1996). *Learning: The treasure within: Report to UNESCO of the international commission on education for the twenty-first century*. Paris: UNESCO Publication.

Field, J. (2006). *Lifelong learning and the new educational order*. Stoke on Trent: Trentham Books.

Hake, B. (2008). Comparative policy analysis and lifelong learning narratives: The "employability agenda" from a life-course perspective. In J. Reischmann & M. Bron Jr. (Eds.), *Comparative adult education 2008. Experiences and examples* (pp. 167–178). Frankfurt a.M: Peter Lang.

Hoskins, B., Cartwright, F., & Schoof, U. (2010). *The ELLI-index. Europe 2010. Making lifelong learning tangible!* Gutersloh: Bertelsmann Stiftung.

Ioannidou, A. (2007). Comparative analysis of new governance instruments in transnational educational space – A shift to knowledge-based instruments? *European Educational Research Journal, H. 6*, 336–347. URL: http://dx.doi.org/10.2304/eerj.2004.3.1.9.

---

[7] The conceptual framework for the ELLI-Index (cf. Hoskins et al. 2010) is loosely based on the UNESCO's International Commission on Education for the Twenty-first Century (Delors et al 1996) and the four major dimensions of learning identified: (a) Learning to Know (includes acquisition of knowledge and mastery of learning tools such as concentration, memory, and analysis), (b) Learning to Do (concerns occupational, hands-on, and practical skills), (c) Learning to Live Together (concerns learning that strengthens cooperation and social cohesion), and (d) Learning to Be (includes the fulfillment of a person, as an individual/member of a family/citizen). The ELLI-Index combines 36 variables of lifelong learning that reflect a wide range of learning activities, including participation rates in formal education and training, literacy skills (PISA), employees participating in CVT courses, labor market policies expenditure, and community engagement through cultural activities, among others.

Ioannidou, A. (2010). *Steuerung im transnationalen Bildungsraum. Internationales Bildungsmonitoring zum Lebenslangen Lernen.* Bielefeld: W. Bertelsmann Verlag.

Istance, D., Schuetze, H. G., & Schuller, T. (Eds.). (2002). *International perspectives on lifelong learning. From recurrent education to the knowledge society.* Buckingham/Philadelphia: The Society for Research into Higher Education/Open University Press.

Jakobi, A. (2009). *International organizations and lifelong learning: From global agendas to policy diffusion.* New York: Palgrave Macmillan.

Keiner, E. (2005). Zur Konstruktion erziehungswissenschaftlicher Forschung aus der Perspektive der OECD. *Zeitschrift für Erziehungswissenschaften, 8*(4), 13–23.

Kuckartz, U. (2005). *Einführung in die computergestützte Analyse qualitativer Daten.* Wiesbaden: VS Verl. für Sozialwiss.

Landesinstitut für Schule und Medien Berlin-Brandenburg (Deutschland)., Bundesministerium für Unterricht, Kunst und Kultur (Österreich), & Schweizerische Konferenz der kantonalen Erziehungsdirektoren (Schweiz). (Hrsg.). (2008, September). *Bildungsmonitoring, Vergleichsstudien und Innovationen. Von evidenzbasierter Steuerung zur Praxis. OECD/CERI Regionalseminar für die deutschsprachigen Länder in Potsdam vom* (pp. 25–28). Berlin: BWV Berliner Wissenschafts-Verlag.

Lawn, M., & Lingard, B. (2002). Constructing a European policy space in education governance: The role of transnational policy actors. *European Educational Research Journal, 1*(2), 290–307. http://dx.doi.org/10.2304/eerj.2002.1.2.6

Martens, K., Rusconi, A., & Leuze, K. (Eds.). (2007). *New arenas of education governance. The impact of international organizations and markets on education policy making* (Transformation of the state series). Basingstoke: Palgrave Macmillan.

Mayer, K.-U. (2001). The paradox of global social change and national path dependencies: Life course patterns in advanced societies. In A. E. Woodward & M. Kohli (Eds.), *Inclusions and exclusions in European societies* (pp. 89–110). London: Routledge.

Mayntz, R. (1997). *Soziale Dynamik und politische Steuerung. Theoretische und methodische Überlegungen.* Frankfurt a.M./New York: Campus Verlag.

Mayntz, R. (2004). Governance im modernen Staat. In: A. Benz (Hrsg.), *Governance – Regieren in komplexen Regelsystemen: eine Einführung* (pp. 65–76). Wiesbaden: VS Verlag für Sozialwissenschaften.

Mayntz, R., & Scharpf, F. W. (1995). Der Ansatz des akteurzentrierten Institutionalismus. In: R. Mayntz, & F. W. Scharpf (Hg.), *Gesellschaftliche Selbstregelung und politische Steuerung* (pp. 39–72). Frankfurt a.M.: Campus Verlag.

Meuser, M., & Nagel, U. (2005). "Experteninterviews – vielfach erprobt, wenig bedacht. Ein Beitrag zur qualitativen Methodendiskussion". In: A. Bogner, B. Littig, & W. Menz (Hrsg.). *Das Experteninterview. Theorie, Methode, Anwendung* (pp. 71–93). Wiesbaden: VS Verlag für Sozialwissenschaften.

Meyer, J., & Ramirez, F. (2003). The world institutionalization of education. In: J. Schriewer (Hrsg.), *Discourse formation in comparative education* (pp. 111–132). Bern: Peter Lang.

OECD. (1996). *Lifelong learning for all.* Paris: OECD Publishing.

Robertson, S. L. (2008). Producing the global knowledge economy: The world bank, the KAM, education and development. In M. Simons, M. Olssen, & M. Peters (Eds.), *Re-reading education policies: Studying the policy agenda of the 21st century.* Rotterdam: Sense Publishers.

Robertson, S. L., & Dale, R. (Eds.). (2009). *Globalisation and Europeanisation in education.* Oxford: Symposium Books.

Scharpf, F. W. (2006). *Interaktionsformen. Akteurzentrierter Institutionalismus in der Politikforschung.* Wiesbaden: VS Verlag für Sozialwissenschaften.

Schriewer, J., & Martinez, C. (2004). Constructions of internationality in education. In Steiner-Khamsi (Ed.), *Global politics of educational borrowing & lending* (pp. 29–53). New York: Teachers College Press.

Tillmann, K.-J., Dedering, K., Kneuper, D., Kuhlmann, C., & Nessel, I. (2008). *PISA als bildungspolitisches Ereignis. Fallstudien in vier Bundesländern.* Wiesbaden: Verlag für Sozialwissenschaften.

Chapter 19
Vocational Learning: Shifting Relationships Between Education and Working Life

Erik Kats and Jaap van Lakerveld

Introduction

The development of systems of education is strongly connected to the development industrial society. Relationships between education and the vocational practice of people in the companies and organisations where they work are however variable through the times, and there is always some room between both spheres. In this chapter we will describe shifts in the way vocational learning is situated in the growing room between formal education and working life in the Netherlands.

First, we will shortly go into the way vocational learning relates to the traditional broad humanistic approach to adult education. Next, we will discuss a number of shifts that have occurred in the field of vocational learning in the course of economic and political developments in the Netherlands. These shifts are not exclusively tied to specific historic circumstances, and they are neither irreversible. In conclusion we will argue that all shifts we describe have an actual meaning for the debate on lifelong learning.

Education and Learning: Narrowing and Broadening Practices

An important function of adult education, next to the sociocultural development of people, has always been to assign people a useful economic role in society. The economic function however tends to dominate the actual conception of lifelong

E. Kats (✉) • J. van Lakerveld
Centre for Research and Development in Education and Lifelong Learning (PLATO),
Leiden University, Leiden, The Netherlands
e-mail: kats@fsw.leidenuniv.nl

G.K. Zarifis and M.N. Gravani (eds.), *Challenging the 'European Area of Lifelong Learning': A Critical Response*, Lifelong Learning Book Series 19, DOI 10.1007/978-94-007-7299-1_19, © Springer Science+Business Media Dordrecht 2014

learning (Doets et al. 2008). Summarising, the functions of adult education may be described as the acquisition of general knowledge, the training of specific skills and the development of sociocultural competence (van Gent 1996). The relationships between these three functions and the ways they are dealt with are shifting with social and economic developments.

In former days the relation of adult education to labour and economy mainly had an *external* character. The economic function of adult education concentrated on vocational training. It intended to prepare people for work or to support people who had somehow been excluded from employment. Next to that, adult education served as sociocultural compensation to the miserable conditions of early industrial labour, or it tried to open possibilities for development that the economic system denied to many people.

Nowadays we live in a knowledge society. The European Union mainly argues the need for lifelong learning from the ambition to become a competitive knowledge economy (CEC 2000). A knowledge economy implies that all kinds of companies and organisations are bound to the continuous improvement and innovation of business processes. Employees thus are challenged to be engaged in continuous vocational learning and professional development (Kessels 1996). In this sense, adult learning has rapidly pervaded economic life *internally* (Kats 1998). All people are expected to keep up and to improve their competence and their employability. This demonstrates the strong emphasis on the vocational function in the actual discussions on lifelong learning.

The emphasis on learning represents still another shift. Adult *education* traditionally implied the guidance of underprivileged people by privileged educators. Following the individualisation of society, lifelong *learning* is however nowadays primarily a responsibility for each individual himself. People are expected to direct learning themselves; it is a privilege to be able to do so, which of course involves renewed social distinction.

If lifelong learning is a need for everyone, it also has to be lifewide learning. The Dutch Education Council substantiates that all functions mentioned above are involved, whereas traditional training tends to be confined to specific skills (Onderwijsraad 2003). The dominance of the economic function however prevails. In the 2004 *Action Plan on Lifelong Learning*, the Dutch government mainly pays attention to subjects like employability, productivity and economic development (Ministerie 2004).

A knowledge society is marked by a highly developed system of formal education on the one hand. In economic life professional practices show an ever growing complexity on the other hand; a specific training does not suffice anymore for a lifelong career. The link between formal education and economic life is becoming less direct, and the room as well as the need for 'extra' education and learning is growing. Lifelong learning develops in this room; it is connected both with the education system and with the structures of economic life.

For the debate on the challenges of lifelong learning, it is useful to consider historic changes in the position of and approaches to vocational learning. In the following we will describe shifts in the way vocational learning is situated in the growing room between formal education and working life in the Netherlands.

The Dutch sociologist de Swaan (1988) gives a comparative analysis of the development of collective arrangements and public services, like systems of education, in the Netherlands, Germany, Great Britain, France and the United States. Following this analysis we will here consider the development of vocational education in the Netherlands: from a private initiative to a collective arrangement, gradually transformed into a public provision, that eventually has to rediscover its connections with private business life. To describe the shifts and transformations in the field of vocational learning, we will introduce a number of concepts that might be useful to identify comparable shifts and transformations in other countries.

The Rise of Industrial Society

Compared to other Western European countries, industrialisation in the Netherlands had a late start. The 'take-off' did not occur until the 1890s (de Jonge 1976). As in other countries, the need of the industrial economy to rely on a skilled labour force has shaped the development of vocational education and training in the Netherlands (Leune 2003).

The first industrial companies that started their business activities often were at the leading edge in their respective region. The entrepreneurs of the nineteenth century typically were innovators and enlightened citizens. In the Netherlands, such entrepreneurs started establishing company schools from the second half of the nineteenth century. In these schools training is strongly connected to apprenticeships in the company. By taking responsibility for the schooling of the population, they served the common interest as well as their own needs of building up a skilled labour force for their businesses. Following de Swaan (1988) this mechanism of serving public and one's own business interests in combination may be described as enlightened self-interest. The establishment of schools within companies has created a strong tradition that still exists in several companies today.

An unintended consequence of the establishment of company-based schools for skill development is that the trained workers acquire a better position for developing their personal career and may decide to change employers. So other companies may also benefit from the generally better skilled labour force. This is an important reason why groups of companies start to found common vocational schools. Such collective arrangements that serve the common interest constitute an adequate response to this 'free rider' phenomenon. Following De Swaan's analysis, all kinds of arrangements in the modern welfare state originate from seeking solutions to such unintended consequences.

Ultimately, companies are better capable to fulfil the overall qualification needs for a particular sector collectively rather than individually. This eventually led to the creation of common National Vocational Training Bodies (Landelijke Opleidingsorganen) in numerous sectors. These bodies care for the fulfilment of the need for knowledge development and for having qualified personnel for the business sectors involved.

De Swaan points out that the creation of collective arrangements leads to a growing interdependence of actors, in the beginning at the interpersonal level but soon also at the broader institutional level. This process may be typified as *interdependification*. The shift from only training one's own labourers to a broad provision to fulfil the need for a skilled labour force is a clear example of this process.

As the development of industrial society goes along with an ongoing expansion, the process of upscaling requires a guarantee for the growing interdependence of institutions and actors. As the tasks of training bodies were becoming ever broader, the need for formal recognition of certificates was growing as for an arrangement of financing and eventually for a legal foundation. This explains why the state at a certain moment enters the field.

In 1919 the first government act on vocational education (the 'Nijverheidswet') was agreed in the Netherlands. From the industrialisation period of the 1920s onwards, branch-specific initiatives for the training of workers were gradually transformed into technical schools (Meijers 1983). A typical feature of the Dutch society here is that these schools, despite their increasing public funding, continued to be run by the sectors of business concerned, and they remained outside the developing national system of general education. The class differences between brainwork and manual work were thus reinforced (Van Kemenade 1981).

The Reconstruction of a Modern Industrial Society

Despite the industrial development before the Second World War, the Netherlands to a large extent kept the character of an agricultural society until the middle of the twentieth century. In the post-war reconstruction period after 1945, efforts were concentrated on a strong industrial expansion. The 'social partners', employers, trade unions and the government, intensively worked together to bring about full employment. The cooperation between social partners in a so-called polder model is a typical feature of the Dutch society. This cooperation has been institutionalised at a nearly corporatist way in a whole series of public and private bodies.

Windmuller (1969), who made an analysis of the peculiar Dutch system of labour relations, describes the climate in the post-war period as largely influenced by the wish to avoid forever the social and political misery that resulted from the pre-war economic crisis.

The cooperation between social partners in specific branches of industry and business also stimulated the growth of vocational education and training. Originating from the diversity of private initiatives of regional and sectoral groups of business, numerous technical schools, often with only a few hundred pupils, were established (Meijers 1983). All these schools provided education for one or more specific vocational fields. The gradual transformation of diverse training bodies into schools may be typified as *schoolification*.

Another important feature of Dutch society is the so-called pillarisation. Pillarisation implies that each religious and sociopolitical group may establish its own social institutions. This not only means churches and political parties but also newspapers, trade unions, employer organisations, voluntary associations, social service institutions and, especially, schools (Lijphart 1968). As a result of the 'pillarisation', the patchwork of technical schools is even multiplied. To this day, about 75 % of the schools are organised on a denominational (religious or nonreligious) basis; the 25 % 'state' schools consequently have got the character of a separate pillar.

The pillarisation implies that many organisations in the public sphere are in fact no public institutions; they are publicly funded but initiated and governed by the diverse sociopolitical groups. The combination of pillarisation and cooperation gives the Dutch society the character of 'living apart together' in those days; for large parts of the population communication for a long time only took place within the own 'denomination'. The elites of the different 'social streams' deliberate with each other at the level of the state and make agreements about an equitable distribution of resources. This mechanism is a strong impetus for the development of the Dutch welfare state.

Expansion of the Welfare State and the System of Education

At the beginning of the 1960s, the economy in the Netherlands had gradually developed to a level that allowed not only for a substantial growth of material welfare but also for social transformations in different spheres. After the parsimony of the reconstruction period, from 1963 an explosion of wages occurred, which was reinforced by a shortage on the labour market. In this period the dismantling of traditional industries already started. The increased welfare allowed for this radical economic change without causing large social disadvantages. Negative social consequences were counterbalanced by the rise of a service economy, which was actively stimulated by government policies.

The public sphere was marked by the expansion of the welfare state into a comprehensive system of public provision. In the 1960s, the influence of the 'pillars' diminished, but many of the institutions, and again especially the schools, continued their separate existence. Many of these originally private organisations were however increasingly embedded in the state system and in public bodies.

Public and private services offer ample employment for a well-educated labour force; the need for a skilled labour force gets complemented with a growing wish for more general education. A welfare state needs an integrated system of education that provides equal opportunities to all pupils, regardless of their class origin, to acquire a useful position in society (van Wieringen 1984). The traditional division of brainwork and manual work should be broken down, and technical schools should be integrated in the national system of education. An integrated system of education would allow all pupils, according to their capabilities, to move through the different levels of education.

Against this background, in the 1960s, a major reform of the secondary education system was implemented in the Netherlands through an act surnamed the 'Mammoth Act'. After a development of a century, from this act alone the technical schools that were originally privately founded were integrated into the national system of education.

The technical schools were transformed into 'lower vocational education'; most schools became to form part of comprehensive schools that offer both general and vocational education. The integration of vocational education in the national school system was completed by the creation of a so-called vocational education column, allowing for moving through from lower vocational education to secondary vocational education and higher professional education.

The integration of the schools in the public sector may be typified as *publicification*. An integrated national education system that comprehends all types of education seems to offer the best possibilities for access and moving through to all. Although the formation of this system certainly has contributed to these possibilities, the process of publicification also has problematic consequences that we will discuss below.

Transitions in the Welfare State

The expansion of the welfare state not only took place in the field of education but also involved many other kinds of communal services like the health services and social security. In the end of the 1970s, economic development however declined, unemployment rates grew, and the public deficits increased. In that situation, the expansion of the welfare state appeared to exceed its limits; the costs of the variety of public services took up an ever greater part of the gross domestic product. From the 1980s onwards, subsequent Dutch governments tried to rebalance the relatively expensive welfare state and the underperforming Dutch economy.

But next to problems of financing, the efficacy and the legitimacy of the institutions of the welfare state were also questioned. The absorption in the public system of institutions, that once were founded by social groupings to serve their common interest, led to a growth of legal regulations, to a formalisation of procedures and to bureaucracy in the organisations. As a consequence the commitment of the social groupings that originally created these institutions fades away. As founders and beneficiaries they were directly involved. Instead of supporters they have now gradually become clients who are dependent of anonymous public institutions (van Doorn and Schuyt 1978). This demonstrates the analysis of De Swaan (1988) mentioned above that the well-intended creation of collective and public arrangements also has unintended consequences that are often less favourable.

The embedding of vocational training in the school system extends more autonomy to the institutions concerned, especially towards the social partners. According to Archer (1982) the dynamic of educational systems first develop as a result of the initiatives of social interest groups, but gain autonomy later on. The related policies then mainly develop under the influence of the actors involved in the system.

Once integrated in the national system of education, the internal dynamic of the schools brings about a *generalisation* of the educational programmes. Supplanting trainers with a background in vocational practice, education is increasingly cared for by educational professionals. The curriculum gets organised around subjects, and transfer of knowledge is more emphasised than the training of skills. Generalisation implies that the acquisition of general knowledge supersedes the training of specific skills.

In the Dutch education system, the focus on vocational orientation has gradually faded away in the last decades of the twentieth century; the connection between the sociocultural and the socioeconomical functions of education has vanished (Kats 1998). This has lead to the growing gap between education and vocational practice. Employers were complaining that 'school-leavers can't even handle a hammer'.

However, the process of generalisation is also promoted by economic developments that demand broader qualifications. The majority of jobs in the service and knowledge economy do not correspond anymore with the idealised model of traditional craftsmanship. And since the 1970s, the Dutch economy has gradually been transforming into such a service and knowledge economy (van Hoof and van Ruysseveldt 1996). So the function of vocational schools could no longer be the mere supply of skilled workers to companies, but also building up the general knowledge of pupils.

Vocational Education Turns to the Market

Although economic development turned in positive direction from 1989, the criticism against public services persisted. Their costs, efficacy and legitimacy remained to be disputed. In the 1990s, the emphasis changes towards a withdrawal of the state and towards the privatisation and liberalisation of public services. It was assumed that private institutions would be more economic and more effective than public services and that they would be better capable to fulfil the needs of people, who are here approached as clients or customers.

These ideas were also largely applied in the field of education. Since the beginning of the 1990s, educational institutions at different levels are subject to a process of *privatisation*. That is not to say that they are turned into private enterprises, but they get assigned much more autonomy in designing programmes, recruitment of students, cooperation with stakeholders, human resource management, quality insurance, organisation development, financial management, etc. Vocational education especially gets the task to meet the demands of the market. New connections should be made between vocational education and vocational practice to meet the new qualification needs emerging from the demands of the service and knowledge economy (Moerkamp and Onstenk 1999). In post-industrial society, companies and organisations need employees who command a more general competence and are educated at secondary level.

All new responsibilities require a larger scale than the traditional schools that were often connected to a delimited vocational or professional field. Thus, an extensive reform process of vocational education has started. All secondary vocational schools have gradually been merged into regional education and training centres (ROC: Regionaal Opleidingen Centrum) in the 1990s. At the legislative level, the educational reform was confirmed by the 1996 Adult and Vocational Education Act (WEB: Wet Educatie en Beroepsonderwijs). This act makes secondary vocational education a separate sector in the school system, distinct from general education.

The ROCs have turned into huge institutions. Now, about 70 ROCs and comparable institutions are operational with the largest one having approximately 30,000 students; the total number of students amounts to over 500,000. The ROCs face the complex task to meet both the learning needs of a variety of groups and the qualification needs of a variety of occupations. They offer a broad variety of courses leading to all kinds of traditional and newly emerging vocational qualifications. For all institutions together, the total number of courses amounts to 11,000. The ROCs not only are the providers of vocational education to young people but also guide and train adults and youth with a vulnerable position on the labour market and provide local labour-market-oriented training for employees and the unemployed (Westerhuis 2001). In addition to adult education and 'regular' vocational education, most ROCs also run a private training institute or commercial department, which provides made-to-measure continuing vocational training programmes for companies and organisations.

The Adult and Vocational Education Act (WEB) also involves the transformation of the old National Vocational Training Bodies into Expertise Centres for Vocational Education and Business (KBB: Kenniscentra voor Beroepsonderwijs en Bedrijfsleven). The WEB attributes a new and important role to these Expertise Centres. They have, under this act, the task of translating the needs of the branches they represent into qualification frameworks, profiles of competences and examination requirements for secondary vocational education. It is supposed that the link between vocational education and vocational practice could be restored in this way.

The traditional apprenticeship system that was supported by the National Vocational Training Bodies was widespread in various branches of business. Under the WEB this system is integrated in secondary vocational education. The new role of the Expertise Centres implies the attuning of the curricula to qualification needs of branches of business. The Expertise Centres have experienced that this requires more than one-way traffic; they also take care of the quality of the learning contexts in the companies and organisations that host the apprentices from secondary vocational education.

Many efforts are made to accomplish a new kind of *integration* between learning and working that is required in a knowledge economy. It remains an open question if all far-reaching reforms actually contribute to this integration.

Seeking for New Relations Between Education and Working Life

From 2008 the crisis of credits and debts has ended the belief in the self-resolving and self-correcting capacity of markets in numerous fields. The adoption of the idea of a market in the field of vocational education also shows serious disadvantages. The formation of ROCs that make their way in the market, create their supply and answer the demands of branches of business appears to carry several unintended negative consequences.

The market-oriented creation of an educational supply opens the possibility to think up fashionable courses that may attract students, but does not offer a solid basis for a sustainable vocational practice. The introduction of competence-based learning that was promoted to meet the demands of employers sometimes leads to curricula with little substance. Self-directed learning sometimes seems a licence to cut down on professionals who support the direction of learning. The quality of education and the meaning of certificates are consequently affected in such cases. The huge institutions give room to a growing management layer; when they are more interested in results instead of contents and the core process of education, the problems mentioned are reinforced. The autonomy of the management of the institutions induced to take unwarranted financial risks in a number of cases. It is not surprising that teachers who find themselves in such situations feel abandoned. Many students for their part get lost in the gigantic and anonymous institutions. A growing number of students nowadays already deal with risks in the personal developmental and behavioural sphere; this loads teachers with expanding coaching tasks.

Against this background various attempts are nowadays made to restore the human scale and the original function of vocational schools. It may be said that *schoolification* is revalued. There is also a demand for a rehabilitation of the educational professionals and their ability in transferring knowledge and training skills that have a lasting function instead of fashionable competencies. So, *generalisation* is again at stake. The restoration of the school also implies a return of public authorities that hold inspection and guarantee the quality of education; so, *publicification* is also back on the agenda. This does not mean a return to the rigid statist model, now the role of local authorities is especially emphasised. Tasks in employment policies and social security as well as the planning of educational provision are increasingly being decentralised towards local authorities in the Netherlands.

Many companies and organisations also experience the disadvantages of the scaling-up of vocational schools and the vapourisation of qualifications. A recent development is that private parties are now resuming their role by setting up newborn company schools. For instance, the Dutch Railways are involved in such a project and also some large hospitals do so. It may be said that the opportunities of new forms of *privatisation* are thus explored. In a way this resembles a return to the situation of individual companies and organisations caring for their own schools. Nowadays they however operate in close cooperation with the learning experts from vocational education.

The cooperation between vocational schools, local authorities and local employers does not run automatically. New forms of *interdependification* are needed. Local authorities are concerned with their new tasks in the field of (un)employment policies. Employers need strategies for human resource management and development to deal with the changing composition of the labour market. Vocational schools want to develop learning projects that open up new prospects. Both schools and employers are seeking for forms of *integration* of learning and working. These efforts may add to bringing learning opportunities closer to learners, which is an aim of European policy (CEC 2000).

The Expertise Centres described above may fulfil a vital mediating role in this context. This role is especially important against the growing economic crisis and rising unemployment rates (Kats et al. 2011). They have the know-how to answer and to connect the needs of the different actors involved. They bring together the various stakeholders, especially at the regional level, to promote the simultaneous upgrading of education and employment. They help in translating labour market developments in employment policies that also provide room for people who are threatened on that labour market. They advise companies and organisations on how they may become a favourable environment for vocational learning and professional development of employees with diverging backgrounds. And they support schools in setting up learning projects that anticipate core problems that arise in vocational practice. By making a connection between employment policies, organisational development and innovation of education, the Expertise Centres contribute to the structural conditions for economic recovery. So, we may describe this shift as a *structuralisation* of the approach to vocational learning.

Epilogue

In this chapter we have identified a number of shifts in the way vocational learning is situated and dealt with in the growing room between formal education and working life. We described these shifts in view of economic and political developments that have taken place in the Netherlands. This is not to say that these shifts are exclusively tied to specific conditions or that they constitute a fixed sequence. We suppose that comparable shifts may be recognised in other countries as well. All shifts represent impetuses that keep working, also in circumstances when they are less fashionable.

In vocational learning, many actors are involved: companies, employers, employees, unemployed, trade unions, trainers, teachers, advisors, students, schools, administrators, local and national authorities and other institutions. Many approaches, like the ones discussed above, seem to be dominated by the problem definitions of some of the actors. This often attributes a subordinate role to other actors who are expected to follow the leading definitions. For instance, when the state monopolises the school system, employers have to deal with the resulting qualifications, for better or for worse. Or, when schools become large-scale private institutions directed by managers, the professional role of teachers may be affected. Then, at a certain moment the price will always to be paid and things will turn around. When shifts in vocational learning occur, it is useful to consider which actors take the lead and which ones have to follow. Because without an involvement of relevant actors, there is every chance that systems and approaches come to a deadlock.

References

Archer, M. S. (1982). *The sociology of educational expansion: Take-off, growth and inflation in educational systems*. London: Sage.

CEC (Commission of the European Communities). (2000). *A memorandum on lifelong learning*. Brussels: European Commission.

de Jonge, J. A. (1976). *De industrialisatie in Nederland tussen 1850 en 1914*. Nijmegen: SUN.

de Swaan, A. (1988). *In care of the state; health care, education and welfare in Europe and the USA in the modern era*. Cambridge: Polity Press.

Doets, C., van Esch, W., & Westerhuis, A. (2008). *Een brede verkenning van een leven lang leren*. 's-Hertogenbosch: CINOP.

Kats, E. (1998). De vermaatschappelijking van de agogische norm. In J. Katus et al. (Eds.), *Andragologie in transformatie*. Amsterdam/Meppel: Boom.

Kats, E., van Lakerveld, J., & Smit, H. (2011). Linking vocational practice and vocational education; the mediating role of expertise centres in the Netherlands. In S. Kirpal (Ed.), *National pathways and European dimensions of trainers' professional development*. Frankfurt am Main: Peter Lang.

Kessels, J. W. M. (1996). *Het corporate curriculum*. Leiden: Rijksuniversiteit Leiden.

Leune, J. M. G. (2003). Onderwijs en overheid. In N. Verloop & J. Lodewyck (Eds.), *Onderwijskunde*. Groningen: Wolters Noordhoff.

Lijphart, A. (1968). *The politics of accommodation; pluralism and democracy in the Netherlands*. Berkeley: University of California Press.

Meijers, F. (1983). *Van ambachtsschool tot L.T.S.; onderwijsbeleid en kapitalisme*. Nijmegen: SUN.

Ministerie van Onderwijs, Cultuur en Wetenschap. (2004). *Actieplan Leven Lang Leren*. Den Haag: Ministerie van Onderwijs, Cultuur en Wetenschap.

Moerkamp, T., & Onstenk, J. (1999). *Beroepsonderwijs en scholing in Nederland*. Thessaloniki: Cedefop.

Onderwijsraad. (2003). *Werk maken van een leven lang leren*. Den Haag: Onderwijsraad.

van Doorn, J. A. A., & Schuyt, C. J. M. (Eds.). (1978). *De stagnerende verzorgingsstaat*. Meppel: Boom.

van Gent, B. (Ed.). (1996). *Opleiden en leren in organisaties; ontwikkelingen, benaderingen, onderzoekingen*. Amsterdam: Boom.

van Hoof, J., & van Ruysseveldt, J. (1996). *Sociologie en de moderne samenleving; maatschappelijke veranderingen van de industriële omwenteling tot in de 21ste eeuw*. Amsterdam: Boom.

van Kemenade, J. A. (1981). *Onderwijs; Bestel en beleid*. Groningen: Wolters-Noordhoff.

van Wieringen, A. M. L. (1984). Alleen is erger; over de dynamiek van de betrekkingen tussen onderwijs en arbeid. In J. D. C. Branger, N. L. Dodde, & W. Wielemans (Eds.), *Onderwijsbeleid in Nederland*. Amersfoort: Acco.

Westerhuis, A. (2001). *European structures of qualification levels*. Luxemburg: Cedefop.

Windmuller, J. P. (1969). *Labor relations in the Netherlands*. Ithaca: Cornell University Press.

Chapter 20
Evaluating Learning and the Work of a Researcher in the Era of Lifelong Learning

Kristiina Brunila

Introduction

After Finland joined the European Union, educational politics have taken a turn towards decentralisation and marketisation. In education, the challenges of decentralisation and marketisation are many and include new interests and linkages between different actors as well as problems related to financing and continuity. Consequently, the state has to some extent lost ground to the European Union and has become a more controlling body by applying new governing techniques to the politics and practices of education. In recent years, the role of the global economy and supranational organisations (especially the EU) as factors which contribute to education and research has become increasingly important (Kallo and Rinne 2006).

Today, EU-funded projects have permeated the public sector (Sjöblom 2009) including the educational sector (Brunila 2011a).[1] Projects have also become a common form of academic short-term and project-based employment (Ylijoki 2010; Sjöblom 2009). Publicly funded academic research has been increasingly forced to apply for EU funding for project-based activities (Brunila 2009, 2011b). A significant proportion of domestic funds has been steered towards projects that specifically reflect European Union policies (Sjöblom 2009; Sjöblom et al. 2006). Consequently, in Finland the number of project researchers in academia has increased between 1994 and 2004 almost two and a half fold (Ylijoki 2010).

In the era of lifelong learning, projects have become an ideological method to introduce a more market orientation, while people involved with projects have been made more accountable for their labour market fates. In education, this has happened

---

[1] By the term "project" I mean an EU-funded short-term project, which usually operates inside or outside the formal educational system and has certain predetermined goals.

K. Brunila (✉)
Unit of Sociology, Politics and Culture of Education, Institute of Behavioural Sciences, University of Helsinki, Helsinki, Finland
e-mail: kristiina.brunila@helsinki.fi

G.K. Zarifis and M.N. Gravani (eds.), *Challenging the 'European Area of Lifelong Learning': A Critical Response*, Lifelong Learning Book Series 19, DOI 10.1007/978-94-007-7299-1_20, © Springer Science+Business Media Dordrecht 2014

alongside the shift from government to (new) governance (Lindblad and Simola 2002; Ball 2007, 2006). New governance and projects have introduced territorially unbounded public and private actors, acting outside of their formal jurisdiction, into political institutions' decision-making processes (Bailey 2006). Projects have represented a form of new governance because they have aimed to bring together individuals, groups, organisations, enterprises, officials and the state in order to solve the problems that the EU has defined and have been brought about by market-orientated interventions. As organised practices through which subjects are governed (e.g. Rose 1999; Miller and Rose 2008), new governance has been strongly linked to the marketisation of education (Ball 2007; Popkewitz and Lindblad 2004).

EU projects have extended marketisation even further into educational research. In spite of the increasing number of project-based activities, there has been much less attention given to critical examination of this phenomenon in educational research. Moreover, EU-driven market-orientated lifelong learning discourse has entailed the view that an individual has endless opportunities and capabilities to learn and act according to her/his desires as long as she/he adopts the right attitude – desire and determination – i.e. the key to lifelong learning (Siivonen 2010). In EU-funded projects, researchers have been supposed to act in accordance to lifelong learning discourse which aims to raise levels of investment in human resources. Researchers have been positioned as responsible, flexible, self-regulating subjects whose personal objectives are congruent with the objectives of marketisation (c.f. Fejes 2008; Siivonen 2010). In this article I will analyse how EU-project-based work represents a form of power that regulates academic research linked to education in accordance to lifelong learning discourse.

Projectisation as a Form of Power in Education

There has been a greater need for the EU to improve its competitive position in the growing global market. In European Union policy documents, education has been repeatedly acknowledged as crucial for a better-qualified work force and for global competition (e.g. The Bologna Declaration 1999; The Copenhagen Declaration 2002; The Helsinki Communiqué 2006; The Lifelong Learning Programme 2006). EU policy documents have repeatedly pointed out that education is most of all the product of an investment in time and money (see Brunila et al. 2011).

The concept of projectisation (Brunila 2009, 2011a) describes an apparatus or dispositive (Foucault 1981) that comprises discourse, institutions, regulatory decisions and knowledge structures. Projectisation as a dispositive enhances and maintains the exercise of market-orientated power within the body. It is a product of new governance and a consequence in EU-driven contemporary societies that increasingly rely on voluntary contracts between individuals, groups, organisations, enterprises, states and their organs or officials. It represents market-orientated self-organising networks by incorporating, producing and positioning everyone involved in project-based work. It is productive in the sense that it shapes and retools in order to fit in with its needs (Foucault 1981, 1977). In the following section I will analyse how projectisation in research implies what can be said and thought, but also who can speak and with what authority.

I utilise research data which I have collected from my earlier research (Brunila 2009, 2011a). Research data consists of interviews with ten researchers who have operated in several research and development projects in education and training. Most of the researchers have worked in academia, but some have also worked in private companies and other institutions in the area of education and adult education. All of them have worked in EU-funded (ESF and EQUAL programmes) research projects. Along with interviews, my research data includes documents from almost 100 EU-funded research and development projects from the field of education and working life. I have also utilised my own research diary which I wrote while working as a project researcher in various EU-funded research projects. Research data was collected between 2003 and 2010. I have chosen not to mention the names of the projects (see, e.g. Vehviläinen and Brunila 2007).

Foucault's thinking offers me a lens through which to carry out discourse analysis (Foucault 1981, 1977). This lens helps, on one hand, to read discourses regarding project-based activities as being infused with power/knowledge and, on the other hand, to play a role in producing power/knowledge networks. In the analysis, the concept of discourse as a productive and regulative practice with material effects is central (Davies 1998). In this research, project-based activities have been analysed by acknowledging the relation of discourse and power as productive and regulative (see Foucault 1981, 1977; Davies 1998) in project work. This kind of approach enables one to see how the forms of power work and what kind of effects they have in forming how one ought to speak in order to be heard. I find this approach relevant because the form of power I am studying is effective as long as it succeeds in staying unnoticed and unrevealed. In exploring the discourses of project-based research, there was a need to explore the ways in which certain elements of the discourses related to project-based research have become more powerful than others. With the analytical concept of projectisation, it was possible to analyse how researchers involved in EU-funded projects were made speaking subjects at the same time as they were subjected to the constitutive force of discourses.

The Marketisation of Educational Research

> It really matters what gets funded: you do what you get funding for. Finland is a small country, with small ministries and small political elite. It's like a merry-go-round. When someone decides that matters about the information society are important in the EU and brings the message here, then all the ministries in Finland offer money for information society projects. (Terhi, researcher and project manager 2003)

> I have learned to sell what I do. (Mari, researcher 2004)

The two researchers' comments above indicate the effects of what has been a central period in defining Finnish education, the EU policy period. Consequently, in the project society run by the EU, one must become flexible, and as Terhi and Mari describe it, the basic idea is you do what you get funding for and you learn to sell it as well. Based on my research results, the majority of EU-funded projects have been implemented with funding specifically reserved for a particular purpose. This is also one of the obstacles for continuity: as soon as the funding is over, the research ends. When the funding is over, a completely new project with a new idea must be sought. This circle of endless projects makes researchers restless and impatient. The extracts above but also the extract below describes how projectisation as a dispositive directs how one ought to speak in order to be heard.

> "The aim of the research was to examine the connections between diversity and diversity management (…) for the sake of the organisation's competitiveness and effectiveness". (EU-funded research and development project report 2008)

Marketisation has become a fundamental element of EU-funded research projects. As the extract above indicates, during the EU period, research has begun to display more market-orientated traits, such as competitiveness, but also effectiveness actions, evaluation and measurement. In projectised work brands, management by results, efficiency and products have become more legitimate discourses than discourses about human rights, justice and equality. Market-orientated projects seem an effective way to impose EU-driven codes and meanings that essentially make education and educational research even more vulnerable by accepting these codes and meanings as new realities.

> European Social Fund projects require bureaucracy, strict accounting, clear distribution of work and liability, and organisations make contracts and carry out the responsibilities of these contracts. (EU-funded research and development project's final report 2002)

> The organisation administering the project was not committed to the contents and objectives of a project, and they appointed clerical staff to administer this project of ours. There was this conflict right from the start. (Rita 2004)

Because of the predetermined schedule and aims that used to be the responsibilities of the Nordic welfare state as well as the various interests of the project partners and project staff, projectised work inherently includes tensions and conflicts as the two extracts above indicate. Projectised work seems to lack reliance and trust among project workers (see also Vehviläinen et al. 2007). As the excerpts above suggest, projectisation causes all kinds of tensions by constant reporting, accounting and hierarchies.

Projectisation also means short-term employment which is interrelated to all kinds of pressures in research. As a consequence, researchers experience pressures and feel that their work has become fragmented and externally scheduled with few opportunities for profound and long-term research work as Outi Ylijoki has argued in her research concerning academic project work (Ylijoki 2010; see also Davies et al. 2006). Even though problems are brought up, they do not necessarily get heard. One reason for this is a rapidly increasing number of evaluation and evaluation professionals who estimate and assess publicly funded projects from their start to their final report (Ylijoki 2010). Research is often evaluated statistically, for example, how many articles, books and other written works have been produced. The problem is that in a project it may be difficult to measure the results achieved in terms of figures. Another problem is the close alliance between EU-funded projects and project evaluation professionals:

> The number of (…) projects has increased pleasingly and growth has even accelerated recently. Growth proves the awakening of interest and the expansion of actors: (…) the theme is considered to be even more important. (EU-funded project evaluation report 2004)

During my analysis I have read several evaluation reports concerning EU-funded projects. Evaluation reports disclose an interesting paradox. On one hand, they pay critical attention to the various problems in project work and even argue that funders' aims are almost impossible to achieve through short-term projects. On the other hand, they end up encouraging an increasing number of projects without regard for equality research (see also, Brunila 2009). It is a circle that benefits many different kinds of professionals, including educationalists.

> Meri: There were a lot of challenges in the beginning.
> Interviewer: Was this surprising or did you think that maybe these things will sort of arise?
> Meri: Well, you know in theory projects are like that, but in practice it always comes as a surprise when it happens. All those clichés become reality. (Meri, who has worked in several EU-funded projects as a researcher 2004)

Meri expressed her tiredness with the way project-based work forms a circle where "new" results ought to be endlessly discovered, and she refers to this as clichés becoming reality. Indeed, projectisation works by producing similar kinds of results as though they were always "new" (Brunila 2009). Meri as well as others who were interviewed were rather critical towards publicly funded projects. They are aware of the circular thinking that projectisation often entails.

The Mastery and Submission of Projectisation

Projectisation regulates research conducted in projects. Consequently researchers face the dilemma of how to speak in order to be heard and try to find a solution to it. From my own research diary the diary I found the following incident:

> I'm in an informal meeting where project researchers meet. I am asked what do you do in your project? I try to find the right words to describe my position in the project, but I am interrupted by another researcher before I get to the end: No, no, seriously, what is your project's product, the core product? (Researcher's diary 2006)

In order to better understand why projectisation works and why researchers end up acting as they do, as in the extract above, the concept of subjectification has been useful. According to Bronwyn Davies and her colleagues, subjectification represents the processes through which we are subjected and actively take up as our own the terms of our own subjection (Davies et al. 2001, see also Davies 1998). In the extract above, subjectification describes the ongoing process where one is placed and takes place in the market-orientated discourses. Speaking for myself, my subjectification was completed when I replied with a little hesitation to the question: "A book".

Subjectification as a form of projectisation involves taking up those discourses in which researchers involved in project work and others speak/write as if these discourses were their own (Davies 1998). Through such discourses, people become speaking subjects at the same time as they are subjected to the constitutive force of those discourses. As Terhi described earlier, in order to get funding, one must speak the right kind of talk, namely, the language of the market and money.

From the perspective of subjectification, projectisation forms a new kind of ideal being who is capable of practising self-discipline, flexibility and continuous self-development. This reflects an ideal being where the entire self must be completely made over as an enterprising individual (cf. Komulainen et al. 2009; Leffler 2009; Komulainen 2006). This, of course, meshes well with policies of lifelong learning, which have been permeated with the narrow utilitarian and technological notions of learning and the competences needed in modern economies (Rasmussen 2000, p. 86). This transformation is linked to changes in the political context including welfare state retrenchment and decentralisation, which have had a significant effect in the form of diminishing resources.

From the perspective of subjectification, there was a noticeable and constant ambivalence in the interviews. It is no surprise that researchers talked about tiredness and were in general rather cynical. One researcher wished she had become an ornithologist instead, and another thought she should have started a career as a gardener. In order to conduct research, one needs to learn the "right" way to talk so that in becoming objects of the disciplinary forms of power, people also become active subjects. In spite of projectisation research is constantly done in various ways. During the interviews, we discussed how crucial it is to recognise these power relations and try to open up channels that allow the creation of some distance from identities and identifications with pre-given meanings and categories.

> The reason why I wanted to shift into the research side was a desire to understand, understand more deeply, and to help others to understand (…) about for example discrimination and inequality, how they form and work. (Tina 2004)

As forms of power, projectisation does not have to be repressive as in Tina's case. Tina had previously worked in administrative tasks but she wanted to start doing research because she saw opportunities that specifically research was able to give. If projectisation is considered a power relation, it is the very constitutivity of the subject that enables them to act in these forms of power that are not just regulatory but are also productive (Butler 1997). Indeed, researchers have already considered this in various ways:

> In Finland, we have learned to utilise what comes from above (…) It is simply turned into an aim to determine what this means exactly. (Sara 2003)

> One can always say that EU has decided to give money for this. So in this way one can get some prestige for his or her project. Money is sort of a good thing. (Marie 2003)

Surviving in the EU-driven contemporary societies means learning to see how funding or aims coming from above are always constructed within societal power relations. When this is realised this notion can be utilised. All the researchers I interviewed have learned this. They utilised different discourses in order to be granted financial resources and continue research. Consequently, researchers are able to gain some leeway by constantly learning to act in various kinds of power relations as well as utilising them, as Marie and Sara have done. In research, instead of being submissive or repressive, projectisation means continuously ongoing negotiations. The negotiations carried out by researchers consist of skills and tacit knowledge that can be called discourse virtuosity (Brunila 2009, 2011b). Discourse virtuosity is a consequence of parallel and contradictory aims and discourses in project-based research, a complex form of competence one performs in order to be heard. Discourse virtuosity when performed the "right" way is capable of satisfying the various interests of funders, project partners, target groups as well as academic audiences. Project research requires a wide range of competences. Discourse virtuosity is especially needed when applying for money for one's own employment and for the next project.

Conclusion

This chapter illustrates the shift EU-driven research and researchers are facing in the era of market-orientated lifelong learning. Education and educational research that used to be related to the Nordic welfare society and was based more on a criticism of market forces is nowadays more likely to gain its legitimisation from marketisation and becomes responsible for individual short-term research and development projects. From the perspective of subjectification, it implies that the person involved in research has to submit to marketisation and must also master the language of the market in order to be heard. Research funding seems to favour large-scale projects that consist of various subprojects and possess extensive international co-operation networks. Consequently, EU-funded projects with a market-orientated policy and using economic discourse have formed a new joint rhetorical discursive framework in the area of educational research. This alliance can be viewed as a response to the needs of a global economy where both education and research are harnessed to market forces and help shape a more flexible and mobile labour force.

Project-based research suggests a shift in which one must become trainable, capable of development and learn to produce the right kind of talk as in accordance to EU-driven market-orientated lifelong learning discourse. The right kind of talk works by ensuring that researchers keep themselves busy by making themselves available to fulfil the needs of the market. This indicates a more instrumental idea in which research is seen as an investment and as a product of money. The rise of project-based activities all over Europe not just in research but in politics and in practices on the whole has resulted in enormous changes in social structure, power relations and knowledge. In the near future, it would be crucial to acknowledge the form of power that maintains project societies and projectisation. This calls for a more critical appraisal including a study of the effects and the perspectives of subjectification, resistance and rebellion.

References

Bailey, D. (2006). Governance or the crisis of governmentality? Applying critical state theory at the European level. *Journal of European Public Policy, 13*(1), 16–33.

Ball, S. (2006). *Education policy and social class: The selected works of Stephen J. Ball*. London: Routledge.

Ball, S. (2007). *Education plc: Private sector participation in public sector education*. London: Routledge.

Brunila, K. (2009). *Parasta ennen. Tasa-arvotyön projektitapaistuminen* (Research report, Vol. 222). Helsinki: University Press.

Brunila, K. (2011a). The projectisation, marketisation and therapisation of education. *European Educational Research Journal*. Special Issue: Philosophy of Education and the Transformation of Educational Systems, *10*(3), 425–437.

Brunila, K. (2011b). Kasvatus ja koulutus projektimarkkinoilla. *Kasvatus, 3*, 222–231.

Brunila, K. (2011c). Rönsyt pois! Tutkija tietokykykapitalismissa. *Aikuiskasvatus, 2*, 111–119.

Brunila, K., Kurki, T., Lahelma, E., Lehtonen, J., Mietola, R., & Palmu, T. (2011). Multiple transitions: Educational policies and young people's post-compulsory choices. *Scandinavian Journal of Educational Research, 55*(3), 307–324.

Butler, J. (1997). *The psychic life of power: Theories in subjection*. Stanford: Stanford University Press.

Davies, B. (1998). *A body of writing 1990–1999*. Walnut Creek: AltaMira Press.

Davies, B., Dormer, S., Gannon, S., Laws, C., & Rocco, S. (2001). Becoming schoolgirls: The ambivalent project of subjectification. *Gender and Education, 13*(2), 167–182.

Davies, B., Gottsche, M., & Bansel, P. (2006). The rise and fall of the neoliberal university. *European Journal of Education, 41*(2), 305–319.

Fejes, A. (2008). Historising the lifelong learner: Governmentality and neoliberal rule. In A. Fejes & K. Nicoll (Eds.), *Foucault and lifelong learning: Governing the subject*. Oxon: Routledge.

Foucault, M. (1977). *Discipline & punish. The birth of the prison*. London: Penguin Books Ltd.

Foucault, M. (1981). *History of sexuality. Vol. 1: The will to knowledge*. London: Penguin.

Kallo, J., & Rinne, R. (2006). *Supranational regimes and national education policies. Encountering challenge* (Research in educational sciences, Vol. 24). Helsinki: Finnish Educational Research Association.

Komulainen, K. (2006). Neoliberal educational policy. A case study of Finnish textbooks of entrepreneurial education. *Nordisk Pedagogik, 26*(3), 212–228.

Komulainen, K., Korhonen, M., & Räty, H. (2009). Risk-taking abilities for everyone? Finnish entrepreneurship education and the enterprising selves imagined by pupils. *Gender and Education, 21*(6), 631–649.

Leffler, E. (2009). The many faces of entrepreneurship: A discursive battle for the school arena. *European Educational Research Journal, 8*(1), 104–116.

Lindblad, S., & Simola, H. (2002). Education governance in transition: An introduction. *Scandinavian Journal of Educational Research, 46*(3), 237–245.

Miller, P., & Rose, N. (2008). *Governing the present: Administering economic, social and personal life*. Cambridge: Polity Press.

Popkewitz, T., & Lindblad, S. (2004). Historizing the future: Educational reform, systems of reason, and the making of children who are the future citizens. *Journal of Education Change, 5*, 229–247.

Rasmussen, P. (2000). Lifelong learning as a social need and as policy discourse. In R. Dale & S. Robertson (Eds.), *Globalisation & Europeanisation in education*. Oxford: Symposium Books.

Rose, N. (1999). *Governing the soul. The shaping of the private self*. London: Free Association Books.

Siivonen, P. (2010). *From a "student" to a lifelong "consumer" of education? Constructions of educability in adult students' narrative life histories* (Research in Educational Sciences 47). Jyväskylä: Finnish Educational Research Association.

Sjöblom, S. (2009). Administrative short-termism: A non-issue in environmental and regional governance. *Journal of Environmental Policy and Planning, 11*(3), 165–168.

Sjöblom, S., Andersson, K., Eklund, E., & Godenhjelm, S. (Eds.). (2006). *Project proliferation and governance: The case of Finland*. Helsinki: University of Helsinki, Swedish School of Social Science.

The Bologna Declaration. (1999). Retrieved September 3, 2011, from http://ec.europa.eu/education/policies/educ/bologna/bologna.pdf

The Copenhagen Declaration. (2002). Retrieved September 3, 2011, from http://ec.europa.eu/education/pdf/doc125_en.pdf

The Helsinki Communiqué. (2006). *Report on enhanced European cooperation in vocational education and training*. Retrieved September 3, 2011, from http://ec.europa.eu/education/policies/2010/doc/helsinkicom_en.pdf

The Lifelong Learning Programme. (2006). Retrieved October 2, 2011, from http://europa.eu/legislation_summaries/education_training_youth/general_framework/c11082_en.htm

Vehviläinen, M., & Brunila, K. (2007). Cartography of gender equality projects in ICT. Liberal equality from the perspective of situated equality. *Information, Communication & Society, 10*(3), 384–403.

Ylijoki, O. (2010). Future orientation in episodic labour: Short-term academics as a case in point. *Time & Society, 19*(3), 365–386.

Chapter 21
Focus on Learners: A Search for Identity and Meaning in Autobiographical Practices

Laura Formenti and Micaela Castiglioni

The aim of this chapter is to put learners, with their experience, questions, and knowledge, at the center of the debate in adult education. The essence of lifelong (and lifewide) learning is precisely in the capacity of adults to redesign and give new meaning to their projects, and even to their identity. A critical aspect in adult education practices and policies is the underestimation of the role of learners in shaping and giving meaning to all educational processes. We claim that autobiographical and narrative methods in adult education, largely developed in Italy, can give voice to learners, and even redefine the overall meaning of lifelong learning.

The first part of the chapter discusses the critical points of European policies. They are too oriented toward the future and the market, focusing on adaptation, flexibility, and qualification, with a poor understanding of individual strategies and tools that adult learners need in order to adapt to this rapidly evolving and uncertain world. Current policies are mainly oriented toward the achievement of key abilities, and there is a lack of attention paid to other competences such as reflexivity, agency, and critical thinking. The focus on objectivity, on the one hand, and institutional policies, on the other, downplays the crucial role of experience and meaning in adult learning. The dominant idea behind lifelong learning as being based on technical abilities and adaptation to the market should be questioned, taking the learner's view into consideration. After all, the learner is a strategic actor within the institutional and social world.

In fact, any learning experience, be it formal or informal, entails participants making sense of it, finding their own way to "adapt" to the situation, even if not always in the expected ways. Through stories, we hear (and learn) from each

L. Formenti (✉)
University of Milano Bicocca, Micaela Castiglioni, Researcher, University of Milano Bicocca, Milan, Italy
e-mail: laura.formenti@unimib.it

M. Castiglioni
General Pedagogy and Adult Education, University of Milano Bicocca, Milan, Italy
e-mail: micaela.castiglioni@unimib.it

G.K. Zarifis and M.N. Gravani (eds.), *Challenging the 'European Area
of Lifelong Learning': A Critical Response*, Lifelong Learning Book Series 19,
DOI 10.1007/978-94-007-7299-1_21, © Springer Science+Business Media Dordrecht 2014

individual how he or she found ways for adapting, leaving, or transforming. Autobiographical work is an occasion to make more explicit choices and strategies, to build agency and reflexivity.

A European Outline: From Policies to Learners

When the *Lisbon Strategy* was announced in March 2000, the European economy appeared to be in better shape than today. Yet, critical aspects and vulnerabilities were pointed out, including low performance in economic growth, unemployment, and growing poverty in underprivileged areas. The overall goal of the European Union (EU), "to become the most competitive and dynamic knowledge-based economy in the world, capable of sustainable economic growth with more and better jobs and greater social cohesion,"[1] defined the strategic areas for education: employment, technology, competition, and *of course* knowledge. In official documents, knowledge appears to be unquestionably connected with economic growth, and both of them are linked to employment, social cohesion, and multiculturalism. Yet, the meaning of a "knowledge-based society" seems to be narrowed down to increased participation in formal education and the development of *key competences*.

The political agenda for EU countries aims at better coordination of teaching/training and research, to make larger numbers of people active in the "economy of knowledge": the ET2010 Program for Education and Training and EU2020 Strategy made further commitments toward collaboration and shared strategies.[2] Without going into detail, we would like to point out some assumptions and recurring themes in these documents: the crucial role of *lifelong learning*; the more realistic and effective implementation of formal education and training; key competences (communication in the mother tongue, communication in foreign languages, mathematical competence and basic competence in science and technology, digital competence, learning to learn, social and civic competence, initiative and entrepreneurship, cultural awareness and expression); and the pursuit of equality, inclusion, social cohesion, and active participation among learners.[3] These goals are not neutral or anodyne. They shape local efforts to identify actions and educational practices addressed to adults, in a social, historical, and cultural context that has been named as a *knowledgeable present* (Biasin 2011; Alberici 1999), a *liquid modernity* (Bauman 2000), and a *flexible* (Sennett 1999) or *risk* (Beck 1998) society. The EU documents offer an outline depicting an ideal learner characterized by learning to

---

[1] Presidency conclusions, Lisbon European Council, 23 and 24 March 2000.

[2] Recommendation of the European Parliament and of the Council of 18 Dec. 2006 on key competences for lifelong learning (2006/962/EC). In *Official Journal of the European Union*, 30.12.2006, L.394/10–18.

[3] Council conclusions of 12 May 2009 on a strategic framework for European cooperation in education and training ('ET 2020') (2009/C 119/02). In *Official Journal of the European Union* 28.5.2009 (C 119/2–10).

learn; personal, social, and professional fulfillment; creativity, initiative, and entrepreneurship; self-direction and access to learning facilities; and increasing flexibility in the learning career, with easier transitions from education to training and openness to nonformal and informal learning.[4] *Learning to learn* seems to be the overall frame of reference: it focuses on the ability to organize one's learning and training, to make choices and take risks.

Italy is late in fulfilling the goals of the Lisbon Agenda, partly due to a rigid, traditional training system and low numbers accessing Higher Education (HE), as well as for cultural reasons. The meaning of this situation is far from clear. It would be naive to see the EU outline as a neutral standpoint in relation to the view of education (Mariani and Santerini 2002; Tramma 2011) and local conditions. Implementation may be unrealistic in this context. A critical reading of the documents, based on empirical research and real practices in adult education, raises fundamental issues about the risk of emphasizing the role of politics and strategic choices, including the rhetoric of lifelong learning as merely oriented to the *future* and the *market*, following the rules of *adaptation, flexibility, and qualification*.

Some researchers who are actively engaged with adults in formal and nonformal learning expressed their concerns about the recent evolution of Adult Education (AE) as a field of research and practice (Castiglioni 2011). What kind of *adaptation* is required here? (Mariani 1997; Mariani and Santerini 2002). How is *flexibility* experienced and interpreted by real people when they are living a dramatic impossibility of change, future, and hope? (Benasayag 2004; Bodei 2002). What does it mean to focus learners on their future, when personal and professional projects appear to be so difficult, poor, or lacking? (Bauman 2000, 2001; Benasayag 2004). Reflection is needed regarding the strategies and tools that education should offer to learners in relation to their future professional lives (Alberici 1999, 2011; Biasin 2011).

We need to make an effort to uncover, discuss, and clarify these assumptions and ambiguities. A new, contextualized debate may reduce the risk of narrowing down Adult Education and training to the economic-political-institutional viewpoint (Marescotti 2011) or mere professionalization (Tramma 2011). In many regards, Adult Education appears to be unable to live up to its original intent. In 2007, a permanent observatory – "*Osservatorio sulla condizione adulta e i processi formativi*" – was established in the University of Milano-Bicocca by a group of researchers and experts from universities around Italy[5] with the goal of monitoring the ongoing situation in the field and to provoke public debate.[6] The group aims at breaking the silence, collusion, and negligence regarding the "mission" of Adult

---

[4] In *Official Journal of the European Union* 28.5.2009 (C 119/2–10), p. 35.

[5] Coordinated by D. Demetrio (Bicocca) and composed by A. Alberici (Roma Tre), D. Bellamio (Bicocca), C. Biasin (Padova), M. Castiglioni (Bicocca), M. Cornacchia (Trieste), P. Di Rienzo (Roma Tre), M. Gallerani (Bologna), B. Mapelli (Bicocca), E. Marescotti (Ferrara), R. Piazza (Catania), and S. Tramma (Bicocca).

[6] A book series "Adult Condition and Educational Processes" is established, whose first volume (see Castiglioni 2011) collects studies on the present situation of Adult Education in Italy and interviews with experts (Bellamio, Morgagni, Pinto Minerva, Varchetta) focusing on the relationship between need and dream in adult learning.

Education (Demetrio 2011).[7] As a matter of fact, many forms of exclusion seem to be present, not only in relation to specific subjects and groups but also in relation to different adult stories and learning experiences, far beyond the so-called "disadvantaged" or "marginal" people. Whole areas of human experience are silenced. In 2011 an anthology was published (Castiglioni 2011), offering reflection on the authentic meaning of adult learning, the so-called proprium of Adult Education (Marescotti 2011), moving toward a rediscovered *humanistic project* (Demetrio 1997). The loss of the complexity and depth of Adult Education – both in practice and research – has negative effects on individuals and on the cultural, social, and institutional contexts. We summarize them as follows:

(a) An undisputed coincidence of Adult Education and training, where

> actions are oriented towards the achievement of instrumental and technical abilities, seen as a basic form of learning, necessary for meeting market requirements and market logic, [...] instead of practices and processes that should be aimed at developing a complex set of competences, in relation to reflexivity and the pro-active attitudes of learners towards their competences and critical thinking skills. (Alberici 2011, pp. 46–47)

(b) A deep crisis and disavowal of biography, experience, and personal meaning as fundamental aspects of adult learning, since the so-called objective conditions and institutional policies are systematically invoked in order to bypass the learner as a subject (Gallerani 2011).

(c) An increasing focus on institutions where education or training is offered, instead of on those who are learning (Toriello 2011).

(d) A paradoxical distance between Adult Education, as a field of practice, and the emerging approach to *lifelong learning*; Adult Education, in fact, could and should be "a field where *lifelong learning* can be observed, hence further developed; and vice versa, *lifelong learning* policies may serve to give a concrete form to the general principles of Adult Education, helping the field to become more than wishful thinking" (Toriello 2011, p. 165).

(e) The disappearance from the field of important notions, as *utopia* and *freedom*, traditionally at the core of the humanistic view in Adult Education; in fact, to consider adult education as gratuitous and an aim in itself seems to make it an unnecessary good, not deserving an investment of resources (Marescotti 2011).

(f) An overemphasis on professionalization, seen as "the adaptation to the changing market, and not as a protection from it" (Tramma 2011, pp. 109–110), with the consequent neglect of the personal, emotional, and existential effects of this "adaptation." People may feel abandoned by institutions, including educational agencies that are too prone to the flexibility model.

Constant flexibility in turn needs to develop emotional and cognitive tools to enable people to "sustain flexibility," by developing some "autobiographical meaning" on their own (Castiglioni 2011). A narrative, subject-centered view leads to a reflexive, introspective framework, able to "reawaken critical thinking" (Nussbaum

---

[7] The group is working to develop a *Manifesto to redesign adult education*.

2010) in relation to key concepts like knowledge, learning, and learning to learn.[8] From this perspective, Adult Education can support adults in the challenge to meet their needs in a rich, subtle, and complex way. Life in a changing world requires a sort of critical empathy toward the self, as well as the capacity to sympathetically represent the other (Nussbaum 2010). Even EU documents contain phrases like *critical thinking, creativity, positive management of feelings, and preparation to adult life*.[9] But how can real learners develop these attitudes and capacities and under what conditions?

The Power of Autobiography: Reflexivity in Adult Learning

> Biographical research can illuminate the complexities of learning and transitional processes, beyond a potentially reductive, one-dimensional rhetoric of people as 'leaders' and change agents, which may characterize contemporary educational discourse. We are given access, instead, to narratives of resilience but also of difficult emotional experience, when working in troubling contexts. (Merrill and West 2009, p. 88)

Autobiographical methods in education aim to develop a stronger sense of identity in the participants, a better understanding of experience, and a more critical, creative, and active attitude. The Italian tradition in *autobiographical education* (Formenti 1998) as an approach to adult learning was initially rooted in social research. Since the 1960s, social researchers have undertaken the task of chronicling rural and urban life, traditions and folklore, along with the evolving lives of working class people and marginalized groups who were trying to adapt to a rapidly changing society. For instance, Montaldi (1961) wrote stories of working class people in rural Northern Italy, while ethnographers as Ernesto De Martino, oral historians as Revelli, Passerini, and Portelli, and sociologists as Ferrarotti (2002) addressed the relationship between individual and collective memories in the ongoing cultural changes. For the first time, marginalized and poorly educated people had the possibility to be heard thanks to those studies that brought a strong ethical-political commitment into the field, still often the case in biographical research.

In the 1970s, self-narration also became a way to gain recognition and build self-awareness as a political subject, for example, in feminist groups. Institutions, however, abandoned these qualitative and reflexive methods of research very rapidly as a more quantitative, statistical trend began to dominate the Social Sciences (Formenti 2012).

In the 1980s, education in Italy was strongly influenced by the French tradition, due to linguistic similarities between Italian and French and a delayed contact with

---

[8] Commission of the European Union (2006). Not published in the Official Journal. See also Opinion of the Committee of the Regions on the 'Action Plan on Adult learning. It is always a good time to learn' (2008/C 257/11) *Official Journal of the European Union*, 9.10.2008, pp. 70–75.

[9] In *Official Journal of the European Union* 28.5.2009 (C 119/2–10), p. 38.

the English literature.[10] The establishment, in the French-speaking countries, of a life history approach in education (*histoires de vie en formation*, quite different from the northern European definition of "life history") challenged the detached, neutral, and objective view of research and education, by asking adults to tell their learning stories with their own voice and words and to make critical sense of it. The seminal work of Pineau (Pineau and Le Grand 1993), Dominicé (1990), Josso (1991), and others inspired the use of personal narratives as a method for the education of adults. Telling the story of "how I learned who I am" in a group setting, where critical and reflexive thinking was favored, opened possibilities to release individuals, at least partially, from their social, cultural, institutional, and also biographical determinants. Awareness of being determined gives to people the power of choice: the final aim of this reflexive work is, in fact, to invite learners to take deliberate action (Dominicé 1990).

In the same years, Adult Education became a discipline and a research field in Italian academia: some universities established courses, and master's degrees in adult education handbooks were published. Previously, adult education was a practice devoted to literacy projects and courses to qualify adults to work, offering merely functional training. The academic recognition of its relevance as a science of education raised new questions about adulthood and the meaning and practice of adult learning. The theoretical and philosophical debate on adult life brought new energy into the field and mitigated its penchant toward excessive pragmatism. Contact between learners and trainers led to a better understanding of the learners points of view, their ways of making sense of experience, and the questions that were relevant to them.

Since the 1990s, many narrative and autobiographical studies have been conducted with different groups of adults in education and vocational training courses: teachers, nurses, managers, doctors, students, social workers, etc. A lot of studies have also focused on nonformal and informal learning, for example, within the family (Formenti 2002, 2011). Many courses and workshops invited participants to write their life experience and use it as a basis for learning; the aim of this self-narration was to favor self-awareness, knowledge, change, and even self-care (see Demetrio 1995, 2008; Formenti 1998, 2002, 2004; Formenti and Gamelli 1998; Gamelli 2003; Cambi 2002; Castiglioni 2008a, b). Autobiographical education is conceived of as a form of self-education within the institutional, social, and/or cultural context, a way to voice subjectivity within structures.

The landscape of autobiography as a method for adult education is broad and diverse. Different ways of doing and contexts for learning are developed through hundreds of projects. Their differences are methodological as well as epistemological and theoretical: some practitioners and researchers draw inspiration from phenomenology, others from Dewey's notion of experience and reflexivity, or embodied

---

[10] The issue of languages is crucial in Europe. The slow but steady movement toward English as the dominating language raises questions about the blur of cultural differences, especially in research and education. What are the risks of these developments, in terms of an impoverishment of ideas in an intended-to-be pluralistic and democratic Europe?

knowledge and aesthetic experience. Many researchers/practitioners are engaged in autobiographical writing, whereas others alternate writing and oral storytelling, or even more expressive and creative forms of communication (Formenti 2009a). Autobiographical methods are used in group sessions, classes, or individual counseling. This diversity nurtures a panoply of practices that are used to foster individual, collective, and institutional learning.

In these projects, life experience is put at the center of attention, valued, shared in speaking and writing, analyzed by participants themselves, considered, and treated as adults. This attitude offers the basis for a more complex idea of learning, in comparison to the EU outline discussed above. It involves a more complex range of dimensions of knowledge (and life experiences): practical, cognitive, emotional, relational, etc. It considers different contexts and levels of learning: private and public, formal and informal, conscious and unconscious. In this view, learning is approached as a *lifewide* as well as lifelong process: for an adult, a course or a workshop can be the occasion to explore different parts of life, different identities, and to connect them. The common idea of learning, based on technical abilities and adaptability to external requests, can be openly questioned and transformed into a notion where the learner's "version of the story" is seriously considered.

Besides differences, there are common aspects between autobiographical methods. They aim to provoke, gather, analyze, and transform stories. They consider adults to be experts and insiders of their own lives: the educator or trainer is interested and respectful of this *insiderness*. They challenge common understandings of the role of education, its methods and aims. They also build a different view of educational research, creating a possible alliance between research and education. Very often they address learners who are at risk of marginalization, listening to their stories, celebrating their differences and diversities, and showing their uniqueness and complexity, quite often unrecognized by institutions. Stories (and voices) claim their own space within the institutional space. Identities tend to become fixed and generalized within institutions, but human experience is larger, and identities are multiple. To deal with this plurality, learners should be seen as strategic actors: even if they are storied by others and by their circumstances, they can tell how they relate to their life contexts – work, family, education – as well as to the educational program or course they are participating in. Hence, learners can learn from their own way of making sense about the learning experience and develop their own concept of "adaptation" to a situation. This concept may be very different from the way it is understood by "the system."

As an example, we can take participation in HE, a core issue in the EU agenda, since dropout rates have become a problem for many universities. Listening to individual stories, we learn that for some people dropping out is not a problem or a failure at all; on the contrary, it can be the beginning of a new and more centered job or life project. We know this from autobiographical workshops with students. Some "adaptation" strategies seem to work better than others; some people are happy to stay in HE, others are not.

Thus, we need occasions (courses, workshops, projects) to help people to become clearer about their choices and strategies. A way to do this is through cooperative and participatory research projects (Formenti 2009a), where core issues in education can be explored directly with the participants. In these kinds of projects, all participants are both learners and researchers, and they take responsibility for the whole process. This is a really rewarding approach in training professionals, in evaluation processes, and in working with people at risk of marginalization. When adults come into contact with their experience, they remember who they are and may become more aware, critical, and open to transformation.

From the researcher's point of view, the stories gathered in these circumstances are "gold mines" as they cast new light on research issues, nourishing knowledge and understanding of "what is going on" in the field. From the learner's point of view, the process of telling and listening to stories brings awareness and mutual recognition regarding adaptation and coping strategies employed, the challenges of being citizens, workers, women, foreigners, or nontraditional students in HE. Generally, this enhances motivation and transformation. Through collective narrative and reflexive work, adult learners develop new ideas and their identity becomes richer and more flexible. They build agency and life skills; they develop strategic positioning toward themselves, others, and the world. They learn how to take care of their own learning (Formenti 2009b).

In this kind of approach, learners *learn to learn*, i.e., they change their theoretical, cognitive, affective, moral, or even physical positioning (Munari 1993) toward knowledge. Any act of knowing, in fact, entails "a strategic decision that implies the totality of the person" (Munari 1993, p. 14). This is a very special opportunity, as adult learners are usually unaware of their own learning, both in the sense of *what* they know and *how* they know. They may become aware only when there is a break in the continuity of everyday experience: when a problem arises or good reflexive questions are posed. It is quite common in autobiographical work to hear things like "*Well, I never thought about this before. It simply happened. Now I wonder... what was* really *happening.*" Agency and reflexivity are outcomes of this kind of context.

Autobiographical work can be understood as the meeting – sometimes the clashing – of different cultures. Learners in the same group may have different ages, genders, statuses, ethnic backgrounds, previous experiences, beliefs, and so on. The *authentic experience* (Formenti 2009a) of these differences challenges their ideas. However, they cannot be taken for granted. Systematic distortions – simplification, purposefulness, de-contextualization, quantification – can undermine reciprocal understanding and reduce stories to simple ideas. Autobiography is *educational* when it develops complexity and critical thinking; good processes are needed to achieve this. The "didactic" of autobiography (Formenti 2004) should include the whole arrangement, especially communication and interaction, in order to sustain respect and curiosity for human differences. This entails, of course, the development of values like cosmopolitanism and inclusiveness, democracy, and citizenship. These are at the basis of the European project. We need models for research, education, and communication that promote good relationships, self-acceptance, and a better reciprocal understanding. Educational autobiography can be a part of this effort, a way to make sense of our journey into human life.

References

Alberici, A. (1999). *Imparare sempre nella società conoscitiva*. Torino: Paravia.
Alberici, A. (2011). Educazione degli adulti nella prospettiva dell'apprendimento permanente. In M. Castiglioni (Ed.), *L'educazione degli adulti tra crisi e ricerca di senso* (pp. 45–59). Milan: Unicopli.
Bauman, Z. (2000). *Liquid modernity*. Cambridge: Polity Press.
Bauman, Z. (2001). *The individualized society*. Cambridge: Polity Press.
Beck, U. (1998). *World risk society*. Cambridge: Polity Press.
Benasayag, M. (2004). *Abécédaire de l'engagement*. Paris: Bayard.
Biasin, C. (2011). Autonomia e vulnerabilità per un'educazione adulta. In M. Castiglioni (Ed.), *L'educazione degli adulti tra crisi e ricerca di senso* (pp. 149–164). Milan: Unicopli.
Bodei, R. (2002). *Destini personali*. Milan: Feltrinelli.
Cambi, F. (2002). *L'autobiografia come metodo formativo*. Laterza: Roma-Bari.
Castiglioni, M. (2008a). *Fenomenologia e scrittura di sé*. Milan: Guerini.
Castiglioni, M. (2008b). Scrivere di sé, della propria pratica di cura e vicenda professionale. In L. Grosso, e S. Galati (Eds.), *I colori della depressione*. Milan: Guerini.
Castiglioni, M. (Ed.). (2011). *L'educazione degli adulti tra crisi e ricerca di senso*. Milan: Unicopli.
Commission of the European Union. (2006). *Adult learning: It is never too late to learn*, 23.11.06-COM(2006)614. Brussels: Commission of the European Union. http://europa.eu/legislation_summaries/education_training_youth/lifelong_learning/c11097_en.htm
Demetrio, D. (1995). *Raccontarsi*. Milan: Raffaello Cortina.
Demetrio, D. (1997). *Manuale di educazione degli adulti*. Laterza: Roma-Bari.
Demetrio, D. (2008). *La scrittura clinica. Consulenza autobiografica e fragilità esistenziali*. Milan: Raffaello Cortina.
Demetrio, D. (2011). Paradossi e responsabilità dell'educazione in età adulta. Riflessioni tra incurie ed equivoci. In M. Castiglioni (Ed.), *L'educazione degli adulti tra crisi e ricerca di senso* (pp. 25–41). Milan: Unicopli.
Dominicé, P. (1990). *L'histoire de vie comme processus de formation*. Paris: L'Harmattan.
Ferrarotti, F. (2002). *On the science of uncertainty: The biographical method in social research*. Boulder/New York/Oxford: Lexington Books.
Formenti, L. (1998). *La formazione autobiografica*. Milan: Guerini.
Formenti, L. (2002). *La famiglia si racconta*. Milan: Guerini.
Formenti, L. (Ed.). (2004). *DIANOIA didactics in autobiography for professionals, teachers and educators*. Anghiari: Libera Università dell'Autobiografia.
Formenti, L. (2009a, March 12–15). *Learning and caring in adult life: How to develop a good theory*. Paper presented at ESREA Life History and Biography Network Conference "Wisdom and knowledge in researching and learning lives: Diversity, differences and commonalities". Milan.
Formenti, L. (Ed.). (2009b). *Attraversare la cura. Relazioni, contesti e pratiche della scrittura di sé*. Gardolo: Erickson.
Formenti, L. (2011). *Re-inventare la famiglia*. Milan: Apogeo.
Formenti, L. (2012). Oltre le discipline. Pratiche e significati del fare ricerca con le vite umane. Introduction to the Italian edition of B. Merrill, & L. West (2009). *Using biographical methods in social research*. London: Sage.
Formenti, L., & Gamelli, I. (1998). *Quella volta che ho imparato*. Milan: Raffaello Cortina.
Gallerani, M. (2011). L'educazione degli adulti tra educabilità, emancipazione e partecipazione. In M. Castiglioni (Ed.), *L'educazione degli adulti tra crisi e ricerca di senso* (pp. 75–106). Milan: Unicopli.
Gamelli, I. (Ed.). (2003). *Il prisma autobiografico*. Milan: Unicopli.
Josso, M.-C. (1991). *Cheminer vers soi*. Paris/Lausanne: L'Age d'Homme.

Marescotti, E. (2011). Per un'autentica educazione degli adulti tra istanze epistemologiche e pressioni politico-economiche. In M. Castiglioni (Ed.), *L'educazione degli adulti tra crisi e ricerca di senso* (pp. 61–74). Milan: Unicopli.

Mariani, A. M. (1997). *Educazione informale tra adulti*. Milan: Unicopli.

Mariani, A. M., & Santerini, M. (Eds.). (2002). *Educazione adulta. Manuale per una formazione permanente*. Milan: Unicopli.

Merrill, B., & West, L. (2009). *Using biographical methods in social research*. London: Sage.

Montaldi, D. (1961). *Autobiografie della leggera*. Torino: Einaudi.

Munari, A. (1993). *Il sapere ritrovato*. Milan: Guerini.

Nussbaum, M. C. (2010). *Not for profit: Why democracy needs the humanities*. Princeton: Princeton University Press.

Pineau, G., & Le Grand, J.-L. (1993). *Les histoires de vie*. Paris: PUF.

Sennett, R. (1999). *The corrosion of character*. New York: W.W. Norton & Company.

Toriello, F. (2011). Legislazione *nel* e *per* l'educazione degli adulti. In M. Castiglioni (Ed.), *L'educazione degli adulti tra crisi e ricerca di senso* (pp. 165–178). Milan: Unicopli.

Tramma, S. (2011). L'educazione degli adulti all'incrocio tra deindustrializzazione e invecchiamento dell'età adulta. In M. Castiglioni (Ed.), *L'educazione degli adulti tra crisi e ricerca di senso* (pp. 107–118). Milan: Unicopli.

Part V
Lifelong Learning and Bringing Learning Closer to Home

Chapter 22
'Bringing Learning Closer to Home': Understanding 'Outreach Work' as a Mobilisation Strategy to Increase Participation in Adult Learning

Barry J. Hake

Introduction: 'Bringing Learning Closer to Home'

During the past decade, discourse with regard to 'bringing learning closer to home' was situated in relation to the uneven development of adult learning policies within the broader strategy of the European Commission (EC) to promote lifelong learning in the Member States. The overarching policy priority in the adult learning sector was the urgent need to identify strategies to raise levels of participation in adult learning activities and to widen participation to those traditionally excluded from adult learning. *Bringing Learning Closer to Home* was regarded as a more specific set of policy measures and practices which could potentially widen participation to excluded individuals and social groups who were identified as 'target groups'.

In the first section of this chapter, the wider policy framework of *Bringing Learning Closer to Home* will be briefly described. Section "EU policy framework for 'bringing learning closer to home'" examines the persistently low levels of participation in adult learning in terms of widely accepted understandings of the so-called problem of articulation between the supply of adult learning provision, on the one hand, and the demand by (potential) adult learners, on the other hand. In terms of strategies and interventions intended to 'bringing learning closer to home',

The author was engaged from the early 1980s until 2005 in a research programme at Leiden University which was devoted to the articulation between adult education providers and the demand for adult learning. Originally based on research into participation and non-participation in adult learning this research programme was increasingly focussed on research into outreach work and the specific role of media. This chapter is based on numerous publications arising from this long-term research programme. The author is intellectually deeply indebted to the published (co-) contributions of Carl Doerbecker (†) Folke Glastra and Erik Kats in the development of this research programme which continues to make a contribution to the theoretical and methodological understanding of research into mobilisation issues in adult learning

B.J. Hake (✉)
Eurolearn Consultants, Bad Nieuweschans, The Netherlands
e-mail: eurolearn@home.nl

G.K. Zarifis and M.N. Gravani (eds.), *Challenging the 'European Area of Lifelong Learning': A Critical Response*, Lifelong Learning Book Series 19, DOI 10.1007/978-94-007-7299-1_22, © Springer Science+Business Media Dordrecht 2014

this section focusses on 'outreach work' towards specific target groups and community-based learning environments as a mobilisation strategy. In section "Strategies to mobilise participation in adult learning closer to home", attention turns to alternative theoretical perspectives which can inform understandings about the problematic articulation between the supply of and the demand for adult learning. These perspectives offer three different approaches to understanding adult learning strategies and interventions in terms of the social organisation of adult learning as communicative social and cultural practices. Section "Theoretical and methodological perspectives on 'bringing learning closer to home'" comprises the further development of a specific theoretical perspective which focusses on understanding organised adult learning activities in terms of public spaces characterised by struggles between conflicting social and cultural meanings about the purposes of adult learning in the everyday lives of adults. The fifth and final section offers some reflections on the historical and contemporary manifestations of the articulation between different social actors and cultural practices.

EU Policy Framework for 'Bringing Learning Closer to Home'

In 2000, the Lisbon European Council set itself the goal of making the European Union (EU) the most competitive and dynamic knowledge-based economy in the world. The European Commission (EC) stressed the importance of lifelong learning and the role of adult learning, including its contribution to personal development and fulfilment, in reaching the key objectives enhancing economic growth, competitiveness and social inclusion. There was subsequently a long drawn-out policy discussion during the following decade about ways to increase the participation of adults in education and training throughout the life course. The key question was how to achieve the EC's benchmark for of the participation of 15 % of adults in lifelong learning and to reduce the traditional imbalance in participation between highly skilled and low-skilled adults. It was also regarded as vitally important that adults continue to learn, to develop and upskill their competences to meet the challenges of demographic change, Europe's role in the global economy and a sustainable society and to invest in their own personal development.

For the purposes of this chapter, however, *A Memorandum on Lifelong Learning* (European Commission 2000), also published in 2000, is used as the baseline for the analysis of problems associated with raising levels of participation in adult learning. The objective of the *Memorandum* was to stimulate Member States to establish structures to reach more adults and to include them in the learning society through their participation in adult learning activities. The *Memorandum* formulated six key messages in order to make lifelong learning a reality. This chapter is focussed on Key Message 6 in the Memorandum: *Bringing Learning Closer to Home*. In the *Memorandum*, the objective of Message 6 was formulated as 'Provide lifelong learning opportunities as close to learners as possible, in their own communities and supported through ICT-based facilities wherever appropriate'. The *Memorandum* pointed out that 'Regional and local levels of governance have become increasingly influential in recent years in line with intensified demand for decision-making and services 'close to the ground'. The provision of education and training was one of the policy areas destined to be part of this trend on the grounds that for most people, from childhood through to old age, learning mainly happens regionally and locally. It was pointed out that regional and local authorities are also largely responsible for providing the infrastructure for access to lifelong learning, including childcare, transport and social welfare services. Mobilising the resources of regional and local authorities in support of lifelong learning was therefore essential' (European Commission 2000, p. 18).

The *Memorandum* also pointed out that civil society organisations and associations have their strongest roots at local level, and that they typically possess vast reservoirs of knowledge and experience about the communities of which they are part. Particular localities may have different characteristics and problems, but they all share a unique distinctiveness of place and identity. It was also argued that 'The familiar distinctiveness of people's home community and region gives confidence and provides social networks. These resources are important for lending meaning to learning and for supporting positive learning outcomes' (European Commission 2000, p. 19). The concluding sentence of Key Message 6 proposed that 'Bringing learning closer to home will also require re-organization and redeployment of resources to create appropriate kinds of learning centres in everyday locations where people gather – not only in schools themselves, but also, for example, in village halls and shopping malls, libraries and museums, places of worship, parks and public squares, train and bus stations, health centres and leisure complexes, and workplace canteens' (European Commission 2000, p. 19). As such this was an implicit recognition of the additional value of non-formal and informal adult learning in regional and local communities which are situated at some distance from the provision of formal learning opportunities intended for adults.

The EC continued throughout the decade to argue the case that it supported the Member States in promoting adult learning as part of lifelong learning processes and placed its commitment firmly on the European political agenda by adopting in 2006 the Communication on adult learning '*It is never too late to learn*' (European Commission 2006), followed by the Communication in 2007 on the adult learning Action Plan '*It is always a good time to learn*' (European Commission 2007). The Action Plan was formulated in terms of helping to remove the high thresholds and obstacles that prevent adults from engaging in learning activities and to improve the quality and efficiency of the adult learning sector. It complemented this with a call to ensure adequate levels of investment in, and better monitoring of, the adult learning sector. The adult learning sector in this context was formulated in terms of embracing all of the forms of learning undertaken by adults training in formal, non-formal and informal settings after they have left initial education.

In order to enhance policy development in the sector, improve governance and deliver better services, the Action Plan suggested five areas of action: analyse the effects of reforms in all sectors of education and training in Member States on adult learning; improve the quality of provisions in the adult learning sector; increase the possibilities for adults to go 'one step up' – to achieve a qualification at least one level higher than before; speed up the process of assessment of skills and social competences and have them validated and recognised in terms of learning outcomes; and, finally, to improve the monitoring of the adult learning sector. There was, however, a significant absence in the Action Plan of any explicit recognition of the importance of 'bringing learning closer to home' which had been made manifest in Key Message 6 of the *Memorandum*. The dominant focus was upon formal adult learning, one step up to higher qualifications, the acquisition and/or recognition of validated qualifications and individual competences via Accreditation of Prior and Experiential Learning (APEL) leading back to formal qualifications, while the overall priority of skills and requalification to enhance re-entry into the labour market. There was no specific reference in the Action Plan to a significant study of local learning centres and regional strategic partnerships which had been commissioned by the EC in 2004 (Buiskool et al. 2005). This much underestimated study had built upon the national responses to the *Memorandum* and their references to the long-standing traditions of non-formal and informal adult learning in regional and local communities.

Strategies to Mobilise Participation in Adult Learning Closer to Home

One of the studies commissioned by the EC as part of the evaluation of the Action Plan was most significant in that it was firmly focussed on the core policy issue of raising participation in adult learning and the contribution of the Action Plan to this end. The study, entitled *Impact of ongoing reforms in education and training on the adult learning sector*, argued that strategies to increase participation could be best understood in terms of the substantial body of theory and empirical research about participation and non-participation in adult learning (Broek et al. 2011). Against the background of different theoretical perspectives and empirical research concerned, for example, with learning motivations, social networks and learners' social capital, influence of social class and initial education, learning careers and autobiographical studies of adult learners, the study focussed on the so-called articulation problem between the prevailing patterns in the supply of adult learning opportunities and the demand for learning by adults. Given the variety of identified barriers to learning for specific social groups, the study argued that different policy measures and specific instruments can be deployed at national, regional and local levels in order to lower prevailing barriers and thus to increase the participation of adults in all kinds of formal, non-formal and informal learning activities. The basic assumption was that policies, measures and instruments intended to increase the participation of adults in learning activities should seek to influence both the structure of provision and the demand from targeted groups in so-called mobilisation strategies. National, regional and local policies for increasing participation in adult learning were described and analysed in terms of six mobilisation strategies which could be identified in both the *Memorandum* and the Action Plan. Six categories of relevant mobilisation strategies were identified: (a) information, counselling and guidance services; (b) flexibility of learning trajectories; (c) quality management; (d) outreach; (e) acknowledgement of prior (experiential) learning; and, finally, (f) economic instruments. In terms of 'bringing learning closer to home', this section will subsequently look at 'outreach work' to specific target groups and the development of community-based non-formal and informal learning environments at regional and local levels.

The final report of the study pointed out that in recent years there had been a considerable development of outreach work to targeted groups in a broad range of educational, health and welfare services throughout the EU. Outreach work can comprise a number of specific interventions to reach out to and involve targeted groups that are not in contact with or do not make use of available services. Outreach work is used in the field of adult learning in order to reach out to targeted groups of adults who are not involved in learning activities but who are at risk of social exclusion. Such groups can include the low qualified, low skilled, single parents, ethnic minorities and increasingly elderly people. Outreach work seeks to lower the thresholds of learning institutions, to 'bring learning closer to home', to enhance learning opportunities within the community and to convince difficult-to-reach adults that learning can enrich their lives, and that adult learning is a realistic option for themselves and their personal development.

On the one hand, information leaflets, brochures and posters are also distributed via intermediary organisations frequently visited by the adult general public such as schools, public libraries, local authority offices, social welfare agencies, employment services and the waiting rooms of family doctors and dentists. Outreach work can also involve, on the other hand, the use of 'ambassadors for learning' in the workplace involving trade union representatives as in the UK; contacting parents via the schools attended by their children; contacting risk groups through front-line health and welfare services via family doctors, dentists, hospitals, social/family services and services for the homeless or drug addicts; reaching out to 'in-debt' individuals and households who are in need of financial literacy education; and outreaching via voluntary organisations. Information is also disseminated via announcements in newspapers and local radio and television stations. In terms of the provision of information about learning opportunities, country studies refer to the development of virtual information systems about the learning opportunities available to adults. These comprise national and institutional virtual portals providing information about providers and their courses at the national, regional and local levels. Current developments in outreach work now include experiments with broadband communication and the potential of social networking software to reach targeted groups and make learning more accessible in user-friendly formats.

Outreach work with regard to participation in adult learning involves proactive measures undertaken by adult education providers to establish contact with specific target groups who are considered to be in need of these services but who do not make use of them. Given the dominance in current policies directed to increasing levels of participation in the labour market, providers of adult learning tend to regard outreach in terms of reducing the institutional barriers that inhibit participation. In this respect, outreach strategies tend above all to focus on young dropouts from secondary and vocational education, low-qualified workers, the unemployed, jobseekers and, increasingly, older workers. In most Member States, this tends, on the one hand, to involve closer co-operation between providers of adult education, employment and social service agencies in order to reintegrate individuals in the labour market. There is convincing evidence, however, that outreach strategies in the Member States also focus on those groups which face severe problems of exclusion from adult learning as a result of their multiple social exclusion resulting from conditions of poverty, illiteracy, indebtedness, migration, refugee status, homelessness and alcohol and drug abuse. This leads to the involvement of adult education providers in outreach activities which are often organised together with intermediaries such as NGOs and front-line health and welfare support services including family-care workers, community nurses, social workers and the health services such as family doctors. Through consultation with those in day-to-day contact with at-risk groups, the outreach strategies of adult education providers seek to explore innovative ways of meeting specific learning needs and to fill the gaps that exist in provision 'closer to home'. There is substantial evidence in the Member States of the development of these so-called 'hybrid' forms for the provision of adult learning activities for adults in order to support them in learning their way out of the threatening experience of social exclusion.

Within the terms of the above-mentioned study on 'local learning centres and strategic partnerships', it was clearly established that the bulk of non-formal and informal learning in the daily lives of adults, especially the low qualified and low skilled, takes place at a considerable distance from formal educational institutions. This non-formal and informal learning takes place primarily in families, households, streets, neighbourhoods, communities, trade unions, political parties, churches, voluntary associations and social movements at the regional and local levels. Such adult learning is related to the everyday experiences of adults in relation to problematic issues such as housing, health, food, transport, pollution and the environment. Such issues are addressed in terms of their potential for learning activities by a broad range of neighbourhood and community centres, community action groups, social movements, etc. The key characteristic of the development of these community-based non-formal and informal learning environments is that the issues and problems arising in daily life are identified as 'social spaces for the development of learning questions' and the development of social capital through active engagement in learning by individuals and social groups and in terms of their engagement in social movements.

Theoretical and Methodological Perspectives on 'Bringing Learning Closer to Home'

The dominant tendency in policy-led studies of 'bringing learning closer to home' is to determine criteria which can facilitate the identification of 'good practices' of outreach work which can be exported to other countries or borrowed by others. This chapter refuses to take the easy option of delving into the murky waters of the language of 'good practices' so much favoured by the Open Method of Coordination in the EU and the Mutual Learning Programme in the area of adult learning. Instead, attention in this section will focus on theoretical and methodological perspectives which analyse 'outreach work' in terms of the social and cultural relations between outreach activities and the target groups of such activities.

Success or failure of outreach work strategies in *Bringing Learning Closer to Home* is to a very significant degree determined by the emergence of an 'audience' or a 'public' which is receptive to the idea of their voluntary engagement in adult learning, in many cases for the first time on their lives. Do the well-intended endeavours of policymakers and 'outreach workers' result in the emergence of new audiences or publics on a large-enough scale to justify the continued investment of, increasingly scarce, public and private resources? This is the point at which 'bringing learning closer to home' becomes a complicated issue of the articulation between social and cultural actors who inhabit different social spheres. Research has suggested that at least 10 % of adults can be regarded as comprising a 'non-audience' or a 'non-public' who are resistant to all endeavours to turn them into voluntary adult learners (de Sanctis 1984). Is this to be interpreted as fool-hardy, plain bloody-mindedness or meaningful resistance in terms of their understanding of their social situation? For many more adults, participation research indicates that while they may regard adult learning as a good thing in general terms, they then proceed to make an exception in their own personal case in the sense of 'A good thing for others, but not relevant to my situation'. Furthermore, many non-participants in publicly provided adult learning are often active participants as learners and members of collective actions organised in order to create their own oppositional social and cultural meanings. Given such insights into participation and non-participation in adult learning, it is perhaps more meaningful to examine the articulation between supply and demand in terms of the social organisation of communication processes which characterise 'outreach work' to target groups. Theoretical and methodological perspectives on the problem of articulation can focus, for example, on the social organisation of communication processes between the providers of adult learning and the target groups or intended audiences. Metaphors of communication play an important role in all discussions of the social relationships between adult learning activities and the target groups, audiences and publics addressed by socially organised learning activities. This section will focus on three distinct metaphors for understanding the articulation between providers of and the demand for adult learning and in particular the historical and contemporary specifics of 'bringing learning closer to home'. These are, respectively, the 'transmission', 'signification' and 'argumentation' metaphors which manifest different assumptions about research into 'outreach' strategies for 'bringing learning closer to home'. The analysis will focus on the argumentation metaphor and the insights it proposes with regard to understanding articulation in outreach work practices.

The *'transmission' metaphor* has long been the dominant theoretical perspective in research seeking to understand the relationships between the providers and users of adult learning activities. In most general terms, this metaphor assumes that the providers of adult learning, both public and private agencies, are responsible for the supply of information for those who are regarded as in need of knowledge, skills and sensitivities. Emphasis is placed on channels of communication between providers and intended users of adult learning. The target groups, audiences or publics addressed by outreach work are those in disadvantaged social situations who are regarded as suffering from a deficit of formal education, a lack of information about the reality of their lives and the absence of the skills to manage their own lives. Such assumptions encourage providers of adult learning to ensure the smooth, effective and successful transmission of information via outreaching activities to target groups, audiences and potential publics. Failure to achieve these objectives is understood in terms of malfunctions in communication channels, 'noise' filtering messages, and 'cultural lags', and 'misunderstandings' by the target groups, audiences and publics. Renewed, and refined, efforts to communicate will ensue, and specific attention is often paid to technical factors in unsuccessful communication. Moreover, 'opinion leaders' and 'intermediary agencies' may be introduced in outreach work who function as a feedback loop and enable the source to attune the message to the reactions of the intended receivers. The reduction of 'noise' in reaching target groups is increasingly resolved by providers adopting social networking software together with possibilities for intended users to indicate 'like', 'send' and 'tweet' options on providers websites. Public and private providers of adult learning themselves increasingly resort to 'tweets' in their well-intentioned messages in order to convince audiences of their 'good intentions'. Any 'tweet' by a disgruntled 'user' or 'client' can be regarded as a message which undermines the messages communicated by providers and even give rise to 'shit-storms'. The increasing use of the transmission metaphor in the E-based rhetoric of outreach work is characterised by the bad taste of product-consumer conceptions of social relations in adult learning. In the new world of virtual reality in social networks, the transmission metaphor largely fails to address questions surrounding the changing positions of authors and readers of messages, the increase of anonymity and distortion of the subject and the reduction of the public sphere of 'communicative action' to a multiplicity of private spaces.

In departing from the transmission metaphor of information sent by authoritative sources to target groups of receivers, the *'signification' metaphor* is informed by a hermeneutic understanding of the interpretation and reinterpretation of outreach messages by senders and intended audiences. Communication is understood as reiterative processes of interpretative activities. This shifts the focus from the source of messages to the receivers of messages and their lifeworlds. Signification recognises that the dissemination and acquisition of cultural meanings is characterised by the cultural capacities of audiences themselves to make sense of any information communicated to them. Individuals and social groups, even collective audiences, are seen as able to create their own frameworks of meaning by selecting information and integrating cultural messages in their own everyday lives. In this perspective, the signification metaphor recognises that potential audiences may evaluate adult learning opportunities in terms of their own cultural capital, codes and meanings. Adult learning no longer has necessarily integrative effects such as happens when dominant cultural meanings are accepted by targeted audiences. Furthermore, adult learning programmes may provide individuals and social groups with the cultural resources to develop their own cultural meanings and *critical cultural awareness*. Adult learning activities never constitute more than a small part of the information and knowledge available to people in their everyday lives. Public and private providers, including for-profit adult learning activities, increasingly have to compete with multiple sources of cultural meanings in the 'tower of Babel' which characterises the modern world of the internet. Publicly provided messages and cultural meanings are now far from as unambiguous as the providers would like them to be. The world of 'messaging' produces an almost unbridled pluralism in the dissemination and acquisition of cultural meanings together with the differentiation of social relations in the public and private spheres. While the transmission metaphor views the failure of information to reach audiences in terms of technical shortcomings and/or cultural lags, the signification metaphor suggests that target audiences can produce their own definitions of problems and possible solutions in the form of adult learning. This can result in a tendency towards cultural relativism in which adult learning activities are inhabited by a collection of subcultures each with its own system of meanings which are equally valid in the cacophony of messages and meanings. It can also result in a failure to take into account the role of social structures and power relationships between social groups, state institutions, adult learning organisations and the marketplace in understanding how outreach work brings about changes in the behaviour of target groups, audiences and publics, or not.

Adult learning programmes are indeed developed and implemented against the background of social forces and power relationships which may have contemporary but also deep historical roots in the broader society.[1] The *'argumentation' metaphor* shifts the focus of analysis to understandings of the social organisation of communication and learning in terms of the *articulation* between adult learning and these broader social and cultural forces. It is assumed that even the most apparently autonomous manifestations of adult learning are subject to the influence of these social forces and have repercussions, however indirect, upon society and the everyday lives of both learners and non-learners. More often than not, adult learning programmes are ridden by different 'arguments' with regard to the reasons why the

---

[1] The author is indebted to the intellectual contribution of Raymond Williams to the analysis of the materialist understanding of social formations and cultural practices. Key texts include: Williams, R. (1961), *The Long Revolution*, London; idem. (1973), 'Base and superstructure in Marxist cultural theory', *New Left Review*, no. 82; idem. (1977), *Marxism and Literature*, Oxford; idem. (1980), *Problems of Materialism and Culture*, Oxford; idem. (1981), *Culture*, Glasgow.

social situations of target groups are regarded as problematic and thus 'in need' of interventions to stimulate their participation in adult learning programme. The argumentation by target groups of their own situation is based upon their own counter-cultural systems of meaning which can easily conflict with the arguments promoted by the providers of the adult learning programmes that are intended to help them. This means that communication processes cannot be divorced from the social relationships in society which are reflected in these different argumentations about adult learning activities. These social relations involve those who are organised by others, or organise themselves, for the purposes of communicating and acquiring knowledge, skills and sensitivities and the struggle for cultural resources to these often differing purposes of adult learning.

Social and Cultural Configurations of Outreach Work Practices

A variety of social actors are involved in the provision of adult learning such as policy-makers, public and private providers of adult learning activities, trade unions and employers' organisations, a plethora of voluntary associations, community action groups and social movements, together with the target groups themselves. These social actors are structurally related at regional and local levels in complex social and cultural configurations in which the distribution of power over adult learning is uneven. Adult learning initiatives aimed at a variety of target groups are developed and implemented in the complex public arena of these institutionalised social forces. These initiatives are concerned with winning consent in a field of contesting social interests, and their definitions of problems have to be continuously established and re-established within social and cultural relationships. When adult learning programmes seek to tackle the adult learning problems identified in these power configurations, they become involved in processes of argumentation concerning different readings of social contexts and ways of dealing with identified problems and the intended results of interventions to resolve these problems. In this sense, adult learning providers are active agents in the argumentation of social problems into specific adult learning interventions. At the same time, target groups and their advocates are also involved as social actors in these social and adult learning configurations. There is no direct or automatic reflection of socially dominant interests in the presentation of the adult learning programmes developed and implemented. State agencies, private providers and other stakeholders, including target groups and their advocates, are engaged in the articulation of argumentations in order to claim, increasingly scarce, resources and especially funding in order to reach specified target groups, audiences and publics.

In the contemporary *contextualisation* of policy-led interventions for *Bringing Learning Closer to Home*, assessments of success and failure are of paramount importance in the search for 'good examples' of 'outreach' work to intended target groups, audiences and publics. At the same time, these notions of success and failure are contentious and have to be handled with great caution. On the one hand, the intentions of those responsible for outreach interventions are important, and they form a legitimate focus of both contemporary and historical research. On the other hand, it needs to be recognised that intentions cannot be studied in any insightful way within the transmission or signification metaphors. Intentions and their effects are actually of subordinate interest in the understanding of outreach interventions; indeed they can be misleading and quite unhelpful. The alternative approach is to come to terms with the inevitable recognition that attempts to change the lives of target groups, audiences and public groups are a vastly complex undertaking. In the contemporary world of voluntary participation in adult learning, the fate of 'outreach' initiatives depends on the emergence of an effective audience among target groups and the persistence of continuing involvement by this 'receptive' public in adult learning programmes.

These processes need to be situated in the historical and contemporary contexts of complex social and cultural relationships which are at the end of the day determined by social and cultural relationships which reflect relationships of power in the distribution of scarce resources. The foregoing analysis has suggested that it is indeed necessary in theoretical terms to refine the use of the terms 'target groups', 'audiences' and 'publics' in relation to different metaphors. Identification of 'target groups' may be appropriate within the transmission metaphor, while the language of 'audiences' is more appropriate for the 'signification' metaphor. The notion of 'publics' is a theoretical category which can effectively address the broader scope of social and cultural influences involved in the argumentation metaphor. This understanding focusses on the formation of 'subject' positions in communicative practices and the force of social and cultural meanings. In terms of 'bringing learning closer to home', outreach work may be better understood in terms of the capacities of social actors, indeed collective cultural agents, who are actively involved in the creation of the social and cultural meanings of 'subject' positions in social communication processes. This serves to distinguish the argumentation metaphor from the position of 'target groups' of the intended end-consumers of messages within the transmission metaphor. The argumentation metaphor is also able to analyse the proto-product position of individuals within the signification metaphor of communication and learning which is based upon the cultural relativism of messages in which the individual experience of social structures is reduced to 'like' positions or expressed in 'tweets', and in effect the individual submits to global market forces in the social and cultural form of a product for Facebook to sell to other capitalists.

Conclusions

Efforts to mobilise target groups, audiences and publics in the field of adult learning have historically come and gone almost endlessly, and they relate to each other in very complex ways in the course of European modernisation (Hake 2010). One historical example, drawn from my own historical research on cultural formations in the Netherlands during the late eighteenth century, may suffice here to argue that outreach work is not something new, and that the providers of adult learning have in the past attuned their efforts for the 'enlightenment' of adults. At the same time they contributed to the argumentation of well-defined differences between the target groups, audiences and publics for their adult learning wares.

Similar conclusions were drawn by a committee (of the Society for the Common Benefit) which was established by the Annual General Meeting in 1820 to investigate the causes of the limited reading and distribution of the popular tracts of the Society and the means for improving their distribution among the 'common man' and arousing his appetite for reading (see Hake 1987). The report by this committee to Annual General Meeting in 1821 came to the conclusion that it was possible to distinguish between three social categories among the less educated sections of the population (see Hake 1987). It spoke firstly of those 'who should they be given books; they only throw these away, or, given the opportunity, sell them and spend the proceeds on drink or other excesses'. In the second place, the committee identified those 'labourers who display little or no interest in reading due to their heavy labours, their limited means of subsistence, dull understanding, or deep ignorance'. While the first public was considered to be responsibility of the public authorities, the second group was thought to be the responsibility of the philanthropic societies. Worthy of the efforts of the Society for Common Benefit were the 'respectable' among those 'with limited means, who as result of their diligent labour and thrifty house-keeping, their gentle disposition and religious feeling, find time for and have an interest in reading, and who are prepared to this end to purchase books, or are able to procure them by borrowing or as gifts'. The 'respectable' working man represented the public to be served (Hake 1987, pp. 380–381).

How can we best understand 'outreach' to the 'difficult to reach' as a mobilisation strategy for the purposes of 'bringing learning closer to home'? It is first of all necessary to understand adult learning programmes in terms of the socially mediated access to cultural resources for specific social groups. On the one hand, this directs attention to the historically wide variety of cultural disseminators which is a question of the contribution of what Carlson (1980) calls peers, poets, propagandists, priest, peddlers, politicians, performers, publishers, pamphleteers, playwrights, publicans and practitioners of the plastic arts.

In the social and political context of the virtual world of internet, we also need to include the 'p' for the 'pirate party' which argues for absolute anonymity in a totalitarian image of virtual reality constituted by messaging. They thus serve to conflate the world of the social and cultural positions of disseminators and publics in social and cultural communication. For the inhabitants of virtual reality, there is no longer any 'public space' available for increasingly decentred 'subjects' in the relativism of the multiplicity of 'private spaces'.

This somewhat discursive and episodic journey through the historical and contemporary representations of the world of outreach work and 'bringing learning closer to home' must conclude with the assertion that our understandings necessarily need to be based on reflection about the broader patterns of change in late modern society and the global hegemony of capitalist social and cultural forms. This is not to argue that adult learning is a cultural epiphenomenon and forms a part of the cultural superstructure, which should be understood as the (over)determined reflection of a determining economic and technological base. Instead one proposes here that the 'objective' economic, social and political conditions of the social order constitute the raw materials for the constitution of social and cultural action in the production of meaning. However, these raw materials of social and cultural production and reproduction do not determine the concrete historical and contemporary manifestations of social and cultural consciousness and struggle. In the classic argumentation of the 'young' Karl Marx, social conditions form the raw materials for the production and reproduction of consciousness by social and cultural actors. There is no place here, however, for formulations of 'false consciousness' which took the form of accepting the 'original' social problem as formulated by conservative, liberal and social-democratic factions in the late nineteenth century. When they were confronted with the capacity of autonomous working-class organisations to organise their own independent adult learning activities, 'the social question' was formulated in terms of outreach activities to incorporate the emergent working class in 'liberal adult education'.

Oppositional argumentations by anarchist, socialist and communist cultural formations in terms of 'knowledge is power' gave rise to the social organisation of counter-hegemonic forms of autonomous adult learning. The cultural sphere of adult learning is indeed influenced by social forces, but the institutions of adult learning may enjoy a degree of historical and contemporary autonomy. Such relative autonomy is not an abstract or given characteristic of any manifestation of cultural institutions and practices, it is a variable social and historical phenomenon. The degree of autonomy of the social organisation of adult learning can only be established by rigorous historical and contemporary research into the influence of economic, social and political forces and the exertion of pressures upon and the setting of limits to the development of outreach work and 'bringing learning closer to home'. The social and cultural processes involved in the 'making' of adult learning activities can still be best understood in terms of the organised efforts of individual and collective cultural subjects in order to deal with their experience and interpretation of 'lived conditions' and 'the ways in which these experiences are handled in cultural terms: embodied in traditions, ideas and institutional forms' (see Thompson 1963).

It is necessary today to study rigorously the cultural forms produced by 'citizens' active in the public sphere of 'making meanings' who seek to change social relationships through their cultural action. It is also necessary to study the social forces and cultural forms which reproduce the false consciousness of the inhabitants of the virtual world and the cultural transformation of 'subject positions' into 'product positions' for the purposes of unbridled capitalist accumulation. To paraphrase the original title of one of Walter Benjamin's (1936) major works, this calls for greater understanding of the social forces engaged in 'making' the 'subject in the age of its digital reproduction'.

References

Benjamin, W. (1936). L'oeuvre d'art à l'époque de sa reproduction mécanisée. *Zeitschrift für Sozialforschung, 5*, 40–363.

Broek, S., Buiskool, B.-J., & Hake, B. J. (2011). *Impact of ongoing reforms in education and training on the adult learning sector. Final report.* Leiden: Research voor Beleid.

Buiskool, B.-J., Grijpstra, D., van Kan, C., van Lakerveld, J., & van den Oudendammer, F. (2005). *Developing local learning centres and learning partnerships as part of Member States' targets for reaching the Lisbon goals in the field of education and training: A study of the current situation.* Leiden: Research voor Beleid.

Carlson, R. A. (1980). The foundation of adult education: Analyzing the Boyd-Apps model. In R. D. Boyd & J. W. Apps (Eds.), *Redefining the discipline of adult education.* San Francisco: Jossey-Bass.

de Sanctis, F. M. (1984). Problems of defining the public in the context of lifelong education. *International Journal of Lifelong Education, 3*(4), 265–278.

European Commission. (2000). *Commission staff working paper. A memorandum on lifelong learning* (SEC (2000) 1832). Brussels: European Commission.

European Commission. (2006). *Communication from the commission. Adult learning: It is never too late to learn* (COM (2006) 614 final). Brussels: European Commission.

European Commission. (2007). *Communication from the commission. Action plan on adult learning: It is always a good time to learn* (COM (2007) 558 final). Brussels: European Commission.

Hake, B. J. (1987). *Patriots, democrats and social enlightenment: A study of political movements and the development of adult education in the Netherlands, 1780–1813* (pp. 380–381). Dissertation, University of Hull.

Hake, B. J. (2010). Rewriting the history of adult education: The search for narrative structures. In K. Rubenson (Ed.), *Adult learning and education* (pp. 14–19). Oxford: Elsevier.

Thompson, E. P. (1963). *The making of the English working-class.* London: Victor Gollancz.

Chapter 23
Lifelong Learning and Schools as Community Learning Centres: Key Aspects of a National Curriculum Draft Policy Framework for Malta

Peter Mayo

Introduction

The island of Malta has been engaged in policy document formulations for curriculum renewal in the country's educational system (4–16 years of age) since 1988 when the first National Minimum Curriculum (henceforth NMC) was launched (Wain 1991; Borg et al. 1995). In 1999 a revamped NMC (Ministry of Education 1999) was developed following a long process of consultation involving various stages and stakeholders. It was a compromise document (Borg and Mayo 2006) which emerged as a result of reactions to a more radical and coherent draft document produced in 1998. Both curricular documents were subject to debates and critiques (Wain 1991; Darmanin 1993; Borg ct al. 1995; Giordmaina 2001; Borg and Mayo 2006). More recently a series of volumes providing guidelines, key principles and aims for a national curriculum framework (henceforth NCF) have been produced (MEEF 2011a, b, c, d) and are currently the target of debate and the focus of reactions by various stakeholders in education including teachers who were asked to read the volumes and provide reactions in the form of answers to a set questionnaire.

In this chapter, I will focus on one aspect of the documents, the first of its three aims: 'Learners who are capable of successfully developing their full potential as lifelong learners'. It is that aspect of the framework documents that falls within the purview of the title for this book on lifelong learning. The use of this notion attests to the influence of the EU's policy communications on member states, Malta having joined the Union in 2004 (Mayo 2007).

The NCF documents base their vision for the future of education in Malta around the now widespread concept of lifelong learning in keeping with the dominant

P. Mayo (✉)
Department of Education Studies, Faculty of Education, University of Malta, Msida, Malta
e-mail: peter.mayo@um.edu.mt

G.K. Zarifis and M.N. Gravani (eds.), *Challenging the 'European Area
of Lifelong Learning': A Critical Response*, Lifelong Learning Book Series 19,
DOI 10.1007/978-94-007-7299-1_23, © Springer Science+Business Media Dordrecht 2014

discourse which has emerged from not only the European Union but also the OECD. One notices the discursive shift from the old UNESCO discourse on lifelong education (Tuijnman and Boström 2002). Much has been written about this discourse from a critical perspective (Murphy 1997; Williamson 1998; Brine 1999; Wain 2004; Borg and Mayo 2004; Field 2001, 2010), to make policymakers aware of the shift in emphasis that has occurred from the broad, humanistic concept of lifelong education (Faure et al. 1972) to that of lifelong learning. This shift is not innocent and ties in with some of the hegemonic ideas that are often taken on board uncritically without the slightest concern for the kind of ideology that underpins such terminology. It is felt that one needs to eschew the current meanings attributed to the notion of lifelong learning if one is to engage in a commitment to education for social justice. The dominant discourse on lifelong learning, as adopted in the NCF, is one that shifts the onus of responsibility onto the individual rather than the state and the social collectivity. Learning and adequate provision for it become a matter of individual rather than social responsibility. This is all in keeping with the politics of *responsibilisation* that is hegemonic these days, shifting the responsibility for learning onto individuals and communities (Darmanin 2011 in talk delivered to Dept. of Education Studies, University of Malta).

Collective Dimension of Learning

In contexts such as these, a reversal to the old UNESCO discourse of lifelong education would help only if we avoid the rather individualistic orientation of some (not all) of the relevant writings and follow those writings that place emphasis on not only the individual but also the collective dimensions of learning as indicated in passim by Dave (1976) and more in depth by Suchodolski (1976), Williamson (1998), Gelpi (2002), Walters et al. (2004), Livingstone and Sawchuk (2004), Borg and Mayo (2004) and Wain (2004). Related concepts such as lifewide learning and the learning society have often (not always) been developed within the context of a vision for collective learning in addition to individual learning, especially in the literature just cited.

While criticality is mentioned in the NCF documents, as a component of a genuine process of lifelong learning, a key point in the above literature, this has not been spelt out. There is an emphasis on 'solving problems'. (MEEF 2011b, p. 28) This sounds quite fair. However, the question that arises is whether learning entails more than this. Is it just a matter of solving problems with the mistaken belief that there is a clear answer to any question raised? What about handling complexity? What about problem posing in addition to problem solving? Surely, a genuine study of literature at the later stages of secondary education should help drive this point home. Confining oneself to the latter (problem solving) could lead to the emergence of very resourceful people, including a pool of technocrats (very much suited to a human capital theory approach), while the former can serve the purpose of developing a healthy democracy with people serving as social actors and not atomised individuals who simply embody certain attributes and are attuned to acting in ways that allow them to be governed indirectly and by proxy, what Foucault would call *governmentality*.

The documents (MEEF 2011b) place emphasis on the imagination, defined, following Ken Robinson and Lou Aronica (2009), as 'the capacity for original thought' with creativity meaning 'applied imagination' (MEEF 2011b, p. 28). This is a welcome development in the dominant Maltese policy discourse. And it is imperative that approaches to teaching/learning are imaginative and involve the constant arousal of 'epistemological curiosity' as Freire (1998) would put it. Unless this occurs schools would be providing little in the way of creating the right milieu for lifelong learners, both individually and collectively. Boring and mind-numbing teaching can either put off students from wanting to learn formally and possibly non-formally or alternatively make them seek alternative sources of knowledge as a reaction to formal schooling, part and parcel of a 'counter culture' (which has frequently been the case with some but not all). Developing a counter-discourse and culture is not necessarily a bad thing and has been a survival strategy for several artists, writers, dissidents and other intellectuals. It would however serve to underline a dissonance between conventional schooling and the emancipatory or self-creative (individual and collective) aspirations of its students.

The notion of students as lifelong learners also has implications for guidance and counselling (Sultana 2003). Guidance and counselling needs to be broadened to become a lifelong learning service. It should not be confined to school age and not be 'remedial' in its approach but serve a proactive purpose throughout a person's lifespan. The officials involved also need to treat persons as lifelong learners. This is in keeping with one of the better six key messages of the EU's Memorandum on Lifelong Learning (CEC 2001). The objective of Message 5 is to 'Ensure that everyone can easily access good quality information and advice about learning opportunities throughout Europe and throughout their lives' (CEC 2001, 17). This message is of great importance for countries in Europe that still restrict guidance and counselling facilities to schools and tertiary institutions, as well as public and private labour market agencies. Given the variegated and broad nature of the field of education, comprising the formal and non-formal (mentioned in the NCF documents) sectors, not to mention informal learning, a holistic and lifelong approach to guidance and counselling is being advocated in European Commission documents (Sultana 2003). The net result of this strategy at the European level is that more and more guidance and counselling provisions are meant to follow citizens throughout life; enhance social inclusion by engaging reluctant learners in educational and training experiences; present up-to-date information that responds to people and employer needs; network with NGOs (though care is cautioned here given the onset of too much NGOisation in these days of 'Neoliberalism', in lieu of proper and socially committed state intervention) to address specific needs; and avail oneself of the potential of technology-based infrastructures for guidance and counselling purposes (Sultana 2003).

The notion of conceiving of students as lifelong learners also has implications for evaluation (Skager 1978). What do we evaluate? Do we evaluate simply possession and mastery of skills and knowledge, important and crucial in light of learners' entitlement as citizens in a democratic country or *also* the ability to explore and identify new forms of knowledge and insights? In the latter case, this would mean venturing beyond the knowledge provided in the classroom by crossing borders in the manner explained by Young (1998, 2004) with regard to his proposed notion of a mix between in-depth learning of core areas characterised by 'strong framing', in Basil Bernstein's terms, and trans-disciplinary areas. This is intended towards the goal of enabling lifelong learners to take charge, both individually and collectively, of their own learning especially in future.

The school contributes little to lifelong learning if it produces 'failures' who have not learned or achieved from school the skills, knowledge and further learning networks to which they are entitled as citizens. Certain core areas have to be mastered by all. One must be aware of the pitfalls indicated by Gramsci (1971) and others with regard to the adoption of watered-down progressivist ideas. Active learning is important but also entails rigour and mastery of certain skills. While anchoring pupils learning in strong disciplinary knowledge (Young 2004), the school can pave the way, in the later years, for improvisation by encouraging students to venture beyond the 'comfort zone' of such knowledge by crossing boundaries. One requires the right balance between disciplinary cross-borders and in-depth knowledge, with a strong 'framing' and 'classification' of certain disciplines such as Maths and the natural sciences and a weaker 'classification' and 'framing' of others which are very closely related (Darmanin 2011, op.cit.).

The idea of lifelong learning was consolidated in the 1988 draft NMC and the 1999 final NMC document when they promoted the idea of schools as community learning centres (SCLCs).

> Schools should serve as community learning centres that also cater for the adult members of the community. This principle combines the commitment of this Curriculum to a holistic education with the recognition of the importance of lifelong education and the need for stakeholder participation in the educational process. (Ministry of Education 1999, p. 89)

This idea remains a valid one and continues to be mentioned in the NCF especially with regard to parental involvement in schools, with parents being 'subject' in terms of having an active say on the proceedings and not simply serving as adjuncts – in short parents as social actors. This is as it should be, though the SCLCs concept involves much more than this. The SCLCs project should not however be dependent for its implementation on simply ESF (European Social Funds) funds which are intermittent, as was the case in Malta around 2005 with regard to the abortive funding of the short-lived community learning centres in different towns and villages and are geared solely towards 'employability' which does not necessarily mean employment, as Ettore Gelpi (2002) once remarked. There is more to community learning than 'employability'. There is a need for indications regarding how the community can serve as a learning enhancing resource.

The final document, for which this draft provides a basis for discussion, also needs to spell out the educational, democratic and economic reasons why we need to conceive of schools as community learning centres, a concept found in some of the literature on small states. Summing up this literature, I would submit that there are at least three arguments to be made:

1. *Democratic argument*: Schools, especially state schools, are public resources. This proposed project constitutes an attempt to make democratic use of public resources.
2. *Economic argument*: The cost per capita of public resources in a microstate such as Malta is higher than that incurred in larger states. One must make better and maximum use of resources, lest these resources become 'idle capital' for several hours during the day and entire months during the calendar year.
3. *Educational argument* (with regard to schooling): It is not only adult members of the community who benefit from such schools but also children. Links between schools and the community would create greater space for the involvement of more stakeholders, such as parents, in the school process. This would create closer ties between schools and their pupils' immediate home environment, without confining the latter to a 'campanilismo' (very parochial) style of education. On the contrary, there should be both a global and local dimension to the education provided; otherwise, one would be restricting the children's different 'universes of knowledge'.

The work of Didacus Jules (1994/5) from St. Lucia, in the Caribbean, is instructive here. He helped develop a multipurpose learning school in Trinidad and Tobago on the lines of a school as a community learning centre (Mayo et al. 2008, p. 230). State funding is crucial for such a project which entails teachers' and heads' continuing professional development in this area (this is a crucial area in courses on educational administration and leadership). It also involves restructuring buildings to accommodate adults and building new schools as community learning centres from the very start. This entails liaison between the areas of education and architecture. It represents a new vision for schools born out of the reality of small jurisdictions, a vision that turns scale (Baldacchino 2010) into a virtue rather than an impediment.

Conclusion

As a recent member of the European Union, Malta has been quick to embrace the notion of lifelong learning which can be regarded as the Union's master concept for learning just as it was UNESCO's master concept for education in the past. This particular interpretation of lifelong learning within the EU policy context differs considerably from the more expansive notion used by UNESCO. Though contested within different epistemic communities within the EU, which must not be seen to be monolithic, the overarching notion that emerges from its main policy documents thus far (one awaits an overdue and revised document 10 years after the launch of the EU Memorandum in 2001) is that of lifelong learning for employability and a narrowly defined notion of active citizenship which overlooks the collective dimension of education for social change and which provides a very problematic notion of individualised learning. This notion does not reflect any cognisance of the way concepts, assumptions and practices are influenced by mechanisms that prey on people's sensibilities. Any further development of the Maltese curriculum discourse should be predicated on an awareness of these mechanisms in the interest of providing guidelines for an education geared towards an enhancement of social justice. One hopes to see the overriding notion of lifelong learning for this proposed renewed curriculum fleshed out, in the final National Curriculum document, in a manner that takes on board some of the criticisms levelled at the current discourse emanating from the EU. One hopes that it would do this in the spirit of developing a more holistic approach to lifelong learning/education that eschews its reduction to simply matters of production and consumption and encourages an alternative conceptualisation of persons as collectively and individually engaged social actors. Options for learning and living a full life would thus be broadened, while the basic necessary knowledge, to which every citizen is entitled, would be made available without any dilutions.

References

Baldacchino, G. (2010). Entrepreneurship on smaller jurisdictions: Appraising a glocal elite. In P. Mayo (Ed.), *Education in small states. Global imperatives, regional initiatives and local dilemmas*. London/New York: Routledge.

Borg, C., & Mayo, P. (2004). Diluted wine in new bottles. The key messages of the EU memorandum on lifelong learning. *Lifelong Learning in Europe (LlinE), 9*(1), 19–25.

Borg, C., & Mayo, P. (2006). *Learning and social difference. Challenges for public education and critical pedagogy*. Boulder: Paradigm.

Borg, C., Camilleri, J., Mayo, P., & Xerri, T. (1995). Malta's national curriculum. A critical analysis. *International Review of Education, 41*, 337–356.

Brine, J. (1999). *Under educating women: Globalizing inequality*. Milton Keynes: Open University Press.

CEC. (2001). *Commission staff working paper. A memorandum on lifelong learning*. Brussels: European Commission.

Darmanin, M. (1993). More things in heaven and earth: Contradictions and co-optation in education policy. *International Studies in Sociology of Education, 3*, 147–167.

Darmanin, M. (2011, July 4). A reading of the national curriculum framework 2011. Powerpoint presentation to Department of Education Studies, University of Malta, Seminar on draft NCF documents, Corinthia San Gorg, Malta.

Dave, R. H. (1976). Foundations of lifelong education: Some methodological aspects. In R. H. Dave (Ed.), *Foundations of lifelong education*. Oxford/Hamburg: Pergamon Press/ UNESCO Institute for Education.

Faure, E., Herrera, F., Kaddoura, A.-R., Lopes, H., Petrovsky, A. V., Rahnema, M., & Champion Ward, F. (1972). *Learning to be. The world of education today and tomorrow*. Paris: UNESCO.

Field, J. (2001). Lifelong education. *International Journal of Lifelong Education, 20*(1 and 2), 3–15.

Field, J. (2010). Lifelong learning. In P. Peterson, E. Baker, & B. McGaw (Eds.), *International encyclopedia of education* (3rd ed.). Amsterdam: Elsevier.

Freire, P. (1998). *Pedagogy of freedom. Ethics, democracy and civic courage*. Lanham: Rowman & Littlefield.

Gelpi, E. (2002). *Lavoro Futuro. La formazione professionale come progetto politico*. Milan: Edizioni Angelo Guerini e Associati SpA.

Giordmaina, J. (Ed.). (2001). *National curriculum – Proceedings of a national conference, June 2000*. Msida: Publishers Enterprises Group. Malta.

Gramsci, A. (1971). In Q. Hoare & G. Nowell Smith (Eds.), *Selection from the prison notebooks*. New York: International Publishers.

Jules, D. (1994/5). Adult education policy in micro-states. The case of the Caribbean. *Policy Studies Review, 13*(3 and 4), 415–432.

Livingstone, D. W., & Sawchuk, P. (2004). *Hidden knowledge: Organized labour in the information age*. Toronto/Lanham: Garamond Press/Rowman & Littlefield.

Mayo, P. (2007). *Adult education in Malta*. Bonn: DVV International.

Mayo, P., Pace, P., & Zammit, E. (2008). Adult continuing education in small states. The case of Malta. *Comparative Education, 44*(2), 229–246.

MEEF. (2011a). *Towards a quality education for all. The national curriculum framework consultation document 1: Executive summary*. Valletta: Ministry of Education, Employment & the Family. Malta.

MEEF. (2011b). *Towards a quality education for all. The national curriculum framework consultation document 2: Rationale and components*. Valletta: Ministry of Education, Employment & the Family. Malta.

MEEF. (2011c). *Towards a quality education for all. The national curriculum framework consultation document 3: The three cycles*. Valletta: Ministry of Education, Employment & the Family. Malta.

MEEF. (2011d). *Towards a quality education for all. The national curriculum framework consultation document 4: The way forward*. Valletta: Ministry of Education, Employment & the Family. Malta.

Ministry of Education. (1999). *Creating the future together. National minimum curriculum*. Valletta: Ministry of Education. Malta.

Murphy, M. (1997). Capital, class and adult education: The international political economy of lifelong learning in the European Union. In P. Armstrong, N. Miller, & M. Zukas (Eds.), *Crossing borders. Breaking boundaries: Research in the education of adults, proceedings of the 27th annual SCUTREA conference*. London: Birkbeck College, University of London.

Robinson, K., & Aronica, L. (2009). *The element: How finding your passion changes everything*. New York: Viking Penguin.

Skager, R. (1978). *Lifelong education and evaluation practice*. Oxford: Pergamon Press.

Suchodolski, B. (1976). Lifelong education – Some philosophical aspects. In R. H. Dave (Ed.), *Foundations of lifelong education*. Oxford/Hamburg: Pergamon Press/UNESCO Institute for Education.

Sultana, R. G. (2003). *Lifelong guidance and the European challenge. Issues for Malta*. Floriana: Euroguidance. Malta.

Tuijnman, A., & Boström, A.-K. (2002). Changing notions of lifelong education and lifelong learning. *International Review of Education, 48*(1/2), 93–110.

Wain, K. (1991). *Malta's national curriculum. A critical evaluation*. Msida: Mireva. Malta.

Wain, K. (2004). *The learning society in a postmodern world*. New York: Peter Lang.

Walters, S., Borg, C., Mayo, P., & Foley, G. (2004). Economics, politics and adult education. In G. Foley (Ed.), *Dimensions of adult learning. Adult education and training in a global era*. Sydney/London: Allen & Unwin/McGraw Hill/Open University Press.

Williamson, B. (1998). *Lifeworlds and learning. Essays in the theory, philosophy and practice of lifelong learning*. Leicester: NIACE.

Young, M. F. D. (1998). *The curriculum of the future. From the 'new sociology of education' to a critical theory of learning*. London: Falmer Press.

Young, M. F. D. (2004). Curriculum studies and the problem of knowledge: Updating the enlightenment? In H. Lauder, P. Brown, J. A. Dillabough, & A. H. Halsey (Eds.), *Education, globalization and social change*. Oxford: Oxford University Press.

Chapter 24
The Rise and Fall and Rise Again of Learning Cities

Lynette Jordan, Norman Longworth, and Michael Osborne

Introduction

In this chapter we provide an overview of an aspect of lifelong learning implementation that has waxed and waned in importance over since the 1970s, the notion of creating learning cities and regions. It may be that this field of endeavour is about to attract international attention once again, with the impetus coming from Asia, in particular China, Korea, Vietnam and Japan, where activity now seems to be burgeoning at a time when initiatives in Europe seem with some notable exceptions haphazard and uncoordinated at EU, national and regional level. We provide a brief history of developments of within the field of learning cities and regions in Europe in recent decades and then focus on one particular project, EUROlocal, which has sought to gather and analyse the current state of development within the continent.

A Brief History of the City and Regional Learning Space

Over the past four decades, lifelong learning has increasingly become a priority for policymakers throughout Europe largely because of the demands of a more knowledge-intensive economy in which continuing learning at all levels has been

L. Jordan
Bachelor of Arts in Community Development (BACD), University of Glasgow, Glasgow, UK

N. Longworth
UNESCO/OECD, Paris, France

M. Osborne (✉)
Centre for Research and Development, Adult and Lifelong Learning,
University of Glasgow, Glasgow, UK

Place Management, Social Capital and Lifelong Learning, PASCAL Observatory, Glasgow, UK
e-mail: michael.osborne@glasgow.ac.uk

G.K. Zarifis and M.N. Gravani (eds.), *Challenging the 'European Area of Lifelong Learning': A Critical Response*, Lifelong Learning Book Series 19, DOI 10.1007/978-94-007-7299-1_24, © Springer Science+Business Media Dordrecht 2014

prioritised. In this context the role of the learning region and city as a vehicle for stimulating lifelong learning has taken on greater significance. Longworth (2001) claims that a rapid change in the 'learning economy', for example, the explosion of information and knowledge and increasing individualisation amongst other factors, has provoked a significant movement from the paradigm of 'education and training' to one of 'lifelong learning'. The emphasis now is much more on the learners themselves and how their perceptions of the importance of learning throughout life can be fostered and translated into the kind of skills, attitudes and values that will enable them to cope with deep changes in lifestyles and work demands. Such a transformation requires new approaches on the part of learning providers and a re-examination of assessment methods, ensuring that learners are not discouraged at a young age and that their personal circumstances are taken into account. This suggests a shift from a supply-side concept of education with an education offer determined by providers to the principle of continuous learning for everyone controlled at least to some extent by individuals themselves. As part of that change in emphasis, many European cities have been encouraged to develop themselves as learning cities in order to tackle the new challenges posed in the post-industrial period and faced by all countries in the developed world (see Hassink 2004; Gustavsen et al. 2007; Longworth and Osborne 2010). Similarly, there have been a number of initiatives in Europe promoted under the aegis of the *Learning Region*, most notably the R3L programme of the European Commission (2002), which states:

> A learning city, town or region recognises and understands the key role of learning in the development of basic prosperity, social stability and personal fulfilment, and mobilises all its human, physical and financial resources creatively and sensitively to develop the full human potential of all its citizens. European Commission (2002, p. 11)

Similarly the definition of a learning region or city from Faris (1998) refers to:

> ...communities of place using lifelong learning as an organising principle and social/ cultural goal as they mobilise the learning resources of all five of their community sectors, economic, civic, public, education and environmental to enhance their social, economic, and environmental conditions on a sustainable, socially inclusive basis. Faris (1998, p. 5)

As Duke et al. (2005) have observed, the concept of a learning city has been interpreted in a number of ways with the emphasis at one end of a continuum being about creating an underlying infrastructure of educational opportunity that might attract inward investment from business through to the creation of learning networks that promote and enhance social cohesion and inclusion. The terms learning region and learning city have in fact been used interchangeably throughout the period of growth in Europe and the notion of 'learning region' is useful in that it extends the learning city in scale and scope.[1] The literature suggests that over the last 30 years, some European cities have sought this status enthusiastically and that the rationale for wanting to become a learning city may principally be economic, social or environmental, but usually contains elements of each stimulus (Longworth and Osborne 2010).

---

[1] See reports from the recently completed R3L+ project funded by the European Commission at http://www.learning-regions.net/ and within Eckert et al. (2012).

The origins and subsequent development of learning cities has been well documented. In brief, the learning city was defined geographically in the 1970s when the Organisation for Economic Co-operation and Development (OECD) invited seven cities around the world to become an 'Educating City' (Adelaide, Edmonton, Edinburgh, Gothenburg, Kakegawa, Pittsburgh and Vienna). This status was offered on the basis that the cities concerned placed the broad concept of learning at the heart of their strategies. This idea is at the core of the objective of the learning region and city methodology, namely, that activities across a broad portfolio of services should revolve or stem from learning. The notion of using learning as a medium to foment positive change was perceived as being more effective than simply using economic levers to stimulate development. The popularity of the concept in the 1980s and 1990s reflected a tendency to emphasise the agency of both social and economic actors. In 1992, a Gothenburg conference organised by the OECD led to the formation of the International Association of Educating Cities (IAEC). Some of the values and aspirations which emerged at Gothenburg continue to have currency, not least the idea that partnerships and collaboration of interested regions and cities are essential if the ambitions of learning cities are to be realised (OECD/CERI 1992).

Subsequent developments have meant that *lifelong* learning now lies firmly at the heart of the learning city concept, emphasising the importance of learning throughout life for everyone. At a European level it has been the European Community (EC) that has taken the lead in making this link. In 1998 it initiated the TELS (Towards a European Learning Society) project, which surveyed 80 European municipalities from 14 countries by measuring their progress towards becoming 'learning cities, towns and regions' in 10 domains and 28 subdomains. TELS became the European Commission's major source of information on the local and regional dimension of lifelong learning, offering ten recommendations to governments and a further ten recommendations for embryo learning cities. As a result of TELS, seminars were held in Brussels for interested regional organisations and papers were produced. This in turn resulted in the production of a European Policy Paper on the 'Local and Regional Dimension of Lifelong Learning' (European Commission 2001a) distributed to all member states for comments. This in turn led to the European Commission's R3L pilot initiative, *European Networks to promote the local and regional dimensions of Lifelong Learning*, within the background of which is suggested that the learning region 'goes beyond its statutory duty to provide education and training…and instead creates a vibrant, participative, culturally aware and economically buoyant human environment through the provision, justification and active promotion of learning opportunities to enhance the potential of all of its citizens' (European Commission 2003, p. 11).

Already in 2000, both the Lisbon and Feira European Councils had provided impetus for the European Commission to focus on lifelong learning. The Lisbon Council set the now well-known strategic goal over the decade from 2000 to 2010, for the EU 'to become the most competitive and dynamic knowledge-based economy in the world, capable of sustainable economic growth with more and better jobs and greater social cohesion'. This was accompanied by a number of targets for raising employment rates across the continent, and it emphasised the importance of lifelong learning, setting targets in various parts of the education and training system in order to create an alignment in achieving the Lisbon goals.

Regionally based lifelong learning was stressed in relation to these targets because of the substantial disparities that exist between regions in the EU (European Union). Strategies for lifelong learning would have to be tailored to the specific requirements of each region. This emphasis was included in the subsequent *Memorandum on Lifelong Learning* (European Commission 2000), which in turn initiated EU-wide consultation on an updated strategy for implementing lifelong learning policies. The results culminated in the European Commission's communication, *Making a European Area of Lifelong Learning a Reality* (European Commission 2001b). The R3L programme was announced in 2002 as the principal way in which the European Commission would seek to develop this emerging policy priority for there to be a regional and local dimension of lifelong learning, meeting the commitment of the communication to 'support through its programmes the establishment of networks between those regions and cities with well-developed lifelong learning strategies, to facilitate the exchange of experience and good practice'.

The R3L aimed to:

• To help further develop good practice on issues relating to the 'learning region'
• To encourage a fruitful transnational sharing and exchange of this experience
• To promote the development of European networks between learning regions as a means of placing European cooperation in the lifelong learning field on a more durable and sustainable footing (European Commission 2002, p. 2)

However, despite laudable intentions, the impetus of this initiative was not sustained with most of the 17 pilot projects promoting little activity once their funding from the European Commission ended. Subsequently within the aegis of the Lifelong Learning Programme for the period 2007–2013, there have been further individual projects[2] concerned with learning cities and regions, the foci of which have been described by Longworth and Osborne (2010), but there has been relatively little co-ordinated action or overview of the territory in intervening years.

Initiatives have also occurred at the level of the nation state, with examples of learning city or region networks created in a number of countries including Germany, Italy and the UK. However as with R3L, evidence for the sustainability of such networks is limited (see, e.g. Hamilton and Jordan 2011; Thinesse-Demel 2010). Since the 1990s in some places, the concept of learning cities has been absorbed or mainstreamed into strategic policy and as a consequence may not necessarily be evident through labelling as such. For example, Glasgow in Scotland, which had previously strongly promoted the learning city, now argues that whilst learning is still at the core of their work driving policy and practice forward, the banner of

---

[2] These include the Learning in Local and Regional Authorities (Lilara) (see http://pie.pascalobservatory.org/content/lilara-executive-summary), PASCAL European Network of Lifelong Learning Regions (PENR3L) (see http://eurolocal.info/project/penr3l-european-commission-project-establish-expertise-network-learning-regions) and Quality Framework for Learning Regions (R3L+) (see http://www.learning-regions.net/) projects.

'learning regions or cities' is no longer the preferred current terminology (Hamilton and Jordan 2011). In other places, there has been a lack of sustainability of initial developments whether work initiated within individual cities and regions or through larger-scale network initiatives such as R3L (Souto-Otero and McCosham 2006).

The challenge now for regions and cities throughout Europe is how to sustain a culture of lifelong learning that exploits the potential of contributions of a range of stakeholders in a synergetic fashion to the benefit of all citizens against the backdrop of the current difficult economic circumstances that the continent faces. For Goncalves (2008) the idea of learning cities in the twenty-first century has two key pillars of equity and sustainability, thereby playing a role in ensuring active citizenship and social inclusion alongside economic development that takes into account the reality of a fragile ecosystem.

One example currently being planned is the UNESCO *Global Learning Cities Network* (GLCN), an initiative to provide a Kitemark standard by which learning cities can measure and monitor their progress. The 12 generic indicators used recognise that the concept of the learning city has moved on. Instead of being purely associated with the implementation of lifelong learning principles within the city, the perception is that sustainability issues have expanded the learning city responsibility. No longer is it simply concerned with the well-being of its own citizens, it must now attend to some of the pressing issues raised by climate change, renewable energy sources, air and water pollution and loss of biodiversity. In other words, its remit extends to the survival of the planet, a mission frequently reiterated in the recent RIO+20 summit of June 2012. The duopoly of social and economic which has been the staple of city focus for many years is now a triumvirate of social, economic and environmental, each with their own focuses. Even that is now superseded by the holism of the modern city. For example, economic growth must now be sustainable if we are to avoid the excesses that will destroy our fragile ecosystems. In addition, sustainable economic growth will not happen without the input of a lifelong learning system of education and training. Thus, the future of cities is a fusion of all three: interdependency, interconnectedness and interaction.

The UNESCO model is in three sections. On the one hand, there are the variables that provide the underlying motivation – individual empowerment and social cohesion, sustainable development and cultural and economic prosperity. Secondly come the building blocks that will allow a learning city to establish itself as such. These include creating a culture of learning, learning organisations, local and international partnerships, innovation and change and the engagement and contribution of stakeholders. None of these will, however, take place without the third elements of political will and commitment and good governance. The project is still very much work in progress, but there is a determination to make it succeed with help from the PASCAL Observatory.[3]

---

[3] The PASCAL Observatory for place management, social capital and learning regions has based in Glasgow, Illinois, Melbourne and Pretoria and emerged from work of the OECD in the field of learning cities and regions in the early 2000s.

EUROlocal: The European Storehouse on Learning Regions and Cities

One initiative within Europe that has gathered knowledge of learning regions and cities and analysed the current situation in terms of their development and progress is EUROlocal,[4] a recently completed international project funded by the European Commission through the Transversal Key Activity (KA) 4 of the LLP with partners that included a number of the leading proponents of learning region development. Four collaborating organisations with a history of experience in learning regions and cities were involved: the PASCAL Observatory, University of Glasgow (UK), Learning Regions Deutschland (LRD) (Germany), Universus Bari (Italy) and the University of Pecs (Hungary). The principal aim of this project was to provide a central repository in the form of a website to store more than two decades of data, tools, indicators, reports, videos, projects, recommendations, plans, strategies and learning materials for the benefit of European cities and regions. The approach of EUROlocal project was both collaborative and interactive by providing an easily accessible web-based resource of existing and extant initiatives and by seeking input and feedback from new and prospective entrants.

As well as creating a rich reservoir of materials, EUROlocal has also collated more than 800 regional development contacts from throughout Europe. It has also developed existing audit tools concerned with learning region development and translated and tested these in different sectorial areas, including schools, adult education institutions, local authorities and universities. Learning materials were devised for others interested in learning regions and cities to use. At various points during the project, stakeholders were consulted and recommendations for policy changes in the field were revised on the basis of their comments.

Longer-term targets in relation to dissemination, exploitation and sustainability have also been developed and reached. For example, the work of the project is feeding directly into the developments within UNESCO's GLCN initiative. Interested parties have already met to discuss how the work can be developed in the future. Other objectives were met through the purchase of a dissemination package from the European Association for the Education of Adults (EAEA) which provides a separate web section within its website.

One of the main criticisms of projects funded within the framework of the LLP is sustainability and impact, and this has been a fundamental problem of many previous initiatives in the field of learning cities and regions. By establishing strong sets of connections with other networks, regions and cities as well as individuals, and by being maintained after the life of the project by a global network, the PASCAL Observatory, unusually high prospects for longevity exist for EUROlocal. Furthermore, the project was designed to have maximum impact on

---

[4] See http://eurolocal.info/

the development of linked strategies for lifelong learning regions at a EU level. It does this by having

- Provided a wealth of potentially valuable knowledge for European regions that urgently needed to be brought together and made available in one place. Furthermore, commentary and analysis of these materials, both thematically and by geographic region, add value to content.
- Made the knowledge available in an innovative way. The innovativeness and extensive use of a website that contains many features of modern Internet custom and convention (e.g. blogs, rich media, interaction and 'digging') enhance the project's impact on those who intend to develop learning regions in the future. The design of the site also facilitates the organisation of material in ways that facilitate thematic and geographical analysis and by permitting remote user submissions always to a degree ways in which knowledge can be co-constructed.
- Provided learning and publicity materials that enable all European regions to develop a strategy that exploits the available wealth of knowledge for its stakeholders in VET institutions, universities, schools, enterprises, local administrations and adult education institutions.
- Devised a dissemination plan that targets regional development agencies in all EU countries.
- Provided the guidelines and recommendations for a new expanded European policy in this area.

Each one of the previous targets has a significant impact on the development of lifelong learning. Together they add up to a step forward for local and European policy and practice. Furthermore, EU policies in cognate areas are addressed, including the high level objective of integration, 'the process of overcoming, by common accord, political, physical, economic and social barriers that divide countries from their neighbours, and of collaborating in the management of shared resources and regional commons' (European Commission 2008).

Through the various work packages of the project, the website and the final seminar, EUROlocal was able to make contributions to this objective in several ways. Through the sharing of mutual experiences and the provision of reciprocal support, EU regions have been able to enhance their own regional work. One opportunity came in Ostersund, Sweden, in 2010 at the Jamtli Museum during the '*Heritage, Regional Development and Social Cohesion*' conference. The event was hosted by the PASCAL Observatory and facilitated the sharing of experiences and research findings by regions across a wide range of interests. The themes included whether cultural and natural heritage was a resource for development and how to make links between the heritage movement, social inclusion and lifelong learning for all. The EUROlocal final seminar '*Investing in the Future*: *Building Learning Cities and Regions in Europe*' in October 2011 was held in Murten, Switzerland, and was aimed at for key decision-makers in European regions. This event maximised impact through discussion and exchange of experiences and expertise between

European regions. The culmination of the work provided the guidelines and recommendations for European policy in this area.

In the Interim Report of the LLP (European Commission 2011, p. 14), the Commission talks about how to make the work of the programme more effective and suggests that those active in the lifelong learning programmes should 'Share good practice among the Member States and various stakeholders, ... Make better use of KA1 of the Transversal programme to analyse the needs of the target groups, undertake outreach initiatives to associations of enterprises, non-formal and informal education providers'. EUROlocal has achieved this through the interactive website, the development of an extensive database and learning materials, the dissemination of audits, contacts, information on projects and festivals in both cities and regions. Additionally through stakeholder audits and tools testing, the project has undertaken an analysis of which groups are relevant in which sector and what their actual needs are. Through a final seminar it worked to 'strengthen the involvement of national and sub-national policy makers and other stakeholders in the cooperation process at the EU level (peer learning activities and other fora of learning) as well as in the implementation of the LLP's actions' (p. 89).

EUROlocal Contribution to EU Policy

The first European Commission Policy Document on the Local and Regional Dimension of Lifelong Learning (Longworth 2006) was a result of one of the first European Commission Learning City/Region projects, TELS. It contained a series of recommendations for implementation by local authorities and by the European Commission. As we have reported previously, the recommendation to initiate an European Commission programme on learning regions was implemented in 2002 (R3L), when 17 projects were approved to kick-start the process of lifelong learning region development.

The EUROlocal final seminar provided additional recommendations for the future. EUROlocal urged that the EU strongly consider the following:

1. Reintroduce the concept of learning cities and regions into the new programme for lifelong learning development, *Erasmus for All*.
2. Recognise the place of learning cities and regions in the development of jobs, employment and Europe 2020[5] and promote new projects to establish these as frameworks for development.
3. Recognise the interactivity, interconnectedness and interdependence of economic, social and environmental capital in local development, and promote research and development projects, which activate good practice.
4. Work with active learning city organisations, cities and regions abroad; learn from them and implement projects, which mirror their success.

---

[5] See Europe 2020 at http://ec.europa.eu/europe2020/europe-2020-in-a-nutshell/targets/index_en.htm

5. Encourage member states to implement learning city and region development projects and networks.
6. Work with other intergovernmental organisations (IGOs) such as UNESCO and the OECD to help them establish worldwide networks of good practice in learning cities and regions.
7. Encourage innovative approaches, which link European cities with others abroad to exchange good practice and creative solutions. Use these to help cities and regions in underdeveloped or dangerous parts of the world.
8. Encourage all schools at all levels to establish links with other schools in other countries throughout the world for joint curriculum development and creative projects that promote understanding, tolerance and peace.
9. Make the EUROlocal storehouse available to all, worldwide, and use it to create recommendations for action in the learning cities and regions field.
10. Establish links between the Lifelong Learning Programme and Social and European Regional Development Funds to increase the number of learning regions throughout Europe. Use the experts who have organised and run DG EaC learning region projects to implement these.
11. Embed learning region concepts into all lifelong learning projects in the new *ERASMUS for All* programme (see European Commission 2012).
12. Encourage integration projects and partnerships between learning providers and city/region stakeholders.
13. Accept projects that encourage citizens to identify with, and contribute to, the economic, social and environmental development of their own region.
14. Establish links with the Committee of the Regions to give more attention to learning city and region development.
15. Use the tools and learning materials in the EUROlocal storehouse to increase the number of learning regions and cities in Europe. Encourage the writing of more such tools and materials.

This would enable learning regions throughout Europe to meet the criteria of the policy of the past as well as that of the future. EUROlocal has played a part in the Lisbon Council strategic goal, for the EU 'to become the most competitive and dynamic knowledge-based economy in the world, capable of sustainable economic growth with more and better jobs and greater social cohesion' by gathering the knowledge in one pace which will contribute to this growth and social cohesion.

In the Interim Report for the evaluation of this lifelong learning programme, the European Commission (2011, p. 8) recognised the many achievements of the life-long learning programme such as 'the benefits of improved content and practice of education and training but it also', but it also identified several matters of concern. In terms of effectiveness of the education and training in Europe, the Panel were eager to address these matters before the end of the programme in 2013. One of the issues included 'Inequalities in education hindering individuals from lower-economic backgrounds to acquire the high levels of competence they need to con-tribute to and benefit from a knowledge society'. Through the mutual exchange and knowledge from the EUROlocal site, learning regions will be able to make a difference in terms of both building economies and contributing to social inclusion practices. There will be more links between different and similar organisations and institutes. For example, those dealing with employment will link with those focused on social inclusion.

It was agreed that future European Commission programmes will be even more integrated and cover all aspects of education and training as in the case for the Erasmus for All programme to be introduced in 2014. The Interim Report of the LLP (European Commission 2011) identified that we need to develop as 'partnerships between the education and the world of work, regional and local authorities and NGOs'. The European Commission Interim Panel for this report suggested that EU actors should 'also further enlarge the possibilities of cooperation with non-EU countries' and give more attention to transversal actions. The Commission took note that 'most answers and feedbacks received come from current beneficiaries of the Lifelong Learning Programme and reflect the quite usual tendency to ask for continuity and stability'. Erasmus for All will bring further investment in education and training and 'is the key to unlocking people's potential, regardless of their age or background. It helps them to increase their personal development, gain new skills and boost their job prospects' (European Commission 2012, p. 1).

The Future of the Work

The EUROlocal project created a website, which is a virtual platform for researchers, developers and managers focusing on establishing, managing or developing learning cities, regions or communities. The website frames and sets out the basic precepts of learning cities and regions in Europe so as to engage designers, planners, decision-makers and other stakeholders who are interested in promoting the idea and practice of learning cities and regions. EUROlocal can be used as a reader/source for people wanting to be informed of or to learn about learning cities and regions in Europe. Moreover, the PASCAL Observatory has linked EUROlocal to its website which widens the scope and assures the sustainability of the work.

One precondition for the development of a successful learning region is the identification of dedicated people and institutions that follow the same aim: developing a structure that is reaching people flexibly and creatively and that reduces competitiveness and makes common working fields accessible. Building a network of educational institutions with regional partners from the scientific, social, economic and cultural background is the way towards a knowledge-based economic area, which means a learning region. EUROlocal identified several areas for action, including the:

- Development of new tools for use in cities and regions
- Consolidation of EUROlocal outputs in specific areas of the lifelong learning
- Increased visibility of EUROlocal to European cities and regions
- Expansion of the scope of learning cities and regions into the aspects of learning city/region development other than educational and training that is presently active in Europe

More work needs to be done by EUROlocal in terms of exploitation, and this is an ongoing and never-ending task. However, in order to make the exploitation of the EUROlocal project more effective, there may be a need to reduce the gap between projects and policymakers by considering the creation of an 'observatory' for the Lifelong Learning Programme itself.

During the course of the project, we encountered cities and regions with many other nomenclatures outside of our remit, such as creative cities, resilient cities, transition towns, green cities, healthy cities, smart cities, slow cities, ecowell cities, cities of possibilities, cities alliance for poverty reduction and sustainable development, cool cities, intelligent cities, sustainable cities, educating cities, energy cities, future cities, culture cities, Eurocities and Eurotowns.[6] We know that others exist that may have fallen under the radar.

All of them have created networks; all of them are active in Europe, many of them also interacting with other cities worldwide. Most are active in several aspects of local and regional lifelong learning development; all of them can potentially contribute to the learning of all their stakeholders in formal, non-formal and informal learning; and all of them can learn much from each other. EUROlocal has recognised that there is also further urgent work to be done to collect the knowledge, tools and materials that these new entities have created, in order to further economic, social and environmental development in European cities and beyond.

References

Duke, C., Osborne, M., & Wilson, B. (Eds.). (2005). *Rebalancing the social and economic: Learning, partnerships and place*. Leicester: NIACE.

Eckert, T., Preisinger-Kleine, R., Fartusnic, C., Houston, M., Jucevičienė, P., Dillon, B., Nemeth, B., Kleisz, T., Ceseviciute, I., Thinesse-Demel, J., Osborne, M., & Wallin, E. (2012). *Quality in developing learning cities and regions a guide for practitioners and stakeholders*. Munich: University of Munich.

European Commission. (2000). *A memorandum on Lifelong Learning* Commission of the European Communities Brussels (SEC (2000) 1832 Commission Staff Working Paper). http://www.bologna-berlin2003.de/pdf/MemorandumEng.pdf. Accessed 10 June 2012.

European Commission. (2001a). *The local and regional dimension of lifelong learning – A policy paper*. Brussels: EC.

European Commission. (2001b, November). *Making a European area of lifelong learning a reality*. http://www.bologna-berlin2003.de/pdf/MitteilungEng.pdf. Accessed 15 June 2012.

European Commission. (2002, July 20). *R3L call for proposals*. Call EAC/41/02.

European Commission. (2003, April 7). *Information note: The "R3L initiative" European networks to promote the local and regional dimensions of Lifelong Learning*, Brussels.

European Commission. (2008). *Regional integration for development in ACP countries*. Communication from the Commission to the Council, the European Parliament, the European

---

[6] Some URL examples are as follows: energy cities (http://www.energy-cities.eu/), sustainable cities (http://sustainablecities.net), creative cities (http://creativecities.org/), educating cities (http://www.bcn.es/edcities/aice/) and green cities (http://greencities.com).

Economic and Social Committee and the Committee of the Regions. http://ec.europa.eu/development/icenter/repository/COMM_PDF_COM_2008_604_F_EN_REGIONAL_INTEGRATION.PDF. Accessed 5 Aug 2013.

European Commission. (2011, February 18). *Interim evaluation of the lifelong learning programme – Final report (2007–2013)*. At http://ec.europa.eu/dgs/education_culture/evalreports/index_en.htm#educationHeader. Accessed 15 June 2012.

European Commission. (2012). *Erasmus for all*. At http://ec.europa.eu/education/erasmus-for-all/. Accessed 14 June 2012.

Faris, R. (1998, August 15). *Learning communities: Cities, towns and villages preparing for a 21st century knowledge based economy*. A report submitted to the Resort Municipality of Whistler on behalf of the Centre for Curriculum, Transfer and Technology, Victoria.

Goncalves, M. J. (2008). *Cities and emerging networks of learning communities*. Accessed from http://www.afscet.asso.fr/resSystemica/Lisboa08/goncalvesMJ.pdf on 17 June 2012.

Gustavsen, B., Nyham, B., & Ennals, R. (2007). *Learning together for local innovation: Promoting learning regions*. Thessaloniki: CEDEFOP.

Hamilton, R., & Jordan, L. (2011). Learning cities: The United Kingdom experience. In P. Kearns, S. Kling, & C. Wistman (Eds.), *Heritage, regional development and social cohesion* (pp. 193–228). Jamtli: Ostersund.

Hassink, R. (2004). *The learning region: A policy concept to unlock regional economies from path dependency*. At http://www.diw.de/documents/dokumentenarchiv/17/41724/20040510_hassink.pdf. Accessed 22 June 2012.

Longworth, N. (2001). *The local and regional dimension of lifelong learning: Creating learning cities, towns and regions, a European policy paper from the TELS project*. Brussels: DG Education and Culture.

Longworth, N. (2006). *Learning cities, learning regions, learning communities: Lifelong learning and local government*. London: Routledge.

Longworth, N., & Osborne, M. (2010). *Perspectives on learning cities and regions*. Leicester: NIACE.

Organisation for Economic Cooperation and Development, & CERI. (1992). *City strategies for lifelong learning* (An OECD study prepared for the second congress on educating cities in Gothenburg). Paris: OECD.

Souto-Otero, M., & McCosham, A. (2006). *Ex-post evaluation of the R3L initiative: European networks to promote the local and regional dimension of lifelong-learning. Final report to the European Commission technical report*. Birmingham: ECOTEC.

Thinesse-Demel, J. (2010). Learning regions in Germany. *European Journal of Education, 45*, 437–450.

Chapter 25
Collective Dimensions in Lifelong Education and Learning: Political and Pedagogical Reflections

Françoise F. Laot

Introduction

This chapter[1] offers a look back into the past in order to revisit a period of history when individual and collective adult education and training were two hotly debated alternatives at the national and local levels. These debates occurred in France in the 1950s and 1960s before the continuing vocational education era which started with the law of 16 July 1971, at a moment when lifelong education was emerging as a social project aimed at 'promoting' individuals and social groups.

Drawing on sources from archives, this chapter will first examine the different understandings of 'promotion' in the debates. It will study the arguments of those who defended them from a political point of view and will highlight the content of disagreements. It will then identify the pedagogical arguments for the collective development of adult education, specifically those which pleaded for a collective development even in individualised education, in the framework of 'collective education actions' (ACFs: *actions collectives de formation*). Various documents were analysed from several archive collections, notably those of the *Délégation générale à la promotion sociale* (DGPS),[2] the *Centre universitaire de coopération économique et sociale* (CUCES)[3] in Nancy (Lorraine) and also the archives of some trade unions.

---

[1] A French version of this text was first published in the journal *Savoirs* n° 25, 2011, under the title *La prise en compte du collectif dans la formation individuelle, considérations politiques et péda-gogiques dans les années 1960*, pp. 49–67.

[2] The 'General Delegation for Social Promotion' was the national body in charge of adult education policies from 1961 to 1966.

[3] The 'Adult Education University Centre' was a pioneer in this domain in the 1960s.

F.F. Laot (✉)
Professeure de sociologie, Centre d'études et de recherches sur les emplois et les professionnalisations (CEREP), Université de Reims Champagne-Ardenne, Reims, France
e-mail: francoise.laot@univ-reims.fr

G.K. Zarifis and M.N. Gravani (eds.), *Challenging the 'European Area of Lifelong Learning': A Critical Response*, Lifelong Learning Book Series 19, DOI 10.1007/978-94-007-7299-1_25, © Springer Science+Business Media Dordrecht 2014

The analysis of these documents reveals the fundamental role attributed to the family (notably the couple) in these discussions. Finally, it will examine the decline in intensity of these debates within the framework of the wider European context of discussion over lifelong learning, charting their evolution or their translation into other social spheres.

Individual Education Versus Collective Education: Political and Social Arguments

In the very beginning of the 1960s, instead of adult education or adult training, the word used in France was 'promotion' which was recognised to be equivalent. Vocational improvement and 'recycling' (retraining) constituted alternatives for adult education, albeit extending the expression 'social promotion'. The Chenot report (1964) on social promotion, for example, included in its ambit 'any education or training action, whatever its content or level, when addressed to someone already involved in working life[4]'.

Philippe Casella (2001) emphasises the teleological vision underlying the expression 'social promotion'. Indeed, contrary to adult education or training, this expression neglects the learning process, attaching importance to the result (the promotion). This situation originated in a linguistic shortcut referring to 'promotion courses'. In fact, since 1948, workers could acquire advancement through evening or weekend courses, lasting generally several years (6–8 years), held in the framework of programmes named 'work promotion' or 'worker promotion', later 'work higher promotion', and finally 'social promotion' in the context of the 1959 law.[5] Antoine Prost (2008) remarks that this conception of adult education quickly encountered limits because of the asceticism on which it was based. Pascal Caillaud (2007) forwards the hypothesis that the uncertainty in the legal content of 'social promotion' led to its progressive disappearance from legal texts. As a matter of fact, in 1966, 'vocational training' (understood as continuing or adult vocational training) was added to 'social promotion' in the title of a new law, the law of 3 December 1966. This law constituted the first attempt at rationalisation and coordination of the whole spectrum of adult education activities. 'Promotion' disappeared from the title of subsequent laws, starting from 1971. Nevertheless, before this period the theme of promotion gave rise to heated debates between those who defended collective promotion against those who argued in favour of individual promotion.

---

[4] Report by Bernard Chenot, on behalf of the *Commission d'étude des problèmes de formation et de promotion sociale* (study committee for social promotion and adult education problems), February 1964, (*Livre Blanc de la Promotion sociale*, Paris, La Documentation Française, 1966).

[5] The social promotion law (July 1959) was due to Michel Debré, who was the Général Charles de Gaulle's first prime minister.

Promotion: A Class Betrayal?

The idea associated with individual promotion is that of the 'second chance'. It can lead a worker or a middle-ranking employee to get a diploma[6] or to succeed in a competitive examination after having attended an evening course programme for several years. It is an integral part of upward mobility, either inside their company by climbing the steps of the career ladder, or outside, by changing vocation or employer. This is how some more junior employees became *chiefs* (team managers or workshop foremen) or *cadres* (senior executives). These promoted managers occupy positions which still are more or less well accepted (Gadéa and Pochic 2009). They are considered to be 'defectors' (*transfuges*), abandoning their original social class for something better (or something worse, depending on one's point of view). Upward social mobility grew rapidly at the end of 1950s, in a historical period marked by a transformation of the working class, as described by Jean-Pierre Terrail (1990), through what he calls *worker individualisation*. Adult education issues played their part in this, although always alongside other factors that shaped class identity (relationship to school, patterns of consumption, housing ownership).

Collective promotion should be understood as promotion *inside* and *to the benefit of* one's social group. It is an old idea, already present in the labour movement in the first half of the nineteenth century, long before the creation of trade unions,[7] which later strongly defended this principle. The risk of class betrayal via education constituted a threat and often an important obstacle to workers support for diverse educational initiatives coming from the bourgeois. For instance, in 1845 the worker-editors of the *Atelier* paper wrote: '*In order to perpetuate their power and render people's efforts vain, our adversaries count a lot on selfish feelings that, by their example, they have helped to disseminate among people. 'As soon as one of you – they say – through learning, has prepared himself for the functions that you expect of him, it will be very easy for us to confound your expectations, opening our ranks […] we will show to this man what wellbeing is waiting for him among us and the ingratitude and suspicion which too often affect mass representatives, and, if he is intelligent, his choice won't be incertain'. We have to acknowledge that this hope of the clever conservatives is not unfounded.*[8]'

Yet, they still opted for the path of 'intellectual emancipation', involving reading, discussion and education, a unique path, as they wrote, towards social and political emancipation. However, vigilance was required, with the educator's social origin or class attachment remaining a fundamental question and playing an essential part in the acceptance or rejection of education among workers.

---

[6] For instance, the *Diplôme d'études supérieures techniques*, *DEST* (technical studies graduate diploma), created in 1957 which gave access to engineers' schools.

[7] 1884 in France.

[8] 'Introduction à la sixième année'. *L'Atelier*, n° 1, October, 1845 ('introduction to the sixth year'), pp. 13–14.

This mistrust led workers to organise their own education within the *Bourses du travail*[9] or trade unions and also within the popular education movements,[10] where the term 'milieu' was substituted for 'social class' to avoid the connotations of the latter (Chauvière 2001). For instance in the *Jeunesse ouvrière chrétienne*, the young Christian workers association, education had to be organised 'between them, by them, for them'. After World War II, the slogan became, within *Peuple et culture*,[11] 'in the milieu, by the milieu, for the milieu'. These old reflections affected adult education and training conceptions elaborated in the 1960s.

Collective: A Controversial Term

Many sociological or sociohistorical analyses were conducted on social promotion (Terrot 1997; Palazzeschi 1998; Tanguy 1999; Dubar and Gadéa 1999; Benoist 2004). They all highlight the lack of precision of this policy. Discourses about social promotion were always very general, and the polysemy of the terms tended to smooth over the diversity of objectives (Casella 2001). This blurring probably stemmed from a political will to reduce social divisions in order to facilitate industrial modernisation.

In the context of public policies for adult education, the two dimensions of individual and collective promotion were debated and implemented through diverse laws, identifying two models for collective promotion, firstly 'social worker promotion' conceived as a means to improve employer-employee relations (at least this argument was put forward to push the project through) and, secondly, social agricultural promotion as a means to face the total transformation of the sector.

Marcel David (1976) recounts in detail the debates and strategies of avoidance concerning conflicting terms following the initiative of Minister Gazier to create nonpaid education leaves for workers in 1957. In the midst of the Cold War, 'the word "collective", even when associated with promotion, was likely to alarm large segments of opinion sensitive to the slightest hint of collectivisation' (David 1976: 52). While the acceptance of the principle of collective promotion was finally acknowledged by the following government with its Social Promotion Law of 1959, it was, according to David (1976), a clever concession to the demands of the labour movement. Individual promotion was supported by engineers, managers and employers.

As Guy Brucy has demonstrated, trade unions were not unanimous in their attitude towards issues of promotion. Analyses produced by various union bodies

---

[9] The 'Labour Exchange Institution' run by the workers themselves.

[10] I distinguish between 'worker education' and 'popular education'. In the first, initiatives come from the workers themselves; this is not necessarily the case in the second one.

[11] *Peuple et culture* is a popular movement created in 1945. It acted as a key player in the development of adult education.

'opposed class struggle intransigent advocates to class collaboration defenders' (Brucy 2007: 118). They were particularly divided over individualism at the expense of the collective. For the *Confédération générale du travail* (CGT),[12] the risk of individual promotion was to make workers forget 'their sense of class membership'.[13] Brucy describes how, in the complex economic transformation and with the rise of the mobilisation and power of managers within trade unions, 'the senior executives ('cadres') of the CGT and CFTC (Confédération française de travailleurs chrétiens[14]) finally imposed their conceptions in a domain rather poorly invested by workers' trade unions' (Brucy 2007: 135). These workers' representatives transferred their demands into the field of collective promotion, which was progressively marginalised, thus achieving 'the individual and the collective's graduated separate development' described by David.

Concerning social agricultural promotion, the political confrontations may have been less heated, but the social and economic divides appeared to be considerable. This promotion was twofold aimed at training and giving access to career mobility, 'consisting in leading a whole population destined to remain in agriculture to learn a new trade' (Brucy 2007: 17). The end of the 1950s was marked by a massive rural exodus and by agricultural mechanisation and modernisation. At the same time there was a complete social and political renewal in agricultural organisations' leaders (Cordellier 2003). A new generation coming from youth movements, notable the *Jeunesse agricole catholique*[15] (JAC) and the *Centre national des Jeunes agriculteurs*[16] (CNJA) took on leading positions in trade union or professional bodies. According to Cordellier, while social agricultural promotion did not completely avoid the risk of educating an elite, it nevertheless contributed to local emulation and reflections towards change, as well as sharing the work between training centres, notably the *Institut français des cadres paysans*[17] (IFOCAP) created in 1959, and youth and trade union movements. On the ground, starting in 1966, this emulation gave birth to the development of cooperatives for the shared use of agricultural machines (CUMA[18]) as well as study groups or agricultural popularisation societies. It also permitted interesting wide-ranging pedagogical and e-learning initiatives, for instance Rural Promotion TV (*Télé-promotion rurale*) (Flageul 1972; Hantonne 2000).

---

[12] *Confédération générale du travail*, the largest French trade union federation.

[13] Quotation from an article written by A. Barjonnet, in *Revue des comités d'entreprise*, March 1952, quoted by Guy Brucy (2007) p. 118.

[14] *Confédération française de travailleurs chrétiens*, a Christian trade union which still exists. It was from this union in 1964 that a large group of dissidents created the CFDT (Confédération française démocratique du travail), a secular trade union.

[15] Catholic Agricultural Youth Association.

[16] Young Farmers National Centre.

[17] French Farmer Leaders Institute.

[18] *Coopératives d'utilisation du matériel agricole*.

Reporting on its action in 1966, the *Délégation générale à la promotion sociale* (*DGPS*) noted a constant growth in collective promotion assistance since 1961.[19] Nevertheless, one can detect in the progressive diversification of actions characterised as 'desirable' a change in the targeted public. Initially conceived to reach trade unions leaders, social collective promotion gradually widened to other groups and finally addressed everyone with responsibilities in the social or economic spheres, with, for example, legal, economic or social training open to everyone. Therefore, in light of the fact that responsibilities could be assumed in 'various milieus', collective promotion could even concern senior industry executives:

'Efforts [in collective promotion] have also focused on senior executives ("cadres") economic and social training. Programmes directed towards their participation in the life of companies and their introduction to economic mechanisms and balance were held for them in the *Midi-Pyrénées*, in the *Nord*, in *Alsace* and in *Lorraine* thanks to subsidies of around 50,000 F for each action[20]'.

This example illustrates how blurred the idea of social collective promotion had become. The collective here no longer refers to the working class, but to higher hierarchic grades in the staff of companies. This conception is very far from the militant definition of collective promotion given by the 'Groupe de Grenoble':

The aim of collective promotion is to raise the cultural level of the ensemble of manual workers, i.e. enable them to be aware of their condition, thus to be able ultimately to take in hand their own future within the bodies they have created for themselves (Groupe de Grenoble 1964, p. 1061).

The Pedagogical Argument: The Effectiveness of Individual Education

Is a strictly individual adult education possible? At the CUCES (University centre for social and economic cooperation[21]) of Nancy,[22] a centre for research on adult pedagogy, the question was studied through various surveys and observations of the adult education actions organised by the centre. It appeared to the researchers and trainers who worked in it that limiting education to individuals limits its efficacy, even reducing its effects to zero:

From a 'sociological' point of view, one has to realise that an isolated man, a man whose education is cut off from the globality of his life, has very few opportunities to benefit from education. As evidence we can cite those workers educated in expression and trained to write reports at the CUCES, who, back in their companies, quickly returned to their former

---

[19] From 25,000 in 1962 to 53,000 in 1965. 'La promotion collective', DGPS 5 page unsigned note, January 1967, DGPS Archives, CAC-AN 800405-4.

[20] *Ibid.* p. 3.

[21] The CUCES was both a training centre financed by heads of industry and a university centre (the two bodies were mixed together: an association and a public institution).

[22] Nancy is a big industrial town in Eastern France.

way of writing (in fact, their entourage's way of doing it) so as not to be 'mocked'. We can also cite the case of engineers trained in statistics whom their director asked to avoid abusing the 'so-called sciences' only because they themselves did not know any statistics. The examples are innumerable.[23]

This paragraph was inserted into a chapter dealing with the 'insufficiencies of adult education'. Here, the authors explained that the courses for 'disinterested' improvement and individual promotion were both qualitatively and quantitatively limited; quantitatively limited because of the very small proportion of the whole population who could have access to courses. In comparison with the USA or USSR, France appeared to be lagging behind. But the courses were also considered qualitatively limited, 'and this is an even more serious issue' because the knowledge acquired in these courses appeared to be of very little use. Learning on this model was thus considered not to be very productive.

> The reason for this is that education is superficially 'tacked' on to him [the adult], not rooted in his affective and professional life; it makes him the only beneficiary of the learning within the milieu in which he lives, without any occasion either to use it – and so to benefit from it – or to communicate it to others.[24]

Therefore, knowledge had to be directly useable, but also communicable, and meaningful for the learner's entourage or 'milieu' as well. Even individual education had to be complemented by a collective dimension.

The Family Circle and the Couple: The First Collective to Be Taken into Account

First, we have to note that this adult, this 'man' to be educated, did not refer to a 'neutral male'[25] individual, encompassing women. A detailed examination of the archives led me to bring to light that the social promotion policy had been conceived by men exclusively for men (Laot 2010). This is not surprising if we consider the very slow evolution in the 'feminine condition' at the beginning of the 1960s, which remained the 'golden age of the family and housewife' (Battagliola 2008: 85). However, it would be wrong to think that women were totally forgotten. On the contrary, as learners' spouses, they were supposed to play a key role. As I have explained in detail elsewhere (Laot 2012), in the middle of the 1960s, education programmes were conceived in order to bring wives to support and accompany their husbands in their learning paths. The issue was twofold: First, the aim was to remove 'the obstacle of the family' (DGPS 1966: 63), or the obstruction represented by

---

[23] Le CUCES, 16-page document [unsigned, not paginated, undated, however, probably from the beginning of the 1960s], IMEC – Pierre Schaeffer's archives, PSR 55.

[24] *Ibid.*

[25] French grammatical specificities are at stake here: words can be feminine or masculine. 'Neutral' which does not exist is generally expressed by masculine grammatical gender, something that French gender studies challenged in the 1980s.

family circles, and especially spouses, who stood in the way of men entering into a course programme. The aim was also to prevent high dropout rates from evening courses, due – among other reasons – to family pressure (Thesmar 1965). However, a third dimension had to be taken into account: the risk of imbalance in couples caused by the cultural rise of men as a result of their learning efforts. Following surveys conducted on 'auditors' (as they called the people attending the courses), a rumour of high divorce in the ranks of those benefitting from evening courses of social promotion was widespread. The findings of these surveys (Thesmar 1965; Champagne and Grignon 1969; Glikman 1970) were more or less well understood and somewhat over interpreted.

This affair was very seriously examined at the national level. Guy Thuillier, who was a member of the 'Comité Grégoire'[26] in charge of pedagogical problems in the framework of the DGPS, wanted to draw attention to the dangerous imbalance that adult education programmes could provoke:

> Concerning adult education, one too often forgets that it should not be separated from actions upon the social milieu. Indeed, one cannot seize an isolated subject: he is closely linked to his family and, as soon as one raises the professional and cultural level of the husband, it is necessary to see that no imbalance, no rupture should occur. Any disaccommodation could be dangerous.[27]

Thuillier went to recommend a sort of quasi-education programme for women (in fact for 'spouses'), as he wrote in a book firstly published in 1966:

> All of the observers insist on the necessity to associate the woman[28] with the effort of promotion, almost to give her 'training' in order to avoid any imbalance: a tricky task with still undefined boundaries (Thuillier 1969: 45–46).

One of his suggestions concerning this training directed at women, notably to housewives, was to create radio or TV programmes broadcast at times when children were at school. Reading Thuillier's writings, it is clear that women were absolutely not a direct target of this 'promotion effort' but were only concerned through the intermediary of their husbands. As well, it appears evident that women were uniquely considered as wives and mothers. The same self-evident positioning of women is visible in numerous texts and archives from this period. Even women who had an occupation (even when they were mothers, they were more numerous in the labour market than the members of DGPS then believed[29]) were not considered to be 'promotionable' (*promouvables*[30]).

---

[26] Official group chaired by Roger Grégoire.

[27] Problèmes d'action sur le milieu familial (Actions directed to the family circle), Annexe VI Thuillier Report. Réflexions sur les problèmes de la pédagogie des adultes, (Reflections on adult pedagogical problems) Grégoire Report, April 1965, 2 pages, DGPS Archives, CAC-AN 800405-11.

[28] In French, the same word is used for wife and woman (*femme*).

[29] Indeed a specific study group, the study committee for women vocational training, was created later within new institutions held after the 3 December 1966 law on vocational training and social promotion. In the archives of this group, I found a survey in which it was written that 'contrary to spread ideas, in 1962, more than 50 % of active women were married'. Draft report entitled 'Women's vocational training', November 1968, 31 pages, CAC-AN 800406-48.

[30] In French, this word is incorrect, it is a neologism found in DGPS archives.

At a local level, for instance, at the CUCES in Nancy, taking into account family circles and particularly spouses was a serious consideration, and it gave rise to specific actions.

As early as 1962, it was considered a necessity to inform spouses about their husbands' social promotion programmes, at least by posters if not through information meetings.[31] The beginning of the new school year in 1966 was the occasion for very successful evening conferences open to families (children and spouses).[32] All these initiatives had the same objective: reducing the dropout rate. At the CUCES, the awareness of each adult educator of the importance of the family circles was considered very important, as was confirmed by the study of the film *Retour à l'école?* (Back to School?)[33] in which three evening course auditors were interviewed in the company of their wives.

A New Collective to Promote: The Inhabitants of a Territory

The same arguments used to develop a 'collective' conception of individual education were reused when the CUCES implemented 'collective education actions' (ACFs) in the mid-1960s. In particular, individual isolation, considered very unprofitable, had to be ruled out. However, two new arguments were added, inspired from collective promotion: that of the expected benefits for the social group in its entirety and that of self governance or, at least, workers' participation in decisions about the content and modalities of learning. The first ACF session began in 1966, in the Lorraine iron mining area, based on these principles:

> Adult education is called 'collective' if the collective itself (i.e. the group attending the session) can directly manage the action and if there is a return on the collective life.[34]

ACFs also contributed to changing the conception of the role of 'spouses' in adult education. As wives, specifically miners' wives, they were directly targeted. This time they were invited to participate in sessions in order to 'provoke an effect on men's attendance'.[35] Some archives studied on 'women's education' in the Forbach-Merlebach coal-mining area in 1966–1979[36] show that women's participation

---

[31] CUCES, Session pédagogique, 10–14 September (Pedagogical training session), Rapport des commissions (résumé), 4-page note. René Cercelet's personal archives, CAC-AN 78 0670-25.

[32] Interview with Jean-Marie Péchenart (14 November 2006), who was the instigator of these conferences.

[33] *Retour à l'école?* Alain Bercovitz (Author), Jacques Demeure (Director), 45 min black-and-white film shot at the CUCES of Nancy in 1966, in order to train trainers, produced by the Service de la recherche de l'ORTF, and the DGPS.

[34] Pourquoi 'implanter' une organisation, un 'système' d'éducation des adultes, non daté, 22 p. (meeting minutes February 1968). CUCES. Private Archives, pp. 4–5.

[35] Compte rendu de la réunion du sous-comité de la formation professionnelle et de la promotion sociale pour le Bassin houiller lorrain du 13 mars 1969 (Minutes of meeting) (Fonds Pagel, Archives de Bobigny).

[36] They are Anne-Marie Pagel's archives, ACF former educator in the coal basin, in the east of France (Forbach-Merlebach).

surprised and even caused problems for the organisers (notably concerning the provision of subsidies) because women were more numerous and their attendance more regular than men, the initial target for the ACFs.[37] Progressively, women's place in these ACFs normalised, with conceptions evolving significantly post-1968, notably concerning women's employment. Working and nonworking women were finally recognised as an integral part of the community to be promoted via ACFs.

The geographical territory and its inhabitants also tended to impose itself as a new conception of 'collective' ahead of any specific social or vocational group. ACF had initiated the idea of educating a population in a given territory, and this was adopted as the basis for a draft regional system of adult education by the AUREFA (Regional University Associations for Education and Training), which disappeared in 1969 (Laot 2009). The idea of a representative audience as an indicator of success was developed in the ACFs of Saullumine-Noyelles-sous-Lens[38]:

> The concept of collective education necessarily refers to the social composition of the audience. One can put forward the idea that there's no collective education when the audience is not sufficiently representative of the targeted community. This requires not only a sufficient level of participants [...] but also and most importantly, a distribution of social characteristics in the audience that is as close as possible to that of the entire community's. This is not only an objective "democratic" criterion, but also implies the subjective agreement of the whole milieu with the ACFs. Education is sociologically collective when it implies and integrates in its dynamics a group of people, objectively and subjectively representative of the community to which it belongs (Dubar and Evrard 1973: 6).

Similarly, albeit at a later date, when a form of representativeness of the population of a given territory was sought for in the context of the new urban policies implemented in France at the beginning of the 1980s, the new concept that emerged was that of 'social development' (Donzelot and Estèbe 1994). Rooted in the critique of a unique pattern of development applied to the Third World, and of a normative model for living, this concept also integrated the idea of development in rural areas that came out of Brittany in 1965 (Gontcharoff 2009). Given the fact that many agricultural collective actions were conducted in this region, some connections with collective promotion could doubtless easily be found.

The Weakening of the Collective Dimension in Adult Learning

Between 1960 and 1980, the collective dimension seems to have disappeared from adult education and learning appearing instead in the domain of social intervention.

---

[37] Compte rendu de la réunion du sous comité de Merlebach (Meeting minutes), 27 June 1969, Pagel's archives, Centre d'archives de la Seine-Saint-Denis, Bobigny.

[38] Coal basin in the north of France.

The July 1971 Law that organised 'Continuing Vocational Adult Training' within 'Permanent Education'[39] made no reference to collective promotion or adult education and instead aimed to promote and facilitate individual access to education and training during an employee's work time. Yet, as I have demonstrated, collective actions (ACF), qualified as 'outlaw' actions,[40] continued into the 1990s. Numerous and diverse education actions still exist; however, they are rarely qualified as 'collective'. During a period of individualism and individualised learning (Frétigné and Trollat 2009), the word seems to be outmoded.

Although the word 'collective' is not totally absent from European policies of lifelong learning (it is used twice whereas the word 'individual' is used 29 times in the text *Making a European Area of Lifelong Learning a Reality*[41]), it is 'the centrality of the learner' – understood as the 'individual' learner – that is considered to be 'the key characteristic' of lifelong learning. In this text, the collective (or the group or the society or the labour market) becomes the entity in which the individual learner has to be included (or empowered, or employed), thanks to the learning activities.

Concerning the theme of the family circle as a significant variable in the individual's learning path, it seems to have lost its relevance in French as well as in European policies in the context of the social change in the 'feminine condition' and conjugal life. While inequalities persist within the couple (de Singly 2002), couples themselves now tend towards individualism (Giraud and Mougel 2008). Starting in 1967, a radical change in French policies towards women's adult education (Laot 2010) has led decision-makers to consider that 'continuing vocational education and training has to be identical and accessible to everyone, without sex distinctions[42]'.

However, nobody seems to have raised the question of a need to educate husbands to accompany their wives in their learning paths! Nevertheless, while decision-makers lost interest in the family circle as a relevant theme for public policies, it remained a question for researchers. Even today, knowledge inequality, leading to identity tensions – what Etienne Bourgeois (2006) calls 'cognitive dissonance' – still represents a threat for the learner (man or woman) and their immediate family circle or social group. Learning may raise tensions or conflicts, where before there was no problem at all; it may entail a rupture in communication

---

[39] I intentionally use the words 'Permanent Education' (*Éducation Permanente*) and not 'lifelong learning' (*éducation tout au long de la vie*) because their use into French corresponds to distinct periods. The former is used from the 1950s to the mid-1970s, the latter since the 1990s.

[40] Guy Herzlich, 'Promotion collective. Sallaumine, 4 heures de l'après-midi', *Le Monde*, 13 février 1974, p.22. Guy Herzlich wrote in his article: 'this 1971 outlaw action (ACF), focused on vocational training'. *Ibid*.

[41] European Commission communication, 2001.

[42] *La formation professionnelle féminine* (women vocational adult training), 1968, Rapport de 31 pages du *Groupe d'étude pour la formation professionnelle féminine*, (Study group for Women's Adult Education) set up following the 3 December 1966 law, p. 30. CAC-AN 800406-48.

and make relations between learners and their close relatives or work colleagues difficult. Thus, one can ask, from a social perspective, whose interests are served by strictly individualised learning?

References

Battagliola, F. (2008). *Histoire du travail des femmes*. Paris: Editions La Découverte.

Benoist, P. (2004). Michel Debré et la formation professionnelle. *Histoire de l'éducation, 101*, 35–66.

Bourgeois, E. (2006). Tensions identitaires et engagement en formation. In J.-M. Barbier, E. Bourgeois, G. de Villiers, & M. Kaddouri (Eds.), *Constructions identitaires et mobilisation des sujets en formation* (pp. 65–120). Paris: L'Harmattan.

Brucy, G. (2007). La formation au travail: une histoire de cadres (1945–1970). In G. Brucy, P. Caillaud, E. Quenson, & L. Tanguy (Eds.), *Former pour Réformer. Retour sur la formation permanente (1945–2004)* (pp. 101–137). Paris: La Découverte.

Caillaud, P. (2007). La construction d'un droit de la formation professionnelle des adultes (1959–2004). In G. Brucy, P. Caillaud, E. Quenson, & L. Tanguy (Eds.), *Former pour Réformer. Retour sur la formation permanente (1945–2004)* (pp. 171–210). Paris: La Découverte.

Casella, P. (2001). La promotion sociale comme forme d'intervention publique: le cas de Grenoble (1960–1966). *Travail et Emploi, 86*, 49–62.

Champagne, P., & Grignon, C. (1969). *Rapport d'enquête sur le public du Conservatoire national des arts et métiers*. Paris: Conservatoire national des arts et métiers.

Chauvière, M. (2001). Action catholique, promotion collective et éducation permanente. *Education permanente, 149*, 167–183.

Cordellier, S. (2003). La "promotion collective agricole", un dispositif peu connu. *Education permanente, 154*, 113–122.

David, M. (1976). *L'individuel et le collectif dans la formation des travailleurs: Tome 1, Approche historique 1944–1968*. Paris: Economica.

de Grenoble, G. (1964). La promotion collective, point de départ d'une rénovation. *Esprit, 1964–5*, 1058–1069.

de Singly, F. (2002 [1987]). *Fortune et infortune de la femme mariée*. Paris: PUF.

Délégation générale à la Promotion sociale. (1966). *Livre Blanc de la Promotion sociale*. Paris: La Documentation française.

Donzelot, J., & Estèbe, P. (1994). *L'Etat animateur. Essai sur la politique de la ville*. Paris: Editions Esprit.

Dubar, C., & Evrard, S. (1973). Recherche sur quelques facteurs sociaux des motivations à la formation collective d'adultes. *Education permanente, 17*, 5–27.

Dubar, C., & Gadéa, C. (Eds.). (1999). *La promotion sociale en France*. Lille: Presses universitaires du Septentrion.

Flageul, A. (1972). Six ans de télé-promotion rurale. *Education permanente, 16*, 33–48.

Frétigné, C., & Trollat, A.-F. (2009). L'individualisation de la formation: un objet de recherche. *Savoirs, 21*, 11–40.

Gadéa, C., & Pochic, S. (2009). Des "disparus" bien présents: les cadres issus de la promotion. *Education permanente, 178*, 9–24.

Giraud, C., & Mougel, S. (2008). *Le couple à l'heure de l'individualisme*. Paris: La documentation française.

Glikman, V. (1970). *Etude sur la population des élèves du CNAM ayant obtenu leur diplôme d'ingénieur en 1965–1966 et 1966–1967*. Paris: Conservatoire national des arts et métiers.

Gontcharoff, G. (2009). *Dix territoires d'hier et d'aujourd'hui pour mieux comprendre le développement local*. Paris: Adels.

Hantonne, P. (2000). *Evolution de l'utilisation du film de formation dans le monde agricole et rural: l'exemple de la Télé promotion Rurale.* Thèse de Sciences de l'information et de la communication, sous la direction d'Armand Mattelart, Université de Paris 8.

Laot, F. F. (2009). Un modèle universitaire et régional de la formation des adultes dans les années 1960. L'épisode oublié des AUREFA et leur échec face à la loi de 1971. *Éducation et sociétés, 24,* 143–157.

Laot, F. F. (2010). La promotion sociale des femmes. Le retournement d'une politique de formation dans les années 1960. *Le mouvement social, 232,* 29–45.

Laot, F. F. (2012). Les épouses des auditeurs. Le film *Retour à l'école?* Couples et formation d'adultes dans les années 1960. *Travail, genre et sociétés, 27,* 125–146.

Palazzeschi, Y. (1998). *Introduction à une sociologie de la formation. Anthologie de textes français. Vol. 1: Les pratiques constituantes et les modèles. Vol. 2: Les évolutions contemporaines.* Paris: L'Harmattan.

Prost, A. (2008). Jalons pour une histoire de la formation des adultes (1920–1980). In F. F. Laot & E. de Lescure (Eds.), *Pour une histoire de la formation des adultes* (pp. 37–54). Paris: L'Harmattan.

Tanguy, L. (Ed.). (1999). Les chantiers de la formation permanente (1945–1971). *Sociétés contemporaines, 35,* 5–130.

Terrail, J.-P. (1990). *Destins ouvriers. La fin d'une classe?* Paris: PUF.

Terrot, N. (1997 [1983]). *Histoire de l'éducation des adultes en France.* Paris: L'Harmattan.

Thesmar, C. (1965). *Etude sur les raisons des abandons aux cours du soir.* Nancy: Les Documents de l'INFA.

Thuillier, G. (1969). *La promotion sociale.* Paris: PUF.

Chapter 26
Reinstating the Invisible: A Proposed Framework for European Learning Collectives

George K. Zarifis and Maria N. Gravani

In this book we set out to critically examine the context as well as the perspective on which the *European Area of Lifelong Learning* is resting today. The book follows the structure of the *Memorandum on Lifelong Learning* which prescribes the content of the 2001 Communication of the European Commission for *Making a European Area of Lifelong Learning a Reality*. The issues that are discussed in the book reflect on the ideological challenges as well as the policy inadequacies that characterise decision-making in the field.

Based on the content of the book, we identified that the discourse on making the European area of lifelong learning a reality revolves around four distinct objectives: employment, education and training provision, citizenship and inclusion. These objectives that appear in the *Memorandum* messages are very much related to each other and operate as the platform on which a number of more intrinsic topics evolve: skills and competences, learning outcomes, quality, innovation in teaching and learning, access, guidance, values and equity.

The chapters of the book touch upon all these topics that essentially develop in two axes of thought. Reflecting on the contributions, we consider both axes permeating the imagery of lifelong learning in Europe. The first of these axes is built on input[1]

---

[1] This positioning is largely reflected in the contributions by Schmidt-Hertha and Strobel, Milana, Andersson and Wärvik, Tsakiris, O'Brien and Ioannidou.

G.K. Zarifis (✉)
Faculty of Philosophy, School of Philosophy and Education, Department of Education, Aristotle University of Thessaloniki, Old School of Philosophy Building, Office 208, GR-54124, Thessaloniki, Greece
e-mail: gzarifis@edlit.auth.gr

M.N. Gravani
School of Humanities and Social Sciences, Open University of Cyprus, Latsia, Cyprus
e-mail: maria.gravani@ouc.ac.cy

G.K. Zarifis and M.N. Gravani (eds.), *Challenging the 'European Area of Lifelong Learning': A Critical Response*, Lifelong Learning Book Series 19, DOI 10.1007/978-94-007-7299-1_26, © Springer Science+Business Media Dordrecht 2014

from the human[2] and social capital[3] approaches, whereas the second axis is constructed on input[4] from a pragmatist[5] but also from an ethical[6] perspective. We strongly consider these axes serving as a canvas for reinstating what is less represented in the current debate in Europe, and what is less represented are the learners and the validity of their experience. We have concluded that this is not fundamentally the consequence of a dubious policymaking process, but the after-effect of the process of constructing a false European reality based on postindustrial, postcapitalist coinage that does not reflect on learning realities in Europe.

In spite of the deep commitment of European policymaking to the idea of life-long learning, the language of the *Memorandum* and of all relevant texts thereafter echoes the neologies of globalisation. The relevant discourse however does not deserve to be called 'neoliberal', at least not in its intention. As Popović puts it in this volume the devil is in the detail, and the *Memorandum* messages reveal a kind of naivety suggesting steps and solutions that do not respond to the real nature of the proclaimed goals and do not give a realistic direction for reaching them.

The Significance of the Language

It is therefore the language (essentially the English language) and the meanings proclaimed by the usage of neoliberal terminology that consist the underbelly of the current European policy agenda on lifelong learning. And although one could argue that language does create realities, at the time *Memorandum* was released, this was not much the case as it is today. More than a decade later, the neoliberal approach in making the European area of lifelong learning a reality has developed an ecology that is linguistically culminated with the 'Study on European Terminology in Adult Learning' (released in 2010). It is not always with scepticism that we receive European Commission's initiatives and studies as we have contributed in a number of them, but in this case we wish to make an exception simply because it was developed under the framework of the 2007 Action Plan on Adult Learning, '*It is always a good time to learn*', which called for a glossary of terminology and a set of core data to facilitate monitoring of adult learning in Europe. The main argument for

---

[2] Learning reflects the stock of competencies, knowledge, social and personality attributes, including creativity, embodied in the ability to perform labour so as to produce economic value.

[3] Learning reflects on the social connections that exist between people, and their shared values and norms of behaviour, which enable and encourage mutually advantageous social cooperation, identity building and trust.

[4] This is more evident in the contributions by Popović, Lucio-Villegas, Gough, Jõgi, Bernhardsson, Brunila, Formenti and Castiglioni, Hake, Laot and Mayo.

[5] Learning lies in its observable practical consequences, namely, what is defined in most European policy documents as learning outcomes.

[6] Learning lies on sets of values (intrinsic and extrinsic) and principles deriving from the European ideal and the rich history of traditions.

developing this glossary (in English nonetheless) was that an up-to-date common language is prerequisite to overcoming the misunderstandings and lack of comparable data which currently impede monitoring (sic) of the adult learning sector across the European Union. So, out of the need for controlling and overcoming misunderstandings in a field of practice (educational, academic, policy and research), someone had to put an order in the terminological and linguistic 'chaos' in adult education and lifelong learning in Europe.[7] It is intended that recommendations from this study will be tools in the implementation of the Action Plan and that the study will help to create a better understanding of the existing good practices and also of the obstacles to monitoring the adult learning sector. And here is where our scepticism lies, even if we cannot argue the need for making order in the European terminological chaos in our field (as academics we constantly try to put things in order by creating our own little 'chaos' every single time), it is extremely hard not to be sceptical of the actual intention behind the study.

We conclude this part of the final chapter with this simple thought; language is a tool, and the one who knows how to use it can take control of others (individuals, societies or why not fields of study or academic terrains). In other words language is a power(ful) instrument for creating narratives and depending on who develops the codes of communication it may prove worthy of monitoring, supervising, observing, keeping under review, measuring or testing, regulating and controlling these narratives. This essentially affects the way policies look upon people, and as Gough argues in the fifth chapter of this volume, the linguistic and conceptual imperialism of English seems to be the problem. This demands a proper

---

[7] European Commission did exactly that with 67 terms: access to education; accreditation of an education or training programme; accredited learning; adult; adult learning; adult learning provider; adult learning teacher; adult learning trainer; apprenticeship; barriers to learning; basic skills; community-based adult learning; competence; continuing vocational training; disadvantaged; distance learning; early school leavers; formal learning; functional literacy; functional numeracy; funding body; funding stream; guided learning; hard to engage; higher education; ICT skills; individual learning account; individual learning plan; informal learning; information, advice and guidance (IAG); initial vocational training; key competences; learning difficulties/disabilities; liberal adult education; lifelong learning; life wide learning; literacy; low qualified; low-skilled; mentoring; mother tongue; new basic skills; non-accredited learning; non-formal learning; numeracy; off-the-job training; on-the-job training; outreach; participation rate; persistence; post-compulsory education; priority groups; progress; progression; qualification framework; retention; returns to learning; second chance education; self-directed learning (self-study); social partners; tertiary-level attainment; third sector; training of trainers; upskilling; validation of learning outcomes; vocational education and training (VET); and work-based learning. A further nine terms were deemed by the Commission to be key terms. For the reference, these terms are the following: access to learning, adult learner, digital divide, dropout, individual learning route, individualisation of learning, learning module, learning offer and qualification. The terms selected for inclusion in the adult learning glossary were those considered essential for discussion on monitoring adult learning between EU27+ representatives, be these policymakers or adult education specialists. The terms were also categorised in six dimensions: adult learning strategy, policy and legislation; adult skills and competences; access to and participation in adult learning; investment in adult learning; quality of adult learning; and outcomes and impacts of adult learning. The study is available at http://ec.europa.eu/education/more-information/doc/2010/adultreport_en.pdf

consideration in order to uncover the flaw in the analytic reductionist thinking behind the policy developments now infecting all of Europe. An alternative conception, even more so a plethora of alternative narratives, may be then the means for revising such policies.

The Need for Shifting the Paradigm: Towards a New Ecology of Lifelong Learning in Europe

In the midst of an economic crisis with vast sociopolitical repercussions that nearly divide Europe into the 'sluggish South' and the 'diligent North' and revive stereotypes among Europeans largely fomented by certain national and international media, the call for making a European area of lifelong learning a reality seems to be totally out of place. What we need today 10 years after the *Memorandum* and the *Communication* is a new paradigm that will be based on a collective approach on how different appreciations (narratives) of learning in Europe may support the development of participatory learning 'networks'[8] that will involve exchange of ideas, decision-making and collaboration among different actors in a small scale.

This is not new knowledge to European policymakers. Responses to the consultation on the *Memorandum* called for a broad definition of lifelong learning that is not limited to a purely economic outlook or just to learning for adults. In addition to the emphasis it places on learning from pre-school to postretirement, lifelong learning should encompass the whole spectrum of formal, non-formal and informal learning. The consultation also highlighted the objectives of learning, including active citizenship, personal fulfilment and social inclusion, as well as employment-related aspects. The principles which underpin lifelong learning and guide its effective implementation emphasise the centrality of the learner, the importance of equal opportunities and the quality and relevance of learning opportunities (see European Commission 2001: 3–4). Ten years later the ecology of lifelong learning in Europe differs greatly from what the consultation emphasised. As Mayo argues in Chap. 23 of this volume, the overarching notion today is that of lifelong learning for employability and a narrowly defined notion of active citizenship which overlooks the collective dimension of education for social change and which provides a very problematic notion of individualised learning. This notion does not reflect any awareness of the way concepts, assumptions and practices are influenced by mechanisms that prey on people's sensibilities. Today educational policymaking in Europe is exceedingly connected to economic benefits and human capital growth rather than social and cultural capital development. Lifelong learning in Europe is

---

[8] This shared position among many scholars is also highlighted by Chapman (2006) who suggests that *'the important point to make about the concept of 'network' is that it differs in character from other terms that have historically been used in association with education and with the organisational arrangements with which education has been managed and through which innovation and change have been brought about'* (ibid. 2006: 332).

increasingly looking upon the learner as an employable unit that needs to fit in the market rather than a free individual that validates the benefits of its own learning.

This essentially gravitates the discourse towards human capital (with focus on investing in the development of skills and competences) and pragmatist (with focus on learning outcomes) approaches, leaving most other approaches of lifelong learning compromised. Fejes in Chap. 9 of this book concludes that even though there seems to be a consensus perspective promoted via European policy documents – where the state, the employer and the individual are all positioned as being jointly responsible for creating the 'good' future, where lifelong learning and investment in human capital are central – it is still the individual who is positioned as responsible for becoming adaptable and flexible as a way to become and remain employable. One could say that there is a 'responsibilisation' of the individual. The individual needs to take responsibility for using the opportunities for lifelong learning, by means of education and in-service training, offered by the state and the market, thus transforming itself into an employable unit. The role of the state becomes more distanced than in the past. Today, structures for supporting the individual in its own choice are created instead of collectively planning the future by means of legislative measures and regulations. The essence of these arguments is that the conceited mode of delivering the concept of lifelong learning in European policies has largely neglected the role of the individual learner (see Formenti and Castiglioni in Chap. 21) but has also disregarded knowledge that is directly useable but also communicable and meaningful for the learners' entourage or 'milieu' as Laot comments. It may not come as a novelty therefore if we suggest that what we really need in Europe today is a new approach in reframing the disturbed ecology of lifelong learning by putting the learners in the centre.

What we propose therefore as the culmination of the approaches and argumentation presented in this volume is a framework for developing European learning collectives that will reinstate the learners in the centre of the objectives set by the European Commission. Fundamentally this proposed framework stresses the need for a collective promotion of lifelong learning from the learners and for the learners. Although the word 'collective' is not totally absent from European policies of lifelong learning as Laot observes (it is used twice whereas the word 'individual' is used 29 times in the Communication on *Making a European Area of Lifelong Learning a Reality*), it is 'the centrality of the learner' – understood as the 'individual' learner – that is considered to be 'the key characteristic' of lifelong learning. In our context, however, the collective (or the group or the society or the labour market) becomes the entity in which the individual learner has to be included (or empowered or employed) depending on various levels of networking. According to Laot, this collective promotion should be understood as promotion inside and to the benefit of one's social group. It is an old idea, already present in the labour movement in the first half of the nineteenth century in Europe, long before the creation of trade unions, which later strongly defended this principle. The framework is based on the four objectives that appear in the relevant policy documents and are thoroughly analysed by the contributors in this book. These objectives – namely, employment, educational and training provision, equity and inclusion – consist the canvas for developing collective narratives on the targets initially set by the European Commission in the *Memorandum* messages (skills and competences, learning outcomes, quality, innovation in teaching and learning, access, guidance, values and equity).

Epilogue

As Lucio-Villegas argues with reference to John Dewey in the fourth chapter of the current volume, the most important achievement in a democratic society is education's role to encourage both personal and collective development. European policies however subordinate these educational aims to professionalisation and business. The most powerful and important critique that can be made to current lifelong learning policies and practices is that the aims of the education must be for education itself.

In this book we stressed that in the European lifelong learning policy context from its generation in 2000 until today, there is an increase of the approaches that look upon the learner as an employable unit rather than as a free individual that validates the benefits of its own learning. These approaches have fundamentally gravitated the discourse on *Making the European Area of Lifelong Learning a Reality* towards human capital and pragmatist approaches that essentially compromise other equally or more valuable approaches (see O'Brien in Chap. 11 of this volume). We also pointed at the need for changing the existing neoliberal vocabulary, as a response to the call for a more critical appreciation of the concept of lifelong learning (as a modernist distortion) and the urgency of changing the paradigm from the more economic and pragmatist to the more social and ethical.

Ten years after the launch of the Memorandum on lifelong learning and the Communication for making a European area of lifelong learning a reality, our proposed framework for European learning collectives aims to put the learners in the centre while using the main European policy objectives as the core elements of a broad canvas on which the different targets set by policymakers evolve, based on the idea of creating collective narratives among a plethora of stakeholders (individuals, workers, students, employees, policymakers, scholars, etc.) that build agency and life skills, develop strategic positioning towards themselves, others and the world and help them to take care of their own learning. The proposed framework highly reflects upon such approaches as Hake's (Chap. 22 of the book) in which individuals and social groups, even collective audiences, are seen as able to create their own frameworks of meaning by selecting information and integrating cultural messages in their own everyday lives. This understanding of *Making the European Area of Lifelong Learning a Reality* focuses on the formation of 'subject' positions in communicative practices and the force of social and cultural meanings. As Hake himself puts it in this volume, 'it is necessary today to study rigorously the cultural forms produced by 'citizens' active in the public sphere of 'making meanings' who seek to change social relationships through their cultural action. It is also necessary to study the social forces and cultural forms which reproduce the false consciousness of the inhabitants of the virtual world and the cultural transformation of 'subject positions' into 'product positions' for the purposes of unbridled capitalist accumulation'.

References

Chapman, J. D. (2006). An analysis of problems, issues and trends in the provision of lifelong learning: Lessons learned. In J. Chapman, P. Cartwright, & E. J. McGilp (Eds.), *Lifelong learning, participation and equity*. Dordrecht: Springer.
European Commission. (2001). *Making a European area of lifelong learning a reality* (COM (2001) 678 final). Brussels: Communication from the Commission.

Index

G.K. Zarifis and M.N. Gravani (eds.), *Challenging the 'European Area
of Lifelong Learning': A Critical Response*, Lifelong Learning Book Series 19,
DOI 10.1007/978-94-007-7299-1, © Springer Science+Business Media Dordrecht 2014

Printed by Printforce, the Netherlands